URBS ROMA

BY DONALD R · DUDLEY

PHAIDON

URBS ROMA

A SOURCE BOOK OF CLASSICAL TEXTS
ON THE CITY & ITS MONUMENTS
SELECTED & TRANSLATED WITH A COMMENTARY

BY DONALD R · DUDLEY

PHAIDON PRESS

TO MY WIFE

MOST CONGENIAL OF ROMAN COMPANIONS

MADE IN GREAT BRITAIN 1967

PRINTED AT THE ABERDEEN UNIVERSITY PRESS

PREFACE

THIS book is neither a history of the architecture of classical Rome nor a guide to its antiquities. It is rather, as the sub-title indicates, a selection of the ancient *testimonia*—texts, coins, inscriptions—for the city and its monuments. They illustrate the public rather than the private life of Rome: they are bounded in space by the Walls of Aurelian and in time by the death of Constantine in A.D. 337, though sometimes the story of a monument has been continued beyond that date.

The evidence they have to offer is subject to limits of its own. Strange as it may seem, no classical writer, so far as we know, set himself to write a systematic description of Rome, such as Procopius gives in the *Buildings* for the Constantinople of Justinian. Vitruvius, admirable as a guide to the practice of Augustan architecture, mentions rather more than a score of Roman buildings without describing any of them at length. And the *testimonia* themselves are capricious in their scope. Sometimes they are almost silent, as for the Tabularium or the Arch of Titus; sometimes inadequate, as for the Thermae or, notably, for the Pantheon. But it is also true that it is largely thanks to them that we can form any idea of such major buildings as the Temple of Jupiter Optimus Maximus, or Nero's Golden House, or the Temple of Apollo on the Palatine. And of course, full or scanty, they claim the authority of primary sources.

Texts are given in translation where the originals are readily accessible (as in the Loeb series), save where, for one reason or another, the reader needs to have the original before him. The illustrations have in most cases been chosen as working documents, and provided with extended captions to that end. Most of the photographs reproduced have been taken by Fototeca Unione, Rome. The Notes to the Text contain suggestions for further reading.

In compiling this book, I have had in mind the needs of students in school and universities—and, especially, of teachers of classics or Latin or Roman History in the schools of Britain. Because of the shoddy utilitarianism that now dominates our education, they often have to work in an atmosphere of discouragement. Yet they have one great advantage over their more privileged predecessors, which is not exploited as much as it ought to be. Travel is easy: much of the classical world is accessible: it is possible, and should be mandatory, to ensure that all our pupils see Rome for themselves. I hope that this book, which provides a link between literature and the study of the topography and monuments of Rome, will be used to make such visits more profitable. I hope, too, that visitors to Rome who have no previous knowledge of the ancient world—the great majority, nowadays—may find it a *vade-mecum* of an unusual kind, and that many will be stimulated to explore further into classical literature.

I have to acknowledge obligations of many kinds. Dr. Ernest Nash kindly advised me on the choice of illustrations and allowed me to draw on the rich resources of his collection at the Fototeca di Architettura e Topografia dell'Italia Antica, now so conveniently housed at the American Academy in Rome. The Director and staff of the British School at Rome showed me much kindness when I stayed at that agreeable institution. My Birmingham colleague, Dr. John Wilkes, has been good enough to read through my manuscript. I am grateful to the Columbia University Press for permission to quote an extract from N. Lewis and M. Reinhold, *Roman Civilization*; also to the Editor of the *Transactions of the American Philosophical Society* for allowing me to use sections of Professor James H. Oliver's translation of Aelius Aristides. Finally, those who have had the privilege of working with Dr. I. Grafe of the Phaidon Press will understand my debt to his patience and guidance.

Birmingham 1967 D. R. Dudley

CONTENTS

SECTION I

THE SITE OF ROME AND THE GROWTH OF THE CITY · AQUEDUCTS · THE TIBER

THE SITE OF ROME

The city of the Romans is situated in the western parts of Italy on the banks of the Tiber, which flows through the midst of the peninsula, being distant 120 stades (15 miles) from the Tyrrhenian Sea.

DIONYSIUS HALICARNASSUS, *Roman Antiquities*, II. l. I

Inland, the first city above Ostia is Rome, and it is the only one situated on the Tiber. It is said to have been founded from necessity rather than by choice; one should add that even those who founded later sections of it were not free to act for the best, but were the prisoners of existing conditions.

STRABO, *Geography*, V. 3. 7

The site of the city—a matter which calls for the most careful consideration of a founder who wishes to set up a state that will long endure—was chosen by Romulus with almost unbelievable foresight. . . . With admirable prudence he realized that maritime sites are by no means the most advantageous for cities founded in the hope of permanence and empire, firstly, because cities so placed are exposed not merely to numerous dangers, but also to those that cannot be foreseen.

How, therefore, could Romulus have combined with more god-like skill the advantages of a maritime position with the avoidance of its drawbacks, than to found his city on the banks of a copious and smooth-flowing river, with a broad estuary on the sea? This river would enable his city to receive from the sea what she needed, and to export by it her own surplus. This same river, too, would make possible not only the import by sea of all that is most necessary for life and civilization, but also those goods carried by it from the land: even at that early date, I believe, Romulus foresaw that this city would provide a visiting place and a home for a world empire: for certainly no city placed in any other part of Italy could more readily have wielded such great authority as Rome.

Again, as to the natural defences of the city itself, is there anyone so indifferent as not to have surveyed them and to keep them firmly fixed in his mind? The extent and siting of the wall was determined with so much wisdom by Romulus and the other kings, being set on all sides upon steep and precipitous hills, that the one natural approach, between the Esquiline and the Quirinal, was protected by a huge ditch with an enormous rampart surrounding it. The citadel, too, was so well fortified by its sheer circuit, with the rock, as it were, cut to fit it, that even in that appalling storm of the Gallic invasion it remained secure and impregnable.

Moreover, Romulus chose a site with a good supply of springs, and healthy though in an unhealthy district: for there are hills which themselves catch the breezes and also provide shade for the valleys.

CICERO, *On the Republic*, II. 3, 5: 5, 10: 6, 11

So much then, for the advantages which the nature of the land conveys on the city: but the Romans have added others by their own foresight. For while the

Greeks bore the reputation of being discerning choosers of sites for the foundation of cities, aiming at beauty, defensive siting, harbours, and fertile soil, the Romans showed good discrimination in points neglected by the Greeks, such as the construction of roads and aqueducts, and of sewers that could wash the filth of the city into the Tiber. They have built paved roads throughout the country, levelling ridges and filling up hollows, so as to make possible the movements of heavily loaded waggons. The sewers are vaulted with close-fitting slabs and in some places are wide enough for waggons with a full load of hay to pass through them. And such is the quantity of water brought in by the aqueducts, that veritable rivers flow through the city and its sewers: almost every house has cisterns, water-pipes, and copious fountains. It was Marcus Agrippa who particularly concerned himself with this amenity, though of course he beautified the city with many other benefactions. One may say that the earlier Romans cared little for the beauty of their city, since they were preoccupied with other, more utilitarian measures. But later generations—and especially those of the modern age and our own times, have by no means fallen short on this score, but have filled the city with many and splendid endowments of their munificence. For example, Pompey, the late Julius Caesar, Augustus, his friends and sons, his wife and sister have surpassed all others in their zeal for building and willingness to meet its expenses. The Campus Martius is the site for most of these buildings. It is of impressive size, and allows chariot-racing and other equestrian exercises to go on without interfering with the crowds of people exercising themselves with ball games, hoops, and wrestling. The many works of art that surround it, the ground covered throughout the year with grass, the ridges of the hills rising above the river, or sloping down to its edge, all look like the painted backcloth to a stage, and form a spectacle from which it is hard to tear yourself away. . . . There, too, is the Mausoleum, a huge mound near the river on a high base of white marble, covered with evergreen trees to its summit. It bears on the summit a statue of Caesar Augustus, and within the mound are the tombs of himself, his kinsmen, and his friends. Behind it is an enclosed precinct with superb walks, and near the centre of the Campus, by the crematorium (*ustrinum*) of Augustus is a wall, also of white marble, surrounded by a circular fence of iron and planted inside with black poplars.

Again, if one should go to the Old Forum, and see one Forum after another ranged beside it, with their basilicas and temples, and then see the Capitol and the great works of art on it, and the Palatine, and the Porticus of Livia, it would be easy to forget the world outside. Such, then, is Rome.

STRABO, *Geography*, v. 3. 8

(Southern peoples have the keenest wits, but lack valour, northern peoples have great courage but are slow-witted). . . . Such being the way Nature has arranged the universe, and allotted to all these peoples temperaments lacking in moderation, the really perfect land, which is under the middle zone of heaven, and has on either side of it the whole extent of the world and its several countries, is that inhabited by the Roman people.

The fact is that the peoples of Italy have the optimum constitution in both respects—both in physique and in the mental intelligence that is a match for their valour. . . . So Italy, lying between the North and the South, combines the advantages of each, and her pre-eminence is well founded and beyond dispute. So by her wisdom she can repel the assaults of the northern barbarians, by her courage she can defeat the ploys of the southerners. It was, therefore, a divine intelligence that placed the city of the Roman people in an excellent and temperate country, so that she might acquire the right to rule over the whole world.

VITRUVIUS, *On Architecture*, VI, I, II

Not without reason have gods and man chosen this site for the founding of a city . . . health-giving hills, a navigable river for the carriage of produce from the interior of the country, or for the import of goods by sea, a position where the sea is near enough for profitable use, but not exposed unduly to the attacks of foreign fleets, a site in the middle of Italy—in fact, a site uniquely endowed to foster the growth of the city.

LIVY, V. 54, 4

From my own home, I turn to the sights of splendid Rome, and in my mind's eye I survey them all. Now I remember the fora, the temples, the theatres covered with marble, the colonnades where the ground has been levelled—now the grass of the Campus Martius and the views over noble gardens, the lakes, the Waterway, the Aqua Virgo. . . .

OVID, *Letters from Pontus*, I. 8. 33–38

Cicero is the earliest writer to be quoted for the site of Rome: the others belong to the age of Augustus. They looked back over seven centuries, in which the tiny settlement of shepherds on the hills above the Tiber had become the mistress of an empire that covered most of the known world. Small wonder that they were so ready—especially the Romans—to invoke divine providence and geographical determinism in almost equal measure. Cicero's account, in particular, is highly coloured, and blind to the disadvantages of the site. The climate was not so healthy, nor the Capitol so impregnable, nor the water so salubrious, as he would have them. And the Tiber is really an unsatisfactory river—much given to flooding, not easily navigable, and with the drawbacks of an estuary exposed to winds and always silting up. Enormous labour and cost had to be devoted to minimizing these disadvantages: they were never really overcome. Strabo does well to see that Rome was founded 'by necessity', and that later generations were the 'prisoners of existing conditions'. Naples, on purely geographical grounds, would be a much better site for the ruling city of the Mediterranean world.

The passage from Vitruvius represents a view of the world that had become well established in the time of Augustus. Rome is the destined seat of empire: Italy, the land providing the optimum conditions for human settlement. This view permeates the *Aeneid*, and is expressed at the highest level of poetic intensity in the Second Georgic. It is, of course, an adaptation by the Romans of ideas very common in classical Greece to explain Greek superiority, and its origins may be traced through Posidonius and Aristotle to the treatise *On Airs, Waters, and Sites* attributed to Hippocrates.

A modern geographer would begin trying to identify the factors favourable to early settlement. These were: the good grazing afforded by the Palatine and Quirinal on defensible sites, the Tiber island, which made possible a crossing of the river on the line of communication between the more highly civilized regions of Campania and Etruria, and an inland position, free from the attacks of pirates (this last a point well recognized by the ancient sources). Thereafter, Rome's development can be explained by Toynbee's theory of 'challenge and response': i.e. the vigour and intelligence shown by her people in exploiting the potential, and overcoming the disadvantages, of their site. Of this there is some prevision in the passage of Strabo.

AENEAS AT THE SITE OF ROME

Vix ea dicta, dehinc progressus monstrat et aram
et Carmentalem Romani nomine portam
quam memorant, nymphae priscum Carmentis honorem,
vatis fatidicae, cecinit quae prima futuros
Aeneadas magnos et nobile Pallanteum.
Hinc lucum ingentem quem Romulus acer Asylum
rettulit et gelida monstrat sub rupe Lupercal,
Parrhasio dictum Panos de more Lycaei.
Nec non et sacri monstrat nemus Argileti
testaturque locum et letum docet hospitis Argi.
Hinc ad Tarpeiam sedem et Capitolia ducit,
aurea nunc, olim silvestribus horrida dumis.
Iam tum religio pavidos terrebat agrestis
dira loci, iam tum silvam saxumque tremebant.
'Hoc nemus, hunc' inquit 'frondoso vertice collem
—quis deus, incertum est—habitat deus: Arcades ipsum
credunt se vidisse Iovem, cum saepe nigrantem

aegida concuteret dextra, nimbosque cieret.
Haec duo praeterea disiectis oppida muris,
reliquias veterumque vides monumenta virorum.
Hanc Ianus pater, hanc Saturnus condidit arcem:
Ianiculum huic, illi fuerat Saturnia nomen.'
Talibus inter se dictis ad tecta subibant
pauperis Euandri passimque armenta videbant
Romanoque foro et lautis mugire Carinis.
ut ventum ad sedes, 'haec' inquit 'limina victor
Alcides subiit, haec illum regia cepit.
aude, hospes, contemnere opes et te quoque dignum
finge deo, rebusque veni non asper egenis.'
dixit, et angusti subter fastigia tecti
ingentem Aenean duxit stratisque locavit
effultum foliis et pelle Libystidis ursae.

VIRGIL, *Aeneid*, VIII. 337–68

Hard on these words, he stepped forward and showed Aeneas an altar, and then a gate which now the Romans call Porta Carmenta. This name commemorates that ancient honour conferred on the prophetic nymph Carmenta, the first to foretell the high destiny of the line of Aeneas, and the renown of Pallanteum. Next Evander showed the huge grove which bold Romulus was later to make his sanctuary, and, under a chill crag, the Lupercal, the Wolf's Cave, which the Arcadians have named after their fashion from Pan, the Wolf-god of Lycaeus. He also showed the sacred grove of the Argiletum, and explained how on this spot Argos met his death, although a guest. Thence to the Tarpeian Fortress and the Capitol; it is all golden now, then it was thickly covered with rank shrubs. Yet even then some unknown dread possessed the country people, even then they feared the forest and the rock. 'This grove,' said Evander, 'this hill with its wooded crest, is the abode of some god—which god, we do not know. My Arcadians believe they have seen Jupiter here, shaking the dark aegis in his right hand to gather the storm-clouds. Then again, you see these two towns whose walls have been shattered?—relics these of the men of ancient times. Father Janus founded one of them: Saturn the other: so their names have long been Janiculum and Saturnia.' With these words, they were drawing near to Evander's home—that of a poor man. On all sides they saw cattle, where now is the Roman Forum, and heard them lowing on wealthy Carinae.

When they reached his dwelling, Evander said 'Hercules as victor crossed this threshold, this was the palace that received that mighty hero. My guest, do you have the courage to scorn wealth, and make yourself worthy of the god: be not overbearing as you enter a humble home.' So he led mighty Aeneas under the roof of the little building, and gave him a bed on a couch strewn with leaves, and spread with the skin of an African she-bear.

Virgil has employed all his art on the high theme of Aeneas at the site of Rome, in a passage which evokes the simplicity of humble beginnings and the grandeur of imperial destiny. Aeneas is imagined as landing at the Navalia, where Procopius tells us that an ancient ship, 'the bark of Aeneas', was piously preserved. He finds Evander and his Arcadians sacrificing to Hercules, at the forerunner of the Great Altar of Hercules in the Forum Boarium, joins the feast, hears the story of Hercules' encounter with the fire-breathing demon Cacus, and gets a brief account of earlier settlements.

Then Evander conducts him to the Palatine, to a simple dwelling on the site of the House of Augustus (see p. 163). Every visitor to Rome should take this walk—and model himself on Aeneas, whose *pietas* includes how to behave as an intelligent tourist:

> miratur facilisque oculos fert omnia circum
> Aeneas, capiturque locis et singula laetus
> exquiritque auditque virum monimenta priorum.
>
> *Aeneid*, VIII. 310–12

(Aeneas was filled with admiration, and eagerly turned his eyes on all around him: he was charmed with the place, and gladly asked questions about every relic of the men of an earlier age . . .)

First he is shown the Altar and Gate of Carmenta. The first—also called a *fanum* or *sacellum*—stood in the Forum Boarium, while the Porta Carmentalis was a gate in the Servian Wall. Then, as they pass up the Velabrum, Aeneas is made to look up left to the Asylum *inter duos lucos* on the Capitol, and right, to the Lupercal, on the slope of the Palatine. Thus the Trojan legend and that of Romulus are brought together. Next, the Tarpeian Rock and the Capitol: the rough hill is already instinct with divinity, and the visions of Arcadian shepherds foreshadow the Golden Capitol of Virgil's day. The two deserted towns, on the Janiculum and the Capitol, go back to earlier settlements still, like the infinite reflections of one mirror in another. From a point perhaps high on the Clivus Capitolinus, the walkers look out over cattle grazing in the marshy valley that was to be the Forum, and on the keel-shaped ridge of the Esquiline called Carinae.

The climax is at Evander's palace, a kind of conflation of the House of Augustus and the Casa Romuli. The keynote is simplicity, goodness, and the service of mankind; we look back to Hercules and forward to Augustus.

THE GROWTH OF THE CITY

THE NEW ROME AFTER 390 B.C.

The proposal was therefore defeated (of migration to Veii), and they began to build the city without a plan of any kind. Tiles were furnished at the public expense: the right of taking stone and other building materials from wherever they pleased was granted, and pledges were required that they would complete their buildings within a year. Such was their hurry that they did not pause to lay out the streets, for all boundary distinctions had been lost and they were building *in vacuo*. This explains why the ancient sewers, once aligned through public property, now frequently pass underneath private houses, and why the city resembles one that is lived in rather than planned.

LIVY, V. 55. 2–5

So the population of Rome increased, and everywhere buildings arose, since the state provided certain grants, and the aediles encouraged building as though it were a public emergency, and also private builders were in a hurry, since the need to use their buildings spurred them on. Within a year the new city was standing.

LIVY, VI. 4. 6

THE REPUBLIC

193 B.C.

The aedileship of M. Aemilius Lepidus and L. Aemilius Paullus in that year was noteworthy. They levied many fines on the cattle-grazers: from this money they placed gilded shields on the roof of the temple of Jupiter, built one colonnade beyond the Porta Trigemina, and added a market to it, and extended a second from the Porta Fortunalis to the Altar of Mars, thus making a road to the Campus (Martius).

LIVY, XXVI. 27. 1–5

179 B.C.

(Building by the censors M. Aemilius Lepidus and M. Fulvius Nobilior.) From the moneys raised and divided between them, Lepidus built a theatre with a proscaenium by the Temple of Apollo, restored the Temple of Jupiter on the Capitol, and had the columns surrounding it scoured and painted white: he removed from these columns statues that seemed inconveniently placed, and removed shields and military standards placed upon them. M. Fulvius carried out still more works, and of greater utility—a harbour and bridge piles in the Tiber (P. Scipio Africanus and L. Mummius as censors later placed contracts for the arches to be added to these piers), a basilica behind the new shops, and a fish market surrounded by shops which he sold to private owners: a forum and colonnade outside Porta Trigemina, and another by the Navalia, by the shrine of Hercules, behind the Temple of Spes by the Tiber, by the Temple of Apollo the Physician. They had also certain funds in common, from which they placed contracts for bringing in water and for building arches (for an aqueduct). M. Licinius Crassus hindered this work, by refusing to grant way leave over his property. Of the censors, M. Aemilius requested the Senate to allow him money for the games, so permitting the dedication of a temple to Juno the Queen and to Diana, which he had vowed eight years earlier during the war against the Ligurians. 20,000 *asses* were voted and he dedicated these two temples, in the Circus Flaminius.... He also dedicated the Temple of Lares Marini on the Campus (Martius).

LIVY, XL. 51. 2–8

THE SPOILS OF SYRACUSE, 212 B.C.

When Marcellus captured Syracuse, he brought to Rome the treasure of that city—pictures and statues, which were plentiful in Syracuse. . . . This was indeed the origin of that passionate admiration for the products of Greek art, and due to this licence came the habit of despoiling everything, sacred or profane.

LIVY, XXV. 40. I. 2

When Marcellus was recalled by the Romans to fight in Italy, he took back with him the greater and most beautiful part of the dedicatory offerings from Syracuse, intending these both for display at his triumph and to beautify the city. Previously Rome neither possessed nor knew about such fine and sophisticated works, nor was there any taste for delicate and refined art. She was filled rather with the arms of barbarian peoples and with the spoils of war, and crowned with the memorials and trophies of her triumphs—no pleasing or reassuring sight, indeed, nor one calculated to gladden unwarlike or luxury-loving visitors. As Epaminondas called the plain of Boeotia 'the dancing-plain of Ares', and Xenophon spoke of Ephesus as 'the workshop of war', so might the Rome of those days have been called, in Pindar's words 'the sacred temple of the God steeped in battle'. So Marcellus won favour with the common people, because he had graced Rome with objects that had all the beauty and charm and faithfulness to life of the arts of Greece. But with an older generation it was Fabius Maximus who was thought of better, for when Tarentum was captured he did not remove or carry off works of art: money and other valuables he did indeed bring away, but the statues he allowed to remain, adding the famous comment 'Let us leave the Gods here: they are angry with the people of Tarentum'. And they censured Marcellus for bringing Rome into invidium, seeing that she displayed not merely men but also gods in her triumphs: again, here was a people used only to war and agriculture, unused to luxury and idleness, a people like the Hercules of Euripides, plain and unadorned, but true in great issues—and now he had filled them with idleness, and with empty chatter about art and artists, so that they filled much of the day in such pretentious discussions. But despite all this criticism, Marcellus spoke with pride of his actions even to Greeks, claiming that he had taught the ignorant Romans to admire and prize the beautiful and wonderful works of Greece.

PLUTARCH, *Marcellus*, XXI

THE SPOILS OF CORINTH, 143–2 B.C.

Signa statuas tabulas Corinthias L. Mummius distribuit circa oppida et Romam ornavit.

Lucius Mummius distributed sculptures, statues, and paintings from Corinth around the towns (of Italy), and with them ornamented Rome.

LIVY, LIII, frag. Oxyr. 165

And indeed, of the other works of art in Rome, the most numerous and the best came from Corinth.

STRABO, *Geography*, viii. 6. 23.

JULIUS CAESAR

Lex Julia Municipalis

QVAE VIAE IN VRBE[[m]] ROM(a) PROPIUSVE V(rbem) R(omam) P(assvs) (mille), VBEI CONTINENTE HABITABITVR, SVNT ERVNT, QVOIVS ANTE AEDIFICIVM EARVM QVAE VIAE ERVNT, IS EAM VIAM ARBITRATV EIVS AED(ilis), QVOI EA PARS VRBIS H(ac) L(ege) OB VENERIT, TVEATVR . . .

AED(iles) CVR(vles), AED(iles) PL(ebei) . . . IN DIEBVS V PROXVMEIS, QVIBVS EO MAG(istratvi) DESIGNATEI ERUNT EVMVE MAG(istratvm) INIERINT, INTER SE PARANTO AVT SORTIVNTO, QVA IN PARTEI VRBIS QVISQVE EORVM VIAS PVBLICAS IN VRBE[[m]] ROMA, PROPIVSVE V(rbem) R(omam) P(assvs) [M], REFICIVNDAS STERNENDAS CVRET EIVSQUE REI PROCVRATIONEM HABEAT. . . .

QVO MINVS AED(iles) ET IIIIVIR(ei) VIEIS IN VRBEM PVRGANDEIS, IIVIR(ei) VIEIS EXTRA PROPIVSVE VRBEM ROM(am) PASSVS [M] PVRGANDEIS . . . VIAS PVBLICAS PVRGANDAS CVRENT . . .

QVAE LOCA PVBLICA PORTICVSVE [p]VBLICAE IN V(rbe) R(oma) P(ropivs)VE V(rbem) R(omam) P(assvs) [M] SVNT ERVNT, QVORVM LOCORVM QVOIVSQVE PORTICVS AEDILIVM [e]ORVMVE MAG(istratvom),

QVEI VIEIS LOCEISVE PVBLICEIS V(rbis) R(omae) P(ropivs)VE V(rbem) R(omam) P(assvs) M PVRGANDEIS PRAERVNT, LEGIBVS PROCVRATIO EST ERIT, NEI QVIS IN IEIS LOCEIS INVE IEIS PORTICIBVS QVID INAEDIFICATVM INMOLITOMVE HABETO, NEVE EA LOCA PORTICVMVE QVAM POSSIDETO, NEVE EORVM QVOD SAEPTVM CLAVSVMVE HABETO, QVO MINVS EIS LOCEIS PORTICIBVSQUE POPVLVS VTATVR PATEANTVE, NISI QVIBVS VTEIQVE LEG(ibvs) PL(ebei)VE SC(itis) S(enatvs)VE C(onsvltis) CONCESSVM PERMISSVMVE E⟨st⟩.

As for the roads which are or shall be within the city of Rome, or within one mile of the city of Rome and within the limits of continuous habitation, it shall be the duty of every person before whose property such a road shall run, to maintain that road to the satisfaction of the aedile in whose charge that portion of the city shall be assigned by this law. . . .

That aediles, whether curule or plebeian, shall within the five days following their nomination or appointment to office, arrange or draw lots among themselves to determine in which part of the city of Rome, and within one mile of the city of Rome, each of them shall have charge of the repair and paving of the roads, and who shall have special responsibility for this matter. . . .

Nothing in this law is intended to prevent the aediles and the *quattuorviri* who bear special responsibility for cleaning roads within the city, and the *duoviri* for cleaning roads outside the city but within the one-mile limit, from attending to the cleaning of public roads. . . .

As regards public places and porticoes which are or shall be within the city of Rome, or within one mile of the city of Rome, which shall by law be under the charge of aediles or of those magistrates who supervise the cleaning of roads and public places within the city of Rome or within one mile of the city of Rome: no person shall in such public places or porticoes have any such place closed or blocked off in such a manner as to deprive the public of free access to and free use of such places and porticoes, except for such persons and in such manner as shall be allowed by laws, plebiscites, or decrees of the Senate.

CIL, I², 593; ILS, 6085, 20–21; 24–27; 50–51; 68–72

Caesar undertook daily great works for the embellishment and convenience of the city. Notable especially were his plans for a Temple of Mars, to be the biggest in the world, for which he would have filled in and paved the lake in which he had displayed the sham naval battles. There was also to have been a great theatre, built into the side of the Tarpeian Hill. . . . He also planned Greek and Latin libraries on the largest possible scale, entrusting to Marcus Varro the task of collection and classification. Death overtook him in the midst of these projects and plans.

SUETONIUS, *Caesar* 44

A little later came P. Capito with Titus Carrinas. I could scarcely get them to take their coats off, still, they did stay and all went well. But Capito did happen to talk about a plan for improving the city. The Tiber is to be canalized from the Milvian Bridge past the Vatican hills, the Campus Martius to be built over, the Campus Vaticanus to be used for the same purposes as the Campus Martius is at present. 'Such is the law to be passed: Caesar wills it.'

CICERO, *Letters to Atticus*, XIII. 33a, 1

Here's an intolerable thing! Your fellow countryman is improving Rome—which he saw for the first time within the last couple of years. And he finds it too unimpressive, though it was large enough to contain his greatness! Write to me on these matters.

(45 B.C.) CICERO, *Letters to Atticus*, XIII. 35. 1

Legends of the foundation and dedication of early temples will be found in their place in the sections which deal with early sites in the Forum, and on the Palatine and the Capitol. The passages given here provide the bald outline of a building history of Rome from the Gallic invasion of 390 B.C. to the fourth century A.D.

Intelligent Romans of Livy's generation were puzzled by their city. Why, apart from some fine public buildings, was it so unplanned and disorderly—not merely unworthy of a world capital, but lacking even the gridded street-plan of a Roman *colonia*? As Livy saw it, a great opportunity was lost when Rome was rebuilt after the destruction of 390 B.C., which was on a scale not repeated for the next four centuries. Public pressure and private urgency failed to turn this circumstance to advantage. It is very doubtful whether this view has much basis in reality. It was not within the mental horizon of the generation of Camillus—nor, perhaps, their financial means—to provide themselves with an up-to-date specimen of Greek town-planning. They rebuilt the city in the same haphazard way in which it had grown, and so it continued, in the older part at least, despite the building programmes of Julius Caesar and Augustus, down to the Great Fire of Nero.

The republican system of city-government, indeed, discouraged town-planning on a large scale. Public buildings and amenities were the responsibility of the censors and the aediles—magistrates who held short-term offices, and who disposed neither of large funds nor of adequate staff. Forward planning could not be looked for, though sometimes able or ambitious men could carry through a considerable programme, as happened in 193 and 179 B.C. Most of their works, it will be seen, served either religion or social utility. For her embellishment, Rome depended on generals who conquered cities such as Syracuse or Corinth, two major art-centres of the Greek world. While Marcellus was an enlightened philhellene, tradition represents Mummius as a philistine. Both, however, brought to Rome the seductive delight of Greek art and thereby corrupted her native innocence, as Plutarch agrees (so oddly) with the older generation of Marcellus' contemporaries.

In the last fifty years of the Republic, Sulla had a period of dictatorship, and Pompey brought back huge sums of money from his eastern conquests. Both were able to build on a scale not previously known in Rome—witness Sulla's work on the Tabularium, the Capitol, and in the Forum (pp. 55, 72), and the *opera Pompeii* in the Campus Martius (p. 183).

Neither, however, conceived of town-planning as would a Wren or Haussmann. Julius Caesar did. It is a pity that we do not know more of his plans for Rome, and that some of what we do know comes from political opponents. The eminent Greek architect whose condescension provoked Cicero's ire remains anonymous. But clearly a development plan for the city as a whole was drawn up, and such bold schemes as those for canalizing the Tiber and for developing the Campus Martius speak for themselves. Caesar had power, money, and vision—what he was not granted was time. Some of his great projects were never carried out, others that he began, such as the Forum Julium and the Basilica Julia, were completed by Augustus. In building, as in politics, time was to be Augustus' strongest card.

AUGUSTUS

CVRIAM ET CONTINENS EI CHALCIDICVM TEMPLVMQVE APOLLINIS IN PALATIO CVM PORTICIBVS, AEDEM DIVI IVLI, LVPERCAL, PORTICVM AD CIRCVM FLAMINIVM, QVAM SVM APPELLARI PASSVS EX NOMINE EIVS QVI PRIOREM EODEM IN SOLO FECERAT OCTAVIAM, PVLVINAR AD CIRCVM MAXIMVM, AEDES IN CAPITOLIO IOVIS FERETRI ET IOVIS TONANTIS, AEDEM QVIRINI, AEDES MINERVAE ET IVNONIS REGINAE ET IOVIS LIBERTATIS IN AVENTINO, AEDEM LARVM IN SVMMA SACRA VIA, AEDEM DEVM PENATIVM IN VELIA, AEDEM IVVENTATIS, AEDEM MATRIS MAGNAE IN PALATIO FECI.

CAPITOLIVM ET POMPEIVM THEATRVM VTRVMQVE OPVS IMPENSA GRANDI REFECI SINE VLLA INSCRIPTIONE NOMINIS MEI. RIVOS AQVARVM COMPLVRIBVS LOCIS VETVSTATE LABENTES REFECI, ET AQVAM QVAE MARCIA APPELLATVR DVPLICAVI FONTE NOVO IN RIVVM EIVS INMISSO. FORVM IVLIVM ET BASILICAM, QVAE FVIT INTER AEDEM CASTORIS ET AEDEM SATVRNI, COEPTA PROFLIGATAQVE OPERA A PATRE MEO, PERFECI, ET EANDEM BASILICAM CONSVMPTAM INCENDIO AMPLIATO

EIVS SOLO SVB TITVLO NOMINIS FILIORVM M[EORVM I]NCOHAVI ET, SI VIVVS NON PERFECISSEM, PERFICI AB HEREDIBVS [MEIS IVS]SI. DVO ET OCTAGINTA TEMPLA DEVM IN VRBE CONSVL SEX[TV]M EX [AVCTORI] TATE SENATVS REFECI, NVLLO PRAETERMISSO QVOD E[O] TEMPORE [REFICI DEBEBA]T. CONSVL SEPTIMVM VIAM FLAMINIAM A[B VRBE] ARI[MINVM REFECI PONTES]QVE OMNES PRAETER MVLVIVM ET MINVCIVM.

IN PRIVATO SOLO MARTIS VLTORIS TEMPLVM [F]ORVMQVE AVGVSTVM [EX MA]N[I]BIIS FECI. THEATRVM AD AEDE(M) APOLLINIS IN SOLO MAGNA EX PARTE A P[R]I[V]ATIS EMPTO FECI, QVOD SVB NOMINE M. MARCELL[I] GENERI MEI ESSET. DON[A E]X MANIBIIS IN CAPITOLIO ET IN AEDE DIVI IV[L]I ET IN AEDE APOLLINIS ET IN AEDE VESTAE ET IN TEMPLO MARTIS VLTORIS CONSACRAVI, QVAE MIHI CONSTITERVNT HS CIRCITER MILLIENS.

I built: the Curia, and the Chalcidicum which adjoins it, the Temple of Apollo on the Palatine and its colonnades, the Temple of Divus Julius, the Lupercal, the Colonnade by the Circus Flaminius (which I allowed to be called the Porticus Octavia, from the name of the Octavius who built an earlier colonnade on the same site), the imperial box in the Circus Maximus, the Temple of Jupiter Feretrius, on the Capitol, and also that of Jupiter Tonans, the Temple of Quirinus, the Temples of Minerva and of Juno Regina and of Jupiter the Giver of Freedom on the Aventine, the Temple of the Lares on the summit of the Sacred Way, the Temple of the Penates on the Velia, the Temple of Juventas, the Temple of Magna Mater on the Palatine.

I repaired the Capitol and the Theatre of Pompeius—both works calling for lavish expenditure—without any inscription of my own name. I repaired water conduits which had become derelict with age in very many places: I doubled the Aqua Marcia by enriching its flow from a new source. The Forum Julium, and the Basilica between the Temples of Castor and of Saturn—works which had been begun and carried forward by my Father—I brought to completion. When the Basilica Julia was destroyed by fire I began its restoration on an enlarged site under the name of my sons, giving instructions that my heirs should complete it if I did not live to do so. As Consul for the sixth time and on the authority of the Senate, I restored eighty-two temples of the gods within the City, neglecting none that then stood in need of repair. In my seventh consulship I repaired the Via Flaminia from Rome to Ariminum, together with all its bridges except Pons Milvius and Pons Minucius.

From the spoils of war, I built the Temple of Mars Ultor and the Forum of Augustus on land which I owned in person. I built the Theatre by the Temple of Apollo, on land which was mostly bought from private owners, which should bear the name of my son-in-law, M. Marcellus. From the spoils of war I consecrated gifts in the Capitol, the Temple of Divus Julius, the Temple of Apollo, the Temple of Vesta, and the Temple of Mars Ultor. The cost to myself was some 100,000,000 sesterces.

AUGUSTUS, *Res gestae*, 19–21

Rome was unworthy in her architecture of the position she held in the world, and also prone to damage from floods and fire. Augustus so embellished her that his boast was justified 'I left Rome a city of marble, though I found her a city of bricks'.

As for public safety, he provided against future disasters so far as human foresight could do so. He constructed a very large number of public buildings, the most notable of which were the following—the Forum (of Augustus) with the Temple of Mars Ultor, the Temple of Apollo on the Palatine, the Temple of Jupiter Tonans on the Capitol. . . . The Temple of Apollo was built in that part of his home on the Palatine which the soothsayers pronounced that Apollo had indicated by striking it with lightning . . . he consecrated the Temple of Jupiter Tonans (because he escaped from danger on a night march in Cantabria, when a flash of lightning struck his litter, killing the slave who was going in front of it and carrying a torch). Some of his public works were dedicated in the names of other persons, notably his grandsons, his wife, and his sister, for example the colonnades and basilica of Gaius and Lucius, the colonnades of Livia and Octavia, the Theatre of Marcellus.

He also frequently urged other leading public men to embellish the city by constructing new public monuments or restoring old ones, according to their means. Many did so: for example, Marcius Philippus built the Temple of Hercules and the Muses, Lucius Cornificius, the Temple of Diana, Asinius Pollio, the Hall of Freedom, Munatius Plancus, the Temple of Saturn. There were also a theatre by Cornelius Balbus, an amphitheatre by Statilius Taurus, and many splendid buildings by Marcus Agrippa.

Augustus divided the city into regions and wards, placing the former under the control of magistrates chosen annually by lot, while the wards were under supervisors elected by the people in each neighbourhood. Against fires, he organized water-companies and firemen: against flood he cleared and scoured the channel of the Tiber, which had been filled up with rubble and choked with the debris of fallen buildings.

He restored ruined or burned temples and enriched them with the most princely gifts: for example, a single benefaction gave the shrine of Capitoline Jupiter 16,000 pounds of gold, and jewels and pearls to the value of 500,000 sesterces.

SUETONIUS, *Augustus* 28. 3; 30. 1

The most authentic document we have for the growth of the city is the lapidary description of his vast programme of public works contained in the *Res Gestae* of Augustus. It includes new buildings of the first importance, such as the Temple of Apollo and Forum of Augustus, the completion of projects begun by Julius Caesar, a generous policy of restoration, including all the temples in the city then in need of repair, public works such as roads, bridges, and aqueducts, and the dedication of treasures of art in the great temples. Suetonius amplifies what Augustus omits—the encouragement he gave to the generosity of others. Agrippa, in particular, must rank among the greatest of the builders of Rome for his development of the Campus Martius. This, together with the imperial fora, gave Rome a splendid new quarter which may be compared with the New Town of Edinburgh. The passage from Strabo describes it not long after it was built (see p. 4).

Hardly less important were Augustus' arrangement for municipal administration and services. The division into regions and wards in the charge of local officials was of lasting importance. The City could not have supported its huge population of imperial times without the police force, and the measures against damage by fire and flood, which he set on a permanent footing.

There can therefore be no doubt that Augustus left Rome a city, at last, *pro maiestate imperii ornata*. Yet it would be wrong to suppose that the high peak of city development was reached in his reign. His programme was concerned with public building, the housing of its citizens he left untouched. *Vetus Roma*, the ancient and often squalid city, with its Subura and other slums, continued unchanged. Moreover, it has been pointed out that the architecture to which he gave official sanction was conservative and even reactionary, neglecting the technical advances that had begun to appear in the time of Sulla for what was in effect a Classical Revival, based on the styles of Hellenistic and Periclean architecture. The possibilities opened up by the use of concrete and its application to great vaulted buildings were left for later generations to exploit. So it is that the curve for Roman architecture does not correspond with that for literature. No one can deny that, in Latin literature, the Age of Augustus was indeed the Golden Age. In architecture and the allied arts, it was surpassed by the great projects of Nero, the Flavians, Trajan, and Hadrian. And for the story of urbanism in ancient Rome, technological advance and public disaster contrived that the first name should be that of Nero.

THE GREAT FIRE OF NERO

Sequitur clades, forte an dolo principis incertum (nam utrumque auctores prodidere), sed omnibus, quae huic urbi per violentiam ignium acciderunt, gravior atque atrocior. Initium in ea parte circi ortum, quae Palatino Caelioque montibus contigua est, ubi per tabernas, quibus id mercimonium inerat, quo flamma alitur, simul coeptus ignis et statim validus ac vento citus longitudinem circi corripuit. Neque enim domus munimentis saeptae vel templa muris cincta aut quid aliud morae interiacebat. Impetu pervagatum incendium plana primum, deinde in edita assurgens et rursus inferiora populando anteiit remedia velocitate mali et obnoxia urbe artis itineribus hucque et illuc flexis atque enormibus vicis, qualis vetus Roma fuit. Ad hoc lamenta paventium feminarum, fessa aetate aut rudis pueritiae [aetas], quique sibi quique aliis consulebant, dum trahunt invalidos aut opperiuntur, pars mora, pars festinans, cuncta impediebant. Et saepe, dum in tergum respectant, lateribus aut fronte circumveniebantur, vel si in proxima evaserant, illis quoque igni correptis, etiam quae longinqua crediderant in eodem casu reperiebant. Postremo, quid vitarent quid peterent ambigui, complere vias, sterni per agros; quidam amissis omnibus fortunis, diurni quoque victus, alii caritate suorum, quos eripere nequiverant, quamvis patente effugio interiere. Nec quisquam defendere audebat, crebris multorum minis restinguere prohibentium, et quia alii palam faces iaciebant atque esse sibi auctorem vociferabantur, sive ut raptus licentius exercerent seu iussu.

Eo in tempore Nero Anti agens non ante in urbem regressus est, quam domui eius, qua Palatium et Maecenatis hortos continuaverat, ignis propinquaret. Neque tamen sisti potuit, quin et Palatium et domus et cuncta circum haurirentur. Sed solacium populo exturbato ac profugo campum Martis ac monumenta Agrippae, hortos quin etiam suos patefecit et subitaria aedificia extruxit, quae multitudinem inopem acciperent; subvectaque utensilia ab Ostia et propinquis municipiis, pretiumque frumenti minutum usque ad ternos nummos. Quae quamquam popularia in irritum cadebant, quia pervaserat rumor ipso tempore flagrantis urbis inisse eum domesticam scaenam et cecinisse Troianum excidium, praesentia mala vetustis cladibus adsimulantem.

Sexto demum die apud imas Esquilias finis incendio factus, prorutis per immensum aedificiis, ut continuae violentiae campus et velut vacuum caelum occurreret. Necdum positus metus aut redierat plebi spes: rursum grassatus ignis, patulis magis urbis locis; eoque strages hominum minor, delubra deum et porticus amoenitati dicatae latius procidere. Plusque infamiae id incendium habuit, quia praediis Tigellini Aemilianis proruperat videbaturque Nero condendae urbis novae et cognomento suo appellandae gloriam quaerere. Quippe in regiones quattuordecim Roma dividitur, quarum quattuor integrae manebant, tres solo tenus deiectae, septem reliquis pauca tectorum vestigia supererant, lacera et semusta.

Domuum et insularum et templorum, quae amissa sunt, numerum inire haud promptum fuerit; sed vetustissima religione, quod Servius Tullius Lunae, et magna ara fanumque, quae praesenti Herculi Arcas Euander sacraverat, aedesque Statoris Iovis vota Romulo Numaeque regia et delubrum Vestae cum Penatibus populi Romani exusta; iam opes tot victoriis quaesitae et Graecarum artium decora, exin monumenta ingeniorum antiqua et incorrupta, (ut) quamvis in tanta resurgentis urbis pulchritudine multa seniores meminerint, quae reparari nequibant. Fuere qui adnotarent XIIII Kal. Sextiles principium incendii huius ortum, quo et Senones captam urbem inflammaverint. Alii eo usque cura progressi sunt, ut totidem annos mensesque et dies inter utraque incendia numerent.

Disaster followed, in the form of the most terrible and destructive fire Rome has ever known. Whether this was accidental, or elaborately contrived by the Emperor, is uncertain; historians give both versions. It began in the part of the Circus Maximus which is close to the Palatine and Caelian Hills, and among shops whose wares included inflammable goods. The fire took hold at once, and the wind very quickly spread it the length of the Circus, where there were no palaces with outer walls nor temples within precincts nor indeed anything else to check it. First it swept through all the level ground, then climbed the hills, then returned again to destroy the lower districts. The speed with which it spread, and the all-too-inflammable nature of the old city, with its narrow winding streets and irregular buildings, nullified all attempts to contain it. All movement was blocked by the terrified, shrieking women, by helpless old people or children, by those who sought their own safety or tried to help others—some carrying invalids, others waiting for them to catch up, some rushing headlong, others rooted to the spot. When people looked back, outbreaks of fire threatened them from the front or the flanks. When they reached a neighbouring quarter, that too was alight: even what they had supposed to be remote districts were found to be affected. Finally, utterly at a loss as to what to avoid or where to go, they filled the streets, or collapsed in the fields. Some died because they had lost everything they had—even their food for the day. Others had lost their loved ones in the flames, and preferred death, though they could have escaped. No one dared to fight the flames. Menacing gangs threatened anyone who dared to put out the fire; indeed, some men openly cast on torches, and said they had their instructions. They may have been acting under orders, they may simply have wanted a freer hand to loot.

Nero was then at Antium. He did not return to Rome until the flames were threatening the house he had built to link the Palatine with the Gardens of Maecenas. But the fire could not be checked before it had destroyed the Palatine itself, the palace, and everything in the vicinity. As a refuge for the terrified, homeless people he threw open the Campus Martius and the buildings of Agrippa. He also opened his own gardens, and constructed emergency huts to house the thousands of helpless refugees. Supplies were brought in from Ostia and the neighbouring towns, and the price of corn was reduced to 3 sesterces a peck. These were meant to be popular measures, but they earned no gratitude, for a widespread report had it that as the city was burning Nero entered his private theatre and sang 'The Fall of Troy', comparing the modern with the ancient calamity.

The fire was brought to a halt on the sixth day at the foot of the Esquiline, where enormous demolition of houses faced its unbroken violence with open space and bare ground. But before terror was allayed, or hope could revive in the people, there was a fresh outbreak in the more open parts of the city. Here actual loss of life was less, but the destruction of temples and amenities such as colonnades was even more widespread. This second fire was the more suspicious because it started on the estates of Tigellinus in the Aemilian district. Nero, it seemed, longed for the glory of founding a new city, and giving it his own name. For indeed, of the fourteen regions into which Rome was divided, only four remained intact, three were destroyed to ground level; in the other seven a few houses survived, but half-burned and severely damaged.

It would be a long task to enumerate all the palaces, blocks of apartments, and temples that were destroyed. Among famous and ancient shrines, there perished Servius Tullius' Temple of the Moon-Goddess, the Great Altar and Shrine which Evander dedicated to Hercules, the Temple of Jupiter Stator, the Regia, the work of Romulus and of Numa, and above all, the Shrine of Vesta and the Penates of the Roman People. There perished too the spoils of so many victories, the masterpieces of Greek art, and the ancient and authentic manuscripts of so many of the great writers of Roman literature. For all the beauty of the re-built city, there are many of an older generation who remember those losses as unique and irreplaceable. It was noted in some quarters that the fire began on July 19th, the very day on which the Senonian Gauls burned the city. Others inquired so as to discover that between the two fires there elapsed the same number of years, plus months, plus days.

TACITUS, *Annals*, XV, 38–41

HAEC AREA, INTRA HANC DEFINITIONEM CIPPORVM CLAVSA VERIBVS, ET ARA, QVAE EST INFERIVS, DEDICATA EST AB IMP. CAESARE DOMITIANO AVG. GERMANICO EX VOTO SVSCEPTO, QVOD DIV ERAT NEGLECTVM NEC REDDITVM, INCENDIORVM ARCENDORVM CAVSA, QVANDO VRBS PER NOVEM DIES ARSIT NERONIANIS TEMPORIBVS. HAC LEGE DEDICATA EST, NE CVI LICEAT INTRA HOS TERMINOS AEDIFICIVM EXSTRVERE, MANERE, NEGOTIARI, ARBOREM PONERE ALIVDVE QVID SERERE, ET VT PRAETOR, CVI HAEC REGIO SORTI OBVENERIT, SACRVM FACIAT, ALIVSVE QVIS MAGISTRATVS VOLCANALIBVS X K. SEPTEMBRES OMNIBVS ANNIS VITVLO ROBEO ET VERRE. . . .

This open space, as enclosed within the limits of this ring of *cippi*, and the altar which is below, were dedicated by the emperor Caesar Domitianus Augustus Germanicus, in discharge of a vow undertaken, but long neglected and not honoured, for the purpose of preventing fires, when the City burned for nine days in the reign of Nero. It is dedicated on condition that no-one may within these limits be permitted to build a house, remain, carry on a trade, plant a tree or any other crop: also that the praetor to whom charge of this district of the city shall fall by lot, or some other magistrate, shall at the Festival of Volcanus on the 23rd of August in every year offer a red calf and a boar. . . .

CIL, VI. 826

The Great Fire of A.D. 64 was the most calamitous of the many that afflicted Rome, such as those under Augustus in A.D. 6, under Tiberius in 27 and again in 37, when the Circus was also involved. In the fire of A.D. 191 (see p. 171) destruction was almost on the same scale as under Nero. Although Augustus had set up a fire-brigade of 7,000 men, it was not very effective. Lacking fire-fighting apparatus, the chief methods of containing a fire were by means of specially built fire-breaks, such as the wall behind the Forum of Augustus (see p. 127), or by clearing buildings in the path of the flames. The account of Tacitus suggests that fire-storms developed which, as shown in the incendiary raids of the Second World War (e.g. at Dresden), are hard to stop even by modern methods.

The fire of 64 started in the shops on the outside of the north wall of the Circus Maximus, which were a major fire-risk. It is to be noted that all the surviving accounts of the fire (especially Pliny, *N.H.* 17. 1. 5) attribute the blame to Nero. Suetonius (*Nero* 31) expressly says that gangs of Nero's slaves were at work spreading the flames. Suetonius and Dio both give the story about Nero's recital: the private theatre may have been in the Gardens of Maecenas. Despite the apparent precision of Tacitus and the other sources, it is not easy to establish the area of destruction. The four Augustan regions which were intact were presumably the XIVth (Transtiberina), Ist (Porta Capena), Vth (Esquilina), and VIth (Quirinal). Total destruction overtook the IIIrd (Subura), Xth (Palatine) and XIth (Circus Maximus).

The Aemilian district was in the southern part of the Campus Martius, where the City Prefect, Tigellinus, owned slum property. The fire broke out on July 19th, A.D. 64, i.e. 417 years, 417 months, and 417 days after the entry into Rome of the Senonian Gauls. According to the inscription quoted (see also Plate 11) it burned for nine days: this presumably includes the second outbreak mentioned by Tacitus.

Comparable as a disaster to the Fire of London in 1666, it was also a landmark in the building history of the city. Severus and Celer were probably the counterparts of Wren in the plans for the Nova Urbs or New City which arose after the fire had done its work.

THE NERONIAN NOVA URBS

In the part of the city not reserved for the Palace, the re-building was not at random nor uncontrolled, as after the Gallic fire. Regulations prescribed the alignment of roads, the width of streets, and the height of houses. They stood in spacious building-plots and colonnades were added to the blocks of apartments so as to protect their street frontage. Nero undertook to construct these colonnades at his own expense, and to clear up all building-sites before restoring them to their owners.

Rewards were announced, in proportion to the standing and resources of individual citizens, for the completion of private houses or blocks of apartments by a given date.

The marshes by Ostia were designated for the dumping of rubble, and instructions were given that the ships employed to bring corn up the river should make the return trip loaded with rubble.

A portion of all buildings had to be made without timber and of stone from Gabii or Albano, which is fire-proof. Water-inspectors were appointed to ensure a better and more efficient service from the public supply, which had suffered from the tapping of unauthorized individuals. Each householder had to keep fire-fighting apparatus ready to hand. Party walls were forbidden, buildings must be surrounded by walls of their own. Necessity caused these measures to be accepted, and they certainly added to the city's amenities. Some, however, thought the old city had been a healthier place to live in, arguing that the narrow streets and tall buildings offered protection against the intense heat of the sun, while now the open spaces, devoid of shade, reflect the suns rays much more intensely.

TACITUS, *Annals*, XV, 43. I

Ceterum Nero usus est patriae ruinis extruitque domum—with these words Tacitus inserts into his account of the Great Fire the egocentric folly of the building of Nero's Golden House (see p. 139). But, as he makes clear in the passage quoted above, Nero also used the disasters of his country to build a Nova Urbs or New City, conceived on the most advanced lines of architecture and town-planning, and liberally subsidized from imperial treasury. Severus and Celer, whom Tacitus only mentions in connection with the Golden House, were most likely the architects employed. Note the efficient measures taken for the clearance of sites and disposal of rubble, the regular planning of broad streets on, presumably, a grid pattern, and the restrictions on the height of buildings.

The provision for fire-fighting will sound familiar to those who were in England between 1940 and 1945. Fire-proof material was to be used in all new buildings, fire fighting apparatus to be available on a lavish scale, porticoes to be built as platforms for controlling fire in adjacent buildings—everything, in fact, short of compulsory fire-watching.

MacDonald has recently argued that the phrase *aedificia ipsa certa sui parte sine trabibus saxo Gabino Albanove solidarentur* should be read as meaning that a fixed portion of all buildings must be of concrete, and that those parts that were of stone must be made of (comparatively) fire-resistant kinds. Certainly it is from this period that the use of concrete for large vaulted buildings was resumed and vigorously pushed ahead. In this Neronian Nova Urbs, Rome took on, substantially, the aspect which she bore during the High Empire and down to the end of the imperial period. There would be other great buildings, and great projects such as the Forum of Trajan, but no further re-shaping of the city as a whole.

Tacitus pays tribute to the beauty (*decus*) of the new Rome. But it was progress that came at a price, and he understandably records the nostalgia felt at the loss of the old city with its associations. Others have felt the same at later transformations of Rome.

VESPASIAN TO CONSTANTINE

Romulus left a city with three gates, or to accept the highest figure traditionally recorded, with four. But, when Vespasian and Titus were emperors and censors, in the 826th year since the foundation of the city, its walls had a circuit of 13·2 miles, and covered the seven hills. The city is divided into fourteen regions, and has 265 crossroads with shrines of the Lares. A measurement taken from the Golden Milestone (p. 81) in the Roman Forum to each of the gates—37 in all if the Twelve Gates are counted as one and the seven disused ancient gates omitted—would add up to 20·765 miles. From the same milestone to the edge of the built-up area, including the Castra Praetoria, the measurement of all the roads through the various districts would total a little over 70 miles. If one takes into account the height of the buildings, he would have a proper estimate, and would have to admit that no city in the whole world would stand comparison with Rome. On the east it is bounded by that remarkable work, the rampart of Tarquin, for he built it as high as the walls where the approach was level and the city exposed to attack. On all other sides it was protected by high walls or steep slopes, though now the spread of building has added many whole cities.

PLINY, *Natural History*, III. 66–67 (A.D. 73)

VESPASIAN

The city was disfigured by the marks of old conflagrations and ruined houses: Vespasian allowed anyone to take over vacant sites and to build on them, if the owners had left. In person he began the restoration of the Capitol by clearing away marble, and carting off several basketfuls of it on his own shoulders . . .

He also constructed new works in the Temple of Peace by the Forum, the Temple of Claudius on the Caelian Hill (begun by Agrippina, but virtually destroyed by Nero), and the amphitheatre in the midst of the city, a project once contemplated by Augustus.

SUETONIUS, *Vespasian*, 8. 5–9

DOMITIAN

Domitian restored a great many buildings that had been destroyed by fire: notably the Capitol, which had again burned down (in A.D. 80. See p. 56) but refused to allow the inscription of any other name than his own—even that of the original builder. He did, however, raise a new Temple to Jupiter the Preserver on the Capitol, and also built the forum now called the Forum of Nerva, the Temple of the Flavian House, a stadium, an Odeon, and a place for naval battles.

SUETONIUS, *Domitian*, 5

HADRIAN

Although Hadrian built many buildings, in all parts of the world, he only inscribed his name on one—the Temple of his father, the deified Trajan. At Rome he restored the Pantheon, the Saepta, the Temple of Neptune, and countless other temples, the Forum of Augustus, the Baths of Agrippa, and he dedicated them all in the names of the original builders. Under his own name he built a bridge, the Mausoleum by the Tiber, and the Temple of Bona Dea. He also moved the colossal statue, standing and upright, by the agency of the architect Decrianus, from the place where now stands the Temple of (Venus and) Rome. This was a gigantic piece of engineering, requiring the use of twenty-four elephants.

HISTORIA AUGUSTA, *Hadrian*, 9–12

ALEXANDER SEVERUS

He restored the works of former emperors, and constructed many new ones of his own—among them the Thermae, standing in a park, next to the Thermae of Nero. He gave the aqueduct now called Alexandrina. He made the park for his Thermae by pulling down private houses which he had bought and owned. By adding colonnades, he completed and adorned the Thermae of Caracalla. He was the first to use on the Palatine the 'Alexandrinum opus'—marble made of two kinds of porphyry and Lacedaemonian stone—using slabs of marble so decorated. He placed colossal statues at many points in the city, employing artists imported from all parts of the world.

HISTORIA AUGUSTA, *Alexander Severus* 24, 3

AURELIAN

He built a superb Temple of the Sun-God. He so extended the walls of the City of Rome that their circuit covered almost fifty (sic—really *c.* 12) miles.

HISTORIA AUGUSTA, *Aurelian*, 39. 2

DIOCLETIAN AND MAXIMIAN

When Diocletian and Maximian were Emperors there were repairs to many public buildings: the Senate, the Forum of Caesar, the *Scaena* of the Theatre of Pompey, two colonnades, three *nymphaea*, the two temples of Isis and of Serapis, a new triumphal arch, the Thermae of Diocletian.

ZONARAS, I, p. 279

CONSTANTINE

All the famous sites of the city shine bright with new works: nor is it merely a matter of making conspicuous buildings that had of late become obsolete through the lapse of time, but even those formerly thought most splendid now shine with the gleam of gold and show up the scandalous meanness of our ancestors.

Panegyrici Latini, IV. 35. 4 (A.D. 321)

The seventy-year period from the accession of Vespasian in 69 to the death of Hadrian in 138 has been conveniently termed the High Empire. Of the six emperors, Titus and Nerva had only short reigns, but the other four were all great builders. Vespasian and Trajan both had the spoils of war (*manubiae*) to finance their schemes: Domitian, from vainglory, and Hadrian, as himself an amateur architect, were ready to spend lavishly on building above everything else. Architects flocked to Rome, attracted by the great commissions available. Enough is known of the work of two of them, Rabirius and Apollodorus, to show that they must rank among the most eminent of any period. Under their direction and that of their contemporaries, and within the framework of the Neronian Nova Urbs, the new style of Roman architecture was directed, especially, to serve two major ends—the dignity and achievements of the Imperial House, and the pleasures and amenities of the Roman People. To the former belong the work of Rabirius on the Domus Augustiana on the Palatine (see pp. 168, 172), temples in honour of deified emperors, triumphal arches, columns, and other commemorative monuments. To the latter, the Flavian Amphitheatre, the thermae built by Titus and by Trajan, the Stadium and Odeon of Domitian, the repairs and enlargements to the Circus Maximus. To judge from the Third Satire of Juvenal, all this did no more than alleviate the miseries of the life of the poor. After its many vicissitudes, the Capitoline Temple was restored in new grandeur by Domitian; with the Temple of Venus and Rome and the Pantheon Hadrian endowed Rome with the most remarkable, as architecture, of all her temples. The imperial fora were completed on a yet more splendid scale, for the Temple of Peace and above all, the Forum of Trajan, outdid the work of Julius Caesar and Augustus. Unfortunately the literary sources for the buildings of Trajan and Hadrian are wretchedly inadequate. It was also a period of great engineering in Rome and its vicinity, witness the construction of new aqueducts such as the Aqua Trajana, and the magnificent new harbour built by Trajan at Ostia.

Throughout these seventy years the pace and vigour of building at Rome was sustained. After the death of Hadrian it fell away, and for the next two centuries there were only occasional outbursts of energy. Rome was already splendidly equipped as a world metropolis, and the sheer burden of maintenance and repair of her vast heritage of architecture must have been very great. Political and economic circumstances, and the tastes of individual emperors, determined what new building would be done. Antoninus Pius (138–161) was thrifty, Marcus Aurelius (161–180) was preoccupied with wars, Commodus (180–192) had other interests. The great fire of 191 left an opportunity of which Septimius Severus (193-211) was glad, as the founder of a new dynasty, to take advantage: restoration and new building went on through the reign of Caracalla (211–217) to that of Alexander Severus (222–235). The next fifty years were a period of economic and military disaster. Aurelian (270–275) completed two gigantic projects, a Temple of the Sun, and the Walls which bear his name. The reforms of Diocletian (284–305) brought a new period of comparative prosperity, and the last great works of pagan architecture in a Rome which now counted for less in the world. For though Diocletian built his thermae for 'his beloved Romans' (*Romanis suis*) his own palace was built at Spalato in Dalmatia. The Forum fire under Carinus (283) made room for the great Basilica begun by Maxentius and finished by Constantine (see p. 116). Constantine himself (312–337), apart from his restorations and new work in Rome, especially the first Christian basilicas, was above all concerned with the new capital in the eastern half of the Empire: he must take a high place among the building emperors, although the foundation of Constantinople was disastrous for the political primacy of Rome.

THE 'CURIOSUM URBIS REGIONUM XIV'

BIBLIOTHECAE XXVIII.

OBVLISCI VI. IN CIRCO MAXIMO DVO . . . IN VATICANO VNA . . . IN CAMPO MARTIO VNA . . . IN MVSILEO AVGVSTI DVO . . .

PONTES VIII. AELIVS. AEMILIVS. AVRELIVS. MOLBIVS. SVBLICIVS. FABRICIVS. CESTIVS ET PROBI.

MONTES VII. CAELIVS. ADVENTINVS. TARPEIVS. PALATINVS. EXQVILINVS. VATICANVS ET IANICVLENSIS.

CAMPI VIII. VIMINALIS. AGRIPPES. MARTIVS. CODETANVS. OCTAVIVS. PEQVARIVS. LANATARIVS ET BRVTIANVS.

FORI XI. ROMANVM MAGNVM. CAESARIS. AVGVSTI. NERVAE. TRAIANI. AHENOBARBI. BOARIVM. ⟨SVARIVM⟩. PISTORVM. GALLORVM ET RVSTICORVM.

BASILICAE X. IVLIA. VLPIA. PAVLI. VESTILIA. NEPTVNIA. MATIDIES. MARCIANES. VASCOLARIA. FLOSCELLARIA. CONSTANTINIANA.

THERMAE XI. TRAIANAE. TITIANAE. COMMODIANAE. ANTONINIANAE. ⟨DECIANAE⟩. SYRANAE. AGRIPPIANAE. ALEXANDRINAE. DIOCLETIANAE. CONSTANTINIANAE. SEVERIANAE.

AQVAE XVIIII. TRAIANA. ANIENA. ⟨ANIENA⟩ ALTERA. MARCIA. CLAVDIA. HERCVLEA. CAERVLEA. IVLIA. AVGVSTEA. APPIA. ALSEATINA. CIMINIA. AVRELIA. DAMNATA. VIRGO. TEPVLA. SEVERIANA. ANTONINIANA. ALEXANDRINA.

VIAE XXVIII⟨I⟩. TRAIANA. APPIA. LATINA. LAVICANA. PRAENESTINA. TIBVRTINA. NVMENTANA. SALARIA. FLAMMINEA. AEMILIA. CLODIA. VALERIA. AVRELIA. CAMPANA. OSTIENSIS. PORTVENSIS. IANICVLENSIS. LAVRENTINA. ARDEATINA. SETINA. TIBERINA. QVINTIA. CASSIA. GALLICA. CORNELIA. TRIVMFALIS. PATINARIA. ASINARIA. CIMINIA.

HORVM BREBIARIVM.

CAPITOLIA II. CIRCI II. AMPHITHEATRA II. COLOSSI II. COLVMNAE COCLIDES II. MACELLI II. THEATRA III. LVDI IIII. NAVMACHIAE V. NYMFEA XV. EQVI MAGNI XXII. DEI AVREI LXXX, EBVRNEI LXXIIII. ARCI MARMOREI XXXVI. PORTAE XXXVII. VICI CCCCXXIII. AEDICVLAE CCCCXXIII. VICOMAGISTRI DCLXXII. CVRATORES XXVIIII. INSVLAE PER TOTAM VRBEM $\overline{\mathrm{XLVI}}$.DCII. DOMOS $\overline{\mathrm{M}}$.DCCXC. HORREA CCXC. BALNEA DCCCLVI. LACOS $\overline{\mathrm{M}}$.CCCLII. PISTRINA CCLIIII. LVPANARIAE XLVI. LATRINAE PVBLICAE CXLIIII. COHORTES PRAETORIAE X, VRBANAE IIII, VIGILVM VII, QVORVM EXCVVITORIA XIIII. VEXILLA COMMVNIA II. CASTRA EQVITVM SINGVLARIORVM, PEREGRINORVM, RAVENNATIVM, LECTICARIORVM, SILICARIORVM, MISENATIVM, TABELLARIORVM, VICTIMARIORVM. MENSAE OLEAREAE PER TOTAM VRBEM $\overline{\mathrm{II}}$.CCC.

28 Libraries
6 Obelisks . . . 2 in the Circus Maximus . . . 1 in the Vaticanus . . . 1 in the Campus Martius . . . 2 on the Mausoleum of Augustus.
8 Bridges. The Aelius, Aemilius, Aurelius, Milvius, Sublicius, Fabricius, Cestius, and Pons Probi.
7 Hills. Caelian, Aventine, Tarpeian, Palatine, Esquiline, Vatican and Janiculum.
8 Parks. (Campi) Viminal, Agrippa, Martius, Codetanus, Octavius, Pecuarius, Lantarius and Brutianus.
11 Fora. The Forum Romanum or Great Forum. Fora of Caesar, of Augustus, of Nerva, of Trajan, of Ahenobarbus, the Forum Boarium, Suarium, Pistorum, Gallorum and Rusticorum.
10 Basilicas. Julia, Ulpia, Paula, Vestilia, Neptunia, Matidia, Marciana, Vascolaria, Floscellaria, Constantiniana.
11 Thermae. Those of Trajan, Titus, Commodus, Antoniniana, (or Baths of Caracalla), Suranae, of Agrippa, of Alexander (Severus), of Diocletian, of Constantine, of (Septimius) Severus.
19 Aqueducts. Traiana. Aniena, the second Aniena, Marcia, Claudia, Herculea, Caerulea, Julia, Augustea, Appia, Alseatina, Ciminia, Aurelia, Damnata, Virgo, Tepula, Severiana, Antoniniana, Alexandrina.
29 Chief roads. Traiana etc. etc.

A Summary of the above. 2 Capitols. 2 Circuses. 2 Amphitheatres. 2 Colossi. 2 *Columnae Cochlides*. 2 Market Halls. 3 Theatres. 4 Training-Schools. 5 Naumachia. 15 Nymphaea. 22 major equestrian statues. 80 statues of gods of gold. 74 ditto, of ivory. 36 triumphal arches of marble, 37 city gates, 423 wards, 423 shrines. 672 parish officers. 29 superintendents. Total of blocks of apartment houses in the whole city 46,602: private houses 1790, warehouses 290, baths 856, fountains, 1,352, corn-mills 254, brothels 46, public lavatories 144, 10 Praetorian cohorts, 4 of the City Force, 7 of the City Watch, with 14 stations and 2 joint detachments. Barracks for the Equites Singulares, the peregrini, sailors from Ravenna, the *lecticarii*, the *silicarii*, the sailors from Misenum, the *tabellarii*, the *victimarii*. Tables for the distribution of the oil ration, throughout the city 2300.

Two fourth-century documents are (*faute de mieux*) of prime importance for the topography of Rome. They are the *Curiosum Urbis Regionum XIV* or *Inventory of the Fourteen Regions of the City*, and the *Notitia Regionum XIV* or *Catalogue of the Fourteen Regions*. Both are editions of a description originally written in the reign of Constantine: it is now thought that the *Notitia* should be dated to A.D. 354 and the *Curiosum* to 375. They differ in minor points only. Both list the most noteworthy objects in each of the fourteen city regions, and conclude with an Appendix and a Summary (*breviarium*): the Appendix and Breviarium of the *Curiosum* are given here. Their interpretation raises many problems; a few points only are noted below.

Platner and Ashby list 9 libraries, against the 28 of the *Curiosum*. The obelisks have their height given in Roman feet: the highest (122 ft.) being that erected in the Circus Maximus by Constantius II (see p. 30). No logical order seems to govern the listing of bridges, hills, aqueducts, or roads. Of the fora, those of Ahenobarbus, Pistorum, and Gallorum et Rusticorum, are unknown: so, among the *basilicae*, are Floscellaria and Vascolaria. The Basilica Pauli is Basilica Aemilia: those of Matidia and Marciana presumably stood near the Templum Matidiae, close to the Pantheon. All the *thermae* can be identified: the Thermae Suranae were on the Aventine. Of the aqueducts, 'Alseatina' is the Alsietina built by Augustus; Ciminia is unknown. The roads are the 28 (or 29) main roads approaching the city gates.

The 'two Capitols' are the Capitol proper and the Capitolium vetus, on the Quirinal. The Circuses are Circus Maximus and Circus Flaminius. The Amphitheatres, the Colosseum and the Amphitheatrum Castrense. The two Columns, those of Trajan and of Marcus Aurelius, the *macella*, the Macellum Liviae and Macellum Magnum, the theatres, those of Pompey, Balbus, and Marcellus. The statues listed will have been publicly maintained by the *curator statuarum*. The *curatores* included such major officers as the *curatores alvei et riparum Tiberis*, the *quattorviri viarum curandarum*, in charge of street repairs, officials in charge of sewers, of aqueducts, of public temples, buildings, and places. The *balnea* were private bath-buildings, to be distinguished from the great thermae: some 40 are listed in Platner and Ashby. The brothels were licensed and taxed; the public lavatories let out to contractors.

Finally, the *breviarium* gives a list of troops and of public workmen housed in the city. The Praetorian Guard was in fact abolished by Constantine. The *cohortes urbanae* were under the *praefectus urbi* or City Prefect: the *vigiles*, at once police and firemen, under that of the *praefectus vigilum*, with a station (*excubitoria*) in each of the city regions. The sailors from Ravenna and Misenum handled the awning and scenery in the Colosseum. The litter-bearers and messengers were at the disposal of public officials. The *silicarii* or roadmenders came under a *procurator silicariorum*, who was in the department of the *praefectus vigilum*. The *mensae oleareae* were distribution points for the free ration of olive-oil (*oleum*) administered by the *annona*.

THE VISIT OF THE EMPEROR CONSTANTIUS II

Deinde (imperator Constantius II) intra septem montium culmina, per adclivitates planitiemque posita urbis membra conlustrans et suburbana, quicquid viderat primum, id eminere inter alia cuncta sperabat: Iovis Tarpei delubra, quantum terrenis divina praecellunt: lavacra in modum provinciarum exstructa: amphitheatri molem solidatam lapidis Tiburtini compage, ad cuius sommitatem aegre visio humana conscendit: Pantheum velut regionem teretem speciosa celsitudine fornicatam: elatosque vertices scansili suggestu concharum, priorum principum imitamenta portantes, et Urbis templum forumque Pacis, et Pompei theatrum, et Odeum, et Stadium, aliaque inter haec decora urbis aeternae. Verum cum ad Traiani forum venisset, singularem sub omni caelo structuram, ut opinamur, etiam numinum adsensione mirabilem, haerebat adtonitus, per giganteos contextus circumferens mentem, nec relatu effabiles, nec rursus mortalibus adpetendos. Omni itaque spe huius modi quicquam conandi depulsa, Traiani equum solum, locatum in atrii medio, qui ipsum principem vehit, imitari se velle dicebat et posse. Cui prope adstans regalis Ormisda . . . respondit astu gentili: 'Ante' inquit 'imperator, stabulum tale condi iubeto, si vales: equus quem fabricare disponis, ita late succedat, ut iste quem videmus.' Is ipse interrogatus, quid de Roma sentiret, id tantum sibi placuisse aiebat, quod didicisset ibi quoque homines mori.

[So Constantius entered Rome, the native home of Empire and of all the virtues. When he came to the Rostra, he marvelled at the renowned Forum, seat of ancient dominion: wherever he turned his gaze, the crowded display of wonderful sights was overwhelming. He addressed the Senate in the Curia, spoke to the People from the Tribunal, was received in the Palace with elaborate attentions, and there enjoyed a pleasure for which he had ardently longed. . . .] Finally, as he surveyed all the various parts of the city, disposed over the seven hills and along the plains, together with its suburbs, he thought that whatever he saw first towered above the rest. There was the Temple of Tarpeian Jove, excelling as divine things do human: the baths, built like whole provinces: the enormous bulk of the Amphitheatre in its framework of Travertine stone, to whose highest points the human eye can scarcely reach: the Pantheon, almost a domed district of the city, vaulted over in lofty beauty: the great columns with their spiral staircases, bearing the likenesses of former emperors. There was the Temple of Rome, the Forum of Peace, the Theatre of Pompey, the Odeum, the Stadium of Domitian, and among them all the other embellishments of the Eternal City.

But when he came into the Forum of Trajan, a construction in my view unique under the whole canopy of heaven, admired even by the unanimous verdict of the gods, then he stood still in amazement, turning his attention upon the vast complex around him, which is far beyond any description, and not again to be rivalled by mortal men. All hope of attempting anything like it was put aside, and he simply said that Trajan's horse, which stands in the middle of the court and carries the emperor, was something that he could and would imitate. Then the Persian prince Hormisdas . . . remarked with his native wit 'Sire, first you must order a like stable if you can: the horse you propose to make must be as free to exercise as this which we see.' And when Hormisdas was asked what he thought of Rome, he said 'The only thing I am delighted to find is that there, too, men are mortal.' [So, when the emperor had seen the many sights with awe and amazement, he began to rail at Fame as incompetent or spiteful because, although always exaggerating everything, in describing what there is in Rome she is so inadequate. After thinking for a long time what he might do there, he determined to add to the beauties of the City by an Obelisk in the Circus Maximus.]

AMMIANUS MARCELLINUS, XVI. 13–18

The Emperor Constantius II visited Rome in A.D. 357. After twenty years on the throne, he saw the historic capital of the Empire for the first time. He came as an Easterner and a stranger: Ammianus is at pains to emphasize the hieratic dignity of his bearing, aloof and formal in the manner later prescribed for emperors of Byzantium. He stayed in Rome for a month (28th April–29th May), and carried out a heavy programme of public engagements and of sight-seeing. Three things seem to have broken through the affected impassivity of the imperial visitor—the cosmopolitan nature of the people, their free spirit as displayed in the Circus Maximus, and the magnificence of the city. On the free spirit of the people, Ammianus' admiring comment is, characteristically, taken for the worse by Gibbon: 'when Constantius visited Rome, he was assailed by the importunate solicitations of a people who had preserved, as the last remnant of their ancient freedom, the right of treating their sovereign with familiar insolence.'

Constantius saw Rome in its late imperial splendour, reinforced by the new buildings and restorations carried out by his father Constantine. Not only were the great pagan temples and their worship still maintained, but they were for the first time matched in beauty by the new basilicas and churches of the Christian community, most notably those of St. Peter's and St. John Lateran. Of these Ammianus says nothing: pagan in sympathy and an admirer of Julian, they did not rank for him *inter decora urbis aeternae*. Constantius was a devout Christian, and his reactions will have been very different. It was after all on this visit that he gave the famous, and contentious, order for the removal of the Statue of Victory from the Senate House.

Ammianus' description of the visit was written more than twenty years later, sometime after A.D. 378, when the historian himself visited Rome. Apart from those ascribed to the Emperor and the Persian prince, the architectural comments must be those of the historian. They suggest that a kind of hierarchy of buildings to be admired was now established: this is reflected in such later compilations as the *Mirabilia Urbis Romae*. The Forum of Trajan holds first place in this ranking, and Ammianus' attempt to do justice to it is not only admirable in itself, but gains in value because it is almost the only description to survive. A metaphor is sustained throughout the rest of the passage: Rome is the asylum or microcosm of the whole world: of this *orbis* the great Thermae are the provinces: the Pantheon is 'a domed city-district'—*regio teres*. Ammianus' style often strains for effects, but this rather laboured metaphor could be a commonplace of the guide-books.

The raising of the Obelisk in the Circus Maximus is described in a later passage of Ammianus (XVII, IV. 1–23), which includes a digression on notable obelisks and their inscriptions. It now stands outside St. John Lateran, where it was re-erected by Fontana in 1588.

A *NOVELLA* OF MAJORIAN

De aedificiis publicis. Impp. Leo et Maiorianus A(ugusti) Aemiliano P(raefecto) U(rbi). Nobis r(em) p(ublicam) moderantibus volumus emendari, quod iam dudum ad decolorandam urbis venerabilis faciem detestabamur admitti. Aedes si quidem publicas, in quibus omnis Romanae civitatis consistit ornatus, passim dirui plectenda urbani officii suggestione manifestum est. Dum necessaria publico operi saxa finguntur, antiquarum aedium dissipatur speciosa constructio et ut parvum aliquid reparetur, magna diruuntur. Hinc iam occasio nascitur, ut etiam unusquisque privatum aedificium construens per gratiam iudicum in urbe positorum praesumere de publicis locis necessaria et transferre non dubitet, cum haec, quae ad splendorem urbium pertinent, adfectione civica debeant etiam sub reparatione servari.

Idcirco generali lege sancimus cuncta aedificia quaeve in templis aliisque monumentis a veteribus condita propter usum vel amoenitatem publicam subrexerunt, ita a nullo destrui atque contingi, ut iudex, qui hoc fieri statuerit, quinquaginta librarum auri inlatione feriatur; adparitores vero atque numerarios, qui iubenti obtemperaverint et sua neutiquam suggestione restiterint, fustuario supplicio subditos manuum quoque amissione truncandos, per quas servanda veterum monumenta temerantur. Ex his quoque locis, quae sibi conpetitorum hactenus vindicavit revocanda subreptio, nihil iubemus auferri: quae ad ius publicum nihilominus redeuntia ablatarum rerum volumus reformatione reparari, submota in posterum licentia conpetendi. Si quid sane aut propter publicam alterius operis constructionem aut propter desperatum reparationis usum necessaria consideratione deponendum est, hoc apud amplissimum venerandi senatus ordinem congruis instructionibus praecipimus adlegari et, cum ex deliberato fieri oportere censuerit, ad mansuetudinis nostrae conscientiam referatur, ut, quod reparari nullo modo viderimus posse, in alterius operis nihilominus publici transferri iubeamus ornatum, Aemiliane p(arens) k(arissime) a(tque) a(matissime). Quapropter inlustris magnitudo tua saluberrimam sanctionem propositis divulgabit edictis, ut, quae pro utilitate urbis aeternae provide constituta sunt, famulatu congruo et devotione serventur. Dat. V Id. Iul. Rav(ennae) D(ominis) n(ostris) Leone et Maioriano A(ugustis) Conss.

On Public Buildings. The Emperors Leo and Majorian to Aemilianus, City Prefect. While we govern the state, we are anxious to correct obnoxious practices which have long been allowed to deface the appearance of the Venerable City. For it is obvious that public buildings, wherein consists the whole beauty of the Roman state, are on all sides being destroyed by the most deplorable connivance of the city administration. While the requisite materials for public buildings are being collected, the noble constructions of antiquity are torn down, and a great desecration is committed to allow a trivial repair. This has given rise to the practice that allows even individuals building private houses to filch and transport without hesitation, and with the indulgence of the city magistrates, what they require from public buildings, although all that contributes to the magnificence of the city should be kept in good repair by the zeal of the citizens.

We therefore proclaim by a general law that all public buildings, and everything deposited in temples or monuments by our ancestors for public use or amenity, may not be destroyed by anyone: further, that a justice who shall permit such a contravention, shall be fined fifty pounds weight of gold: further, that public servants and account-keepers who obey such a command and do not withstand it by objections on their own account, should be forced to undergo cudgelling, and should have amputated those hands by which they violated those monuments of antiquity which we are bound to protect. And from those places, where the claimants have obtained right of removal which is now to be repealed, we order that nothing is to be taken away: such places none the less we wish to be restored to public use by the restitution of material carried away, and the licence to make application shall henceforth be abrogated. However, if for the construction of some other public building, or after due consideration of the unavoidable necessity of repair, some material has to be laid aside, we order that this is to be commissioned by the noble order of the Senate, and under proper instructions, and if on deliberation they deem it advisable, it is then to be referred to the conscience of our clemency, so that any amenity which we find to be beyond possibility of repair, may none the less be used for the adornment of some other public building, dearly beloved Aemilianus. So let Your Excellency publish this prohibition in a general edict, to ensure that measures wisely taken for the good of the Eternal City may be observed with the proper obedience and devotion.

Given at Ravenna on the 12th July in the Consulships of Our Lords the Emperors Leo and Majorian.

NOVELLAE MAIORIANI, IV (A.D. 458)

The document is one of an endless and largely unsuccessful series of attempts by the emperors to preserve Rome from her most relentless enemies—her own citizens, who from the fourth century onward worked at her destruction with a sustained assiduity far more effective than the occasional onslaughts of the barbarians. It is a *novella* of the emperors Leo and Majorian, written from Ravenna to the city prefect Aemilianus. The date is A.D. 458, three years after the sack of Rome by the Vandals under Gaeseric. Those barbarians made their name a synonym for destruction by pillaging Rome for fourteen days. But their vandalism was mainly directed at precious objects that could be removed; what the emperors try to restrain is the destruction of public buildings through the greed of the citizens and the corruption and apathy of the administration. The effects of that combination need not be stressed in modern Britain. Peculiar features of the Roman scene in the fifth century A.D. were the shrinking population and their hostility to buildings associated with pagan cults. The great buildings of the past became public quarries, and their marbles were valued only as sources for lime. So began that centuries-old process of destruction set out in melancholy detail by Lanciani in *The Destruction of Ancient Rome* (1951).

The Theodosian Codex gives other such preservation orders in 364, 365, 376 and 390. A determined effect to halt and reverse the work of destruction was made by Theoderic, especially in the years 507–511.

THE 'WALL OF SERVIUS TULLIUS'

Servius Tullius added the Quirinal and the Viminal to Rome: next he extended (settlement) on the Esquiline, and dwelled there in person, to add to its prestige. He surrounded the City with an earthwork, a ditch, and a wall. . . .

LIVY, I. 44. 3

Not long before the city was captured (by the Gauls) a voice was heard in the Grove of Vesta—which extended from the roots of the Palatine to the Nova Via—bidding them repair the Wall and its gates.

CICERO, *On divination*, I. 45. 101

The Gauls reached Rome shortly before sunset. Cavalry who had been sent forward reported that the gates were not closed, no watch was kept in front of them, no defenders were posted on the walls. . . . Fearing the night, and the topography of a city they did not know, they camped between Rome and the Anio, and sent scouts round the walls and gates to discover what were the plans of the enemy in this desperate position.

LIVY, V. 39. 2–3 (390 B.C.)

Guards were placed on the gates, to prevent anyone from leaving Rome, and to force men to abandon hope of safety unless the City and its walls remained secure.

LIVY, XXII. 55. 8 (216 B.C.)

Hannibal moved his camp forward to the River Anio, three miles from the city. Then pickets were placed, and he himself with 2,000 cavalry rode up to the Porta Collina and as far as the Temple of Hercules, surveying the walls and the lay-out of the city from the closest possible points of vantage. . . .

LIVY, XXXVI. 10. 3 (211 B.C.)

The name is now given to a wall of large blocks of stone which does not appear to antedate the Gallic invasion of 390 B.C. Earlier defences on the Capitol and the Palatine may in fact belong to the regal period. The first passage gives the traditional ascription to Servius Tullius: the second and third suggest that Rome had no adequate defences at the time of the Gallic invasion. During the Second Punic War, however, the Wall was an effective obstacle, and Hannibal was unable to assault the city. It saw fighting in the Civil Wars of 82 B.C. and A.D. 69, but was in decay (*ἦν γὰρ τῷ χρόνῳ φθαρέντα*—Chron. Pasc. P 273 B) in the mid-third century A.D. See Plate 6.

THE WALLS OF AURELIAN

At that time (the reign of Aurelian), Rome was fortified, having been without walls previously. The work began under Aurelian and was completed by Probus.

ZOSIMUS, *Histories*, I. 49

His actis, cum videri posset fieri, ut aliquid tale iterum, quale sub Gallieno evenerat, proveniret, adhibito consilio senatus muros Urbis Romae dilatavit. Nec tamen pomoerio addidit eo tempore sed postea.

After the end (of the Marcomannic War) when it seemed possible that what happened under Gallienus could recur, he took the advice of the Senate and enlarged the walls of Rome. He did not enlarge the Pomoerium at that time but later on.

HISTORIA AUGUSTA, *Aurelian*, 21. 9

His (Aureliano II et Marcello) consulibus Aurelianus templum Soli aedificavit, Romam firmioribus muris vallat.

In their consulship (Aurelian and Marcellus, A.D. 275), Aurelian built the Temple of the Sun, and fortified Rome with stronger walls.

CASSIODORUS, *Chronica* (M. G. H., A. A. XI, p. 148) (A.D. 275)

Aurelian had scarcely begun his reign, when he began to embellish the Walls of Rome, which were dilapidated with age. He supervised the work himself, and compelled the guilds of Rome to labour on it (*καὶ ἠνάγκαζε τὰ συνέργεια Ῥώμης ὑπουργεῖν τῷ κτίσματι*). The wall was very soon completed, and he issued an imperial decree that from that time all the Guilds of workmen should be called Aurelians, receiving the distinction of the imperial name as a reward for all their toils.

JOHN MALALAS, *Chronicles* XII, p. 299

[M]VRVS ROM⟨A⟩E VRBIS HABET TVRRES SIMPLICES CCCLXXI ET TVRRES CASTELLATAS XLVIIII, PROPVGNACVLA SEXMILIA DCCCC, PORTAS XV, PVSTERVLAS XV, IN CIRCVITO VERO EIUS SVNT MILIA...

The wall of the City of Rome has 371 ordinary turrets, 49 fortified turrets, 6900 bastions, 15 gates, and 15 postern gates. Its circuit is . . . miles.

Index coemeteriorum (*Rend. Pont. Accad. Arch.*, 1922–23, p. 194)

Sic oculis placitura tuis insignior auctis
collibus et nota maior se Roma videndam
obtulit. Addebant pulchrum nova moenia vultum
audito perfecta recens rumore Getarum,
profecitque opifex decori timor, et vice mira,
quam pax intulerat, bello discussa senectus
erexit subitas turres cunctosque coegit
septem continuo colles iuvenescere muro.

So, to please your eyes, Rome has added to her hills and presents herself to view as greater than she was. The new walls, completed because of reports of the Goths, have given her this fair new face. Fear has served as the architect of beauty: and a miraculous change has caused Rome to slough off the old skin of peace, to build towers in haste, and to make all her seven hills to gleam bright again with an unbroken wall.

CLAUDIAN, *On the Sixth Consulship of Stilicho*, 529–36

S.P.Q.R. IMPERATORIBVS CAESARIBVS DOMINIS NOSTRIS DVOBVS PRINCIPIBVS ARCADIO ET HONORIO VICTORIBVS AC TRIVMFATORIBVS SEMPER AVGVSTIS OB INSTAVRATOS VRBIS AETERNAE MVROS, PORTAS AC TVRRES, EGESTIS IMMENSIS RVDERIBVS, EX SVGGESTIONE VIRI CLARISSIMI ET INLVSTRIS, COMITIS ET MAGISTRI VTRIVSQVE MILITIAE STILICHONIS, AD PERPETVITATEM NOMINIS EORVM SIMVLACRA CONSTITVIT, CVRANTE FLAVIO MACROBIO LONGINIANO VIRO CLARISSIMO, PRAEFECTO VRBIS, DEVOTO NVMINI MAIESTATIQVE EORVM.

The Senate and People of Rome set this up to the Imperial Caesars, our Lords the two princes Arcadius and Honorius, victorious, triumphant, ever Augusti, to commemorate the restoration of the walls, gates, and towers of the Eternal City, after the removal of huge quantities of rubble. At the suggestion of the distinguished and noble Count Stilicho, Master of both of the Armed Forces, their statues were set up to preserve the memory of their name. Flavius Macrobius Longinianus, City Prefect, devoted to their majesty and divine power, was in charge of the work.

CIL, VI. 1189 (Porta Maggiore)

The danger of barbarian invasions of Italy was renewed in the third century A.D. Under Gallienus the Alamanni penetrated as far as the Apennines; Aurelian, before leaving for the campaigns against Zenobia on the eastern frontiers, decided to protect Rome itself. The passage from the Historia Augusta refers presumably to the completion of the Wall, which seems to have been begun in A.D. 271. Malalas' account of the forced labour exacted from the *collegia* has been doubted, but Richmond accepts it: such *corvée* certainly fits the context. The Wall so built was normally 26 feet high and 12 wide, provided with gates, posterns, towers for artillery, the whole having a circuit of some 12 miles, or 18·8 kilometres. This would have prevented the capture and pillage of the city by a mobile force of barbarians: it was not meant to withstand siege by a civilized enemy. This Wall had at least one major restoration, perhaps in the time of Maxentius. A much more radical one took place in 401–403 under Arcadius and Honorius, when the military position was far more serious. The Wall was raised, gates remodelled, a continuous footwalk provided, and stress laid on archers rather than artillery. Rome was now a fortress. The Wall was the major factor in the strategy of the Gothic Wars (537–549); siege and counter-siege followed rapidly, the Romans led by Belisarius and Narses, the Goths by Vitigis and Totila. All this is told in the dramatic account of Procopius. The Wall, repaired and renewed (see plate 7), remained an effective defence until it was confronted with artillery in the nineteenth century.

AQUEDUCTS

Ab urbe condita per annos quadringentos quadraginta unum contenti fuerunt Romani usu aquarum, quas aut ex Tiberi aut ex puteis aut ex fontibus hauriebant. Fontium memoria cum sanctitate adhuc extat et colitur: salubritatem aegris corporibus adferre creduntur, sicut Camenarum et Apollinis et Iuturnae. Nunc autem in urbem confluunt aqua Appia, Anio vetus, Marcia, Tepula, Iulia, Virgo, (Alsietina) quae eadem vocatur Augusta, Claudia Anio novus.

For 441 years from the foundation of the city the people of Rome were content with a supply of water derived from the Tiber, from wells, or from fountains. Even today these fountains are remembered and a certain worship is paid them; they are believed to bring health to the sick, as, for example, those of the Camenae, of Apollo, and of Juturna. But now the city enjoys the water jointly supplied by the Appia, Anio Vetus, Marcia, Tepula, Julia, Virgo, Alsietina (also called Augusta), Claudia, and Anio Novus.

FRONTINUS, *De aquis*, I, 4

APPIVS CLAVDIVS C. F.CAECVS CENSOR, COS. BIS, DICT(ATOR), INTERREX III, PR(AETOR) II, AED(ILIS) CVR(VLIS) II, Q(VAESTOR), TR(IBVNVS) MIL(ITVM) III, COM PLVRA OPPIDA DE SAMNITIBVS CEPIT, SABINORVM ET TVSCORVM EXERCIT VM FVDIT, PACEM FIERI CVM TYRRHO (*sic*) REGE PROHIBVIT, IN CENSVRA VIAM APPIAM STRAVIT ET AQVAM IN VRBEM ADDVXIT, AEDEM BELLONAE FECIT.

Appius Claudius Caecus, son of Gaius, censor, consul twice, dictator, interrex three times, praetor twice, aedile twice, quaestor, military tribune three times. He won numerous towns from the Samnites, defeated the armies of the Etruscans and Sabines, and prevented the conclusion of peace with King Tyrrhus (*sic*). As censor, he paved the Via Appia, brought water to the City, and built the Temple of Bellona.

CIL, I_2, 1827

IMP. CAESAR DIVI IVLI F. AVGVSTVS, PONTIFEX MAXIMVS, COS. XII, TRIBVNIC(IA) POTESTATE XIX, IMP. XIIII, RIVOS AQVARVM OMNIVM REFECIT.

The Emperor Augustus . . . tribunician power for the nineteenth time (5 B.C.), repaired the channels of the aqueducts.

CIL, vi. 1244

RIVOS AQVARVM COMPLVRIBVS LOCIS VETVSTATE LABENTES REFECI, ET AQVAM QVAE MARCIA APPELLATVR DVPLICAVI, FONTE NOVO IN RIVVM EIVS INMISSO.

I repaired the channels of aqueducts which had fallen into decay through age in many places. I doubled the aqueduct called Aqua Marcia, and tapped a new supply for its channel.

AUGUSTUS, *Res gestae*, 20

II B.C.

. . . quoniam fere omnes specus per privatorum agros derecti erant et difficilis videbatur futurae inpensae praeparatio, nisi aliq⟨ua⟩ iuris constitutione succurreretur, simul ne accessu ad reficiendos rivos redemptores a possessoribus prohiberentur, S(enatus) c(onsultum) factum est quod subieci.

'Quod Q. Aelius Tubero Paulus Fabius Maximus cos. V(erba) F(ecerunt) de rivis, specibus, fornicibus ⟨a⟩quae Iuliae, Marciae, Appiae, Tepulae, Anienis reficiendis, Q(uid) D(e) E(a) R(e) F(ieri) P(laceret) D(e) E(a) R(e) I(ta) C(ensuerunt) uti cum ii rivi, ⟨specus,⟩ fornices, quos Augustus Caesar se refecturum impen⟨sa⟩ sua pollicitus senatui est reficerentur [- - -] ex agris privatorum terram, limum, lapidem, testam, harenam, ligna ceteraque quibus ad eam rem opus esset, unde quaeque eorum proxime sine iniuria privatorum tolli, sumi, portari possint, viri ⟨boni⟩ arbitratu aestimata darentur, tollerentur, sumerentur, exportarentur; et ad eas res omnes exportandas earumque rerum reficiendarum causa, quotiens opus esset, per agros privatorum sine iniuria eorum itinera, actus paterent, darentur.'

Moreover, since all aqueducts run through private property and it seemed difficult to provide for future expenditure without proper legislation, and further, to prevent proprietors from denying access to the conduits to contractors carrying out repairs, the Senate passed a resolution in the following terms:

'The consuls, Q. Aelius Tubero and Paulus Fabius Maximus, having submitted a report on the restoration of canals, conduits, and arches of the Julia, Marcia, Appia, Tepula, and Anio, and having asked the Senate what it wished to do in the matter, IT IS HEREBY RESOLVED: That when the canals, conduits, and arches which Augustus promised the Senate to repair at his proper charge, shall come to be repaired, then all the earth, clay, stone, tiles, sand, wood, etc. which shall be necessary, shall be granted, removed, taken, and brought from the property of private owners: that some disinterested person shall assess their value: that they shall each of them be removed, taken and brought from whatever point is most convenient and without damage to private property: and that rights-of-way and roads through private property shall, without injury to the same, remain open and their use permitted, whenever it shall be necessary to transport all such material for repairs needed to the above working.

FRONTINUS, *De aquis*, 124–5

In hoc senatus consulto crediderim adnotandum quod senatus tam augeri quam minui salientium publicorum numerum vetuerit. Id factum existimo, quia modus aquarum quae is temporibus in urbem veniebant, antequam Claudia et Anio novus perducerentur, maiorem erogationem capere non videbatur. Qui aquam in usus privatos deducere volet, impetrare eam debebit et a principe epistulam ad curatorem adferre; curator deinde beneficio Caesaris praestare maturitatem et procuratorem eiusdem officii libertum Caesaris protinus scribere. Procuratorem autem primus Ti. Claudius videtur admovisse, postquam Anienem novum et Claudiam induxit.

It is to be noted in the above resolution that the Senate prohibited any increase, as well as any decrease, in the number of public fountains. This I think was because the supply then available to the City, before the Claudia and Anio Novus had been brought in, ruled out any more lavish distribution. Whoever wishes to have a private supply must seek for a grant and bring the commissioner authorization in writing from the emperor: then the commissioner must at once expedite Caesar's grant, appointing a freedman from the imperial household as his deputy for this purpose. Claudius would seem to have been the first to appoint such a deputy after the construction of the Claudia and Anio Novus.

FRONTINUS, *De aquis*, 104–5

Whosoever, after the passage of this law, shall maliciously tap or of set purpose break, or shall allow the tapping or breaking, of the channels, conduits, arches, pipes, tubes, reservoirs or water-tanks brought into the City of Rome . . . or who shall damage the same . . . or who shall prevent the issue, distribution and allotment or discharge into reservoirs or basins of any water in Rome . . . he shall be condemned to pay a fine of 100,000 sesterces to the Roman People . . . and, whoever shall maliciously do any of these things . . . shall repair, restore, reconstruct, re-establish, or replace all that he has damaged . . . The water-commissioners are authorized to remove, pull-up, dig up, uproot, any trees, vines, brambles, banks, thickets, hedges, or beds of reeds, etc., etc.

I should consider anyone who transgressed so beneficent a law well worthy of the penalties prescribed. But the long-standing neglect of the administration had deceived many, and this called for lenient reform. I therefore decided to allow those who had erred to remain anonymous so far as possible. Those who sought the Emperor's favour after due warning received should thank me for the indulgence. However, I hope in future it will not be necessary to invoke the laws, since it will be proper to maintain the dignity of my office even if it means giving offence.

FRONTINUS, *De aquis*, II. 129–30

Sed dicantur vera aestimatione invicta miracula, Q. Marcius Rex, iussus a senatu aquarum Appiae, Anienis, Tepulae ductus reficere, novam a nomine suo appellatam cuniculis per montes actis intra praeturae suae tempus adduxit; Agrippa vero in aedilitate adiecta Virgine aqua ceterisque conrivatis atque emendatis lacus DCC fecit, praeterea salientes D, castella CXXX, complura et cultu magnifica, operibus iis signa CCC aerea aut marmorea inposuit, columnas e marmore CCCC, eaque omnia annuo spatio. Adicit ipse aedilitatis suae commemoratione et ludos diebus undesexaginta factos et gratuita praebita balinea CLXX, quae nunc Romae ad infinitum auxere numerum. Vicit antecedentes aquarum ductus novissimum inpendium operis incohati a C. Caesare et peracti a Claudio, quippe a XXXX lapide ad eam excelsitatem, ut omnes urbis montes lavarentur, influxere Curtius atque Caeruleus fontes et Anió novus, erogatis in id opus HS $\overline{\text{MMM}}$ D. Quod si quis diligentius aestumaverit abundantiam aquarum in publico, balineis, piscinis, euripis, domibus, hortis, suburbanis villis, spatia aquae venientis, exstructos arcus, montes perfossos, convalles aequatas, fatebitur nil magis mirandum fuisse in toto orbe terrarum.

But let us go on to describe marvels whose real value makes them incontestable. Q. Marcius Rex, being ordered by the Senate to repair the conduits of the Aqua Appia, the Anio, and the Tepula, tunnelled through the mountains to bring to Rome a new water-supply that bore his name and was finished during his praetorship. Again, Agrippa as aedile added to these the Aqua Virgo, repaired and restored the others, and constructed 700 basins, besides 500 fountains and 130 distribution points, many of which were finely decorated. To these works he added 300 statues of bronze or marble and 400 columns of marble; all this was done in a year. In the account he wrote of his aedileship he added that games lasting 59 days were celebrated in honour of this achievement, and that the 170 baths were thrown open to the public *gratis*—a number now of course very greatly increased. But all previous aqueducts have been completely outclassed by the very lavish schemes begun by the Emperor Gaius and completed by Claudius, by which the water from the Curtian and Caerulean Springs, as well as the Anio Novus, were conducted into Rome from the 40th milestone at such a high altitude as to supply all the seven hills of Rome. 350 million sesterces were expended on this project. If we take careful account of all the abundant supply of water for public buildings, baths, settling-tanks, pools, private mansions, gardens, and country estates close to the city, and of the distance the water travels before entering the city, the height of the arches, the tunnelling of mountains, the levelling of routes across deep valleys, one must rate all this as the most remarkable achievement anywhere in the world.

PLINY, *Natural History*, XXXVI. 121–2

Pliny is right in saying that the need for an adequate water supply for Rome gave rise to the most remarkable feats of civil engineering performed in the ancient world. According to Frontinus the nine major aqueducts of his day (A.D. 97) had a total length of some 264 English miles, with a capacity of 222,237,060 gallons in twenty-four hours. To these figures must be added those for the later Aqua Trajana (A.D. 109) and Aqua Alexandrina (A.D. 226). Imperial Rome was lavishly supplied indeed, though we must not think in terms of piped water in every house. Only the well-to-do could afford to apply for a private grant: the inhabitants of the great *insulae* would have used the public fountains. Besides the problems of engineering and hydraulics posed by the aqueducts, there were also those of law and administration. Thanks to the work of Sextus Julius Frontinus, who was appointed *curator aquarum* by Nerva in A.D. 97 to overhaul the aqueducts and their administration, we know a good deal about the organization of the water-supply, its history, and its abuses.

The first water-course was built by Appius Claudius Caecus in 312 B.C.: it was an underground conduit with bridges where necessary. The second, Anio Vetus (272–269 B.C.), was similar, but the Aqua Marcia (144–140 B.C.) was a high-level aqueduct of cut-stone. Later landmarks were the work of Agrippa, who took charge of the aqueducts as aedile in 33 B.C. and maintained it till his death in 12 B.C.; of Augustus, who established the *curatores aquarum* and renovated the whole system (see p. 38); of Claudius and Nero, who built the Aqua Claudia and the Anio Novus, and finally of Trajan and the reforms carried out by Frontinus. Three passages relating to the laws on aqueducts are quoted, one concerning way-leaves and access (cf. the maintenance of modern power-lines), one the granting of concessions to private users, and one renewing sanctions against illegal tapping and misappropriation. See Plates 9–10.

THE TIBER

quod per amoenam urbem leni fluit agmine flumen.

the river that flows with gentle stream through the fair city.

ENNIUS, *Annals*, *fr.* 173

These (docks) are built beside the Tiber, where it is some four plethra (*c.* 100 yards) wide at the most, yet deep enough to float large ships. Its current is notably strong and produces large whirlpools.

DIONYSIUS HALICARNASSUS, *Roman Antiquities*, IX. 68. 2

'Ego sum, pleno quem flumine cernis
stringentem ripas et pinguia culta secantem
caeruleus Thybris, caelo gratissimus amnis.
hic mihi magna domus, celsis caput urbibus exit.'

I am he whom you see, cleaving these banks and cutting through rich farmland with my full stream—Tiber of the blue waters, the river most dear to heaven. Here is my great palace (at Ostia), my fount is among cities high on the hills.

VIRGIL, *Aeneid*, VIII. 62–65

IMPERATORES DIOCLETIANVS ET MAXIMIANVS AVGVSTI PERPVRGATIS FONTIVM RIVIS ET ITINERIBVS EORVM AD PERENNEM VSVM REFECTIS TIBERINO PATRI AQVARVM OMNIVM ET REPERTORIBVS ADMIRABILIVM FABRICARVM PRISCIS VIRIS HONORI DEDERVNT CVRANTE AQVAS L. AELIO DIONYSIO CLARISSIMO VIRO.

The emperors Diocletian and Maximian, having scoured thoroughly the channels of the fountains, and repaired their courses to serve for many years, dedicated this to Tiberinus, Father of All Waters, and in honour of the men of old who invented these admirable works. Lucius Aelius Dionysius was in charge of the water-supply.

CIL, VI. 773

That year (400 B.C.) the winter was remarkable for frost and snow, so much so, that the roads were closed, and the Tiber unnavigable.

LIVY, V. 13. 1

That year (193 B.C.), there were great floods, and the Tiber invaded the low-lying parts of the city: some buildings round Porta Flumentana collapsed in ruins.

LIVY, XXXV. 9. 2–3

That year (192 B.C.) the river rose more savagely than in the year before, flooded the city, and carried away two bridges and many buildings, especially round Porta Flumentana.

LIVY, XXXX. 28. 4

Vidimus flavum Tiberim retortis
litore Etrusco violenter undis
ire deiectum monumenta regis
templaque Vestae
Iliae dum se nimium querenti
iactat ultorem, vagus et sinistra
labitur ripa Iove non probante u-
xorius amnis.

We have seen tawny Tiber, his waves flung back violently from the Etruscan shore, go to overthrow the monuments of the King and the Temple of Vesta. He boasts himself the avenger of Ilia's loud complaints, and overflows—a river too complacent to his wife—his whole left bank. Jove does not approve.

HORACE, *Odes*, I. 2. 13–20 (43 B.C.?)

TIBERIVS CLAVDIVS DRVSI F. CAESAR AVGVSTI GERMANICVS . . . TRIB. POT. VI . . . FOSSIS DVCTIS A TIBERI OPERIS PORTVS CAVSSA EMISSISQVE IN MARE VRBEM INVNDATIONIS PERICVLO LIBERAVIT.

Tiberius Claudius Augustus etc. etc. (A.D. 46), having dug channels from the Tiber in the course of harbour works, and led them to the sea, freed the city from the danger of floods.

CIL, XIV. 85

M. VALERIVS M. F. M' NEPOS MESSALLA P. SERVEILIVS C. F. ISAVRICVS, CENSORES, EX SENATVS CONSVLTO TERMINAVERVNT.

M. Valerius Messalla and P. Serveilius Isauricus, Censors, delimited the banks of the river, by decree of the Senate.

CIL, I^2, 766a

C. MARCIVS. L. F. L. NEPOS CENSORINVS. C. ASINIVS C. F. GALLVS COS. EX SENATVS CONSVLTO TERMINAVERVNT. RECTO RIGORE PROXIMVS CIPPVS PEDES CXX.

C. Marcius Censorinus . . . and C. Asinius Gallus . . . consuls, delimited the banks of the river, by decree of the Senate. The next *cippus* is 120 ft. distant in a straight line.

CIL, VI. 31451. I

C. PLINIO L. F. OVFENTINA, CAECILIO SECVNDO. COS. AVGVRI. CVRATORI ALVEI TIBERIS ET RIPARVM ET CLOACARVM VRBIS . . .

To C. Plinius Caecilius Secundus, of the tribe Ufentina, consul, augur, Curator of the channel and banks of the Tiber and of the sewers of Rome . . .

CIL, v. 5263

STATIO ALVEI TIBERIS ET CLOACARVM SACRAE VRBIS CVRANTE AVRELIO ARTEMIDORO . . .

The office of the Tiber Channel and Sewers of the Sacred City, under the charge of Aurelius Artemidorus.

CIL, VI. 224 (A.D. 244)

TI. CLAVDIO ESQVILINA SEVERO DECVRIALI, LICTORI, PATRONO CORPORIS PISCATORVM ET VRINATORVM, QVINQVENNALI III EIVSDEM CORPORIS, OB MERITA EIVS, QVOD HIC PRIMVS DVAS STATVAS, VNAM ANTONINI AVGVSTI DOMINI NOSTRI, ALIAM IVLIAE AVGVSTAE DOMINAE NOSTRAE S. P. POSVERIT, VNA CVM CLAVDIO PONTIANO FILIO SVO EQVITE ROMANO ET HOC AMPLIVS EIDEM CORPORI DONAVERIT SESTERTIVM X MILIA NVMMVM, VT EX VSVRIS EORVM QVOTANNIS NATALI SVO XVII KALENDAS FEBRVARIAS SPORTVLAE VIRITIM DIVIDANTVR, PRAESERTIM CVM NAVIGATIO SCAPHARVM DILIGENTIA EIVS ADQVISITA ET CONFIRMATA SIT EX DECRETO ORDINIS CORPORIS PISCATORVM ET VRINATORVM TOTIVS ALVEI TIBERIS QVIBVS EX SENATVS CONSVLTO COIRE LICET S. P. POSVERVNT. . . .

To Tiberius Claudius Severus, of the Esquiline tribe, a *decurio*, lictor, and patron of the Guild of Fishermen and Divers, on the third *quinquennalia* of that body, for his services in being the first to set up two statues, one of our Lord Antoninus Augustus (Septimius Severus), the other of our Lady, Julia Augusta, at his own expense and that of his son Claudius Pontianus, a Roman knight, with whom he gave a sum of money of more than 10,000 sesterces to the aforesaid guild, the interest whereof every year is to be divided as a gift to each member on his birthday the 16th of January: and in particular, because the right of using boats was acquired and confirmed by his diligence, set up by decree of the Council of the Guild of the Fishermen and Divers of the whole channel of the Tiber, who are authorized by a resolution of the Senate, at their own expense.

CIL, VI. 1872 (A.D. 206)

In spite of Ennius, the Tiber, then as now, was an uneasy bedfellow for the city. Numerous floods are recorded, some of them disastrous: three of the most notable are mentioned in the passages given, besides one occasion when the river froze over. The Porta Flumentana was on the left

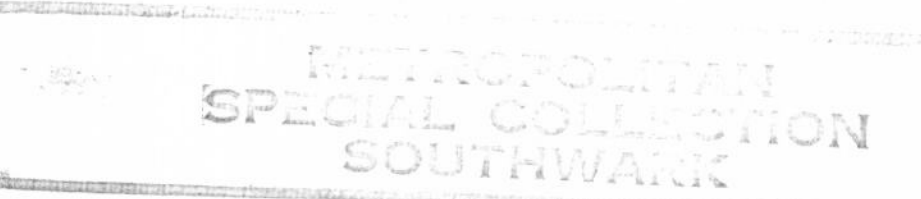

bank by the Tiber Island. Neither the embankment of Augustus nor the canals of Claudius completely solved the problem of Tiber floods, and indeed Pliny was of the opinion that the body of water in the river was equal in volume to that of the Nile (*N.H.* XXXVI. 9. 70). But in normal circumstances it seems that the *curatores alvei et riparum Tiberis* were effective in keeping the channel clear and the river under control. The banks were under their charge for a defined distance, which they delineated by a line of *cippi*, regularly renewed. No fewer than 124 of these inscribed *cippi* survive: they are mostly to be seen in the Museo Nazionale, and are collected in Lugli, *Fontes*, Vol. V, pp. 69 ff. Many of the *curatores* are also recorded on inscriptions, among them Pliny the Younger. It is not known when they were first provided with a *statio*. The third-century *corpus* of Fishermen and Divers (*urinatores*), complete with its *patronus*, its Council, and its benefactions, is interesting as an example of those *collegia* so guardedly licensed and supervised under the empire.

INSULA TIBERINA

The land of the Tarquins, which lay between the city and the Tiber, was consecrated to Mars and known as the Campus Martius. Now it happened that there was a field of grain growing there, ripe for the harvesting. It would have been sacrilegious to consume it, so a large body of reapers were sent in to gather it. They threw it, straw and all, into the Tiber, which was at a low level, since it was midsummer. And so the corn stuck in the shallows, and formed heaps covered with mud. Little by little, an island was formed at that place, and the silt brought down by the river enlarged it. It was later, I suppose, that it was artificially raised and strenthened, so that there should be a platform high above flood level and firm enough to support temples and colonnades.

LIVY, II. 5

When Rome was harrassed by a pestilence, a delegation was sent to bring the statue of Aesculapius from Epidaurus to Rome. They brought away with them a snake, which had boarded their ship: the operative power of the god is known to exist in this snake. It went ashore on the Tiber island, and there a shrine of Aesculapius was founded.

LIVY, *Epitome of Book* XI

January 1st
Now for what I have learned from the calendar itself. On this day the Senate dedicated two temples. The island, which the river hems in with its parted waters, received the son of Phoebus and the nymph Coronis. Jupiter shares the site: a single place accommodates them both, and the temples of the grandson and his mighty grandsire are joined together.

OVID, *Fasti*, I. 289–294

AESCVLAPIO. ET. HYGIAE. M. VLPIVS. HONORATVS DEC. EQ. SING. IMP. N. PRO. SALVTE. SVA. SVORVMQVE. ET. L. IVLI. HELICIS. MEDICI. QVI. CVRAM. MEI. DILIGENTER. EGIT. SECVNDVM. DEOS.

To Aesculapius and Hygieia, Marcus Ulpius Honoratus . . . set this up for the health of himself, his family, and his doctor, Lucius Julius Helix, who (under Heaven) has been most diligent in undertaking my care.

CIL, VI. 19

The passages on the Tiber Island illustrate its legendary origin, the foundation of the Temple of Aesculapius, and the cult of Aesculapius in Rome. Livy gives this story after his account of the murder of Tarquinius Superbus. The later building operations were probably those of 62 B.C., when the Pons Fabricius was constructed. A stone platform was built, and the island 'landscaped' into the form of a ship. Part of the poop is still to be seen.

The date of the second passage is 291 B.C. A further account is given in Valerius Maximus I. 8. 2. This adds that Aesculapius appeared to the Roman envoys at Epidaurus in the form of a snake, that he promised to accompany them to Rome, but swam ashore when the ship was off Antium, and wriggled up a palm-tree. After three anxious days he was persuaded to re-embark.

Epidaurus was the chief shrine of Asclepius, from which many others were founded—notably at Athens, Cos and Pergamum. It developed into a curative and cultural centre of great splendour. The cult may have originated in Thessaly.

The snake curled round the staff is the symbol of Asclepius: Aesculapius is the Latin form of the name. In the third passage Ovid followed Hesiod and Pindar on the parentage of Asclepius. This is confirmed by a hymn on an inscription (*Eph. Arch.* iii. 65ff.) in honour of the god. The other temple was to Vediovis rather than Jupiter: though also founded on January 1st, it was not in the same year. Some twenty inscriptions to Aesculapius are known from Rome. Hygieia or Salus was often associated with him. The dedicator of the inscription quoted here was a soldier: the mention of the doctor (a Greek freedman?) is noteworthy.

SECTION II

BUILDINGS AND MONUMENTS

THE CAPITOL

Meanwhile the city grew by continually enclosing fresh pieces of land within its fortifications, a policy which had regard rather to the large population hoped for in the future than to the actual number of inhabitants for whom defences were then required. Finally, so as not to leave empty this enlarged city, Romulus had recourse to the time-honoured device of founders of cities, who attract to themselves a large number of people of humble origins and condition, and pretend that a race rose from the earth for their benefit—that is, he opened up as an Asylum that space which is now enclosed (on the left) as you pass down between the two groves. There a crowd of refugees, both free men and slaves, collected from all the neighbouring territories, all in search of a new life. Such was an increase of population to match the ample scale of the plans for the city.

LIVY, I. 8.

Prodiderat portaeque fidem patriamque iacentem,
  nubendique petit, quem velit ipsa, diem.
At Tatius (neque enim sceleri dedit hostis honorem)
  'Nube' ait 'et regni scande cubile mei!'
Dixit, et ingestis comitum super obruit armis.
  Haec, virgo, officiis dos erat apta tuis.
A duce Tarpeia mons est cognomem adeptus:
  O vigil, iniustae praemia sortis habes?

She had betrayed her watch on the gate and her country in its need: now she tried to name the wedding-day she wished herself. But, foe that he was, Tatius gave treachery no honour. 'Marry then!' he cried 'and ascend my bed!', and with the words his comrades threw their shields on her and smothered her. So, maiden, you had a dowry to match your merits. Now the hill has taken its name from Tarpeia; maiden who stood guard, was your fate unjust?

PROPERTIUS, *Elegies*, IV. IV. 79–86

When he had recovered Gabii, Tarquin made peace with the Aequi and renewed the treaty with the Etruscans. Then he turned his mind to public works in Rome. The chief of these was his design to found a Temple of Jupiter on the Tarpeian Hill as a memorial of his reign and dynasty—of the two Tarquins, the father founded, the son completed, this Temple. To free the whole area from other cults and to reserve it entirely for Jupiter and the Temple which was being built, he wished to deconsecrate certain shrines and chapels which King Tatius had first vowed to the gods during the struggle against Romulus, and which had been consecrated later in that place. It is said that the gods gave a sign of the greatness of the coming empire at the outset of this project, for the auguries allowed the deconsecration of all the shrines, except that of Terminus. The omen and portent was interpreted as follows: 'Terminus will not change his place: alone of all the gods he refuses to be removed from his consecrated shrine: it is a sign of the stability and permanence of the State as a whole.' This prophecy of long life was followed by another, which foretold the greatness of the empire, for during the consecration of the Temple's foundations it is said that a human skull came to light, its features perfectly preserved. This discovery announced in unambiguous fashion that this place would be the seat of empire and the capital of the world: such indeed was the interpretation of the soothsayers, not only those of Rome, but also those brought from Etruria to study the case.

All this added to the king's expenditure. The spoils of war from Pometium, which he had intended to defray the whole building costs, including the roof, were barely sufficient for the foundations. This is why I follow Fabius—the earlier authority, in any case—for his figure of 40 talents only, whereas Piso speaks of 400 talents being earmarked for this expenditure. This latter is a sum which could hardly be expected from the spoils of a single city, and indeed it would more than meet the costs of the foundations of buildings constructed even on the modern scale of extravagance.

LIVY, I. 55

So, 'Rabirius killed Saturninus'. I wish he had. I should not be defending him from punishment, but demanding a reward! For if Scaeva, a slave of Quintus Croto, who did kill Lucius Saturninus, was given his freedom, what would be the appropriate reward for a Roman *eques*? And of C. Marius, who ordered them to cut the water-pipes supplying the temple and precincts of Jupiter Optimus Maximus, and thereby caused the deaths of these criminals on the Clivus Capitolinus? . . .

CICERO, *Pro Rabirio*, 31

Martialis had scarcely regained the Capitol when the furious Vitellians were at hand, under no command, but each man acting for himself. At the double they advanced through the Forum and the temples which overhang it, then moved forward ready for action, up the hill as far as the outer defences of the Capitol. At this point there were formerly some colonnades, on the right as you ascended the slope: the defenders ran out along their roofs and assailed the Vitellians with tiles and stones. They had nothing but their swords, and it seemed a tedious delay to send for javelins and siege equipment. So they hurled firebrands on to a projecting colonnade, followed up the flames, and would have broken through the half-destroyed gates of the Capitol had not Sabinus pulled down all the statues—the glory of an earlier day—to form a barricade across the gap. They next attacked the approaches to the Capitol, both at the Grove of the Asylum and where the Hundred Steps ascend the Tarpeian Rock. Both attacks were unexpected: but that by the Asylum was the closer and more fiercely pressed. There was no checking the attackers, who climbed by the continuous row of buildings which over the long years of peace had grown up to a height which brought them level with the Capitol plateau. At this point it is doubtful whether the attackers hurled fire on the roofs or whether, as majority report has it, it was the defenders who tried to check them as they fought their way upwards. The flames passed from here to the colonnades next the temples, then the Eagles supporting the pediment, being made of old timber, took up and fed the flames. So the Capitol, its gates shut, undefended and undespoiled, went up in flames.

This criminal act was the most grievous and shameful disaster to befall the Commonwealth of the Roman People since the foundation of the City. Assailed by no foreign foe, with the gods—had our morals allowed it—propitious to us, the seat of Jupiter Optimus Maximus, founded by our ancestors as the pledge of Rome's Empire, the temple inviolate when the city surrendered to Porsenna and when it was captured by the Gauls, this temple was burned in the frenzied strife between our own Emperors. It was publicly besieged and publicly set on fire, and what were the motives for conflict? What prize counter-balanced this enormous disaster? Were we fighting for our country? King Tarquinius Priscus vowed its erection in the war against the Sabines, and laid its foundations, on a scale more suited to a destiny of greatness than to the modest resources of the Roman people at that time. Later, Servius Tullius, with the support of our allies, and Tarquinius Superbus, with the spoils of wars after the capture of Suessa Pometia, advanced its building. But the true glory of the work belongs to the days of freedom. It was Horatius Pulvillus, in his second consulship, who dedicated a building so magnificent that all the vast wealth of the Roman People in a latter age has seemed to embellish rather than to enlarge it. It was rebuilt on the same site after the fire which, 415 years later, destroyed it—the consulship of Lucius Scipio and Gaius Norbanus. After his victory was won, Sulla undertook its restoration: but this one thing eluded his usual good fortune. It bore the name of Lutatius Catulus, amid all the great buildings of the Caesars, to the time of Vitellius. This was the temple that was then burned down.

TACITUS, *Histories*, III. 71–72

The Capitol was the acropolis of Rome, at once cult-centre and fortress. The names ARX and CAPITOLIUM, originally applied to the twin summits of the hill, also reflect its dual role. When this began is uncertain, but the most likely period is in the sixth century B.C., and under Etruscan influence (see p. 51). Legend, however, tries to associate it with the Latin and Sabine settlements: the asylum which existed in historic times is ascribed to Romulus: an eponymous traitress, Tarpeia, is invented to account for the name Mons Tarpeius, which is now regarded as of Etruscan origin and associated with Tarquinius. Tarpeia's story—of which there are several variants—is told at some length in the Fourth Elegy of Propertius' Fourth Book: it was also one of the early Roman legends shown in the frieze of the Basilica Aemilia (see p. 99). Livy's description of the founding of the Temple to Jupiter by the Tarquins has several features of interest. Intended as a memorial of Tarquin and his line, the Temple is shown by portents to be prophetic of the world-empire of Rome. The story of Terminus may well be ancient, but that of the human head *integra facie* does not seem to be earlier than the third century B.C. But here is the origin of that idea of Rome as *caput rerum*—still as dear to Romans as it is infuriating to the inhabitants of Florence and other historic Italian cities.

Cicero's speech at the trial of Rabirius was delivered in 63 B.C., but the events with which it was concerned had happened 37 years earlier, and were resuscitated in an arbitrary spirit by Julius Caesar. In 100 B.C. Saturninus and his friends had taken refuge on the Capitol: Marius, by depriving them of their water-supply, forced them to surrender, and to death at the hands of the mob.

The passage from the *Histories* describes the fateful, and in Tacitus' view wholly unnecessary, clash between the partisans of Vitellius and Vespasian on December 19th, A.D. 69, which resulted in the destruction of the Temple of Jupiter by fire. It gives incidentally some topographical details of the approaches to the Capitol from the Forum. Vespasian's elder brother, Flavius Sabinus, was killed: the future emperor Domitian barely escaped with his life. The destruction of the Capitol made a deep impression throughout the world, especially in the northern provinces of Gaul, where the rebellion of Civilis was coming to a head. The Druids, we are told, took it as a sign that Rome's day was over, and that the Empire of the World was passing to the northern peoples.

THE TEMPLE OF JUPITER OPTIMUS MAXIMUS

Tarquinius was now intent on completing the Temple, and workmen had been summoned from every part of Etruria. Not only were public funds expended for this purpose, but the plebeians were also compelled to provide labour for the work. This was no small burden to be added to their military service, but the people were less annoyed at having to build a temple of the gods by the toil of their hands than they were when, on later occasions, they were employed on other public works which were less spectacular but somewhat more laborious—such as the building of seats in the Circus and the construction of a huge underground sewer, designed to dispose of all the waste-matter from the city.

LIVY, I. 56

As yet the Temple of Jupiter on the Capitol had not been dedicated. The consuls Valerius and Horatius drew lots as to which should perform the dedication. The lot fell to Horatius, and Valerius set out for the war against Veii. But Valerius' supporters were more resentful than they should have been that the dedication of so famous a temple should have been entrusted to Horatius. They tried to obstruct it by every possible means, and after they had exhausted all other methods, they brought the consul—who was already holding the doorpost of the Temple and uttering the prayer to the gods—the ill-omened news that his son was dead, and that therefore his family was under the shadow of death, and thus he could not dedicate the Temple. Whether he did not believe that this was true, or whether he had such tenacity of purpose, tradition does not make clear, nor is it easy to decide. But he allowed himself to be interrupted only long enough to give orders that the corpse should be buried: then still holding the post, he finished the prayer and dedicated the Temple.

LIVY, II. 8. 6

Varro . . . says that the art of clay modelling was brought to perfection in Italy, especially in Etruria. He says too that Vulca was summoned from Veii to receive from Tarquinius Priscus a contract for the statue of Jupiter to be consecrated on the Capitol, this Jupiter being made of clay and so regularly painted with cinnabar: also, that the four-horse chariots on the ridge of the temple were made of clay. . . .

PLINY, *Natural History*, XXXV. 157

At Silvium it is said that a slave of Pontius met Sulla, in a state of trance, and told him that he brought from Bellona a message of war and victory. But, if he did not make haste, the Capitol would be burned down: this actually happened and, we are informed, precisely on the day the man had foretold, namely, the sixth day of Quintilis, or, as we should say, July.

PLUTARCH, *Sulla*, 27, 6

The same fortune marked the second dedication of the Temple. As I have said, the first was built by Tarquin, but dedicated by Horatius: this was burnt down in the Civil Wars. The second was built by Sulla, but his death left the honour of the dedication to Catulus. When this again was burnt in the rebellion of Vitellius, Vespasian, fortunate in this as in other enterprises, began the building of a third temple and lived to see it finished. But he did not live to see it destroyed again as it soon was: he was as fortunate in dying before its destruction, as Sulla had been unfortunate in dying before the dedication of his building. No sooner was Vespasian dead than the Temple was again destroyed by fire. The fourth, still standing, was both built and dedicated by Domitian. Tarquin, they say, spent 400 silver talents on the foundations alone of his temple: but in our times the entire fortune of the richest private citizen in Rome would not pay for the gilding of the roof, which cost 12,000 talents. The pillars were made of Pentelic marble, and their length was most aptly proportioned to their thickness. So they were when we saw them at Athens: but they were spoiled when they were re-cut and polished at Rome, for they were made too thin and tapering, and the embellishment was bought at the cost of symmetry.

PLUTARCH, *Publicola*, 15

CAPITOLIVM ET POMPEIVM THEATRVM VTRVMQVE OPVS IMPENSA GRANDI REFECI SINE VLLA INSCRIPTIONE NOMINIS MEI.

I restored the Capitolium and the Theatre of Pompey, both works requiring great expense, without recording my own name by any inscription.

AUGUSTUS, *Res gestae* 20

The task of restoring the Capitol was entrusted to Lucius Vestinus, an equestrian, but commanding a power and reputation second to none. The *haruspices* he consulted advised that the remains of the old building should be carted off to the marshes, but the temple re-erected on the former site: the gods were averse to any change in its design. On the 21st of June, in fine weather, the whole area to be consecrated for the temple was surrounded with wreaths and garlands. Soldiers entered, men of lucky names, carrying branches from propitious trees. Then Vestal Virgins, with boys and girls whose parents were both alive, purified the whole space with water drawn from sacred springs and rivers. Then Helvidius Priscus, the praetor, having hallowed the whole area by the sacrifice of a bull, a stallion, and a boar, and placed the entrails on the altar, solemnly repeated after the Chief Pontiff, Plautius Aelianus, a prayer to Jupiter, Juno, and Minerva, and the gods who protect the Empire, to enlist their support for the project, and to bring divine aid to prosper the plans for their temple which had been begun by the efforts of man. He then touched the wreaths with which the foundation stone and the ropes around it were bound. At the same time the other magistrates, the priests, the senate, the knights, and a large part of the common people, vied with each other in their zeal to drag along the huge stone. In every part of the foundations were placed ores of gold and silver, never melted down, but in their original state. The augurs had forbidden that any metal or stone intended for some other purpose should be allowed to profane their work. The height of the building was increased: this was the sole innovation that religion would allow, and the only respect in which the ancient temple seemed less than magnificent.

TACITUS, *Histories*, IV, 53

Domitian restored many magnificent buildings destroyed by fire, notably the Capitolium, which had been burned yet again: but in every case only his name was used on the inscription, without reference to the original builder.

SUETONIUS, *Domitian*, V

In Alexandria there are great temples with high-pitched roofs, notably the Temple of Serapis. Words cannot do justice to it, but for its spacious columned halls, its statues that seem to breathe, its numerous other works of art, it is such that, next to the Capitol, by which venerable Rome maintains her claim to eternity, the whole inhabited world sees nothing more magnificent.

AMMIANUS MARCELLINUS, XXII. 16, 12 (A.D. 363)

So Gaeseric sailed to Carthage with a huge amount of imperial treasure, sparing neither bronze nor anything else in the Palace. He also sacked the Temple of Jupiter Capitolinus, bearing off half the roof. This roof was made of bronze of the first quality, with a heavy overlay of gold, so that it presented the most marvellous and striking appearance as it shone.

(A.D. 455) PROCOPIUS, *Vandal War*, III. V. 8

Nothing remains of the great temple of Jupiter Optimus Maximus, the most venerable in Rome, except the foundations still to be seen under Palazzo Caffarelli. Here, surely, is the single most grievous gap in our knowledge of Roman architecture. It is fortunate that the literary sources are abundant; those given above are selected from the most important. The passage of Tacitus (p. 53) gives the salient facts of the Temple's history down to the fire of A.D. 69. First comes the great project, conceived by the first Tarquin, advanced by the second (who was not, of course, his son, despite Livy), but dedicated after the expulsion of the kings and the establishment of the Republic. Note the *corvée* which its building is said to have imposed on the Roman people, the only means of obtaining a large labour-force at that time. Pliny adds the details of the cult statue of Jupiter being made of terra-cotta (*fictilis*) by the great Etruscan artist Vulca, to whom are ascribed the superb statues of gods found at Veii, and now in the Museum of the Villa Giulia. Livy (p. 54f.) gives a vivid account of the dedication in the year 509 B.C.: the consul Horatius 'grasping the door-post', pronounces the formula of dedication undeterred by the announcement which, Plutarch says, was fictitious, of his son's death. This temple, with its three *cellae* dedicated to Juno, Jupiter and Minerva, must have been the most magnificent of all the archaic temples in Italy. Restored and embellished from time to time, it survived until its destruction by fire on July 6th 83 B.C.

Like the Tabularium, the second Temple was largely the work of Sulla, but bore the name of Lutatius Catulus, who dedicated it in 69 B.C. It was this building which had the gilded bronze roof to which Virgil refers in the famous lines in *Aeneid* VIII (347–8)

'hinc ad Tarpeiam sedem et Capitolia ducit
aurea nunc, olim silvestribus horrida dumis'

Perhaps their regilding may have caused the heavy expenses which Augustus defrayed in 26 B.C., after the temple had been damaged by lightning. This late republican temple as repaired by Augustus was the one destroyed in A.D. 69. The second passage of Tacitus describes the inaugural ceremony of 21st June, A.D. 70: the tone is one of a *pietas* recalling Augustus after the excesses of Nero and the Civil Wars. But this was the unluckiest of the four temples: it took five years to build, and had a life of only five years before its complete destruction by fire in A.D. 80. The fourth temple was built with all the magnificence associated with Domitian's major schemes. Plutarch's comment on the cost of the gilded roof is telling: also his criticism of the columns, which he had seen in Athens, rough-cut from the Pentelic quarries, and shipped to Rome to be finished and, in his opinion, spoiled. Domitian's building had a life of some four centuries at least, outliving the cult which it served. For Ammianus in the late fourth century it is still the finest building in the world, and, in his moving words, Rome's claim to eternity—*quo se venerabilis Roma in aeternum adtollit.*

The gilded roof lasted till A.D. 455, when Gaeseric the Vandal carried half of it to Africa; but a comment of Cassiodorus shows that it must have been restored, probably by Theoderic.

The removal of statues by Narses in A.D. 571 probably put an end to the splendour of the temple. In the centuries to come the hill became Monte Caprino, the Goat's Hill: we hear no more of the Golden Capitol.

TRIUMPHS

T. Quinctius Flamininus, 194 B.C.

The triumph of Quinctius Flamininus lasted three days. On the first there was a display of arms, weapons, and statues of bronze and marble: more of these had been captured from Philip (of Macedon) than received from the Greek cities. On the second day, the gold and silver were displayed, whether unwrought and wrought, or minted and unminted. There were: 43,270 pieces of unwrought silver: of wrought silver, a great assortment of vases, many embossed, some of them of high artistic quality: also many vases of bronze, besides ten silver shields. Of coin there were 84,000 Attic 'tetrachma', each being the equivalent in weight of three silver denarii. Of gold, 3,714 pounds weight, one shield of pure gold, and 14,514 gold coins of Philip. On the third day 114 gold crowns, presented by the various cities, were displayed. The victims who marched before the chariot included many noble prisoners and hostages, among them Demetrius, son of Philip, and Armenes of Sparta, son of the tyrant Nabis. Crowds of soldiers followed the chariot, since the entire army had been brought back from the province. In the distribution the infantry received 250 *asses* per head, the centurions twice, and the cavalry, three times that amount. A striking feature of the procession was a group of prisoners who had been set free from slavery, and whose heads had been shaved.

LIVY, XXXIX. 52

L. Aemilius Paullus, 167 B.C.

First, the people having set up sundry scaffolds, as well in the lists and field (called circus by the Latins) where the games and common running of horses and chariots are made, as also about the market-place, and in other streets of the city, the which the show of the triumph should pass: they all presented themselves in their best gowns to see the magnificence and state thereof. All the temples of the gods also were set wide open, hanged full of garlands of flowers and all perfumed within: and there were set through all the quarters of the city, numbers of sergeants and other officers holding tipstaves in their hands to order the straggling people, and to keep them up in corners and lanes' ends, that they should not pester the streets, and hinder the triumph. Furthermore, the sight of this triumph was to continue three days, whereof the first was scant sufficient to see the passing of the images, tables, and pictures, and statues of wonderful beings, all won and gotten of their enemies, and drawn in the show upon two hundred and fifty charrets. The second day, there were carried upon a number of carts, all the fairest and richest armour of the Macedonians, as well of copper, as also of iron and steel, all glistering bright, being newly furbished, and artificially laid in order (and yet in such sort, as if they had been cast in heaps one upon another, without taking any care otherwise for the ordering and laying of them) fair burganets upon targets: habergions, or brigantines and corselets, upon greaves: round targets of the Cretans, and javelins of the Thracians, and arrows amongst the armed pikes: all this armour and carriage, being bound one to another so trimly (neither being too loose, nor too strait) that one hitting against another, as they drew them upon the carts through the city, they made such a sound and noise, as it was fearful to hear it: so that the only sight of these spoils of the captains being overcome made the sight so much more terrible to behold it. After these carts loden with armour, there followed three thousand men, which carried the ready money in seven hundred and fifty vessels, which weighed about three talents apiece, and every one of them were carried by four men: and there were others that carried great bowls of silver, cups and goblets fashioned like horns, and other pots to drink in, goodly to behold, as well for their bigness, as for their great and singular embossed works about them. The third day early in the morning, the trumpets began to sound and set forwards, sounding no march nor sweet note, to beautify the triumph withal: but they blew out the brave alarum they sound at an assault, to give the soldiers courage for to fight. After them followed six-score goodly fat oxen, having all their horns gilt, and garlands of flowers and nosegays about their heads, and there went by them certain young men, with aprons of needlework, girt about their middle, who led them to the sacrifice, and young boys with them also, that carried goodly basons of gold and silver, to cast and sprinkle the blood of the sacrifices about. And after these, followed those that carried all coins of gold divided by basons and vessels, and every one of them weighing three talents as they did before, that carried the great holy cup, which Aemilius had caused to be made of massy gold, set full of precious stones, weighing the weight of ten talents, to make an offring unto the gods. And next unto them went other that carried plate, made and wrought after antique fashion, and notable cups of the ancient kings of Macedon: as the cup called Antigonus, and another Seleucus: and to be short all the whole cubberd of plate of gold and silver of King Perseus. And next them came the charret of his armour, in the which was all King Perseus' harness, and his royal band (they call a diadem) upon his armour. And a little space between them, followed next the king's children, whom they led prisoners, with the train of their schoolmaisters and other officers, and their servants, weeping and lamenting: who held up their hands unto the people that looked upon them, and taught the king's young children to do the like, to ask mercy and grace at the people's hands. There were three pretty little children, two sons, and a daughter amongst them, whose tender years and lack of understanding, made them (poor souls) they could not feel their present misery, which made the people so much more to pity them, when they saw the poor little infants, that they knew not the change of their hard fortune: so that for the compassion they had of them, they almost let the father pass without looking upon them. Many people's hearts did melt for very pity, that the tears ran down their cheeks, so as this sight brought both pleasure and sorrow together to the lookers on, until they were past and gone a good way out of sight. King Perseus the father, followed after his children and their train, and he was clothed in a black gown, wearing a pair of slippers on his feet after his country manner. He shewed by his countenance his troubled mind, opprest with sorrow of his most miserable state and fortune. He was followed with his kinsfolks, his familiar friends, his officers and household servants, their faces disfigured by blubbering, shewing to the world by their lamenting tears, and sorrowful eyes cast upon their unfortunate maister, how much they sorrowed and bewailed his most hard and cruel fortune, little accounting of their own misery. The voice goeth, that Perseus sent unto Aemilius to entreat him, that he should not be led through the city in the show and sight of the triumph. But Aemilius mocking (as he deserved) his cowardly faint heart, answered: As for that, it was before, and is now in him, to do if he will. Meaning to let him understand thereby, that he might rather choose to die, than living to receive such open shame. Howbeit his heart would not serve him, he was so cowardly, and made so effeminate, by a certain vain hope he knew not what, that he was contented to make one among his own spoils.

PLUTARCH, *Aemilius Paullus*, 33–35. NORTH's translation

L. AIMILIVS L. F. III PAVLLVS PROCOS. AN. DXXCVI. EX. MACEDON ET REGE PERSE PER TRIDVVM IIV. III. PRIDIE KAL. DEC.

L. Aemilius Paulus . . . Proconsul, in the 586th year since the foundation of Rome, over Macedonia and King Perseus, a three-day triumph, on the 28th, 29th, 30th November.

CIL, I. p. 459

Pompey, 61 B.C.

So lavish was his triumph that two days were devoted to it, and even they were not enough. Much of what had been got ready for it did not find a place in the actual spectacle—indeed, there was enough left over to fit out completely another triumph. Placards were borne in front of the procession giving the names of the conquered countries, namely—Pontus, Armenia, Cappadocia, Paphlagonia, Media, Colchis, Iberia, Albania, Syria, Cilicia, Mesopotamia, Phoenicia and Palestine, Judaea, Arabia: besides these, the pirates defeated on land and sea. It was explained that during the campaigns, he had captured no fewer than 1,000 fortresses, just short of 900 cities, and 800 pirate ships. He had founded 39 cities. Moreover, whereas in the past the revenue of the state from taxation had been 50 million drachmas, now Pompey's extensions of the Empire were bringing in a further 85 million. He was paying in to the Treasury 20,000 talents of minted currency and in gold and silver plate. This did not include the money distributed to his soldiers, none of whom had been granted less than 1,500 drachmas. There were led prisoners in the procession: the pirate chiefs, a son of King Tigranes of Armenia, with his wife and daughter, Zosime, one of Tigranes' wives, Aristobulus, King of the Jews, Mithridates' sister and five of his children, some women from Scythia, hostages taken from the Iberians, Albanians, and the King of Commagene. Great numbers of trophies were paraded, one for every battle he had won, either in person or through his legates. Yet the greatest glory—and one without precedent in Roman history, was that on his third triumph he triumphed over three continents. Others had previously had three triumphs: but his first was over Europe, his second over Africa, his third over Asia. In a sense, then, he could be said to have led the entire world captive. . . .

It would have been fortunate for him if his life had ended at that point. Up to that time he had enjoyed all Alexander's good fortune: the years to come brought him successes that made him unpopular and defeats that could not be repaired.

PLUTARCH, *Pompey*, 45

CN POMPEIVS . . . MAGNVS III COS. PROCOS A. DCXCII EX ASIA, PONTŌ, ARMENIA, PAPHLAGONIA, CAPPADOCIA, CILICIA, SYRIA, SCYTHEIS, IVDAEIS, ALBANIA, PIRATEIS PER BIDVVM III PRID. KAL. OCTO.

Cn. Pompeius Magnus . . . thrice consul, proconsul, in the 692nd year since the foundation of Rome, over Asia, Pontus, Armenia, Paphlagonia, Cappadocia, Cilicia, Syria, the Scythians, the Jews, Albania and the Pirates, a two-day triumph, on the 29th and 30th of September.

CIL, I, p. 460

Julius Caesar, 46 B.C.

This brought Caesar's campaign in Africa to an end. When he returned to Rome he celebrated four triumphs together. One was for the Gallic wars, in which he had subjugated many great peoples, and brought back others to their allegiance: one was for the war in Pontus against Pharnaces: one was for the war in Africa against the allies of Lucius Scipio (in this the historian Juba, son of King Juba, appeared as an infant). Between the Gallic and Pontic triumphs there was a kind of Egyptian triumph, for the naval victory in the Nile. He took good care not to inscribe the names of any Romans in his triumph—he would himself have thought it improper, and the Romans would have thought it wicked and ill-omened to triumph over fellow-citizens. But their misfortunes were all represented by pictures and statues in the triumphal procession—except for Pompey. Him he feared to exhibit, since he was still mourned by all. Although fear restrained the people, they groaned at these misfortunes of civil war—especially when they saw the picture of Lucius Scipio, the commander, hurling himself into the sea, after stabbing himself in the breast, and Petreius committing suicide at a banquet, and Cato tearing himself open like some wild beast. They clapped for the death of Achilles and Pothinus, and laughed at the flight of Pharnaces.

60,500 talents of silver are reported to have been borne in the procession, also 2,822 gold crowns, with a total weight of 20,414 pounds. Immediately after the triumph Caesar made grants to the troops, paying all he had promised and more. Each soldier got 5,000 Attic drachmas, each centurion twice, each infantry tribune or cavalry prefect four times that sum. Each citizen from the plebs got one Attic mina.

On the day of Caesar's Gallic triumph, the axle of the triumphal car broke as he rode through the Velabrum, and he nearly fell out. Later, he went up to the Capitol between two rows of elephants—of which there were forty in all. In the Pontic triumph, on one of the floats, instead of the usual tableau showing scenes from the campaign, there was an inscription of three words only

VENI, VIDI, VICI,

thus showing the speed of the whole operation.

A ribald song was sung by the troops at the Gallic triumph:

urbani, servate uxores: calvum moechum adducimus
aurum in Galliam effutuisti, hic sumpsisti mutuum.

'Citizens, your wives defend!
Here's a baldhead man of parts
All the moneys that you lend,
Squandered on his Gallic tarts!'

SUETONIUS, *Caesar*, 37, 51

Augustus, Aug. 13th, 14th, 15th, 29 B.C.

BIS OVANS TRIVMPHI, TRIS EGI CVRVLIS TRIVMPHOS, ET APPELLATVS SVM VICIENS SEMEL IMPERATOR. CVM AVTEM PLVRIS TRIVMPHOS MIHI SENATVS DECREVISSET, IIS SVPERSEDI. LAVRVM DE FASCIBVS DEPOSVI

IN CAPITOLIO VOTIS QVAE QVOQVE BELLO NVNCVPAVERAM SOLVTIS . . . IN TRIVMPHIS MEIS DVCTI SVNT ANTE CVRRVM MEVM REGES AVT REGVM LIBERI NOVEM.

I triumphed twice with an *ovatio*, and three times in full fashion: twenty-one times I was saluted *imperator*. When the Senate voted me additional triumphs, I set them aside. I deposited on the Capitol the laurels from my fasces when I had performed the vows I undertook in each war. . . . Nine kings or sons of kings were led before my chariot in my triumphs.

AUGUSTUS, *Res gestae*, 4

Cvrvles trivmphos tris egit, Delmaticvm, Actiacvm, Alexandrinvm, continvo tridvo omnes.

He celebrated three regular triumphs, on three successive days, for the war in Dalmatia, for Actium, and for Alexandria.

SUETONIUS, *Augustus*

IMP. CAESAR DE DALMATIS EID SEX TRIVMPHAVIT PALMAM DEDIT IMP CAESAR AIGYPTO XVIII K SEPT. TRIVMPHAVIT.

The Emperor (Augustus) Caesar triumphed over the Delmatae on August 13th and dedicated the palm of victory. The Emperor (Augustus) Caesar triumphed over the Egyptians on August 15th.

Tab. Triumph. Barb., CIL, I. p. 478

Claudius, A.D. 44

His triumph was on a very lavish scale, and he invited provincial governors and a number of exiles to see it. As symbolic of his victory was a naval crown, adorned with the beaks of ships, and representing the crossing and, so to speak, the subjugation of the Ocean . . . Messalina followed the triumphal car in her town-carriage, behind her came the generals who had won triumphal *ornamenta* in Britain. All wore cloaks of purple, except M. Crassus Frugi: he had been awarded these honours previously, he wore the *tunica palmata* and so rode on a horse specially caparisoned.

SUETONIUS, *Claudius*, 17

Titus and Vespasian, A.D. 71

It is impossible to give any adequate description of these spectacles, which were in every way magnificent, whether in works of art, or wealth of many lands, or in diversity of natural objects. All the works which rich collectors have laboriously acquired one by one, as the chief products of various nations—all of these were exhibited simultaneously, on a single day, as a testimony of the might of the

Roman Empire. Silver, gold, ivory . . . seemed to flow like a river, there were tapestries . . . gems, some transparent, others variously set, in such profusion that one had to revise the belief that such things were rare. . . .

Yet nothing was more astonishing than the movable stages: so massive that there was some alarm as to their stability, for many of them were three and four storeys high. . . . Here was shown the war, in many representations, and in all its episodes. Here was to be seen the devastation of a prosperous countryside, there the slaughter of enemy regiments . . . here powerful fortifications were being demolished by siege-engines, strong fortresses were captured, defences were over-run and the assault force poured in, the whole scene a deluge of blood . . . houses pulled down, temples set on fire. Amid calamity and destruction, the rivers flowed, not over tilled land to bring water to men and animals, but through a country blazing on all sides. Such were the sufferings in store for the Jews when they began the war: now the refinements of art and workmanship brought all these incidents home to those who had not seen them, as though they were happening before their eyes. . . .

Conspicuous above all the spoils were those taken from the Temple at Jerusalem. These were a gold table, many talents in weight, and a gold lampstand, constructed in a quite unusual pattern. A slender shaft, fastened to a pedestal, carried slender branches, arranged like a trident, with a lamp on the end of each branch: of these there were seven, that being a sacred number among the Jews. Finally—last of all the spoils—came a copy of the Jewish Law. . . . Vespasian was followed by Titus: beside him was Domitian, splendidly accoutred and on a superb horse.

The procession ended at the Capitol, where they halted, following the traditional custom of pausing there until the execution of the enemy general was announced. This was Simon ben Giora, who had marched in the procession of prisoners, been scourged . . . and then dragged to the appointed place of execution. The announcement was made, to general applause, that Simon was no more: then the princes began the sacrifices.

JOSEPHUS, *Jewish War*, V. 123–60

The most important ceremonies at the Temple of Jupiter Optimus Maximus were the celebrations of triumphs. Jupiter was the guarantor of the stability and empire of Rome: *imperium sine fine dedi*, in Virgil's words. Victorious Roman generals were carrying out his will, and in a sense were his *legati*: thanks must be paid to him in his temple at the culmination of their triumphs. There were traditionally 320 triumphs from the earliest times to that of Vespasian and Titus in A.D. 71, and a further 30 or so between that date and the end of the Empire. They were a unique combination of thanksgiving service, military parade, political propaganda, and public spectacle. Before 200 B.C. a standard pattern had evolved for the religious ceremonies used, for the composition and marshalling of the procession, and for its route through the city. They are well seen in the description of one of the most lavish of republican triumphs, that of Quinctius Flamininus over Macedonia. Henceforward novelty lay in the exoticism and lavishness of the *apparatus* or furnishings, the rank and demeanour of the principal captives, the splendour of the booty, and the gifts distributed to soldiers and citizens. The statistics of the booty were carefully recorded, and formed a kind of balance-sheet of Roman imperialism. No less important was the psychological side. The victorious general, standing at the pinnacle of human felicity, was peculiarly vulnerable to the *invidia* of fortune or the gods. Hence the poignancy of Aemilius Paullus losing his two sons 'in the hour of triumph': hence the reflection that it had been well for Pompey if he had died shortly after. The ribald songs of the soldiers—of which that sung at Caesar's triumph is a sample—had a ritual purpose; deflated to the human level, the *triumphator* was less of a target. The captives could earn admiration or contempt for their demeanour. Plutarch feels keenly the cowardice of Perseus, unworthy of a king of the realm of Alexander. Most important—and not always predictable—was the behaviour of the spectators. Appian notes how they responded to the various incidents depicted in Caesar's triumphs. It was known that it would have been explosive to show the defeat and death of Pompey, but those of Scipio and Cato evoked a dangerous sympathy. Triumphs over Roman citizens were always invidious: Augustus may record a three-fold triumph, *Delmaticum*, *Actiacum*, *Alexandrinum*: the official *Acta* fuse the last two into a single triumph AEGYPTO 'over Egypt'. Plutarch's description of the triumph of Aemilius Paullus is the most detailed, as it is the most perceptive, of any to be found in a classical author. I reproduce it in the noble translation of North.

The triumphs of Pompey to commemorate his victories and settlement in the East were undoubtedly the most lavish of the Roman Republic. Note what has been called the 'battle-roll' of conquered nations, among them exotic peoples from Russia and the Caucasus. Caesar's concern, as always, was to outdo Pompey. Augustus was a master of the plain statement of fact—when the facts were good enough. So there is the lapidary record of two lesser triumphs: three full triumphs: more had he wanted them: nine royal captives. Claudius' triumph over Britain was the first by a reigning Princeps for more than seventy years. Once more the figure of Oceanus appears, as at the triumph of Caesar, but this time the 'conquest' is more than ephemeral. (See also p. 186).

Singular interest attaches to the description of the triumph of Vespasian and Titus by the Jewish historian Flavius Josephus. That enigmatic individual had fought bravely for his people, then made terms with the Romans in dubious circumstances, and done well out of the patronage of the conquerors. Two things impressed him as he watched the triumph—the miseries that their unyielding obstinacy brought on the Jewish people, and the majesty of the Roman Empire. It is a pity that we lack a good account of the triumph of Trajan over the Dacians, the high-water mark of Roman expansion.

The influence of the triumph on Roman art and architecture was far-reaching. Coins, medallions, cameos, gems, statues and sculpture were all used for commemoration. Specific architectural forms were evolved for the same purpose—notably the triumphal arch and the *Columna cochlida*, the column with spiral bands of reliefs, like those of Trajan and of Marcus Aurelius. Here the pictures and models carried in the triumphal procession itself will have created a repertory of themes and conventions for the sculptures which translated them into permanent form. Indeed, 'official' Roman art with its characteristic blend of symbol and fact, of myth and historical *res gestae*, may well have owed more to the art forms evoked by the triumph than to anything else. Above all, the access of wealth from booty made possible the embellishment of Rome by such splendid architectural schemes as the Theatre of Pompey, the Temple of Peace, and the Forum of Trajan.

AGON CAPITOLINUS

Domitian established a festival to be held at intervals of four years in honour of Jupiter Capitolinus. There were three main divisions—literary (*musicum*), horsemanship, and athletics: prizes were awarded for rather more events than nowadays. For example, there was a competition for Greek and Latin prose declamation: besides the competition for lyre-players, there were other events for both chorus and solo performances with the lyre, without singing: in the stadium there were actually races for young girls. The emperor presided at these competitions in person, dressed in Greek fashion with a purple toga and wearing half-boots, and wearing a golden crown with Jupiter, Juno, and Minerva represented on it. At his side, in similar costume, sat the priest of Jupiter and members of the college of the Flavians.

SUETONIUS, *Domitian*, 4

DEIS MANIBVS SACRVM Q. SVLPICIO. Q. F. CLA. MAXIMO DOMO ROMA VIXIT. ANN XI. M.V. D.XII. HIC TERTII CERTAMINIS LVSTRO INTER GRAECOS POETAS DVO ET L PROFESSVS, FAVOREM QVEM OB TENERAM AETATEM EXCITAVERAT, IN ADMIRATIONEM INGENIO SVO PERDVXIT ET CVM HONORE DISCESSIT. VERSVS EXTEMPORALES EO SVBIECTI SVNT NE PARENTES ADFECTIBVS SVIS INDVLSISSE VIDEANTVR. Q. SVLPICIVS

MAXIMVS ET LICINIA IANVARIA PARENTES INFELICISSIMI F. PIISSIMI FEC. ET. SIBI. POST. S.

To the departed spirits of Q. Sulpicius Maximus, son of Quintus, whose home was at Rome, and who lived 11 years 5 months 12 days. At the third celebration of the (Capitoline) contest this boy submitted a poem in the Greek poetry event with 52 Greek poets competing. The sympathy aroused by his tender age was sustained by his genius to the point of admiration, and he was awarded a high commendation. His extempore verses are quoted below, lest his parents should be thought to be giving rein to their natural feelings. His most unhappy parents Q. Sulpicius Maximus and Licinia Januaria set this up to their dear son, also for themselves and their descendants.

CIL, VI, 33976

tu paene ab ipsis orsus incunabulis
  dei poeta nobilis
sertum coronae praeferens Olympiae
  puer celebrasti Iovem.

Almost from your cradle you appeared as the poet of the noble god: bearing the wreath of the Olympic garland, as a mere boy you sang of Jupiter.

AUSONIUS, *Professores* V. 5 (Delphidius)

The Agon Capitolinus was established by Domitian in A.D. 86. It was the most successful of a series of attempts by philhellene emperors to domesticate Greek athletic and literary contests in Rome. Domitian built the Stadium for the athletic contests, and the Odeon for singing and music. The chariot races were held in the Circus Maximus. Because he presided in person and presented the awards on the Capitol, the festival took root at once and attracted competitors from all parts of the Empire (fifty-two Greek poets competed in the year A.D. 94): it was still maintained in the fourth century, when Ausonius' colleague Delphidius was a competitor. Certain events, such as the races for girls, clashed with Roman prejudice and were soon dropped. Most prestige attached to the athletics, and to the contests in Greek and Latin poetry. It is known that both Statius and Fronto competed unsuccessfully, but it cannot be said that either Greek or Latin literature profited greatly from the stimulus provided by the *agon*. The surviving evidence, indeed, suggests that boy prodigies were unduly favoured: in A.D. 106 the Latin poetry prize went to a boy of thirteen. The well-known tomb of the eleven-year-old Q. Sulpicius Maximus shows another precocious talent. The extemporary verses consist of 43—rather jejune—Greek hexameters, in which Zeus rebukes Helios for allowing Phaethon to borrow his chariot. They do not clear the bereaved parents of undue admiration for the effort of their dutiful offspring.

THE CITADEL AND TEMPLE OF JUNO MONETA

While this was happening at Veii, the Citadel of Rome and the Capitol were in grave danger. For either the Gauls had seen the footprints of the man who had got through from Veii, or had noted for themselves a promising line of ascent from the shrine of Carmenta. So, on a night with stars, they first sent an unarmed man to find the route, then by handing up their arms where the slope was steep, and by supporting and being supported as the ascent required, they finally reached the summit in such silence that they did not even rouse the dogs—animals easily disturbed by noises in the night. But the geese they did not evade: these creatures, being sacred to Juno, had not been killed even though food was desperately short. This was salvation for the Romans. The geese honked and flapped their wings: they aroused M. Manlius, who had been consul three years earlier. An excellent warrior, Manlius snatched up his weapons, summoned others to arms, and, while they were still in the grip of fear, struck a Gaul who was already on the summit with the base of his shield and hurled him backwards. In his fall he knocked down those nearest to him, and the others in their alarm dropped their weapons and clung tight to the rocks—to be killed by Manlius. By now the rest of the Romans had come up, and harrassed the attackers with stones and weapons: soon the entire Gallic force lost their footing and fell headlong to their deaths. At dawn the trumpet summoned the soldiers to meet before the tribunes. Rewards and punishment were then distributed. First, Manlius was praised for his courage, and given a present, not only by the tribunes, but also by the soldiers, who agreed to bring each half a pound of spelt and a gill of wine to his house in the Capitol. It does not sound much in the telling, but it was in fact a signal token of affection, since each man was depriving himself of food and subtracting from the necessities of life to honour a single man. Next they summoned the men who had been posted to watch the cliff by which the enemy ascended. Q. Sulpicius, the tribune, said he was going to enforce the full military punishment, but the cries of the soldiers, who attributed all the guilt to a single watchman, deterred him, and he spared the others. But there was no doubt of the guilt of this last watchman, who was hurled over the cliff with general approval.

Livy, v. 47

Lucius Furius . . . in the heat of battle vowed a temple to Juno Moneta . . . when he returned to Rome . . . the Senate ordered that two commissioners should be created to build it in a style proper to the dignity of the Roman People. A site was approved on the Capitol, where the house of Marcus Manlius Capitolinus had formerly stood. . . . The Temple was dedicated the year after it was vowed, when G. Marcius Rutulus was in his third consulship, and Titus Manlius Torquatus in his second (343 B.C.).

LIVY, VII. 28

January 16th

Candida, te niveo posuit lux proxima templo
qua fert sublimes alta Moneta gradus:
nunc bene prospicias Latiam, Concordia, turbam
nunc te sacratae constituere manus.

Bright goddess! the next day set you on your temple, where high Moneta lifts her slope sublime. Now Concordia, look kindly on the people of Latium, since consecrated hands have established your worship.

OVID, *Fasti*, I. 637–40

FLAVIAE. EPICHA(RI). SACERDOTI. AE. DEAE. VIRGIN(IS). CAELESTIS PRAESENTISSIMO. NVMINI LOCI. MONTIS. TARPEI. SEXTIA. OLYMPIA. S. H(onorifica). F(emina). (*sic*) ET. CHRESTINA. DORCADIVS H(onorifica) F(emina) HONORIFICAE. FEMINAE. CONIVGI. IVNI HYL(A)E. SACERD(otis). VNA. CVM. SACRATAS. ET. CANISTRARIIS. (*sic*). DIGNISSIMAE.

To the Honourable and Most Worthy Lady, Flavia Epicharis, Priestess of the Maiden Goddess. Dea Caelestis, a divinity most potent on the Tarpeian Hill, and wife of the Priest Junius Hylas: set up by the Honourable Ladies, Sextia Olympia and Chrestina Dorcadius, together with the Initiates, and the Basket-bearers. (A.D. 259)

ILS. 4438

The most recent commentator on Livy has well said of the story of Manlius and the Geese 'no modern scepticism can seriously shake its claims'. To those who recall how other Celtic soldiers stormed the Heights of Abraham, Livy's spirited narrative carries conviction. So do the geese. They cannot of course have belonged to the temple of Juno Moneta founded by the Senate in 344 B.C., but there may have been an earlier shrine of the goddess on the citadel. Or, more likely, they may have been attached as sacred birds to the *auguraculum*, or observation-post for diviners, known to have stood on that part of the hill.

The Temple built *pro amplitudine populi Romani* has left no archaeological trace, though it is clear that the church of S. Maria in Aracoeli stands directly above it. It is therefore valuable to learn from the passage of Ovid that it stood on a high podium, and was reached by a flight of steps leading up from the Temple of Concord at the north-west end of the Forum. It housed the Roman mint until the end of the first century A.D.: with its removal the temple seems to have lost its public importance. But the cult of the Queen of Heaven (Juno Regina Caelestis) continued to be observed on the Capitol, and indeed to exfoliate. This is seen from the inscription of the cult of Dea Caelestis. Described as *potens in monte tarpeio* in the late empire, it may have led on to the foundation of the church of S. Maria in Aracoeli.

CARCER AND TULLIANUM

So Marius entered Rome in triumph, displaying Jugurtha as a prisoner to the Roman people—a sight they had given up hope of ever seeing. While he lived, no-one could hope to subdue the enemy in Africa: so resourceful was he in adapting himself to fortune, so indomitable, and so subtle. But it is said that being led in triumph drove him out of his mind. Later, he was thrown into prison, where some tore off his clothes, and others, struggling for his gold earring, wrenched it out of his ear. Then he was thrown naked into the dungeon, and in his madness and confusion, called out with a maniacal laugh 'Hercules, how cold your bath is!' Here he struggled against hunger for six days, fighting for life to the last, but was finally overtaken by the proper reward for his wickedness.

PLUTARCH, *Marius*, 12 (104 B.C.)

When, as I have said, the Senate adopted the motion of Cato, the consul, thinking it better not to await nightfall for fear of a fresh *coup*, ordered the triumvir to make all preparations for the execution. He himself conducted Lentulus to the prison: the others were brought by the praetors. There is in the prison a place called the Tullianum. It is on the left as you go up, and is some twelve feet underground. Walls surround it on every side, and it is roofed by a vault made of dressed stone: its squalor, darkness, and stench make it a foul and dreadful place. Lentulus was lowered into that place; then the executioners garrotted him with a cord according to their instructions. So this aristocrat, a scion of the great house of the Cornelii, a former consul at Rome, met an end worthy of his character and deeds. A similar punishment was inflicted on Cethegus, Statilius, Gabinius, and Caeparius.

SALLUST, *Catiline*, LV (63 B.C.)

C. VIBIVS C.F. RVFINVS. M. COCCEIVS. NERVA. COS. EX. S.C.

(Built by) the consuls C. Vibius Rufinus and M. Cocceius Nerva, by order of the Senate. (See Plate 14.)

CIL, VI. 1539

Doryphorianus also was sentenced to death, and imprisoned in the Tullianum: later he was taken out of it by the Emperor, on his mother's appeal, but was put to death with hideous torture after he was taken back to his own country.

AMMIANUS MARCELLINUS, XVIII. 37 (A.D. 368)

The Tullianum of Sallust is the lower and more ancient of the two surviving rooms of the Carcer. It may originally have been a well-house over a natural spring (*tullus*) at the foot of the Capitol: later a bogus etymology attached it to King Servius Tullius. Its use as a prison, and the addition of an upper room or rooms above the archaic vault, would seem to date from the early republic. By the time of Jugurtha the upper level is the prison proper, and the Tullianum is the death cell. The 'triumvirs' who supervised the execution of the Catilinarian conspirators were the *tresviri capitales*: their assistants carried out the death sentence. Other enemies of the state to die here were Vercingetorix (46 B.C.) and the Jewish zealot Simon Ben Giora (A.D. 71). The passage of Ammianus shows that the prison continued to be used to the late empire: indeed, it is the only state prison known to have existed in Rome. See Plates 14–15.

The inscription relates to a restoration in (probably) A.D. 22.

The legend that St. Peter and St. Paul were imprisoned here does not seem to be early, but it led to the building of the two churches San Pietro in Carcere and San Giuseppe dei Falegnami in and above the ancient levels, and thus contributed to the survival of the monument.

TABULARIUM

Q. LVTATIVS. Q.F.Q.N. CATVLVS COS DE SEN. SENT. FACIVNDVM COERAVIT EIDEMQVE PROBAVIT.

Q. Lutatius Catulus, son of Quintus, grandson of Quintus, consul, by a decree of the Senate, saw to the erection of this building and approved it as satisfactory.

CIL, VI. 1313

Q. LVTATIVS Q.F.Q.N. COS . SVBSTRVCTIONEM . ET . TABVLARIVM . DE . S . S . FACIVNDVM . COERAVIT . EIDEMQVE . PROBAVIT.

Q. Lutatius Catulus, son of Quintus, grandson of Quintus, consul, by a decree of the Senate, saw to the erection of this substructure and the Tabularium, and approved it as satisfactory.

CIL, VI. 1314

There is still *in situ* part of the first of these inscriptions, which were found in 1845. The second, now lost, was copied by the humanists Poggio and Signorili, and contains the important words *substructio* and *tabularium*. They are our only source for the history of a building which, from its use as the State Record Office, must have been one of the most important in Rome, and certainly one of its architectural glories. Q. Lutatius Catulus was consul in 78 B.C.: at this period and under the patronage of Sulla an architect whose name we do not know was at work on the astonishing complex of buildings which adorns the shrine of Fortuna Primigenia at Praeneste. Here, on an even ampler scale than with the Tabularium, an opportunity to exploit a hill-side position was offered to a master of mass, level, and elevation. It has been supposed that the two projects were the work of the same man. The builder of the Tabularium, whoever he was, is worthy of the symbolic link with Michelangelo, whose Palace of the Senators now stands on the surviving portion of the republican building, and perpetuates its long connection with the administration of the city.

The interior shows signs of a repair late in the first century A.D. Suetonius (*Vespasian* 8) mentions the destruction in the fighting of A.D. 69 of over 3,000 bronze tablets containing decrees of the Senate, acts of the people, and treaties granted to states and private persons. The context suggests, however, that these were in the Temple of Jupiter Optimus Maximus rather than the Tabularium.

THE ROMAN FORUM

Talibus inter se dictis ad tecta subibant
pauperis Euandri, passimqua armenta videbant
Romanoque Foro et lautis mugire Carinis.

Talking so together, they came to the house of humble Evander: on all sides they saw cattle lowing in the Forum Romanum and on wealthy Carinae.

VIRGIL, *Aeneid*, VIII. 359–61

hic ubi nunc fora sunt, udae tenuere paludes:
  amne redundatis fossa madebat aquis.

Here, where the fora now are, was once deep swamp:
  a ditch would drip with water that had flooded back from the river.

OVID, *Fasti*, VI. 401

Forum sex modis intelligitur. Primo negotiantis locus, ut forum Flaminium, forum Iulium, ab eorum nominibus, qui ea fora constituenda curarunt: quod et etiam locis privatis et in viis et agris fieri solet. Tertio, in quo iudicia fieri, cum populo agi, contiones haberi. . . .

The word Forum has six meanings. The first, a place of business, as forum Flaminium, forum Julium, and taking its name from those who established it as a forum: as is done for private estates, roads, country districts, etc. Another, a place where lawsuits are tried, public assemblies held, and speeches delivered. . . .

FESTUS, 74

Romulus and Titus Tatius, by cutting down the wood which grew on the level ground at the foot of the Capitol, and by filling up the lake which, lying in a hollow, was constantly fed by the streams coming down from the hills, created the Forum used even to-day by the Roman people. There they held their assemblies, transacting their business in the temple of Vulcan, which stands slightly higher than the Forum proper.

DIONYSIUS HALICARNASSUS, *Roman Antiquities*, II. 50

It is believed that the Forum and the Capitol were added to the city by Titus Tatius, not by Romulus.

TACITUS, *Annals*, XII. 24

From that moment (peace with the Latins) King Tarquin devoted himself with even greater enthusiasm to the unfinished tasks of peace . . . he drained the Forum and the low-lying parts of the city between the hills—flat places with no good run-off for flood waters—by means of sewers constructed with a slope towards the Tiber.

Livy, I. 38

So from the same origin are *novitas* 'newness', *novicius* 'a novice', *novalis* 'a new-ploughed field': part of the buildings in the Forum is called *Sub Novis* 'by the New Shops', although the name is ancient, as indeed is *Nova Via* 'New Street', which is old enough by this time.

Varro, *De lingua Latina*, VI. 59

In the cities of Italy we cannot use the same forum plans as do the Greeks, since our ancestors have handed down the custom of giving gladiatorial shows in the Forum.

Vitruvius, *On Architecture*, I. 1

In honour of Marcus Aemilius Lepidus, twice consul, augur, his three sons Lucius, Martius, and Quintus, gave funeral games lasting three days, and exhibited twenty-two pairs of gladiators in the Forum. (216 B.C.)

Livy, XXIII. 30

At the funeral of Publius Licinius Crassus there was a public distribution of meat, a contest between one hundred and twenty gladiators, three days of funeral games, followed by a public banquet (*epulum*). At the banquet, tables had been set up throughout the Forum, but a storm got up, accompanied by violent gusts of wind, and forcing most people to set up tents in the Forum. Later, when there was a general clearance, these were all taken down: common opinion now declared that the omen was fulfilled, since the soothsayers had declared that fate decreed that tents should be set up in the Forum. (183 B.C.)

Livy, XXXIX. 46

(At his triumph, 46 B.C.) Caesar entertained the whole people at a single banquet, where 22,000 dining tables were set out: and he showed gladiators and a naval battle, to honour, as he said, his daughter Julia, though she had been dead long since.

Plutarch, *Caesar*, 55

In my own name, or that of my sons and grandsons, I gave hunts of African wild beasts on twenty-six occasions, in the circus, the forum, or the amphitheatre. About 3,500 animals were killed.

Augustus, *Res gestae*, 22

Verginius, seeing no help at all, said 'Appius, pardon a father's grief . . . let me question the nurse here, in the girl's presence, to see how this matter stands. If

I am not the girl's father, I shall go away with a quieter mind.' Permission was given, and he led the girl and the nurse aside to the shops near the shrine of Cloacina—the New Shops, they are now called. There, snatching up a knife from a butcher, 'My daughter,' he cried, 'I give you your freedom in this, the only way that I can!' With these words he stabbed her to the heart. Then, looking back to the tribunal, he called out 'Appius, I devote you and your life to destruction with the blood that has been shed!' Appius heard the shout that greeted this fearful deed, and ordered Verginius' arrest. But Verginius hacked his way through with his knife, and protected by a crowd of supporters, reached the city gate in safety.

LIVY, III. 48

sed dum hic egreditur foras commostrabo quo in quem-
que hominem facile inueniatis loco,
ne nimio opere sumat operam si quem conuentum uelit,
uel uitiosum uel sine uitio, uel probum uel inprobum.
qui peiiurum conuenire uolt hominem ito in comitium;
qui mendacem et gloriosum, apud Cloacinae sacrum,
dites, damnosos maritos sub basilica quaerito.
ibidem erunt scorta exoleta quique stipulari solent;
symbolarum conlatores apud forum piscarium.
in foro infumo boni homines atque dites ambulant;
in medio propter canalem, ibi ostentatores meri;
confidentes garrulique et maliuoli supra lacum,
qui alteri de nihilo audacter dicunt contumeliam
et qui ipsi sat habent quod in se possit uere dicier.
sub ueteribus, ibi sunt qui dant quique accipiunt faenore.
pone aedem Castoris, ibi sunt subito quibu' credas male.
in Tusco uico, ibi sunt homines qui ipsi sese uenditant.
in Velabro uel pistorem uel lanium uel haruspicem
uel qui ipsi uortant uel qui aliis ubi uorsentur praebeant.

(Company Manager): Now, till he comes back, I'm going to tell you where you can find people of every kind. After this it won't call for any great exertion whatever kind of fellow you want to meet, good or bad, honourable or the reverse. Now, for perjurers, try the Comitium. Liars and braggarts, by the shrine of Cloacina: rich married wastrels, in stock by the Basilica. A good supply of harlots, too, if not in prime condition: also men for hire-purchase. In the Fish-market, members of dining-clubs, in the Lower Forum, respectable and well-to-do citizens out for a walk: flashier types, in the middle Forum, along the canal. By the Lacus Curtius, bold fellows with a tongue in their head, and a bad purpose in mind—great slanderers of other people and very vulnerable to it themselves. By the Old Shops, the money changers—loans negotiated or accepted. Behind the Temple of Castor—but you'd better not trust yourself there. In the Vicus Tuscus, homosexuals, very versatile, turn and turn about. . . .

PLAUTUS, *Curculio*, 466–82

For more than five centuries the Forum was the centre of the life of the Roman republic, political, legal, commercial, cultural, and to a large extent, religious. The number of literary references is very large, and those given above do no more than throw some light on its origins, growth, and function. More will be said under individual sites and monuments, and especially on their political life.

Virgil and Ovid show the Forum in its natural state, the marshy valley between the Capitol, the Palatine, and the Esquiline. In the passage of the *Fasti*, it is wild nature yet: in that from the *Aeneid* there is already a little band of Arcadians on the Palatine hill, and their cattle graze in the valley below. Modern archaeology will have none of the Arcadians, but would ascribe the first cattle to those Latin pastoralists who sometime about 800 B.C. founded a little settlement on the Palatine (see p. 147). Note Virgil's adjectives: the Roman Forum will be the centre of the world, wealthy Carinae, its Parioli or Park Lane. And there the cattle low, as they would do centuries after Virgil's day, when the Forum was again the Campo Vaccino, the Cow's Field. Of Festus' six meanings, two only concern us. Etymologists are doubtful of the word's derivation, but it may mean a space enclosed for some definite purpose (compare *forma*) and two of the most lasting purposes of the Roman Forum were for law and business, as Festus says: indeed, both were transacted there until the end of the Empire. Both, too, are to be read in the names of such Roman towns as Forum Julii (Fréjus) in Gallia Narbonensis.

Ancient sources differ as to when the Forum was first used, while agreeing that it was later than the earliest origins of Rome. Dionysius ascribes it to Romulus and Titus Tatius; Tacitus to the Sabine King alone. But a far more likely version is that it was neither Latin nor Sabine, but, as Livy says, an Etruscan foundation, following directly on the draining of the swamps by means of the Cloaca Maxima, and the founding of a new religious centre on the Capitol (see p. 51). The passage of Varro gives us two Forum place-names, the Nova Via or New Street, which ran under the Palatine, and the New Shops (new since the fire of 210 B.C.) in front of Basilica Aemilia. Like New College at Oxford, both had acquired antiquity.

The use of the Forum for public ceremonies and a wide range of spectacles meant that the open space had to be preserved, and temporary seating and other apparatus provided on an increasingly lavish scale. The funeral games and 22 pairs of gladiators of 216 B.C. have grown to funeral games, 120 gladiators, a *visceratio* or distribution of meat, plus a public banquet, by 183 B.C. Julius Caesar—whose conquests gave him the money to do it—entertains the entire Roman people at 22,000 tables, which must have imposed a heavy strain on the caterers. The naval battle (*naumachiae*) did not of course take place on the Forum: the need for specialized places of amusement was now apparent, and special ponds were dug for them by the Tiber. But throughout the reign of Augustus gladiatorial shows were given in the Forum. It has recently been shown that the series of underground galleries in the centre of the Forum were connected with these displays: they were provided with lifts whereby gladiators or wild beasts could be hoisted up to the ground level. Such machinery was developed on a very large scale at the Colosseum.

The lines from the *Curculio* of Plautus give a lively picture of the Forum crowds at the beginning of the second century B.C. Put in the mouth of the manager of the stage company, it provides a kind of shopper's guide to human types among the *forenses*, good and bad—mostly bad. The perjurers are by the Comitium, where politicians address the people and hard by the courts are in session. Around the shrine of Cloacina, the braggart warriors (*milites gloriosi*) back from the wars—a rich source of fun for the Roman comedians. The Basilica could only be Basilica Sempronia, known to have been built in 184 B.C.: this is usually given as the year of Plautus' death. There is a problem here. The members of the dining-clubs were choosing in person the delicacies for their meeting: this they would do in the fish-market, then on the fringes of the Forum by the Argiletum, but later (179 B.C.) moved to the Macellum or Market-Hall. Along the canal, the idlers, parasites and drunkards, whose collective name *canalicolae* gives the derivative *canaglia* and *canaille*. The bankers' booths are among the Old Shops, whose street fronts ran along the south side of the Via Sacra by Basilica Sempronia. The dark alleys behind Castor under the Palatine are best avoided; there too, in the Vicus Tuscus, the inverts have their pitch. By this time the action of the play can proceed, but the manager's interlude has not been wasted. We know the Roman *forenses*, and can see in them the same varied fauna that now frequent the Spanish Steps and Piazza di Spagna.

Finally, there are two passages which should be read in full, though they are too long to be given here. The first is Livy's improving story of Appius Claudius and Verginia (Livy III. 42–51). It shows the life of the Forum in the early republic (the traditional date is 449 B.C.) as Livy thought it to have been. Verginia, accompanied by her nurse, has gone to one of the schoolmasters' booths in the Forum. There she is seized by a man suborned by Appius Claudius, who claims her as his runaway slave. As the story unfolds, we note the appeals to the crowd by the outraged Verginia and her father: on the day of her trial she and her father enter the Forum in mourning garb; the verdict of the court is always liable to be upset by popular indignation. If we quote the episode of Verginia's death, it is rather for reasons of topography than morality. The reason the poor girl was drawn aside from the tribunal to the shrine of Cloacina—a few yards only—is that there among the Tabernae Novae was a butcher's shop, from which Verginius could snatch the fatal knife. 'Much hatred, little room': one senses the intimate, stifling scale of life in the early Republic. The other and better known passage is the Ninth Satire of Horace's first book—Horace and the Bore. The time is about 9 a.m.: the setting, the Via Sacra between the Velia and tribunal of the Forum. Horace is occupied first with his thoughts, and second with the Bore, the Forum is only the background. But we can follow him on his stroll of perhaps three hundred yards, past the Temple of Vesta, and ending when the Bore is trapped and hauled into court.

Of set purpose, the passages on the Roman Forum in general do not go beyond Augustus. With the Empire its character changed drastically. Political changes controlled the Senate and left the people powerless. Much of the legal and business life, and a good deal of the ceremonial, went to the new imperial fora. The Forum Romanum, almost covered with great buildings and crowded with triumphal arches, was on its way to becoming a historical monument itself. The reliefs on the Plutei Trajani (see p. 89), now housed in the Curia Julia, and illustrated on plates 23–25, show the Forum as it was early in the second century A.D.

THE TEMPLE OF SATURN

This hill (the Capitol) was once called the hill of Saturn. . . . On it was an old town called Saturnia. Three things recall it even today: that there is a shrine of Saturn on the approach to the hill, also a Saturnian gate, which Junius writes of, called Pandana nowadays: that behind the Temple of Saturn, where the laws for the building of private houses are displayed, the back walls are called 'the walls of Saturn'.

VARRO, *De lingua Latina*, V. 42

The consuls were Q. Cloelius and T. Larcius, next Aulus Sempronius and M. Minucius. In their year (497 B.C.) the temple of Saturn was dedicated, and the day of the Saturnalia made a festal day.

LIVY, XXII. I. 29

C XVI SAT. NP. FER SATVRNO SATVRN AD FOR.

On the sixteenth day (before the Kalends of January: i.e. Dec. 17th): the Saturnalia. Festival of Saturn: at the temple of Saturn in the Forum.

Fasti Amiternini, CIL, 1^2, p. 245

L. PLANCVS L. F. COS. IMP. ITER. DE. MANIB.

L. Munatius Plancus, consul and imperator, renewed this temple out of the spoils of war.

CIL, VI. 1316

L. MVNATIVS PLANCVS . . . AEDEM SATVRNI DE MANIBIIS FECIT . . .

L. Munatius Plancus built the Temple of Saturn out of the spoils of war.

CIL, X. 6087

SENATVS POPVLVSQVE ROMANVS INCENDIO CONSVMPTVM RESTITVIT

The Senate and People of Rome restored (this temple) destroyed by fire.

CIL, VI. 937

The Roman people chose the Temple of Saturn for their public treasury, because, when he lived in Italy, no theft was ever committed. Alternatively, because under him private property did not exist: 'It was not right to set a mark upon the soil, nor to portion out the fields with a boundary stone.' They sought land for the common good. So they entrusted the common prosperity of the people to that deity under whom all things had been owned in common by all.

MACROBIUS, *Saturnalia*, I. 8

Old olive oil is useful for certain kinds of disease, and is held to be effective in preventing ivory from decay: it is a fact that the inside of the statue of Saturn at Rome has been filled with oil.

PLINY, *Natural History*, XV. 32

protinus abducto patuerunt templa Metello,
tunc rupes Tarpeia sonat magnoque reclusas
testatur stridore fores; tunc conditus imo
eruitur templo multis non tactus ab annis
Romani census populi, quem Punica bella,
quem dederat Perses, quem victi praeda Philippi,
quod tibi, Roma, fuga Pyrrhus trepidante reliquit,

quo te Fabricius regi non vendidit auro,
quidquid parcorum mores servastis avorum,
quod dites Asiae populi misere tributum
victorique dedit Minoia Creta Metello,
quod Cato longinqua vexit super aequora Cypro,
tunc Orientis opes captorumque ultima regum
quae Pompeianis praelata est gaza triumphis
pauperiorque fuit tunc primum Caesare Roma.

At once, the temple was thrown open, Metellus pushed aside. Then there was an echo from the Tarpeian rock, as loud gratings proclaimed the opening of the doors. Then came forth from the temple the treasure of the Roman people, untouched for many years—spoils that had come from the Punic War, from Perses, booty from conquered Philip, the gold that the panic-stricken Gaul had abandoned to Rome in his flight, the money that could not bribe Fabricius to sell her to the king. Everything that our ancestors' thrift had put together, everything that the wealthy peoples of Asia had sent as tribute, all that Minos' realm of Crete handed over to the conqueror Metellus, all that Cato brought across the seas from far Cyprus. Last of all came the riches of the East, the treasure fetched from far off captive kings and borne in Pompey's triumph. Ill-omened the spoil that robbed a temple! Then, for the first time, was Rome poorer than a Caesar.

LUCAN, *Pharsalia*, III. 154–68

Julius Caesar, when he first entered the city in the civil war that bears his name, took out of the Treasury 15,000 bars of gold, 30,000 of silver and 30,000,000 sesterces in coin.

PLINY, *Natural History*, XXXIII. 56

M. ACILIO M.F. CANINO QVAESTORI VRBANO NEGOTIATORES EX AREA SATVRNI.

The merchants trading in the *area Saturni* set this up to the city quaestor M. Acilius Caninus, son of Marcus.

CIL, VI. 1265

Much is obscure about the cult of Saturn, but there is no doubt that the god was associated from the earliest times with the area at the west end of the Forum and under the Capitol. This association accounts for the 'Saturnian Walls' and 'Porta Pandana' (site uncertain) of Varro. Doubt surrounds the foundation of the temple—*aedes Saturni*—late in the regal period or early in the republic?—but Livy's date of 497 B.C. is perhaps the most likely. The day is certain, if not the year, the calendar quoted gives it as December 17th, the original date of the midwinter festival *Saturnalia*, which later extended to seven days.

This ancient building seems to have received no major repair until 42 B.C., when it was restored by L. Munatius Plancus, whose action is also recorded in the epitaph on the great family tomb at Gaeta. Early in the fourth century A.D. came the restoration after a fire, recorded by the inscription on the gable, an ill-done piece of botching, but perhaps all that the times could afford.

The cult statue of the god was obviously wooden: not only was it filled with oil, but also bound with wool. The Temple was the state treasury from very early times; the high *podium* providing suitable vaults. Two passages illustrate the famous occasion when in 49 B.C. Caesar helped himself to public funds, despite the brave resistance of the tribune Metellus Cotta. Lucan brings a poet's imagination to a description which fired the mind of Dante. Pliny notes the amount extracted in bullion and cash. Under the empire the *aerarium Saturni* was less important than the imperial fiscus.

The last inscription shows a group of business men operating in the square by the Temple, and presumably paying rent to the state.

In the illustration (Plate 17) the entrance to the vaults of the treasury can be seen on the side of the Temple facing the Forum.

MILLIARIUM AUREUM

At this time (20 B.C.), Augustus was appointed the Commissioner for all roads in the neighbourhood of Rome. As such, he set up the Golden Milestone, as it is called, and also appointed ex-praetors, each attended by two lictors, to see to their actual maintenance.

DIO CASSIUS, *Roman History* LIV. 8

Shortly after dawn on that day Galba was sacrificing in the presence of his friends . . . Umbricius, the officiating priest . . . announced in plain words that the signs showed a great upheaval, and that danger and treachery hung over the Emperor's head. Thus the god almost delivered Otho to arrest. For Otho was standing just behind Galba, and heard what was said. . . . As he stood there in fear and confusion . . . his freedman Onomastus came up and said that the architects had come and were waiting in his house. This was the agreed password that the moment had come for Otho to meet the soldiers. Saying that he had bought an old house and now wished to point out its defects to the vendors, he went away. Passing through the Domus Tiberiana, he went down into the Forum, where stands the golden column which is the terminal point of all the roads that pass through Italy.

Here it is recounted that the soldiers, the first to greet him and salute him as Emperor, numbered no more than twenty-three.

PLUTARCH, *Galba*, 24

On the 15th of January, as Galba was sacrificing in front of the Temple of Apollo, the priest Umbricius declared that the omen was unfavourable, and foretold imminent treachery and a domestic foe. Otho, standing close by, overheard this, and using the interpretation by contraries took it as a good sign for himself and his plans. Then his freedman Onomastus came to say that the architect and contractors had arrived: this was the pre-arranged signal that the soldiers were mustering and the conspiracy in train. To those who asked why he was leaving, Otho answered that he was buying some property whose age made him doubtful of its value, and that he wished to have it surveyed. Then, on the arm of his freedman, he walked through the Domus Tiberiana to the Velabrum, thence to the golden milestone by the Temple of Saturn. There twenty-three men of the bodyguard hailed him as Emperor: he was alarmed that they were so few, but they put him on a covered litter, and hurried him away with swords at the ready. About the same number of soldiers joined as they marched along, some in the plot, others out of curiosity. So they went, some cheering and with drawn swords, others in silence, ready to let the event determine their mood.

TACITUS, *Histories*, I. 27

In 20 B.C. Augustus set up a body of roads commissioners, *curatores viarum*, of senatorial rank, to look after the roads of Italy: those in the provinces being presumably the responsibility of the governors. But Rome was at the centre of the Italian road network, and thus of that of the whole Empire: of this the golden milestone was the symbol. It is said to have been engraved with the distances from the principal cities of the empire, measured from the gates of the city. Pliny says that the distances of the major roads within the city between the golden milestone and each of the 37 gates added up to 20 (Roman) miles and 765 paces, which would be just under 13 English miles. In England there still survive from the days of the stage-coach a number of milestones giving the distance to several important cities: one such is at Craven Arms in Shropshire.

Part of a marble shaft and a plinth (see Plate 18) have long been ascribed to the monument. The discovery of a foundation in 1959 makes the identification certain.

The passages from Plutarch and Tacitus refer to its use as a rendezvous at a crucial point in the rise to power of Otho in the year A.D. 69. Note, incidentally, the contrasts between them. That of Tacitus is the more detailed and, on the whole, more convincing (especially the route via the Velabrum instead of the Forum): Plutarch brings out better the irony of Otho's words of excuse.

VOLCANAL

There is a smack of the Sabine language about the altars which King Tatius dedicated in Rome, for as the *Annales*[1] tell us, he dedicated them to Ops, Flora, Vediovis and Saturn, Sun, Moon, Volcanus, and Summanus. . . .

VARRO, *De lingua Latina*, v. 74

As a result of the expedition against the Camerini, Romulus celebrated a second triumph. From the spoils he dedicated a bronze *quadriga* to Hephaestus (Vulcan), and close to it erected his own statue, with an inscription written in Greek letters recording his deeds.

DIONYSIUS HALICARNASSUS, *Roman Antiquities*, II. 54

(On old trees in Rome). There is another lotus tree in the precincts of Vulcan, which Romulus dedicated from the spoils of war. According to Masurius, it is as old as Rome. Its roots stretch right under the offices of the municipalities as far as the Forum of Caesar. It had a contemporary, a cypress which at the end of Nero's principate fell down and was left on the ground.

PLINY, *Natural History*, XVI. 236

VOLCAN. FERIAE VOLCANO.

(Aug. 23rd) Volcanalia, the feast of Volcanus.

CIL, I^2, p. 217, Kal. Arv.

IMP . CAESAR. DIVI . F . AVGVSTVS . PONTIFEX . MAXIMVS . IMP . XIII . COS . XI . TRIB . POT . XV . EX . STIPE . QVAM . POPVLVS . ROMANVS . ANNO . NOVO . ABSENTI . CONTVLIT . NERONE . CLAVDIO . DRVSO . T . QVINCTIO . CRISPINO . COS . VOLCANO .

The Emperor Augustus . . . in the consulship of Nero Claudius Drusus and T. Quinctius Crispinus (9 B.C.) dedicated this to Volcanus from the money which the Roman People sent to him because he was absent at the beginning of the year.

CIL, VI. 457

The old Italian firegod Volcanus had a sacred area at the western end of the Forum. It comprised a precinct and an altar; a temple never developed, and the cult seems to have retained its archaic features until

[1] i.e. the *Annales Maximi*.

the early Empire. The first two passages recall the legendary associations of the place with Romulus and the Sabine king Titus Tatius. It seems likely that a chariot and a statue of Romulus stood in the *Area Volcani*: they must have been of early date if, as Dionysius says, the inscription used Greek letters (cf. that on the *cippus* under the *Lapis Niger*, see pp. 89 ff). Note the reverence attached to the two ancient trees. If the roots did stretch to the Forum of Caesar they must have been at least 150 yards long. The *stationes municipiorum* were offices maintained at Rome by provincial *municipia* or free cities.

The dedication of an altar to Volcanus by Augustus accords with his policy of fostering traditional Roman cults. In 9 B.C. Augustus was at Ticinum (Pavia) awaiting the return of Tiberius from Pannonia.

What is now visible at the Volcanal is some shaped stonework, which may be the foundation of the altar, resting on the rock.

THE ARCH OF SEPTIMIUS SEVERUS

IMP . CAES . L . SEPTIMIO . M . F . SEVERO . PIO . PERTINACI . AVG . PATRI . PATRIAE . PARTHICO . ARABICO . ET . PARTHICO . ADIABENICO . PONTIFICI . MAXIMO . TRIBVNIC . POTEST . XI . IMP . XI . COS . IIII . PROCOS . ET . IMP . CAES . M . AVRELIO . L . FIL . ANTONINO . AVG . PIO . FELICI . TRIBVNIC . POTEST . VI . COS . PROCOS . OPTIMIS . FORTISSIMISQVE . PRINCIPIBVS . OB . REM . PVBLICAM . RESTITVTAM . IMPERIVMQUE . POPVLI . ROMANI . PROPAGATVM . INSIGNIBVS . VIRTVTIBVS . EORVM . DOMI . FORISQVE . S . P . Q . R .

To the Imperator Caesar Lucius Septimius (son of Marcus) Severus, Pius Pertinax Augustus, Father of his country, conqueror of Parthian vassals in Arabia and Adiabene, chief Pontiff, tribunician powers for the eleventh time, hailed Imperator eleven times, consul four times, proconsul: and to the Imperator Caesar Marcus Aurelius (son of Lucius) Antoninus Augustus Pius Felix, tribunician power for the sixth time, consul, proconsul, most excellent and valorous princes, because the commonwealth was restored and the empire of the Roman People enlarged by their outstanding virtues at home and abroad: set up by Senate and People of Rome.

CIL, VI. 1033

To celebrate the giving of these titles (honorific titles to himself and his two sons) Severus granted the soldiers a most lavish donative, none other, indeed, than the right to loot the Parthian capital. He then returned victorious to Syria. However, when the Senate offered him a triumph for his Parthian campaign, he had to forgo it, because he was so crippled by gout that he could not stand up on the triumphal car.

HISTORIA AUGUSTA, *Severus*, 16. 5–6

Two arches commemorate the triumphs of the African Emperor Septimius Severus, one at Leptis Magna, the other, the triple arch that dominates the north-western corner of the Forum Romanum. This latter was erected to Severus and his sons, Caracalla and Geta, when they returned to Rome in A.D. 203 after victorious campaigns in the East. The restoration of the commonwealth presumably refers to the victories over Albinus and Niger. But the most remarkable feature of the inscription is the rewording of the fourth line, where the words *Optimis Fortissimisque Principibus* replaced the name and style of Geta—*P. Septimio Getae Nob. Caesari.* Geta was murdered by Caracalla in A.D. 211, and all over the Empire his name was erased from inscriptions. This is the most spectacular instance of this *damnatio memoriae.*

The triumph was celebrated lavishly, coinciding as it did with the Decennalia, the commemoration of Severus' ten years reign. Whether gout did prevent the Emperor's personal appearance may be doubted. But certainly he gave his soldiers leave to loot Ctesiphon, where according to Dio some 100,000 prisoners were taken.

A coin shows an arch surmounted by a quadriga, drawn by six(?) horses. Note how the reliefs fall into two quite distinct styles. The scenes of the capture of Parthian cities, such as that reproduced (Plate 20) have been taken to be based on popular paintings of triumphal scenes, influenced of course by the columns of Trajan, Antoninus, and Marcus Aurelius. But the figures of prisoners and the Victories on the spandrels of the central arch are purely classical: the latter have played a notable part in the evolution of the Christian angel.

BASILICA JULIA

FORVM IVLIVM ET BASILICAM QVAE FVIT INTER AEDEM CASTORIS ET AEDEM SATVRNI, COEPTA PROFLIGATAQVE OPERA A PATRE MEO PERFECI ET EANDEM BASILICAM CONSVMPTAM INCENDIO AMPLIATO EIVS SOLO SVB TITVLO NOMINIS FILIORVM MEORVM INCOHAVI ET, SI VIVVS NON PERFECISSEM, PERFICI AB HEREDIBVS IVSSI.

I completed the Forum Iulium and the basilica which lies between the Temple of Castor and the Temple of Saturn, works which had been begun and carried far by my father. When this basilica was destroyed by fire I began its restoration on an enlarged site to be inscribed with the names of my sons, leaving instructions that, if I did not live to complete it, it must be completed by my heirs.

AUGUSTUS, *Res gestae*, IV. 20

Caligula surpassed the spendthrifts of every age in prodigality . . . he would say that a man should either be thrifty, or be Caesar . . . Indeed, he even scattered large sums of money among the people for several days in succession from the gable of Basilica Julia.

SUETONIUS, *Caligula*, 37

Our own times have known more fluent speakers, but when he was pleading Trachalus seemed to stand out above his rivals. Such was his lofty stature, piercing gaze, dignified expression, and mastery of gesture: as for his voice, it was not, as Cicero would have it, almost the instrument of a tragic actor—it far surpassed all tragic actors that I have ever heard. I well remember how in Basilica Julia he was pleading before the first tribunal. Four panels of judges were in session, as usual: the whole building was full of noise: yet he was heard and understood by all four panels—not much of a compliment to the others—and, as I remember, he was applauded by all four tribunals.

QUINTILIAN, *Institutio Oratoria*, X. i. 119

The plea I made on behalf of Attia Viriola was notable because of the rank of the plaintiff, the unusual nature of the case, and the size of the bench that heard it. Here was a lady of good family, married to a man of praetorian rank, suing for her patrimony before a full panel of the Centumviral Court. Her father (aged eighty) had disinherited her eleven days after that lovelorn old dotard had brought a new step-mother into the house. One hundred and eighty judges were sitting, that being the total of the four panels. A huge number of counsel were engaged on either side: the benches were crowded: and the court, broad as it was, was encircled by a crowd of spectators standing several rows deep.

Add to this that the tribunal was crowded, and the galleries were packed with men and women; they hung over in their eagerness to hear (which was hard) and to see (which was easy). Fathers and daughters awaited the verdict anxiously —so, I may say, did stepmothers. When the panels gave their judgements we had won two and lost two. An extraordinary divergence, with the same case being pleaded before the same judges by the same advocates and at the same times. It happened by chance, though the chance was not apparent. The stepmother, who stood to gain one sixth of the estate under the will, lost her case.

PLINY, *Letters*, VI. xxxiii

D. M. L. MARCI FORTVNATI NVMMVLARI DE BASILICA IVLIA QVI VIXIT. ANN. XLII. MENS. III. DIEBVS XVIII FECIT MARCIA ZOE CONIVGI B.M. CVM QVO VIX. ANN. XXIIII.

To the departed spirits of L. Marcius Fortunatus, banker from the Basilica Julia, who lived 42 years 3 months 18 days. Set up by Marcia Zoe to a husband of blessed memory, with whom she lived for 24 years.

CIL, VI. 9711

From its position, size, and alignment it is obvious that the Basilica Julia was designed as a 'respond' to the Basilica Aemilia: the two basilicas henceforward determined the lay-out of the western end of the Forum, and formed with the Tabularium an early example, for Rome, of the successful grouping of very large buildings. No literary source confirms this major piece of town-planning. A much discussed letter of Cicero (*Ad Atticum*, iv. 16. 8) speaks of the need to ease congestion in the Forum, and complains of the cost of buying out private landlords: this suggests that the Basilica was planned as early as 54 B.C. Caesar dedicated it, unfinished, in 46 B.C.: it was soon destroyed by fire. Augustus is at pains to set down what he did for it: he completed the building left by Caesar, saw to its restoration and enlarged it after a second fire, and in A.D. 12—in his old age—dedicated it in the name of his adoptive sons Gaius and Lucius Caesar, who had predeceased him. The Forum fire of A.D. 283 destroyed it yet again, but it was restored, and remained in use to the last days of the western empire.

The passage of Suetonius shows it as the scene of one of Caligula's many follies: it was easily accessible from the Domus Tiberiana on the Palatine. Its regular use for the sittings of the Centumviral Court is vividly illustrated by Quintilian and Pliny. Quintilian shows the great orator Galerius Trachalus dominating the building and attracting the attention of the other three panels then in session. Pliny describes how the entire court sat in a crowded basilica for the hearing of a *cause célèbre*.

The inscription is one of several relating to bankers who had their tables set up in the Basilica Julia, as in other public buildings.

CURIA JULIA

CVRIAM ET CONTINENS EI CHALCIDICVM . . . FECI

I built the Curia and the Chalcidicum next to it.

AUGUSTUS, *Res gestae*, 19

QVO PRO MERITO MEO SENATVS CONSVLTO AVGVSTVS APPELLATVS SVM ET LAVREIS POSTES AEDIVM MEARVM VESTITI PVBLICE CORONAQVE CIVICA SVPER IANVAM MEAM FIXA EST CLVPEVSQVE AVREVS IN CVRIA IVLIA POSITVS QVEM IVSSV SENATVM POPVLVMQVE ROMANVM DARE VIRTVTIS CLEMENTIAE IVSTITIAE PIETATIS CAVSSA TESTATVM EST PER EIVS CLVPEI INSCRIPTIONEM

AUGUSTUS, *Res gestae*, 34

To reward my services in this matter I was given the title of Augustus by decree of the Senate: the doorposts of my house were covered with laurels in a public ceremony: a civic crown was placed over my door: a golden shield was set up in the Curia Julia with an inscription to testify that the Senate and the Roman people conferred this on me because of my valour, my clemency, my justice, and my piety.

After celebrating his triumph, Augustus dedicated the Temple of Minerva, also called the Chalcidicum, and the Curia Julia, built in honour of his father. There he set up that statue of Victory which yet survives, signifying, it would seem, that he owed his imperial power to her. It had belonged to people of Tarentum, but it was now brought to Rome, set up in the Senate-House, and adorned with the spoils of war from Egypt.

DIO CASSIUS, *Roman History*, LI. 22

The destruction of the old Curia Hostilia in the riots at the funeral of Clodius left the Senate without a permanent meeting place. Julius Caesar began a new Curia in 44 B.C.; its building was interrupted by the civil wars and it was finally dedicated by Augustus on 28th August, 29 B.C., immediately after the celebration of his triumph. It was then, as Dio says, that the Victory of Tarentum was placed in it, together with an altar. The golden shield with the four imperial virtues of Augustus was placed there in 27 B.C.: stone or marble copies were set up by many cities throughout the Empire. In this building took place many of the meetings of the Senate described by Tacitus, for example, those held at the accession of Tiberius. It was restored by Domitian, burned in the great fire of A.D. 283, and rebuilt by Diocletian to the same dimensions—like the British House of Commons after the Second World War. It is Diocletian's building that Bartoli in the 1930s disengaged from the church which had encased it since the seventh century. In its present state, with the original paving, the three rows of senators' seats on either side, the original windows facing the Forum (but not the original doors, now in St. John Lateran) it is one of the most splendid interiors to survive from classical Rome. This was the scene of the famous debates over the Statue of Victory, which was removed by Constantius, replaced by Julian, and finally ejected in 382 by Gratian, despite the eloquent reminders by the supporters of paganism that with it was indissolubly linked the destiny of Rome.

The Chalcidicum was perhaps the record office of the Senate: it does not appear to have survived the third century fire.

The coin of Augustus (Plate 88) shows a building with a porticus, with a Victory on the gable.

PLUTEI TRAJANI

S. P. Q. R. IMP. CAESARI. DIVI TRAIANI PARTHICI. F. DIVI NERVAE NEPOTI. TRAIANO HADRIANO AVGVSTO PONT. MAX. TRIB. POT II COS II QVI PRIMVS OMNIVM PRINCIPVM ET SOLVS, REMITTENDO SESTERTIVM NOVIES MILIES CENTENA MILIA N. DEBITVM FISCIS. NON PRAESENTES TANTVM CIVES SVOS SED ET POSTEROS EORVM PRAESTITIT HAC LIBERALITE SECVROS.

To the Emperor Hadrian . . . who, first and alone of emperors, remitted nine hundred million sesterces owed to the imperial treasury, and who by this generosity freed from anxiety not only the Roman citizens of his own day, but also their posterity, the Senate and People of Rome (dedicated this).

ILS, 309

The reliefs called the *Plutei Trajani* were found by the Rostra, and are now kept in the Curia Julia. Their interpretation has been much discussed, and even now is not generally agreed. That on the right (Plate 23) shows the burning of records brought out by the clerks of the Tabularium: its most likely context is the year A.D. 118, when Hadrian took measures to conciliate public opinion after the 'conspiracy' of the Four Senators. His generosity in cancelling 900 million sesterces arrears of taxes caused the dedication by a grateful people of the inscription quoted above, of which only a part survives, though an earlier record allows restoration. The reliefs on the left show an Emperor on the Rostra, while on its left a woman gives thanks before the statue of a second Emperor. The first is taken to be Hadrian, and the second Trajan. The scene will then refer to the famous *alimenta*, the subsistence loans granted by Trajan for the support of children in the small towns of Italy. The workings of the *alimenta* scheme are chiefly known from two long inscriptions, one from Veleia in Northern Italy, the other from Ligurum in Samnium. Presumably Hadrian extended its operation in some way which is not clear. Both panels are of interest in showing the buildings of the Forum (see notes to Plates 23–25).

LAPIS NIGER

QVOI HOI	QVI · HV[nc locum violaverit,
SAKROS ⁝ ESE	manibus] SACER · SIT;
ED SORD	ET SORD[ibus qui haec contam-
OKAFHAS	inet l]OCA, FAS

RECEI ⁝ IO	REGI, IV[dicio ei hab-
EVAM	ito, adimere rem pr]EVAM ·
QVOS ⁝ RE	QVOS · RE[x per hanc senserit
M ⁝ KALATO	vehi via]M, KALATO-
REM HAB	REM, HAB[enis eorum, iubeto
TOD ⁝ IOVXMEN	ilic]O · IVMEN-
TA ⁝ KAPAI ⁝ DOTAV	TA · CAPIAT, VT · A V[ia stati-
M ⁝ I ⁝ TER PE	M · ITER PE[r aversum locum
M ⁝ QVOI HA	pergant puru]M · QVI HA[c]
VELOD ⁝ NEQV	VOLET, NEQV[e per purum
IOD ⁝ IOVESTOD	perget, iudic]IO, IVSTA
LOIVQVIOD QO ⁝	LICITATIONE, CO[ndemnetur].

Whosoever defiles this spot, let him be forfeit to the spirits of the underworld: whosoever contaminates it with refuse, after due process of law, it shall be proper for the King to deprive him of his property. And whatsoever persons the King shall discover passing on this road, let him bid the Herald seize the reins of their draught animals, to force them to turn aside forthwith and to take the approved detour. And whosoever shall fail to take the approved detour and shall persist in travelling this road, let him after due process of law be sold at auction to the highest bidder.

CIL, VI. 36840

niger lapis in Comitio locum funestum significat, ut alii, Romuli morti destinatum, sed non usu obvenisse ut ibi sepeliretur, sed Faustulum nutricium eius, ut alii dicunt Hostilium avum Tulli Hostili Romanorum regis.

The Black Stone in the Comitium marks a place of ill-omen. Some say that it was meant for the death of Romulus, though in fact he was not buried there. Others say, of his foster father Faustulus, others of Hostilius, ancestor of Tullus Hostilius, King of the Romans.

FESTUS, 177

The name Lapis Niger is now given to an archaic Forum monument of unknown purpose. It is probably but not certainly to be identified with that mentioned by Festus: the location *in Comitio* fits, but the excavations of 1899 and 1955 found no trace of a funeral monument. What they did find was a small shrine or *sacellum*, and a *cippus* bearing the earliest known Latin inscription. Since its first discovery this famous inscription has been the centre of a controversy on which the last word has yet to be said. Archaic in language and script, it is written in the *boustrophedon* or 'ox-plough' style (i.e. alternate lines run in opposite directions); for good measure, it is mutilated. Above are the surviving part of the original text, an amplification and translation into classical Latin, and a translation into English. See Plate 21.

The black volcanic stone, and the taboos by which it was protected, suggest that the monument was sacred to the gods of the underworld: also, that it was placed across a former right-of-way. The word RECEI is of prime importance: if this is indeed the King and not the *Rex Sacrorum*, it would date the monument before 500 B.C.

The original *cippus* is now in the Forum Antiquarium and a replica has been placed in its position.

COMITIUM

Comitium ab eo quod coibant et comitiis curiatis et litium causa.

The Comitium is so called because they assembled there at the meetings of the Comitia Curiata, and also for lawsuits.

VARRO, *De lingua Latina*, V. 155

What decided the doubtful issue was a chance but significant utterance, made when the Senate was meeting in the Curia Hostilia. Some cohorts returning from guard-duty were marching in column through the forum: the centurion shouted 'Standard-bearer, set up the standard: here we had best remain.' No sooner was this heard than the Senators rushed out of the Senate House, and proclaimed that they accepted the omen, and the people crowded round them and heartily endorsed it. The motion for emigration was defeated, and they began to rebuild the city, though without any plan. . . .

LIVY, V. 55

The position of the early republican Comitium, just to the south of the Curia, is certain, though excavations have revealed five layers of construction whose chronology is doubtful. In our first passage Varro establishes the etymology of the name. The second is Livy's famous story of the debate in the Senate after the sack of Rome by the Gauls (390 B.C.), when Camillus spoke against the proposal to migrate to Veii. The 'omen' or chance utterance by the standard-bearer clinched the matter (cf. Augustine's acceptance of the chance utterance '*tolle, lege; tolle, lege*' at the time of his conversion). The passage shows that the *comitium* was at first an open space, suitable for troops to camp on, and also that it was always close to the Senate House or Curia. In 145 B.C. the tribune Licinius Crassus led the assembly of the people to the Forum.

ROSTRA

Naves Antiatium partim in navalia Romae subductae, partim incensae, rostrisque earum suggestum in foro exstructum adornari placuit, Rostraque id templum appellatum.

The ships from Antium were hauled up to the docks at Rome, and part of them burned. It was agreed to decorate the raised platform in the Forum with their prows, and that open space was called the Rostra.

LIVY, VIII. 14

Lars Tolumnius, King of Veii, put to death four ambassadors of the Roman people: their statues stood on the Rostra within my memory. An honour well-deserved: for thus our ancestors gave those who died for the republic a lasting memorial in place of a transitory life.

CICERO, *Philippics*, IX. 2

Among very ancient statues, one should mention those of Tullius Cloelius, Lucius Roscius, Spurius Nautius, Gaius Fulanius (all assassinated by the people of Fidenae when on a delegation), and now standing on the Rostra.

PLINY, *Natural History*, XXXIV. 23

So passed the year of my consulship, that I did nothing without the advice of the Senate, and the agreement of the people. I always defended the Senate in speaking from the Rostra, the people in speaking before the Senate. . . . Such is a brief account of my consulship.

CICERO, *In Pisonem*, 3

And Antonius also commanded them to whom he had given commission to kill Cicero, that they should strike off his head and right hand, with which he had written the invective orations, called *Philippides*, against Antonius. So, when the murderers brought him Cicero's head and hand cut off, he beheld them a long time with great joy and laughed heartily. . . . Then when he had taken his pleasure of the sight of them, he caused them to be set up in an open place, over the pulpit for orations (where when he was alive he had often spoken to the people), as if he had done the dead man hurt and not blemished his own fortune, showing himself (to his great shame and infamy), a cruel man and unworthy of the name and authority he held.

PLUTARCH, *Antony*, 20–21: NORTH's translation

The ships' prows which gave their name to the republican Rostra—and hence to all orators' platforms—were captured by Gaius Maenius in the wars against the Latins (338 B.C.). The platform was decorated with honorary statues, which were removed from time to time, as Cicero tells us. This was the scene of the great addresses to the people: Cicero refers to his own two speeches against Catiline in the year 63 B.C. The passage juxtaposed shows the cruel revenge taken by Antony: presumably the Rostra on which Cicero's head and hands were exposed was that in use after the reconstruction of the area by Julius Caesar. But the atrocity as such was no innovation: the Rostra had been used in the same way during the wars between Marius and Sulla. See Plate 19.

THE COLUMN OF GAIUS DUILIUS

CONSOL SECEST ANO S, SOCIOS P(OPLI) R(OMANI), CARTACINIENSIOM OPSIDIONE D EXEMET LECIONE SQVE CARTACININESIS OMNIS M AXI-MOSQVE MACISTR A TOS L VCI PALAM POST DIES N OVEM CASTREIS EXFOCIONT MACEL AMQVE OPIDOM P VCNANDOD CEPET. ENQVE EODEM MAC ISTRATVD BENE R EM NAVEBOS MARID CONSOL PRIMOS C ESET COPIASQVE C LASESQVE NAVALES PRIMOS ORNAVET PA RAVETQVE CVMQVE EIS NAVEBOS CLASEIS POENICAS OMN IS ITEM MAXVMAS COPIAS CARTACINIENSIS PRAESENTED HANNIBALED DICTATORED OL OR OM IN ALTOD MARID PVCN AD VICET VIQVE NAVEIS CEPET CVM SOCIEIS SEPTER-ASMAN I. QVIN QVERESM OSQVE TRIRESMOSQVE NAVEIS X XX, MERSET XIII. AVR OM CAPTOM NVMEI (TRIA MILIA SEPTINGENTEI), ARCEN TOM CAPTOM PRAEDA NVMEI (CENTUM MILIA) . . .; OMNE CAPTOM AES (INTER VNDETRICIES ET TRICIES QVATER CENTENA MILIA). TRIVMP OQVE NAVALED PRAEDAD POPLOM DONAVET MVLTOSQVE CARTACINIE NS IS INCE NVOS D VXIT ANTE CVRVM . . . EIS . . . CAPT. . . .

As consul he freed the people of Segesta, allies of the Roman people, from the Carthaginian siege. Nine days later all the Carthaginian legions and their high commanders fled their camps, and he captured by force the town of Macella. In the same office, he was the first to conduct successful naval operations, he was the first to raise and equip a fleet, and with the ships of that fleet he defeated all the Punic fleets, and especially won a victory on the high seas over huge Carthaginian forces commanded in person by their dictator Hannibal. He captured 1 septereme and 30 quinqueremes and triremes, with their crews, and sank 13 ships. The gold coin he captured amounted to 3,700 pieces, the silver captured as booty 100,000 pieces. Total of currency captured for booty. . . . At his triumph he gave the Roman people a share of his naval booty, and led many Carthaginians of high rank captive before his chariot. . . .

CIL, vi. 31611

Commemorating a triumph with a chariot-group is not ancient. . . . The use of a column is older, such as those of C. Maenius(?) . . . or again of C. Duillius, who was the first to celebrate a naval triumph over the Carthaginians. His column remains to this day in the Forum.

PLINY, *Natural History*, XXXIV. 20

In old Latin, d. was often added at the end of a word—witness on the naval column of C. Duilius, set up in the Forum.

QUINTILIAN, *Institutio Oratoria*, I. 7. 12

Aequoreum iuxta decus et navale trophaeum
rostra gerens nivea surgebat mole columna;
exuvias Marti donumque Duilius, alto
ante omnes mersa Poenorum classe, dicabat.

Next to the honours gained at sea and the naval triumph, where the column bearing ships' prows raised its snowy mass: this Duilius dedicated and presented the spoils as a gift to Mars, the first admiral to win a battle on the high seas when he sank the fleet of the Carthaginians.

SILIUS ITALICUS, *Punica*, VI. 663–7

The great naval victory gained by Gaius Duilius over the Carthaginians at Mylae was commemorated by a column adorned with a ship's prow in the Forum, and bearing an honorary inscription in the form of an *elogium*. A portion of this inscription was discovered in 1565, and is now in the Museo Nuovo Capitolino. The wording of the inscription is in a Latin which would fit the third century B.C., yet the inscription is cut in Luna (Carrara) marble, which was not in use in Rome at that date. The simplest of the many theories that have been advanced is that the monument was repaired and a new base provided in, probably, the time of Augustus. The existing inscription was carefully preserved, for its linguistic as well as its historical interest. Most likely it was originally composed shortly after the death of Duilius in 220 B.C. See Plate 22.

FICUS OLEA VITIS AND THE STATUE OF MARSYAS

A self-sown fig-tree flourishes in the middle of the Forum, near the place where, when the basis of Roman rule was collapsing amid portents of disaster, Curtius filled up the chasm with 'the greatest goods', namely, valour, duty, and a glorious death. Self-sown, too, is the vine in the same place: but the olive was planted by the care of the people to give shade. . . .

PLINY, *Natural History*, XV. XX. 78

P. Munatius took a chaplet of flowers from the statue of Marsyas, and put it on his head. The triumvirs ordered him to be put in chains for this offence: an appeal to the tribunes brought no intervention. . . . The only other example of such licence is that of Julia, daughter of the late Emperor Augustus; a letter from him complains that in her night revels she had crowned the statue of Marsyas with a chaplet. . . .

A fig, olive and vine, the three staples of Mediterranean arboriculture, were kept growing in the Forum, as they are to this day. Close by was the famous statue of Marsyas with its Phrygian cap, taken by the people to symbolize liberty, and crowned by them with garlands.

The coin was struck by L. Marcius Censorinus (86-81 B.C.): the statue appears again, together with the fig-tree, on the famous Plutei Trajani (see Plate 24).

LACUS CURTIUS

Mettius Curtius had rushed down from the citadel in front of the Sabines, and was driving the Romans before him over the whole space where the Forum now stands. He had very nearly reached the gate of the Palatine, calling out 'We have beaten them, treacherous hosts and cowardly foes! Now they know the difference between raping girls and fighting with men!' Romulus, with a group of his toughest warriors, charged him as he uttered these boasts. Since Mettius was fighting on horseback, he was easily driven back: the Romans followed up the pursuit: the rest of the Roman forces, encouraged by the *élan* of their King, put the Sabines to flight. Mettius lost control of his horse, which panicked at the noise of his pursuers, and he plunged into a swamp. The plight of their hero attracted the attention of the Sabines, who beckoned to him and made noises of encouragement. Spurred by their cries, he made a successful effort to get out of the mud. . . .

LIVY, I. 12. 8–10

As a memorial of the battle, the spot where the horse first got out of the deep swamp and brought Curtius on to firm ground was called the Lacus Curtius.

LIVY, I. 13, 5

In this same year, it is said that the middle of the Forum caved in, as it were, and collapsed to a prodigious depth. Though everyone brought earth to do so, it was impossible to fill the chasm, until a warning from heaven forced the inquiry as to what it was that the Roman people held most dear (since the soothsayers declared that such a possession must be vowed to the gods on that spot, if they wished Rome to endure). Then Mettius Curtius, an excellent young warrior, reproached them for hesitating to declare that arms and valour were dearest of all to the Romans. Silence fell: he gazed round on the temple of the gods that overhung the Roman Forum, and on the Capitol: now he raised his hands to heaven, now he looked down into the gaping earth towards the gods of the underworld, to show that he had devoted himself to death. Then he mounted his horse, which was decked in all its finery, and leaped into the gulf, fully armed. Offerings and the produce of the fields were heaped on him by a vast crowd of men and women. The name of Lacus Curtius is said to have derived from him, and not from the earlier Mettius Curtius, the warrior of Titus Tatius. If there were any path to lead the enquirer to truth, I should not be wanting in diligence; as it is, we must make do with tradition, when lapse of time has ruled out any firm conclusion. Certainly the name of the lake is better known from this, the more recent account.

LIVY, VII. 6

Cornelius and Lutatius[1] write that the place was struck by lightning, and fenced off by order of the Senate: since this was done by the Consul Curtius, whose colleague was M. Genucius, it got the name of Lacus Curtius.

VARRO, *De lingua Latina*, V. 150

L. NAEVIVS L.F.SVRDINVS PR. INTER CIVIS ET PEREGRINOS.

Lucius Naevius Surdinus, son of Lucius, Praetor for cases between citizens and foreigners.

CIL, VI. 1468

hic, ubi nunc fora sunt, udae tenuere paludes:
amne redundatis fossa madebat aquis.
Curtius ille lacus, siccas qui sustinet aras,
nunc solida est tellus, sed lacus ante fuit.

Here, where the Forum now is, was once dense swamp: a ditch would drip with water that had flooded back from the river. The Lacus Curtius—its altars now are dry, it is solid ground—but once it was true lake.

OVID, *Fasti*, VI. 401–4

Men of all ranks threw a small offering every year into the Lacus Curtius for his (Augustus') welfare.

SUETONIUS, *Augustus*, 57

Legend, art, and archaeology offer a wide range of evidence for this little monument. The results are confusing. In the time of Augustus there

[1] Q. Lutatius Catulus (consul 102 B.C.) and a writer on antiquities. Of Cornelius nothing is known.

were three different traditions as to the origins of the name—a *triceps historia,* as Varro says (loc. cit). The eponymous Curtius is either a Sabine warrior who fought with Titus Tatius against Romulus (*c.* 750 B.C.?), or a noble young Roman who performed an act of *devotio* in the year 362 B.C., or—a tradition passed over by Livy but mentioned with the other two by Varro—the Gaius Curtius who was consul in 445 B.C. Ovid's account makes it clear that the place was already monumentalized in his own day: the paving stones now to be seen are remains of this monument, and the marble bases may represent the altars. At one point it is possible to see how high the water-table in the Forum still stands today. Suetonius' account suggests that the *lacus* was regarded as a *mundus* or sacred pit linking our world with the underworld: this has affinities with the *devotio* story. But the sculptor of the slab pictured in Plate 26 (copy of the 2nd century B.C.? original, found in 1553, now in Museo Nuovo Capitolino) followed the Sabine version. The reeds make it clear that there is a *palus* and not a chasm. It bears on the back an inscription of the praetor Lucius Naevius Surdinus (*c.* 15 B.C.): another by the same man is found on a pavement slab by the Column of Phocas (Plate 27).

BASILICA AEMILIA

Marcus Fulvius contracted for more works and of greater public utility . . . a basilica behind the new shops of the silversmiths, and a fish-market surrounded by shops which he sold off to private purchasers . . . (179 B.C.)

LIVY, XL. 51

(On the erection of public sundials and water-clocks in Rome.) But the hours were uncertain in cloudy weather until Scipio Nasica set up the first water-clock, with equal divisions for the night and day. This timepiece was dedicated in a covered building in the year 595 *a.u.c.* (159 B.C.). For so long a time had the hours of daylight been unmarked at Rome.

PLINY, *Natural History*, VII. 215

After the consulship of Marcellus, Caesar had already sent a copious stream of wealth from his Gallic conquests for all men in a public position to draw upon . . . to the consul Paulus he gave 1,500 talents, which he used to embellish the Forum with the Basilica, a famous building, which replaced the Fulvia. . . (55 B.C.).

PLUTARCH, *Caesar*, 29

Aemilius Lepidus Paulus constructed at his own expense the basilica called Basilica Pauli, and dedicated it during his consulship, he being consul for a part of that year (34 B.C.).

DIO CASSIUS, *Roman History*, XLIX. 42

The next year (14 B.C.) . . . the Basilica Pauli caught fire. The flames spread to the temple of Vesta, and the sacred objects were carried to the Palatine by the Vestal Virgins (all except the eldest, who was blind), and were placed in the house of the priest of Jupiter. The Basilica was rebuilt, under the name of Aemilius, as being in the family of the original builder, but in fact the costs were met by Augustus and the friends of Paulus.

DIO CASSIUS, *Roman History*, LIV. 24

At this time (A.D. 22) M. Lepidus came forward to ask the Senate to allow him to decorate the Basilica Pauli, a monument of the house of the Aemilii, at his own expense. The custom of public munificence was still maintained: Augustus had not forbidden a Taurus, a Philippus, and a Balbus from using the spoils of war or their overflowing wealth to the embellishment of the city and the glory of posterity. On these precedents Lepidus, though a man of moderate wealth, restored the noble memorial of his family.

TACITUS, *Annals*, III. 72

Should we not record among our splendid buildings the Basilica Pauli, with its superb columns from Phrygia, the Forum of Augustus, the Temple of Peace built by his Imperial Majesty the Emperor Vespasian? Those are the most beautiful buildings the world has ever seen.

PLINY, *Natural History*, XXXVI. 102

TENE ME QVIA FVGI ET REBOCA ME IN BASILICA PAVLLI AD LEONE.

Arrest me. I am a runaway slave. Return me to Leo at the Basilica Paulli.

CIL, XV. 7189

Ut illum di perdant, primus qui horas repperit,
Quique adeo primus statuit hic solarium,
Qui mihi comminuit misero articulatim diem!
Nam me puerulo venter erat solarium
Multo omnium istorum optumum et verissimum:
Ubi is te monebat, esses, nisi quom nihil erat;
Nunc etiam quod est, non estur, nisi Sol lubet:
Itaque adeo iam oppletum oppidum est solariis:
Maior populi pars aridi reptant fame.

God damn the man who invented hours, who first set up a sun-dial in this city, and who divided up my day into miserable little bits! When I was a little lad my belly was my sun-dial—much the best and most reliable of the lot! When he said it was time, you ate, if there was any food in the house. Now, even if there is anything, it don't get eaten, unless the Sun gives the word. Nowadays the whole town is full of sun-dials, and most people are crawling around half dead with hunger.

PLAUTUS, *Boeotians*, *Fragment* in AULUS GELLIUS, III. 3, 3

The sources disclose a very long and complex history of rebuilding and restoration, with several changes of name. The first building was in 179 B.C. as part of the programme of public works undertaken by the censors M. Fulvius Nobilior and M. Aemilius Lepidus: hence the name Basilica Aemilia et Fulvia, or sometimes one of these names alone. The next major phase was the reconstruction, on a magnificent scale, set in hand by L. Aemilius Paulus in 55 B.C., and completed by his son in 34 B.C. This was the building called Basilica Pauli. It was destroyed by fire in 14 B.C. There was still an Aemilius to lend his name if not to give his money: perhaps the M. Aemilius Lepidus who in A.D. 22 brought from Phrygia the marble columns which Pliny singles out as the chief feature of the basilica. The coin (Plate 83) shows what may have been one factor in the tenacity and devotion with which later Aemilii maintained their family connection, despite the loss of their fortunes under the proscriptions of the Triumvirs. Struck by M. Aemilius Lepidus in 65 B.C., it shows a building firmly labelled Aemilia embellished with the bronze shields (*clupei*), set up in 78 B.C. by his father, which were adorned with portraits of famous ancestors. These must have been a part of the *decus avitum* emphasized by Tacitus. When Alaric captured Rome in A.D. 410 there was another disastrous fire: destruction was completed by the earthquake of A.D. 847.

A passage of Varro (L.L. VI. 4) establishes that this Basilica was the building in which Scipio Nasica placed the first reliable public timepiece in Rome. Plautus in his *Boeotians* had written a spirited protest against the tyranny of time.

The slave of the inscription will have been attached to the building: Leo was presumably his overseer.

The friezes, with scenes from early Roman history (the foundation of the city, the punishment of Tarpeia, etc.) would seem to be of Augustan date, though whether they belong to the building completed in 34 B.C. or to the restoration of 14 B.C. is yet to be established. (See Plate 28.)

FUNERAL OF JULIUS CAESAR: SPEECH OF ANTONY

Etsi tum, cum optimum te putabant me quidem dissentiente, funeri tyranni, si illud funus erat, sceleratissime praefuisti, tua illa pulcra laudatio, tua miseratio, tua cohortatio: tu, tu inquam, illas faces incendisti, et eas quibus semiustulatus ille est, et quibus incensa L. Bellieni domus deflagravit.

Yet even then, when you (Antonius) were supposed to be acting honourably—not that I ever thought so—even then, you presided in the most irresponsible way at the funeral of the dead tyrant—if such proceedings can be dignified with the name of a funeral—yours was that moving funeral address, yours the stirring of pity and the incitement to riot: you, you, I repeat, lit the flames which only partially consumed the body of Caesar, but which reached the house of L. Bellienus and burned it to the ground.

CICERO, *Philippics*, II. 91

Afterwards, when Caesar's body was brought into the market-place, Antonius making his funeral oration in praise of the dead, according to the ancient custom of Rome, and perceiving that his words moved the common people to compassion, he framed his eloquence to make their hearts yearn the more: and taking Caesar's gown all bloody in his hand, he laid it open to the sight of them all, showing the number of cuts and holes it had upon it. Therewithal all the people fell presently into such a rage and mutiny that there was no more order kept among the common people. For some of them cried out: 'Kill the murderers.' Others plucked up forms, tables, and stalls about the market-place, as they had done before at the funeral of Clodius: and having laid them all on a heap together, they set them on fire, and burned them in the midst of the most holy places. And furthermore, when the fire was thoroughly kindled, some here, some there, took burning fire-brands, and ran with them to the murderers' houses, to set them afire. Albeit the conspirators, foreseeing the danger before, had wisely provided for themselves, and fled.

PLUTARCH, *Brutus*, 44–46; NORTH's translation

When the funeral was approved, a pyre was set up in the Campus Martius, close to the tomb of his daughter Julia. A gilded shrine was set up in front of the Rostra, modelled on the Temple of Venus Genetrix: within was an ivory bier with trappings of gold and purple, and, at its head, a trophy bearing the gown in which he was murdered. A day was too short for all who wished to bring gifts; it was therefore decreed that all should bring their gifts to the Campus, using any of the city's roads, and in no order of rank. At the games, certain lines were recited, aptly chosen to excite pity, and revulsion against the murder, notably from Pacuvius' *Judgement of Arms*:

'Was I saved, that there should be men to destroy me?'—also from the *Electra* of Acilius, to the same effect. In place of a funeral oration, the consul, Antonius, bid the herald read aloud the decree of the Senate which had decreed to Caesar every honour, divine and human, also the terms of the oath, by which they had unanimously sworn to protect his life. To this he added a very few words of his own.

Magistrates and ex-magistrates carried the bier down to the Forum and placed it before the Rostra. As some were proposing to burn it on the shrine of Jupiter on the Capitol, others on the Curia of Pompey, suddenly two beings appeared, wearing swords and carrying each two spears, and set fire to it from below with wax torches. Immediately the crowd of by-standers heaped on dry branches, the seats from the tribune, and all the gifts that could be laid hold of. Then the flute-players and stage hands tore off the cloaks, with which they had been issued for the present occasion from the stores kept in reserve for triumphs, tore them up, and threw them on the flames. The legionaries among the veteran troops did the same with their weapons, which they carried to attend the funeral. Many of the ladies present threw on their jewels, as well as the amulets and dresses of their children.

SUETONIUS, *Caesar*, 84

The best known sources for the funeral of Julius Caesar are Plutarch and Suetonius. They wrote almost at the same time but more than one hundred and fifty years after the event: the *Parallel Lives* appearing between A.D. 105 and 115, the *Lives of the Caesars* about 121. Besides the passage quoted here, Plutarch also described the funeral in the *Lives* of Caesar and of Antony. Except that the passage from Caesar does not mention Antony, they differ only in detail. But the difference between Plutarch and Suetonius is striking. In Plutarch the artful eloquence of Antony works up the crowd to an outburst of spontaneous fury, of which the cremation is only one outcome. In Suetonius Antony's role is minimized. The emotions of the crowd are first engaged by the blood-stained gown and by striking lines in the plays performed: the cremation follows on the 'divine intervention' by the Dioscuri from their temple near-by. This—and the fact that a picture of the Dioscuri was among the works of art dedicated by Augustus in the Temple of Divus Julius (see p. 103)—suggests that Suetonius is here following an 'official' version approved by Augustus. What of Antony's speech? The passage from Cicero certainly suggests that he delivered one: this tradition is further supported by versions given in Appian (B.C. II, 144–5) (short, conciliatory), and Dio Cassius (XLIV. 36ff.) (long, inflammatory). We can be certain that the cremation took place where the Temple of Divus Julius later stood—outside the Regia and hard by the Temple of Vesta. The choice of place cannot have been accidental, for Caesar was Pontifex Maximus. We can further be fairly sure that Antony delivered the funeral oration from the

Rostra. What did he say? That we do not know; but for the English-speaking world he will always be thought to have used the words which Shakespeare put into his mouth when he came to work up this passage of Plutarch fifteen hundred years later.

THE TEMPLE OF CAESAR

(*Aedes Divi Julii*)

Postea solidam columnam prope viginti pedum lapidis Numidici in foro statuit, scripsitque PARENTI PATRIAE. . . .

After this (the People) placed in the Forum a column of Numidian marble, some twenty feet high, with the inscription TO THE FATHER OF HIS COUNTRY.

SUETONIUS, *Caesar*, 84. 2

O mirificum Dolabellam meum! Iam enim dico meum; antea, crede mihi, subdubitabam. Magnam ἀναθεώρησιν res habet, de saxo, in crucem, columnam tollere, locum illum sternendum locare! Quid quaeris? heroica. Sustulisse mihi videtur simulationem desiderii, adhuc quae serpebat in dies et inveterata verebar ne periculosa nostris tyrannoctonis esset.

May 1st. Cumae.

'There's my Dolabella! Mine, I call him now; previously, I had my doubts. But now—*c'est à voir*—hurlings from the rock, crucifixions, pulling down the column, a contract for clearing the site! In a word, heroic deeds. I think he will have made a clean sweep of all that pretence of a longing for Caesar which has been stealthily growing from day to day; once let it harden, and it could be risky for our friends the tyrannicides.'

CICERO, *Letters to Atticus*, XIV. 15

AEDEM DIVI IVLII . . . FECI.
DONA EX MANIBIIS . . . IN AEDE DIVI IVLII . . . CONSACRAVI.

I built the Temple of Divus Julius. . . .
From the spoils of war, I consecrated gifts in the Temple of Divus Julius.

AUGUSTUS, *Res gestae*, 19; 21

Venerem exeuntem e mari divus Augustus dicavit in delubro patris Caesaris, quae anadyomene vocatur . . . consenuit haec tabula carie, aliamque pro eo substituit Nero in principatu suo Dorothei manu.

In the Temple of his adoptive father Caesar, Augustus dedicated that statue of Venus which is called Anadyomene. . . . When the picture began to decay, Nero substituted for it another, from the hand of Dorotheus.

PLINY, *Natural History*, XXXV. 91

Hanc animam interea caeso de corpore raptam
fac iubar, ut semper Capitolia nostra forumque
divus ab excelsa prospectet Iulius aede.

Meanwhile turn his soul—torn from his murdered body—into a star, so that a deified Julius may ever look out over the Roman Capitol and the forum from his lofty temple.

OVID, *Metamorphoses*, XV. 840–2

Verum adhibito honoribus modo bifariam laudatus est: pro aede Divi Iulii a Tiberio et pro rostris veteribus a Druso Tiberii filio.

The limitations set to the honours paid him (Augustus) restricted the funeral ovations to two, one delivered before the Temple of Divus Julius, by Tiberius, the other from the Rostra Vetera by Tiberius' son Drusus.

SUETONIUS, *Augustus*, 100

The passages chosen illustrate the schemes to commemorate Julius Caesar on the site of his cremation. The column in the Forum lasted less than a year, erected by the People, immediately after the funeral on March 20th, it was overthrown sometime after Dolabella assumed the consulship towards the end of April 44 B.C. Cicero's letter, written on May 1st, 43 B.C., recounts triumphantly the measure taken by Dolabella to punish the ringleaders of that popular demonstration. The lasting memorial was the Temple of Divus Julius, built by Octavian and dedicated on August 18th, 29 B.C. Among the works of art with which Octavian endowed it was the famous Venus Anadyomene of Apelles (4th century B.C.). The reference to its irreparable decay by the time of Nero is one of the few pieces of evidence for the life of an ancient masterpiece—in this case, some four hundred years. Other pieces from the same hand in this temple were of the Dioscuri, and a Victory. There was a colossal statue of Caesar, bearing on his head the comet or *Caesaris astrum*. The 'lofty temple' refers to the high floor of the cella. The podium was decorated on its front by the prows of ships captured at Actium. This provided a new Rostra—the Rostra ad Caesaris—for major state occasions. Its use for one of the two funeral orations for Augustus is noteworthy. The second was given from the old Rostra, a gesture to the traditions of the Republic. The two places chosen aptly symbolize the dual nature of the Augustan principate.

REGIA

Numa in colle primum Quirinali deinde propter aedem Vestae in regia quae adhuc appellatur.

Numa lived first on the Quirinal hill, later in the house still called the Regia, next to the Temple of Vesta.

SOLINUS, *Collectanea*, I. 21

(Regia) . . . quod in fanum a pontifice . . . tant quod in ea sacra fiunt quaedam a rege solita usurpari.

(Regia) . . . because in that consecrated shrine rites are practised that were once supervised by the king.

FESTUS, 278

Vidimus flavum Tiberim retortis
litore Etrusco violenter undis
ire deiectum monimenta regis
templaque Vestae . . .

We have seen the tawny Tiber, its waves thrown back violently from the Etruscan shore, advance to destroy the monuments of the King and the temple of Vesta. . . .

HORACE, *Odes*, I. 2, 12–15

is qui belli susceperat curam, sacrarium Martis ingressus primo ancilia commovebat, post hastam simulacri ipsius, dicens 'Mars vigila'.

He who had undertaken the command of the war, would enter the shrine of Mars and shake the *ancilia*, then the spear of the statue of the god, saying 'Mars, awake!'

SERVIUS, *on Aeneid*, VIII. 3

Roman literature is deficient in history. . . . The annals of the chief pontiffs are bald in the extreme, and then we come to Fabius, to Cato . . . to Piso or Fannius or Vennonius—one may be more spirited than another, but what could be feebler than the whole group?

CICERO, *De legibus*, I. 2. 6

The gold usually given for triumphs Calvinus took only from the Spanish cities, even so, he spent part only on his triumph, but a larger sum on the Regia. This had been burned down: he restored it and dedicated it. Moreover, he adorned it splendidly with many things, notably statues, which he borrowed from Octavian on a promise of return. Later, when asked for them, he still did not give them back, but used a witty excuse. Pretending he had too few workmen, he said 'Send your own men, and remove them.' And Octavian, unwilling to commit the sacrilege, allowed the statues to stay as votive offerings.

DIO CASSIUS, *Roman History*, XLVIII. 42

CN. DOMITIVS M.F. CALVINVS PONTIFEX COS. ITER. IMPER. DE MANIBEIS.

Cn. Domitius Calvinus, Pontifex, consul for the second time, Imperator, rebuilt this from the spoils of war.

CIL, VI. 1301

October equus appellatur, qui in campo Martio mense Octobri immolatur quotannis Marti bigarum victricum dexterior. De cuius capite non levis contentio solebat esse enter Suburenses et Sacrarienses, ut hi in regiae pariete, illi ad turrim Mamiliam id figerent: eiusdemque coda tanta celeritate perfertur in regiam, ut ex ea sanguis distillet in focum. . . .

FESTUS, 190

The October horse is the name given to the one sacrificed every year in the Campus Martius to Mars—the right-hand horse of a winning two-horse chariot. There used to be much rivalry between the people of Subura and those of the Sacra Via, the latter trying to set up its skull on the wall of the Regia, the former on Turris Mamilia. Its tail had to be taken to the Regia quickly enough to allow the blood from it to be sprinkled on the altar.

FESTUS, 190

ISDEM CONSVLIBVS XVIII K. IANVARIAS IN REGIA CN. CORNELIVS CN. F. LENTVLVS AVGVR MAG. IN LOCVM CN. POMPEII Q. FIL . . . POMPEIVM AVGVREM ET IN LOC. IMP. CAESARIS AVGVSTI . . . FRATRES ARVALES COOPTAVIT ET AD SACRA VOCAVIT. ADFVERUNT DRVSVS CAESAR TI.F., L. PISO PONTIFEX, T. QVINCTIVS CRISPINVS VALERIANVS. M. CORNVTVS; PER TABELLAS COOPTAVIT TI. CAESAR DIVI AVG. F. AVGVSTVS.

During the same consulship, meeting held on 14th December in the Regia, Cn. Cornelius Lentulus augur, Master, admitted in place of Cn. Pompeius (deceased) . . . Pompeius, augur, in place of the Emperor Caesar Augustus (deceased) as Arval Brethren, and summoned them to attend the sacred rites. Present: Drusus Caesar, son of Tiberius, L. Piso, Pontifex, T. Quinctius Crispinus Valerianus, M.

Cornutus: Voted by token: Tiberius Caesar Augustus, son of Augustus. (Acts of the Arval Brethren.)

ILS, 5026

KALATORES PONTIFICVM ET FLAMINVM.

The attendants of the Pontiffs and Flamens.

CIL. vi. 2184

On a cramped site between the Temple of Vesta and the Sacra Via, the Regia was one of the most important religious shrines in Rome during the Republic, as the headquarters of the Pontifex Maximus; later its importance declined when that office became vested in the Emperor. The passage of Solinus recalls its legendary association with Numa, the traditional codifier of Roman religious usage. The mutilated passage of Festus shows the regal powers being transferred to the Pontifex Maximus under the Republic. The lines of Horace refer to the destruction of the Regia by disastrous Tiber floods; these cannot be dated, although the poem seems to have been written in 27 B.C. However, they occurred presumably before 36 B.C., when the Regia was rebuilt and lavishly decorated by Cn. Domitius Calvinus. The inscription naming him, although found on the Palatine, must refer to the restoration.

In the Regia were housed certain sacred objects, the shields (*ancilia*) and spear of Mars, in a *sacrarium* dedicated to that god. With them the fate of Rome was connected in much the same way as with the *Palladia*, the mysterious sacred objects stored in the temple of Vesta.

In the entrance to the Regia (perhaps) was kept the *tabula dealbata*, the white board on which the Pontifex Maximus recorded the events at which the sacred colleges had assisted during the year, together with certain other events of public importance. The priestly records probably did not go back earlier than Gallic invasion of 390 B.C. However, they formed a kind of rudimentary history in the form of an annual register, and about 123 B.C. the Pontifex Mucius Scaevola put them together and published them as *Annales Maximi*. These are the records of whose dullness Cicero complains. But in Roman literature they are of cardinal importance as determining the prevalent annalistic tradition, of which the *Annales* of Tacitus is the major example.

The regular use of the Regia for the archaic ritual of the October horse is shown in the passage from Festus. An occasional use of the building is attested in the inscription where the Arval Brethren meet to fill two places vacant by deaths. One is that of Augustus himself, who re-founded this ancient priesthood in 21 B.C., and who died A.D. 14. On December

14th the College meets to fill two vacancies in order of seniority, Tiberius being absent and recording his vote by tablet. The *Kalatores* of the last inscription were attendants who assisted the pontiffs and flamens: they had a *schola* or guild of their own, with headquarters in or near the Regia.

What can be seen in the photograph of the site (Plate 32) belongs to the restoration by Calvinus in 36 B.C., which left only a few traces of the building restored after 390 B.C. and again in 148 B.C. Its odd shape is due to the fact that the earlier building had a different alignment.

THE TEMPLE OF VESTA AND ATRIUM VESTAE

Numa is said to have given its circular shape to the Temple of Vesta, where the sacred fire is kept. This was done to imitate, not the shape of the Earth, as if the Earth was Vesta, but rather the Universe, of which the centre, according to the Pythagoreans, is occupied by that fire which they call Vesta and the Monad.

PLUTARCH, *Numa*, XI

Quae nunc aere vides, stipula tunc tecta videres,
et paries lento vimine textus erat.
Hic locus exiguus, qui sustinet atria Vestae,
tunc erat intonsi regia magna Numae.

The brazen roof you now see was once of thatch, the walls were woven of the tough osier. This little spot, which now supports the Hall of the Vestals, was once the great palace of bearded Numa.

OVID, *Fasti*, VI. 261–4

Esse diu stultus Vestae simulacra putavi:
mox didici curvo nulla subesse tholo.
Ignis inextinctus templo celatur in illo;
effigiem nullam Vesta nec ignis habet.

I long supposed (foolishly) that there were images of Vesta: later I learned that none exist within her curved walls. There is an undying fire within the temple: yet neither Vesta nor the fire has an image.

OVID, *Fasti*, VI. 295–8

Ah, how alarmed the Senate was when the Temple of Vesta caught fire, and the goddess was almost extinguished under her own roof! The holy fires were fed by naked flames: profane and sacred flames mingled together. The priestesses wept, their hair unbound: fear had drained them of bodily strength. Metellus rushed

into their midst, shouting 'To the rescue! Weeping is no use. Take up in your virgin hands the pledges fate has given: they need deeds, not words, to save them. What, more delay?' he said (for he saw that they sank down trembling to their knees). Then he took up water, and raised his hands 'Sacred objects,' he prayed, 'forgive me, a man, if I enter a place no man should tread. If it is a crime, let punishment fall on me! Let Rome survive, and the penalty fall on my head!' So he spoke, and burst in: the goddess was carried away, but she approved the deed, and was saved by the devotion of her pontiff.

OVID, *Fasti*, VI. 437–454

Our own day saw a fine example of manhood in the person of Sempronius Densus. He was a centurion of the Praetorian Guard, and Galba had appointed him to protect Piso. He drew his dagger, rushed to meet the armed men, reproached them with their crime, and drew the attention of the murderers to himself by voice and gesture. This gave Piso, wounded though he was, a chance to escape. He made his way to the temple of Vesta: there one of the public slaves took pity on him and hid him in his room. The obscurity of the place—and not the sanctity of the temple and its rites—gave him a respite from instant destruction. But then there came from Otho men with a special mission to kill him—Sulpicius Florus, of a British auxiliary unit, recently granted Roman citizenship by Galba, and Statius Murcius, one of the bodyguard. They dragged Piso out and butchered him in the entrance to the Temple.

TACITUS, *Histories*, I. 43

Domitian was boiling with fury because of the intense public hatred he had aroused. He had conceived a plan for burying alive Cornelia, the distinguished Head of the Vestal Virgins, from the extraordinary idea that severities of this kind reflected glory on his reign. So, as High Priest—or rather as tyrant—he summoned the Sacred College to his Villa at Albanum, not their usual place of meeting. There . . . he condemned her on a charge of incest. (He himself had incestuously seduced his niece.) At once the priests were sent to supervise the carrying out of the sentence of death by burial. Cornelia implored Vesta and all the other gods, frequently calling out 'How can Caesar think me polluted? While I have carried out the sacred rites, he has conquered and triumphed!' . . . As she was carried down into the underground cell, her gown caught in some obstruction. She tried to free it, and the executioner offered her his hand. But she turned her face away: chaste to the last, she refused his polluting touch on her pure and spotless body. So, in this last moment of her life, she neglected no point of modesty 'and took much thought to fall with decency'.

PLINY, *Letters*, IV. XI

FLAVIAE PVBLICIAE .V. V. SANCTISSIMAE AC RELIGIOSISSIMAE QVAE PER OMNES GRADVS SACERDOTII APVT DIVINA ALTARIA OMNIVM DEORVM ET AD AETERNOS IGNES DIEBVS NOCTIBVSQVE PIA MENTE RITE DESERVIENS MERITO AD HVNC LOCVM CVM AETATE PERVENIT. BAREIVS

ZOTICVS CVM FLAVIA VERECVNDA SVA OB EXIMIAM ERGA SE BENIBOLENTIAM PRAESTANTIAM, . . . DEDICATA PR. KAL. OCT. DD. NN. VALERIANO AVG. III ET GALLIENO AVG. III COSS.

To Flavia Publicia, the most devout and most sacred Head of the Vestal Virgins, who, after filling every grade of that priesthood and serving the altars of all the gods and the undying flame with pious mind day and night, very properly succeeded in due course to her high office. Set up by Bareius Zoticus and his wife Flavia Verecunda, for her extraordinary kindness to them, and her constant aid. Set up on September 30th, in the third consulship of our Lords the Augusti Valerian and Gallienus.

CIL, vi. 32416

No ground in Rome was more sacred than that devoted to the cult of Vesta, with the round temple always rebuilt on the original plan, the Atrium or Hall of the Vestals, and the sacred grove. The passages selected refer to the traditional founding by Numa, the archaic temple, the undying fire, the heroic conduct of Caecilius Metellus in the fire of 241 B.C., the murder of Piso in the sacred precincts in A.D. 69, and the savage punishment meeted out to the Head of the Order by Domitian. The inscription is one of several honorific inscriptions to Heads of the Order discovered in the courtyard of the Atrium, mostly of the third century A.D.

Plutarch follows the tradition that Numa was the first to codify Roman religious ceremonies. The Greek for Vesta is Hestia: hence the connection with the Pythagorean belief of the 'Sacred hearth-fire' at the centre of the universe.

The roof of turf and the walls of osier in the first passage from the Fasti represent the earliest form of the temple—one of those *capanne* like the Hut of Romulus (Plate 2), or the hut-models found among the grave-goods in the Forum Necropolis. The Regia (p. 104) stood to the north of the Temple of Vesta. In the second passage Ovid asserts that Vesta never became anthropomorphic: she was simply 'the ever-living fire'. Other references say that an image of Vesta stood among those of the 'twelve great gods', the *di consentes*, at the foot of the Capitol. But Ovid may be right in that there was no image of Vesta in her temple, at least in his time (but cf. Plate 85).

In the fire of 241 B.C. Metellus violated the taboo that forbade any man to cross the threshold of the temple. He rescued the sacred objects—the Palladia or pledge of Rome's safety and Empire—but lost his sight.

In the last days of Galba's power, Licinianus Piso, whom he had adopted, was murdered by Otho. Note the parts played by the *aedituus*, the public slave who was a temple attendant, and by the British assassin, who must have come from one of the British cohorts used in the Civil Wars of A.D. 69.

The punishment of a Vestal Virgin found guilty of incest was to be carried on a funeral bier to the Campus Sceleratus, the place of execution outside the Porta Collina, and there entombed in a subterranean cell, which was then covered with earth. Her paramour was scourged to death with rods. Domitian carried out this exemplary punishment in all its archaic severity on Cornelia, the Vestalis Maxima: three other unchaste Vestals were allowed to commit suicide. The adultery of a Vestal Virgin ranked as incest because she was a daughter of the State. Domitian himself was suspected of incest with his niece Julia in the reign of Titus. Cornelia points out that the Vestal Virgins pray for the success of Roman arms, and that Domitian had in fact triumphed twice against the Germans (in A.D. 84 and 89). This he could not have done if she had been unchaste. The quotation in the last sentence of the passage is from Euripides, *Hecuba* 569.

LACUS JUTURNAE

Fratribus illa deis fratres de gente deorum
circa Iuturnae composuere Lacus.

'Brothers of the race of the gods built this Temple to the Brother Gods by the pool of Juturna.'

OVID, *Fasti*, I. 707–8

The Roman people had already received the joyous tidings of the victory (i.e. the battle of Pydna, 168 B.C.) long before it was announced in the despatches of the victorious general. For, on the day when Perseus was defeated in Macedonia, it was known in Rome, for two young men with white horses washed off the dust and gore at the pool of Juturna. These young men brought the news. Popular belief thought they were Castor and Pollux, because they were twins, that they took part in the battle, because they were dripping with blood, and that they had come from Macedonia, because they were still panting for breath.

FLORUS, *Epitome*, I. 28. 15

Esteem for springs continue today, and their cult is maintained. They are supposed to bring health to the sick, for example, the springs of the Camenae, of Apollo, and of Juturna.

FRONTINUS, *De aquis*, 4

OPTIMO ET VENERABILI D. N. FL. CONSTANTINO MAXIMO VICTORI PIO SEMPER AVG. FL. MAESIVS. EGNATIVS V.C. CVRATOR AQVARVM ET MINIC. D.N.M.Q.E.

To our Lord, the excellent and venerable Flavius Constantinus, ever victorious, Flavius Maesius Egnatius, *vir clarissimus*, curator over the Water Board and the minor channels, devoted to his divinity and majesty.

DEDICATA CVM STATIONE A FLAVIO LOLLIANO V.C. KAL. MARTIS. IANVARINO ET IVSTO COSS.

Dedicated together with the headquarters office by Flavius Lollianus, *vir clarissimus*, on the 1st March in the consulship of Januarinus and Justus (A.D. 328).

CIL, VI. 36951

M.BARBATIVS POLLIO AED. CVR. IVTVRNAI SACRVM. REST. PVTEAL

M. Barbatius Pollio, Aedile Curulis, restored the stone curb of the well dedicated to Juturna.

ILS, 9261

Several strands of cult and tradition unite around the pool of the water-goddess Juturna. The Helping One (*iuvare*) or Immortal One (*diuturna*), her primitive cult became associated with the Dioscuri after their miraculous appearance in 496 B.C. to announce the victory at the Battle of Lake Regillus (see below). Florus records a second and long-distance mission of the Twins after Pydna. Juturna herself was identified by Virgil with the sister of the Italian hero Turnus: the late imperial altar (Plate 33) portrays their parting before Turnus went to his doom. The excavations of 1900 brought to light fragments of the early republican statues of the Dioscuri now in the Forum Antiquarium. They also showed that in imperial times the area was monumentalized, the goddess being provided with a little temple to house the cult statue, and her worshippers with the means of immersion in the sacred waters. A cult of Aesculapius developed next to that of Juturna: later this ground was taken over to form the headquarters of the *curatores aquarum* or Water Board, as testified by the inscription of Flavius Lollianus. The Barbatius Pollio who restored the stone curbs round the well may be the supporter of Mark Antony. (See Plates 33–34.)

THE TEMPLE OF CASTOR AND POLLUX

It is said that in this battle (i.e. of Lake Regillus, 496 B.C.) two horsemen appeared to Postumius, the Dictator, and to those around him. In size and beauty they far exceeded mortal men, and they were just growing their first beards. They charged at the head of the Roman cavalry, striking out with their spears at every

Latin they met, and driving them in a rout before them. After the rout of the Latins and the capture of their camp, the battle came to an end, it being by then late afternoon. And at that time two youths are said to have appeared in the Roman Forum, in the same manner, dressed for battle, tall, beautiful, and of the same age. They still had on their faces the look of those who have come from battle, and the horses they led were lathered with sweat. Then they watered their horses and washed them at the spring that rises by the Temple of Vesta, which makes a small but deep pool. Many stood around them, asking for news of the battle: they described it, and said that the Romans had won. It is further said that after they had left the Forum no one saw them again, and this despite the very strict search made by those in charge of the city. On the next day the authorities received the despatch of the Dictator Postumius, which, among other details of the battles, told them of the appearance of the two divinities. It was concluded—reasonably enough—that both appearances had been of the same gods, and that the phantoms seen were those of Castor and Pollux.

DIONYSIUS HALICARNASSUS, *Roman Antiquities*, VI. 13

Castoris aedes eodem anno idibus Quintilibus dedicata est: vota est Latino bello Postumio dictatore: filius eius duumvir ad id ipsum creatus dedicavit.

The Temple of Castor was dedicated on July 15th of that year. It had been vowed by the Dictator Postumius during the Latin War: his son carried out the dedication, having been made duumvir for that very purpose.

LIVY, II, 42. 5

Now, what shall I say on a topic that was day after day discussed with indignation throughout Rome—Verres' outrageous theft, or rather unprecedented and blatant act of brigandage? To think of the temple of Castor, that famous and noble monument, a temple placed where the eyes of the Roman people see it every day, where the Senate often meets, which is daily thronged by those who come to consult on the gravest issues: and then to think in that temple Verres has left a monument of his criminal conduct that will last for ever on the lips of men! . . . (When Verres was praetor in Rome) he thought what a pity it would be to abandon a vast and elaborate building like that without lining his own pocket—especially since it could be done at the expense of a minor. So he went in person to the Temple of Castor and surveyed it. The whole roof was beautifully panelled, everything else was sound and in good condition. He turned round, and asked what he could possibly do. Then one of his 'hounds'—and he admitted that he always kept a large pack of them around him—said 'There's no jobbery for you here, Verres, unless you'd like to insist that the columns be made perfectly plumb.' 'Plumb,' asked the ignoramus, 'what's that?' They explained to him that no column could be perfectly plumb. 'By God, yes', he said, 'that's it: let's insist that all the columns should be perfectly plumb!'

CICERO, *Against Verres*, II. 133f.

C. VI. KAL. FEBR. CASTORES.

The sixth day before the Kalends of February, dedication of the Temple of Castor and Pollux.

Fasti Praenestini, CIL, 1², p. 308

At quae venturas praecedit sexta Kalendas,
hac sunt Ledaeis templa dicata deis.
fratribus illa deis fratres de gente deorum
circa Iuturnae composuere lacus.

But on the sixth day before the Kalends of February (27th Jan.) the temple was dedicated to the Dioscuri. Brothers, of the race of the gods, built this Temple to the Brother Gods by the pool of Juturna.

OVID, *Fasti*, I. 705–8

dedicavit et Concordiae aedem, item Pollucis et Castoris suo fratrisque nomine de manubiis.

He (Tiberius) dedicated a temple to Concord, and also to Castor and Pollux, in the name of his brother and himself, from the spoils of war.

SUETONIUS, *Tiberius*, 20

. . . partem Palatii ad forum usque promovit, atque aede Castoris et Pollucis in vestibulum transfigurata, consistens saepe inter fratres deos, medium adorandum se adeuntibus exhibebat.

He extended part of the Palace almost to the Forum, and, since the Temple of Castor and Pollux had been turned into a vestibule, would often sit between the Two Brother Gods, offering himself for the adoration of those who visited the temple.

SUETONIUS, *Caligula*, 22

SENATVS CONSVLTVM DE TIBVRTIBVS. L. CORNELIVS CN. F. PR. SEN. CONS. AD. III NONAS MAIAS SVB AEDE KASTORVM.

Resolution of the Senate concerning the people of Tibur, carried by Lucius Cornelius, son of Gnaeus, leader of the Senate, Consul, on May 5th. Recorded at the Temple of Castor (at Tibur, treaty of 166 B.C.).

EXAC. AD X. CASTOR EX AD V. CASTO EX AD III CASTOR. EXACT. AD II CASTO. EX AD I CAST.

Corrected for five pounds at the Temple of Castor, corrected for three pounds at the Temple of Castor, etc., etc.

CIL, v. 8119. 4

The Temple of Castor and Pollux was one of the earliest in the Forum Romanum, occasioned by the help of the Dioscuri at the Battle of Lake Regillus. The traditional date of the dedication of the first temple is 15th July 484 B.C. This building had a long life, and it was not until 117 B.C. that it was rebuilt and much enlarged by L. Caecilius Metellus Dalmaticus. By then the Dioscuri had acted as special messengers at least once more—after the battle of Pydna, the result of which they gave to the Senate in writing. They are also said to have appeared at the time of Julius Caesar's funeral (see p. 101). The third rebuilding was in the reign of Augustus, when the temple was re-dedicated in the names of Tiberius and Drusus on 27th January A.D. 6. It is this building whose remains are so conspicuous today. Always one of the most important temples in Rome, it was used for many purposes both in republican and imperial times. The Senate met there: speeches to the people were delivered from a platform at the front of the podium. The passages selected show it as the scene of one of Verres' meaner rackets, involving fraudulent contract and the cheating of a minor. Also, of one of Caligula's extravaganzas, when he posed as a third Divine Brother. The vaults of its high podium, like those of the Temple of Saturn (*q.v.*) were used for banking, especially by the imperial *fiscus*, but also by private depositors (see 125). Bronze copies of treaties and *senatusconsulta* were kept there: a copy of one of these latter, dated probably 155 B.C., is preserved at Tivoli. In it were housed standard weights: the last inscription quoted refers to a set of bronze weights found at Aquileia, and now preserved at Milan.

THE TEMPLE OF ANTONINUS AND FAUSTINA

In the third year of his reign (Antoninus) lost his wife Faustina. The Senate deified her, and she was voted games, a temple, priestesses, and statues of silver and gold. To these the emperor added that her statue be set up in all the circuses. When the Senate voted her a golden statue, he paid for it to be erected.

HISTORIA AUGUSTA, *Antoninus*, 6

Antoninus Pius was deified by the Senate, and all men vied with each other in bestowing general praise on his piety and mercy, his intelligence and his righteousness. Every honour was decreed him that had previously been bestowed on the best of emperors. And he well deserved the priests and the games, the temple and the priesthood of Antoniniani. Almost alone of emperors, he had lived without shedding the blood of citizen or enemy, so far as he could. He could justly be compared with Numa, whose good fortune, piety, prosperity and religious rites he always maintained.

HISTORIA AUGUSTA, *Antoninus*, 13

DIVO. ANTONINO. ET DIVAE. FAVSTINAE. EX. S.C.

To the deified Antoninus and to the deified Faustina, by decree of the Senate.

CIL, VI. 1005

Much of the temple survives within its transformation to the baroque church of S. Lorenzo in Miranda in 1602. Faustina died in A.D. 140 and Antoninus Pius in 161. The inscription on the architrave makes it clear that the temple was dedicated to them both; fragments of two statues, male and female, have been found and probably belong to cult statues of the imperial pair. The gold statue, erected at the emperor's expense, presumably stood in the Circus Maximus. See Plate 35.

THE ARCH OF TITUS

SENATVS
POPVLVSQVE ROMANVS
DIVO TITO D. VESPASIANI. F.
VESPASIANO AVGVSTO.

The Senate and People of Rome dedicated this arch to the deified Titus Vespasianus Augustus, son of the deified Vespasian.

CIL, VI. 945

At this celebration (i.e. the entry of Belisarius into Byzantium A.D. 534), there were thousands of silver talents, and also the whole of the royal treasure, which came to a very large sum. For Gaeseric had despoiled the Palatium at Rome, as described earlier. Among these was the treasure of the Jewish people, which Titus and others had brought to Rome after the sack of Jerusalem. Now a certain Jew, seeing them displayed, went to one of the Emperor's friends and said, 'These treasures, in my view, should not by any means be deposited in the palace of Byzantium. They must not be anywhere else but in that place where Solomon, King of the Jews, first placed them. Because of them Gaeseric captured the palace of the Romans, and now, because of them, the Roman army has captured the palace of the Vandals.' When this was reported to the Emperor, he grew alarmed, and immediately sent the treasure to the Christian sanctuaries in Jerusalem.

PROCOPIUS, *Gothic War*, IV. 19

There is no literary evidence for this, the simplest and finest of the three triumphal arches that have survived in Rome. Fortunately the reliefs—the most important sculptures of the Flavian period—speak for themselves. The arch, erected to Titus sometime after his death in A.D. 81, commemorates the triumph he had won for the capture of Jerusalem in A.D. 70. The sculptures on the archway form a coherent scheme. On the north side Titus, on his *quadriga*, is led by Dea Roma into the city. On the south the treasures of the Temple at Jerusalem—silver trumpets, the seven-branched candlestick—are carried along in the triumphal procession (Plate 37). Above, in the soffit of the vault, a square panel depicts the apotheosis of Titus, carried aloft by an eagle.

The Arch was completely rebuilt in 1822.

After the triumph of Titus, the Jewish treasures were placed in the Temple of Peace. There they remained until the Vandal King Gaeseric carried them off to Carthage in A.D. 455. The passage of Procopius enables us to carry the story a stage further. Belisarius, having captured Carthage, took them to Byzantium: a patriotic Jew, clever enough to play on Justinian's superstition, induced him to return them to Jerusalem, probably to the church of the Holy Sepulchre. But not for long. The Persians captured Jerusalem in 614, and carried away the Holy Cross and all the most sacred relics. Among them were the Temple treasures, and after that date we hear of them no more.

THE BASILICA OF CONSTANTINE

Adhuc cuncta opera, quae magnifice construxerat, urbis fanum atque basilicam Flavii meritis patres sacravere.

Moreover, all the buildings which he (Maxentius) had lavishly constructed, the shrine of the city[1] and the basilica, the senate dedicated to the just deserts of Flavius (Constantine).

AURELIUS VICTOR, *The Caesars*, 40. 26

IMPERATORI CAES. FL. CONSTANTINO MAXIMO TRIVMFATORI PIO FEL. AUG. S.P.Q.R.

To the Emperor Caesar Flavius Constantinus Maximus, Triumfator, Pius, Felix, Augustus, the Senate and People of Rome dedicated this building.

CIL, VI. 1147

[1] Usually identified with the Temple of Romulus.

This, the last great building in the Roman Forum, was begun under Maxentius in A.D. 307, after a fire which ravaged this quarter of the Forum. It was still unfinished when Constantine won his victory at Saxa Rubra in 312, and was then dedicated by the Senate to him. The dedicatory inscription is now lost, that printed is a conjectural restoration based on copies made by Panvinius and Ligorio.

Constantine did not merely take over Maxentius' building, but fundamentally altered its plan, turning its axis through 90°, and placing the main entrance on the Forum side. Of its three names, Basilica Nova, Basilica of Maxentius, and Basilica of Constantine, the last has been the most durable. But it is not a basilica of the same kind as the Basilica Aemilia or Julia: since their time Roman architecture had discovered new ways of enclosing huge spaces, as in the halls of the Thermae of Caracalla and Diocletian. Of that line of development the Basilica of Constantine is the finest example. But it has itself been a starting point for great architectural projects: much admired in the Renaissance, it haunted the mind of Bramante as he prepared a design for the new St. Peter's. Riboira has suggested that it may have influenced the plan for Sancta Sophia in Constantinople.

THE TEMPLE OF VENUS AND ROME

With the help of the architect Decrianus Hadrian moved the Colossus of Nero away from that place where the Temple of Rome now is, keeping it upright throughout. It was of such great weight that he had to supply as many as twenty-four elephants for the task. The features of Nero, to whom it had earlier been dedicated, were removed, and he consecrated it to the Sun. He also planned to make another statue on the same scale to the Moon, with the help of the architect Apollodorus.

HISTORIA AUGUSTA, *Hadrian*, 19

(Hadrian) first banished and then put to death the architect Apollodorus, builder in Rome of the Forum, the Odeon, and the Gymnasium, the creations of Trajan. Ostensibly, he had committed some offence: in fact, the reason was the comment he had made when Trajan was consulting him on building plans, and Hadrian interrupted with some irrelevance or other . . . 'Oh, go and draw your pumpkins. You know nothing of these matters.' (Hadrian at the time was very proud of some drawings of that kind he had made.) When Emperor, Hadrian remembered this slight, and refused to endure Apollodorus' outspokenness. He sent him the plans of the Temple of Venus and Rome, in plain proof that great projects could be carried out in his absence, and asked Apollodorus whether he approved of the project. In his reply, Apollodorus wrote, first, that the Temple should have been built on a lofty site and the earth excavated from beneath it, to take full advantage of a loftier position as seen from the Sacred Way. This would have allowed the storage of stage machinery in the basement, which could have been assembled unobserved and produced in the amphitheatre without anyone knowing about it. Secondly, he said that the cult statues were out of scale with their *cellae*. 'If the goddesses,' he said, 'ever want to get up and go out, they won't be able to do so.' When he made this blunt reply, the Emperor was annoyed, and much displeased that he had made a mistake it was now impossible to correct. He could not suppress either his anger or his grief, but had Apollodorus put to death.

DIO CASSIUS, *Roman History*, LXIX. 4

It was decreed by the Senate that silver statues of Marcus and Faustina should be set up in the Temple of Venus and Rome, and that an altar should be built where all girls married in the city and their grooms should offer sacrifice.

DIO CASSIUS, *History of Rome*, LXXII. 31

The child . . . would hear the Sacred Way resound with the lowing of cattle before the shrine of Rome. For she too is worshipped with blood like a goddess: what is only the name of a place is invested with godhead: the temples of the City and of Venus rise to a like height: incense is burned to the two goddesses together. . . .

PRUDENTIUS, *Against Symmachus*, I. 221ff.

The plateau at the top of the Velia, looking across the Forum to the Capitol and the Palatine, confronting in one direction the magnificence of the Imperial fora and on the other the bulk of the Colosseum, must have been the most challenging architectural site in Rome in the days of Hadrian. Here the Emperor built to his own design the enormous double temple of Venus and Rome, begun on 21st April (the birthday of Rome) in A.D. 121, but not dedicated until 135. The moving of the Colossus of Nero closer to the amphitheatre was an engineering feat comparable to the removal of the Vatican obelisk in 1586.

In the design of the temple religious symbolism—to which we do not have the key—is combined with architectural virtuosity. The *cellae* of the two goddesses stood back to back, whether or not influenced by the palindrome Roma-Amor, Roma looking to the Forum, Venus to the amphitheatre. Perhaps owing to the strained relations between Hadrian and Apollodorus, the lunar Colossus was never realized. But the conjunction of Sun and Moon may have stood for eternity, conferred on Rome by the patronage of Venus, and on the human plane passed on by marriage from generation to generation.

The passage of Dio on the quarrel between Hadrian and Apollodorus (for whom see also p. 136) has been thought apocryphal. No doubt the details are unreliable. But it catches the excitement and rivalry of an age of great projects, and the dislike of the professional for the amateur. Hadrian's 'pumpkins' are probably the segmented domes and semi-domes, examples of which are to be seen in his Villa at Tivoli.

The temple was one of the sights of Rome admired by Constantius in A.D. 357 (see p. 29). Prudentius shows that the cult was maintained until the end of pagan times: his Christian scepticism is not impressed by architectural magnificence. See Plate 38.

THE IMPERIAL FORA

The building of the imperial fora progressed in five stages, spread over more than one hundred and fifty years from the dictatorship of Julius Caesar to the death of Trajan. This was the most sustained and magnificent programme of city planning anywhere in ancient Rome, and indeed one of the most notable of any period anywhere in the world. Caesar conceived the idea of a monumental centre linking the Forum Romanum with the Campus Martius: the five imperial *fora* carried it into effect, though it must not be thought that they followed a master plan. The appearance of unity is largely due to the care taken in relating the siting and layout of each phase to its predecessors, to the principle of axial symmetry, and also to the fact that the Forum of Trajan, the last and finest, occupies more than half of the entire area. How far its architect, Apollodorus of Damascus, may have undertaken some regularization of the whole is uncertain.

No ancient author describes the general effect, although the magnificence of Trajan's Forum is well recalled in the passage of Ammianus quoted above (p. 29). Today, and despite the devoted work of Italian archaeologists, appreciation of the whole calls for a deliberate effort. Pliny's reminder of the need for space and silence is useful. It is best, then, to go to the upper terrace of the Mercatus Trajani for a good viewpoint, then, with the help of a ground-plan, to visualize each of the five *fora* in terms of design, function, and concept. Something is said under each of these heads below. But there is something more, for this is a whole which is greater than the sum of its parts. These buildings were the visible expression of the experience and ideas of the Roman empire at its best period. They symbolize the end of the Civil Wars, the establishment and maintenance of peace; they provide for the justice and administration, the arts and commerce by which civilization is sustained. And of their triumphal monuments, all but one relate to the great confrontation on the northern frontiers which is the leading theme of the Empire's first two centuries.

It is characteristic of our times that the Via dei Fori Imperiali, created to reveal the imperial *fora*, now carries such a volume of motor traffic that their study is seriously impeded.

THE FORUM OF CAESAR

(Before the battle of Pharsalus) Caesar offered a midnight sacrifice. He invoked Mars, and his own ancestress Venus, for it was believed that the *gens Julia* descended from Aeneas and his son Ilus, with a slight change of name. Should all go well he vowed to build her a Temple in Rome as the Bringer of Victory, as a thanksgiving. And thereupon a bright light in the sky shot from Caesar's camp towards Pompey's, where it went out. The Pompeians interpreted this as the sign of a brilliant victory for them over their enemies: Caesar took it as a portent that he would fall on the power of Pompey and extinguish it.

APPIAN, *Civil Wars*, II. 68

Caesar built the Temple of Venus Genetrix, as he had vowed to do before the battle of Pharsalus. He also built a precinct around the Temple, intending it to be a forum for the Roman people, not for commercial use, but rather for the transaction of public business, and like the public squares of the Persians, where people assemble to seek justice or learn the laws. He put by the side of the goddess a beautiful statue of Cleopatra, which stands there to this day.

APPIAN, *Civil Wars*, II. 102

Julius Caesar gave 100,000,000 sesterces simply for the site on which his Forum was built.

PLINY, *Natural History*, XXXVI. 103

On the last day of his triumphs, Caesar entered his own Forum after dinner, wearing slippers-of-ease, and garlanded with flowers of all kinds. Then he went home, escorted by almost the entire population of Rome, and with elephants as his torch-bearers. He had indeed built the Forum called after him, which is much more beautiful than the Roman Forum, yet has enhanced the reputation of the latter by causing it to be called the Forum Magnum. This Forum, then, and also the Temple of Venus Genetrix, were completed and dedicated at this time.

DIO CASSIUS, *Roman History*, XLIII. 22. 3

FORVM IVLIVM ET BASILICAM . . . COEPTA PROFLIGATAQUE OPERA A PATRE MEO PERFECI. . . .

I completed the Forum Julium and the Basilica Julia . . . works begun and far advanced by my Father.

AUGUSTUS, *Res gestae*, 20

It is known that small pearls of poor colour are found in Britain, since the deified Julius made it clear that the breastplate he dedicated in his temple to Venus Genetrix was made of British pearls.

PLINY, *Natural History*, IX. 116

Caesar as Dictator gave permission for a statue of himself wearing a cuirass (*loricatam*) to be erected in his Forum.

PLINY, *Natural History*, XXXIV. 18

It was the Dictator Caesar who emphasized the public importance of pictures by dedicating paintings of Ajax and Medea in front of the temple of Venus Genetrix.

PLINY, *Natural History*, XXXV. 26

Subdita qua Veneris facto de marmore templo
Appias expressis aëra pulsat aquis,
Illo saepe loco capitur consultus Amori,
Quique aliis cavit, non cavet ipse sibi.
Illo saepe loco desunt sua verba diserto,
Resque novae veniunt, causaque agenda sua est,
Hunc Venus e templis, quae sunt confinia, ridet:
Qui modo patronus, nunc cupit esse cliens.

Where beneath Venus' marble shrine the Appian nymph strikes the air with her spurting water, there many a lawyer is caught by love. He took care of others, but not of himself: words fail the glib speaker: a new case comes to court, and he must plead his own cause. Venus mocks him from her temple hard by: once an advocate, he would be glad to be a client now.

OVID, *Art of Love*, I. 81–88

TI. CAESAR. DIVI AVGVSTI F. DIVI IVLI N. AVGVSTO PONTIF. MAXIMO COS. IIII IMP VIII TRIB. POT. XXXII AVGVSTALES RES PVBLICA RESTITVIT. SARDES . . . VLLORON MAGNESIA PHILADELPHIA TMOLVS CYME TEMNOS (?) CIBYRA MYRINA EPHESOS APOLLONIDEA HYRCANIA MOSTENE (?) HIEROCAESAREA (round edges).

ILS, 156

To the emperor Tiberius Caesar, etc., etc. . . .Tribunician power for the 32nd time (A.D. 30): the college of Augustus set up this (statue): which was restored by the state (of Puteoli), Sardes etc.

ABCDEFGIL . . . MANTVA ME GENVIT . . . ARMA VIRVMQVE CANO TROIAE QVI PRIMVS AB ORIS . . . SORACTI . . . HECTOR . . . CAECILIVS . . . CAECILIVS ALVMNVS . . . SMIRINA VALE

Graffiti from the Basilica Argentaria, BCAR, 61. IIIff.

The passages of Appian trace the origins of the Temple of Venus Genetrix to a vow made by Caesar on the night before the battle of Pharsalus. But we know that the Forum itself had been in Caesar's mind much earlier, and that he had been collecting money to purchase the site in 54 B.C. The Temple and Forum were consecrated, though unfinished, on 29th September 46 B.C.: the full scheme was not completed until the time of Augustus. Appian's description of the Forum is odd, and suggests that he is writing for Greek readers who might not know that the precinct surrounding a temple is a standard Italic pattern for a forum, to which those of Augustus, Vespasian, and Nerva also conform. The reference to Persian practice presumably refers to the great squares of such cities as Ctesiphon and Seleuceia, familiar to Appian's contemporaries from the campaigns of Trajan and Avidius Cassius. In fact, commerce was not excluded from Caesar's Forum, for *tabernae* were ranged along three sides. Ovid's love-sick barristers are professionally more in place, and the passage adds information about the fountain with its water-nymphs, the Appiades, in front of the marble temple. Pliny refers often to the artistic treasures in the Temple and Forum—the statue of Cleopatra, the collection of gowns and jewels so fitting for the Queen of Love, and the paintings by Greek masters. The British pearls were remarkable for their provenance rather than their beauty: they may well have been mussel-pearls, like those used in the Honours of Scotland. Of the statues in the Forum, we know of one of the Dictator and his favourite war-horse, and of a colossal statue of Tiberius, set up by the cities of Asia whom he helped after the disastrous earthquakes of A.D. 17. This statue was reproduced in other cities, among them Puteoli, where a copy of the inscription survives, together with the names of the grateful cities.

It was not until 1932 that Trajan's work in the reconstruction of the Forum Julium was known, thanks to a mention in the Fasti of Ostia (Notizie Scavi, 1932, p. 201). On May 12th, A.D. 113, he rededicated the Temple of Venus, which had probably been damaged by fire: the three columns now re-erected belong to the Trajanic building. Trajan also built the so-called Basilica Argentaria at the north-west corner of the Forum. The last item is a curiosity. Numerous graffiti have been found in the Basilica Argentaria: from the mixture of Virgilian tags, geographical and historical names, letters of the alphabet, and obscenities, they have been thought to indicate the presence of an elementary school, whose *magister* was a certain Q. Caecilius Eros.

THE FORUM OF AUGUSTUS

IN PRIVATO SOLO MARTIS VLTORIS TEMPLVM FORVMQVE AVGVSTVM EX MANIBIIS FECI. . . .

On my own ground I built from the spoils of war the temple of Mars the Avenger and the Forum Augustum.

AUGUSTUS, *Res gestae*, IV. 21

Augustus built numerous public works, notably the following—the forum with the temple of Mars the Avenger. . . .

His reasons for building the Forum were the increase in population and in the number of law suits, so that the two existing fora were inadequate and a third seemed necessary. It was therefore opened as an emergency before the Temple of Mars was complete, and was reserved for public prosecutions and for the selection of jury by lot. He had taken a vow for the temple of Mars Ultor at the battle of Philippi to avenge his father: he therefore decreed that in this Temple the Senate should discuss questions of war and of the granting of triumphs, that from it those who were leaving to take up military commands in the provinces should be ceremonially escorted and to it the returning conquerors should bring the tokens of their victories.

SUETONIUS, *Augustus*, 29

Augustus made his forum less ample than intended, because he did not wish to expropriate the houses of neighbouring owners.

id. ib. 56

The Senate decreed that ovations should be given to Germanicus and Drusus on their entry to the city. Triumphal arches too were erected flanking the temple of Mars Ultor, together with statues of the two Caesars: Tiberius rejoiced more heartily in having secured peace by diplomacy than he would if he had ended a war by victory.

(A.D. 19) TACITUS, *Annals*, II. 64

Claudius was ready for food and drink, everywhere and at all times. Once when he was trying a case in the Forum of Augustus, he caught the appetizing smell of a banquet prepared for the Salii in the temple of Mars close by. Immediately he left the bench, went up to where the priests were, and sat down with them at table.

SUETONIUS, *Claudius*, 33

In Rome . . . Hadrian restored the Forum of Augustus.

HISTORIA AUGUSTA, *Hadrian* 19

Should we not mention among our noble buildings . . . the Forum of Augustus?

PLINY, *Natural History*, XXXVI. 102

Monstro voluptatem egregiam, cui nulla theatra,
nulla aequare queas praetoris pulpita lauti,
si spectes quanto capitis discrimine constent
incrementa domus, aerata multus in arca
fiscus et ad vigilem ponendi Castora nummi
ex quo Mars Ultor galeam quoque perdidit et res
non potuit servare suas.

Now I show you the most agreeable of pleasures—no theatre or wealthy praetor's show is comparable. Observe at what risk to life men increase their fortunes, possess themselves of full treasure-chests bound with brass, or cash that has to be deposited in the guarded Temple of Castor—ever since Mars the Avenger lost his helmet, and failed to protect his own property.

JUVENAL, *Satires*, XIV. 256–62

Next to the gods themselves, Augustus honoured the memory of those great generals who had raised the empire of the Roman people from obscurity to greatness. So it was that he restored the works of these men, with their original inscriptions, and dedicated statues in triumphal dress of them all in the two colonnades of his forum, issuing at the same time a proclamation 'This I have done to bind the Roman people to require me, while I am alive, and also the princes of ages yet to come, to live by the standards set by these great men.'

SUETONIUS, *Augustus*, 31

Mars Ultor himself comes down from Heaven to see the honours paid him, and his splendid temple in the Forum of Augustus. Huge the god and huge the temple . . . on one side he sees Aeneas with his dear burden, and many an ancestor of the Julian house; on the other Romulus carrying the arms of the conquered leader, and all the statues ranged in order, with their famous deeds inscribed.

OVID, *Fasti*, V. 551–3, 563–6

Non incisa notis marmora publicis,
per quae spiritus et vita redit bonis
post mortem ducibus . . .

Not marbles engraved with public inscriptions, which gives back life and strength to dead generals . . . (add to their fame as much as poetry).

HORACE, *Odes*, IV. 8. 13–15

AENEAS VENERIS ET ANCHISAE FILIVS TROIANOS QVI CAPTA TROIA ET INCENSA SVPERERANT IN ITALIAM ADDVXIT OPPIDVM LAVINIVM CONDIDIT REGNAVIT ANNOS TRIS INDE CVM PROELIO FACTO NON COMPARVISSET DICTVS EST INDIGENS ET IN DEORVM NVMERO RELATVS.

Aeneas, son of Venus and Anchises. He led the Trojans who survived the capture and fire of Troy to Italy. . . . He founded the town of Lavinium and reigned there for three years. Then when after the battle he did not appear again, he was hailed as a deified hero, and enrolled among the gods.

CIL, I^2, XX

AENEAS VENERIS FILIVS LATINORVM REX REGNAVIT ANNOS III.

Aeneas, son of Venus, King of the Latins, ruled three years.

Degrassi, Ins. It. XIII. 3. I

ROMVLVS MARTIS FILIVS VRBEM ROMAM CONDIDIT ET REGNAVIT ANNOS DVODEQVADRAGINTA ISQVE PRIMVS DVX DVCE HOSTIVM ACRONE REGE CAENINENSIVM INTERFECTO SPOLIA OPIMA IOVI FERETRIO CONSECRAVIT RECEPTVSQVE IN DEORVM NVMERVM QVIRINVS APPELLATVS EST.

Romulus, son of Mars, founded the city of Rome, where he reigned for 38 years. He was the first general who, having slain an enemy general—Acro, King of Caere—dedicated the *spolia opima* to Jupiter Feretrius. He was received among the gods, and received the name of Quirinus.

(Pompeii) CIL, I_2, XXII

L. AEMILIVS L.F. PAVLVS COS II CENS INTERREX PR. AED. AVG. LIGVRIBVS DOMITIS PRIORE CONSVLATV TRIVMPHAVIT ITERVM COS VT CVM REGE PERSE BELLVM GERERET A POPVLO FACTVS EST COPIAS REGIS DECEM DIEBVS QVIBVS MACEDONIAM ATTIGIT DELEVIT REGEMQVE CVM LIBERIS EXCEPIT.

L. Aemilius Paulus, son of Lucius, twice consul, Censor, Interrex, Praetor, Aedile. . . . He triumphed over the Ligurians in his first consulship. He was made Consul a second time by the people to wage war against King Perseus. He destroyed the King's forces in the ten days needed to reach Macedonia, and captured the King with his children.

Degrassi, Ins. It. XIII. 3. 81

C. MARIVS C.F. CONSVL SEPTIES, PRAETOR, TRIBVNVS PLEBIS . . . EXTRA SORTEM BELLVM CVM IVGVRTHA REGE NVMIDIAE CONSVL GESSIT, EVM CEPIT ET TRIVMPHANS IN SECVNDO CONSVLATV ANTE CVRRVM SVVM DVCI IVSSIT. TERTIVM CONSVL ABSENS CREATVS EST. QVARTVM CONSVL TEVTONORVM EXERCITVM DELEVIT. QVINTVM CONSVL CIMBROS FVDIT, ET IIS ET TEVTONIS ITERVM TRIVMPHAVIT. REM PVBLICAM TVRBATAM SEDITIONIBVS TRIBVNI PLEBIS ET PRAETORIS QVI ARMATI CAPITOLIVM OCCVPAVERANT, SEXTVM CONSVL VINDICAVIT. POST SEPTVAGESIMVM ANNVM PATRIA PER ARMA CIVILIA EXPVLSVS ARMIS RESTITVTVS SEPTIMVM CONSVL FACTVS EST. DE MANVBIIS CIMBRICIS ET TEVTONICIS AEDEM HONORI ET VIRTVTI VICTOR FECIT. VESTE TRIVMPHALI, CALCIS PATRICIIS. . . .

Gaius Marius, son of Gaius. Consul seven times, Praetor, tribune etc., etc. As Consul he waged war with Jugurtha, King of Numidia, took him prisoner, and in the triumph in his second Consulship ordered him to be led captive before his chariot. In his absence he was made Consul for the third time. In his fourth Consulship he destroyed the army of the Teutones. In his fifth Consulship he routed the Cimbri and celebrated a second triumph over them and over the Teutones. In his sixth Consulship, when the State was disturbed by armed risings, he suppressed the tribune and the praetor who had occupied the Capitol in arms. He was more than 70 years of age when he was expelled from his country in civil war: but he was restored by force of arms and made Consul for the seventh time. As Victor he dedicated a Temple to Honour and Valour from the spoils of the Cimbri and Teutones and (entered the Senate?) in triumphal costume and wearing patrician shoes. . . .

CIL, I[2], XXXII. Cf. *Degrassi Ins. It.* XIII. 3, p. 23

SENATVS SVPPLICATIONES DIS IMMORTALIBVS . . . AVCTORE IMP. CAES. NERVA. TRAIANO. AVG. GERM. DACICO. SENATVS ORNAMENTA TRIVMPHAL DECR. STATVAMQ. IN FORO AVG. PONENDAM CENSVIT.

The Senate decreed thanks to the immortal gods . . . and on the authority of the Emperor Trajan Augustus Germanicus Dacicus, voted him (Cornelius Palma) *ornamenta triumphalia*, and the placing of a statue in the Forum of Augustus. (A.D. 107)

CIL, VI. 1386

D.M.T. FLAVIO AVG. LIB. LIBERALI AEDITVO AED MARTIS VLTORIS CLAVDIA EXOCHE CONIVGI BENEMERENTI ET SIBE FECIT VIXIT ANNOS LVII.

To the departed spirits of T. Flavius Liberalis, freedman of Augustus, attendant in the Temple of Mars Ultor, set up by Claudia Exoche for her worthy husband, and for herself. She lived 57 years.

CIL, VI. 8709

Here, for once, literary sources and the evidence of archaeology are both rich and complementary. Augustus failed to get all the land he wanted, and the site is in fact curtailed on the north-east side. Presumably these difficulties account both for the delay in completing the project (begun 37 B.C.: temple dedicated 1st August, 2 B.C.), and for the huge precinct wall (a firebreak?) which shut the forum off from the Subura and now forms its most conspicuous feature. While it followed, basically, Caesar's pattern of a temple in a piazza, surrounded by colonnades, the plan of Augustus' forum is in fact more complex and sophisticated—notably in the two hemicycles, which make better use of a cramped site and add variety and dignity. As so often, Augustus follows Caesar and surpasses him. The ancient college of the Salii, as priests of Mars, were put in charge of the temple: it was the savour from one of their feasts that attracted the wandering attention of Claudius.

The records of the Arval Brethren show that they also met on occasion in the temple of Mars. The epitaph of the *aedituus*—one of two that we have—shows that he was a freedman of Augustus. The use of the temple as a bank for private deposits is attested by the passage of Juvenal: thoughts of sacrilege did not deter the burglars who made the successful break-in, presumably not long before he wrote and perhaps during the Hadrianic restoration. The helmet of Mars which they took away will have been detachable, as parts of statues often were, and probably of bronze, which could be melted down. This later and faintly comic incident must not impede appreciation of the purposes to which Augustus dedicated the temple and forum on high occasions of state. These are at once appropriate to Mars, as god of war and divine ancestor of the Roman people, and to Augustus, founder of the New Order and of the Julio-Claudian line. They are concerned, as Suetonius says, with issues of war and triumph, of maintaining and extending Roman power.

The provincial governors who left for their commands, the returning conquerors who deposited the tokens of their victories, did so before a great crowd of witnesses. These were the illustrious men of the past, and above all the *triumphatores*, whose statues stood along the colonnades, each with the records (*elogia*) of his deeds attached—just as the *imagines* of ancestors stood in the hall of a great Roman house. Only since the excavations carried out by Italian archaeologists between 1925 and 1932, and thanks to the interpretation by Degrassi and others of their findings, has it been possible to form some idea of the programme of this Hall of Fame. Briefly, Degrassi has shown that the niches in the colonnades and the hemicycles provide for a notional 108 statues. These will have been less than life-size and probably of marble rather than bronze. The passage from the *Fasti* is invaluable for their arrangement. On one side (in fact, the colonnade on the right facing the temple), the Julio-Claudians, headed by Aeneas: on the other, the *illustres viri* of the Republic. Thirty-four niches have actually been recovered, and 17 republican statues can be identified from the portions of their *elogia* that survive. Other sources add two to this list: and from the Julio-Claudian side can be added the names, besides 'all the Kings of Alba'. These statues are known to have been copied in provincial cities, notably at Pompeii and Arretium. While the wording of the Pompeian inscriptions differs from the Roman prototypes, it seems that at Arretium it did not. At any rate, the substantial fragment of the *elogium* of C. Marius—found near the Porta del Populo and almost certainly from the Forum of Augustus—is exactly reproduced in the longer inscription from Arretium, which is quoted here (p. 126). The other *elogia* given here are: Aeneas (from Rome and from Pompeii), Romulus (Pompeii), and L. Aemilius Paullus (Arretium).

A full list of those identified will be found in Degrassi (op. cit. p. 8); they include, among the Julio-Claudians, the father of Julius Caesar, the young Marcellus (died 23 B.C.), and Nero Claudius Drusus (died 9 B.C.), whose *elogium* ends EXSTINCTUS IN GERMANIA. Among the Republicans were Camillus, Appius Claudius Caecus, C. Duilius, Ti. Sempronius Gracchus (father of the Gracchi), Scipio Aemilianus and Sulla. Julius Caesar must have been there. What of Pompey? It would be interesting to know: Virgil treats Pompey with consummate skill in the roll-call of Roman heroes in *Aeneid* VI, 825ff: party feelings will have mellowed by 2 B.C. Most important, what of Augustus himself? He will not have included himself among the *illustres viri*, but we know that the *quadriga* voted him for his Spanish victories stood in the forum. Moreover, in the hall at the north-west corner there are traces of a colossal statue (Plate 40), supposed to be that of Augustus. This is not mentioned in any literary source; it may belong to the Hadrianic restoration.

The mention of the honorary statue to Cornelius Palma shows that *triumphatores* were being added as late as the reign of Trajan. The triumphal arches for Germanicus and the younger Drusus (incidentally, excavation has revealed their footings) were of course wholly appropriate: they are both Julio-Claudians and *triumphatores*. The quotation from Horace, which does not refer directly to the Forum of Augustus, shows the role of such statues in bringing back to life the heroic dead.

The cardinal importance of the Forum for Augustus' propaganda should now be apparent. Here, as in the noble passage of *Aeneid* VI—which may indeed have influenced Augustus' design—are gathered together the great men of the Roman past, and their memories are invoked. In words of unquestionable sincerity Augustus binds himself and his successors to live by their rule—the Principate is to be the Republic restored. He adjures the Roman people to see to it that they do. But he does not say what the Roman people are to do if the *principes* fall away.

THE TEMPLE OF PEACE

Vespasian began several new buildings: the Temple of Peace near the Forum etc., etc. . . .

SUETONIUS, *Vespasian*, 9

Should we not count . . . the Temple of Peace, built by the Emperor Vespasian Augustus, as one of the noblest buildings the world has ever seen?

PLINY, *Natural History*, XXXVI. 102

Once the triumph was over, and the Roman Empire established on secure foundations, Vespasian decided to erect a Temple of Peace. This was erected quickly, in a style to surpass all human imagination. He drew on limitless resources of wealth: he embellished it with ancient masterpieces of painting and sculpture, so that in that shrine were assembled and displayed all objects which men had once travelled the world to see, when they were kept separately in different countries. Here too he stored his especial pride, the golden vessels from the Temple of the Jews: but the Book of the Law and the purple awnings from the Sanctuary he ordered to be placed and kept in the imperial palace.

JOSEPHUS, *Jewish War*, VII. 158–62

In the sixth consulship of Vespasian, and the fourth of Titus (A.D. 75), the Temple of Peace was dedicated.

DIO CASSIUS, *Roman History*, LXVI. 15

The following omens occurred before the death of Commodus . . . a night conflagration, starting in a private house, spread to the Temple of Peace and destroyed a portion of the spoils of Arabia and Egypt . . . (A.D. 191).

DIO CASSIUS, *Roman History*, LXXII. 22. 4

Then (Constantius) surveyed . . . the Temple of Venus and Rome, the Forum Pacis, the Theatre of Pompey . . . and all the other splendours of the Eternal City.

AMMIANUS MARCELLINUS, XVI. 10

in foro Pacis per dies septem terra mugitum dedit.

There were rumblings of the earth for seven consecutive days in the Forum of Peace (A.D. 408).

MARCELLINUS in *Chronica Minora*, II. 69

At Rome the vast number of works of art is such, and their effacement from our memory so effective, that this and the endless round of duties and official business render serious study impossible for us all. To appreciate such works of art calls for leisure, and profound silence in our surroundings. So it is that no-one knows the name of the maker of that statue of Venus which the Emperor Vespasian set up in the precincts of the Temple of Peace, although it fully deserves to rank with the old masters.

PLINY, *Natural History*, XXXVI. 27

Among the works I have referred to, all the most celebrated have now been dedicated in Rome by the Emperor Vespasian, in his Temple of Peace and other public buildings. Nero's rapacity had brought them all to Rome, to be placed in the reception-rooms of the Golden House.

PLINY, *Natural History*, XXXIV. 84

The following account I heard personally while staying in Rome, from a Roman gentleman who was a member of the Senate. He said that, when Atalaric . . . ruled Italy, a herd of cattle came into Rome from the country, passing late in the evening through the forum called the Forum of Peace. (There once stood the ancient Temple of Peace, struck by lightning.) In front of this Forum is an ancient fountain, and by it a bronze bull, the work, I think, of either Pheidias or Lysippus. Indeed, in this quarter there are many works of these two artists; in another case the inscription on the statue proves it to be the work of Pheidias. There too is Myron's calf: for the Romans were at pains to carry off all the finest works of Greece to embellish Rome. Now it happened that one of the cattle—a steer—left the herd, mounted up to the fountain, and stood above the bull. And a passing Etruscan—a rustic fellow it would seem—understood the portent, for even today the Etruscans have the gift of prophecy, and he said that one day a eunuch would bring down the ruler of Rome. At the time they only laughed at the Etruscan and his words. . . .

PROCOPIUS, *Gothic War*, VIII. 21

Little remains of Vespasian's addition to the series of imperial fora, though its general plan is known from Colini's interpretation of the excavations of 1935–6. Here again the literary sources help to fill gaps in our knowledge. Officially, the Peace commemorated was that restored to the Roman world by the victorious conclusion of the Jewish War. But the end of the Civil Wars of A.D. 69 must have been no less important.

The Templum Pacis, dedicated in A.D. 75, stood next to the Forum of Augustus: the founder of the second imperial dynasty would have in mind the architectural projects of the founder of the first. The Ara Pacis commemorated the Peace established by Augustus, so too did the Forum of Augustus and the Temple of Apollo. Elements of all three reappear in the design of the Templum Pacis. The *τέμενος* or precinct was a great colonnaded square, in which masterpieces of Greek sculpture were displayed around what may have been formal flower-beds. The Temple, the central of three buildings along the east range, was flanked by one, perhaps by two, libraries. Since the wall of one of these displayed a revised version of Agrippa's *Forma Urbis*, it is tempting to suppose that a version of his map of the Empire was shown on the other.

The Temple housed the spoils from Jerusalem (see p. 116); the cult-statue stood in an apse. In the choice of a theme for the statues on the colonnades, Vespasian could not follow Augustus. Where the Julio-Claudian line went back through Divus Julius and Aeneas to Venus, that of the Flavians went only to a tax-gatherer of Reate in the previous generation. So Vespasian—perhaps *faute de mieux*—turned to Greek art. Pliny, our chief authority, names also a Scylla by Nicomachus, the

'Hero' of Timanthes, and the painting of Ialysus, founder of Rhodes, by Protogenes. There is an obvious discrepancy between Josephus' picture of the imperial collector purchasing from unlimited wealth, and what Pliny says about his taking over the art collection from the Golden House of Nero. The second carries more conviction. Josephus employs the argument still used to justify metropolitan collections, while Pliny adduces the satiety that the agglomeration may bring. Perhaps the display of statues in the Loggia della Signoria at Florence may give some idea of the general effect.

The *Forma Urbis* went through yet another revision, by Septimius Severus, after the fire of A.D. 191. This is the Marble Plan known to us through fragments: others may yet be discovered.

The earthquakes of A.D. 408 probably destroyed the Templum or 'Forum' Pacis beyond repair.

The passage of Procopius gives a vivid and unusual picture of Rome in the early sixth century. The classical world has faded but not quite vanished: the Greek statues have outlived the Temple of Peace: Etruscans still have the gift of prophecy. But the cattle, coming in from the country through the ruins of imperial magnificence, foretell the shrivelled Rome of the Middle Ages, as well as the triumph of the eunuch Narses and the short-lived Byzantine recovery of Italy.

THE FORUM OF NERVA

Domitian . . . built the Forum which now bears the name of Nerva. . . .

SUETONIUS, *Domitian*, 5

Before his death . . . Domitian dreamed that Minerva, whom he adored fervently, came out of her shrine to warn him that she had been disarmed by Jupiter and could save him no longer.

SUETONIUS, *Domitian*, 15

Annorum nitidique sator pulcerrime mundi
publica quem primum vota precesque vocant,
pervius exiguos habitabas ante penates,
plurima qua medium Roma terebat iter:
nunc tua Caesareis cinguntur limina donis
et fora tot numeros, Iane, quot ora geris.
at tu, sancte pater, tanto pro munere gratus
ferrea perpetua claustra tuere sera.

Fair father of the year and of the starry sky, to whom first of all the gods public prayers are made! Once you lived in a little temple, and one open to traffic, worn down by the tread of mighty Rome. Now your threshold is hung with gifts from Caesar, now you count four *fora*, as many as the faces you bear. Honoured god, be thankful for this great gift: guard your temple gate with a bolt that is always shut.

MARTIAL, *Epigrams*, x. 28

IMP. NERVA. CAESAR. AVG. GERMANICVS. PONT. MAX. TRIB. POT. II. COS. III P.P. AEDEM MINERVAE FECIT.

The Emperor Nerva . . . tribunician power for the second time, consul for the fourth (A.D. 97), built the Temple of Minerva.

CIL, VI. 953

In the Forum of Nerva (which they call Forum Transitorium) Alexander Severus set up colossal statues of all the Emperors who had been deified. Some were nude, and on foot, others on horseback: each had bronze columns recording his deeds. This was done after the model of Augustus, who had erected in his Forum marble statues of the great men of Rome, together with a list of their deeds.

HISTORIA AUGUSTA, *Alexander Severus*, 28. 6

Alone of the imperial *fora*, that of Nerva did not trace its origin to any great political event. Its alternative name, Forum Transitorium, reveals its purpose, for it was indeed a passage way, and, as Martial says, on a much frequented route, which led from the Forum Romanum to the Subura. The old Argiletum had earlier served this purpose, but the building of the Templum Pacis must have made it shabby and out of context. Vespasian may have had the idea of a colonnaded street: from that it was a short step to Domitian's plan of an elongated forum containing a temple to his personal protectress, Minerva. But it fell to Nerva to dedicate the temple, and in the Forum too his name has obliterated that of his hated predecessor. The site of the Temple of Janus, mentioned by Martial, is not known, though probably it was in the centre of the Forum, and from it the god, represented by the ancient four-faced statue that came from Falerii in 241 B.C., looked out over the fora of Augustus, Julius, Pacis and Nerva.

THE FORUM OF TRAJAN

SENATVS POPVLVSQVE ROMANVS IMP. CAESARI. DIVI. NERVAE. F. NERVAE TRAIANO. AVG. GERM. DACICO. PONTIF. MAXIMO. TRIB. POT.

XVII. IMP. VI. COS. VI. P.P. AD DECLARANDVM QVANTAE. ALTITVDINIS. MONS. ET. LOCVS. TANTIS. OPERIBVS. SIT. EGESTVS.

The Senate and the People of Rome to the Emperor, Caesar Nerva, son of the deified Nerva, Traianus Augustus, Germanicus, Dacicus, Pontifex Maximus, etc. etc. to demonstrate how lofty a hill and (what area of) ground was carried away for these mighty works.

CIL, VI. 960 (A.D. 113)

And in his Forum he set up a great column, both for his own burial-place, and to show the scale of his works in building the forum. For all that ground was hilly, but he excavated it to a depth equal to the height of the column, and then levelled the whole area.

DIO CASSIUS, *Roman History*, LXVIII. 16

S.P.Q.R. IMP. CAESARI. DIVI. NERVAE F. NERVAE TRAIANO. AVGVSTO. GERMANICO. DACICO. PONTIF. MAX. TRIBVNICIA. POTEST. XVI. IMP. VI. COS. VI. P.P. OPTIME DE REPVBLICA MERITO. DOMI. FORISQVE.

The Senate and People of Rome, to the Emperor. . . . Traianus Augustus etc., etc., for his supreme service to the State in war and peace.

CIL, VI. 959

DIVO TRAIANO PARTHICO ET DIVAE PLOTINAE. DIVI. TRAIANI. PARTHICI. VXORI. IMP. CAES. TRAIANVS. HADRIANVS. AVGVSTVS. P.M. TRIB. POT. COS. III. PARENTIBVS SVIS.

The Emperor, Caesar Traianus Hadrianus Augustus etc., etc. to his parents, the deified Traianus Parthicus and his wife the deified Plotina.

CIL, VI. 966

Having exhausted the treasury in the war against the Marcomanni, Marcus Aurelius could not bring himself to impose an extraordinary taxation on the provinces. He therefore held a public sale of the imperial treasure in the Forum of Trajan, selling goblets of gold and crystal and agate, also the flagons made for Kings, his wife's silken gowns embroidered with gold, and the rich collection of jewels he found in a secret cabinet belonging to Hadrian.

HISTORIA AUGUSTA, *Marcus*, XVII. 4

CL. CLAVDIANI. V.C. CLAVDIO CLAVDIANO V.C. TRIBVNO ET NOTARIO INTER CETERAS DECENTES ARTES PRAEGLORIOSISSIMO POETARVM LICET AD MEMORIAM SEMPITERNAM CARMINA AB EODEM SCRIPTA SVFFICIANT ADTAMEN TESTIMONII GRATIA OB IVDICII SVI EIDEM D.D. N.N. ARCADIVS ET HONORIVS FELICISSIMI AC DOCTISSIMI IMPERATORES

SENATV PETENTE STATVAM IN FORO DIVI TRAIANI ERIGI COLLOCARIQVE IVSSERVNT

ΕΙΝ ΕΝΙ ΒΙΡΓΙΛΙΟΙΟ ΝΟΟΝ ΚΑΙ ΜΟΥϹΑΝ ΟΜΗΡΟΥ
ΚΛΑΥΔΙΑΝΟΝ ΡΩΜΗ ΚΑΙ ΒΑϹΙΛΗϹ ΕΘΕϹΑΝ.

To Claudius Claudianus, *vir clarissimus*, son of Claudius Claudianus, *vir clarissimus*, tribune and notary. Among other liberal accomplishments he excelled in supreme measure in those of the Poet. His poems, by themselves, are enough to win him immortal memory, but, as a testimony of their favour, and at the request of the Senate, Our Noble Lords, the most fortunate and learned Emperors, Arcadius and Honorius, have ordered that his statue should be erected and placed in the Forum of Trajan.

> 'Rome and the Emperors placed the mind of Virgil and the muse of Homer in a single man—Claudian.'

CIL, VI. 1710 (Naples Museum)

> Scinduntur tunicae sartae modo, longa coruscat
> serraco veniente abies, atque altera pinum
> plaustra vehunt, nutant alte populoque minantur,
> nam si procubuit qui saxa Ligustica portat
> axis et eversum fudit super agmina montem,
> quid superest de corporibus? quis membra, quis ossa
> invenit? obtritum vulgi perit omne cadaver
> more animae.

Tunics just patched are torn, the lofty fir-tree quivers as the waggon goes by: others carry a pine that waves about on high, a danger to the people. If there is a broken axle of some truck carrying Carrara marble, and the whole load is poured down over the passers-by—will there be anything left at all of their bodies? Who could find their bones and limbs? Every corpse has been squashed flat and disappeared—just like their souls.

JUVENAL, *Satires*, III. 254–61

The Forum of Trajan is the supreme achievement of city-planning in Rome. It completes the series of imperial fora, and is integrated axially and spatially with its four predecessors. But it is different in scale and kind. The temple-within-a-forum plan is abandoned, for the temple of Divus Traianus in the second courtyard is a Hadrianic addition. Instead the plan is that of a complex of buildings serving administration, law, commerce, and the arts, symmetrically disposed among spacious courts and hemicycles so as to form virtually a city-centre in itself. In certain of its features the architect, Apollodorus of Damascus, clearly set out to challenge and surpass the best work of the past. The great front court—the forum proper—with its hemicycles and colonnades, is an improved version of the Forum of Augustus. Basilica Ulpia, in the same tradition, outdoes the two earlier basilicas, Aemilia and Julia. Other features make their impact by originality. The Mercatus Traiani, with its tiers of shops and great market-hall in terraces against the flank of the Quirinal Hill, has no rival in Rome. It is a combination of the *macellum* or market-hall, with rows of shops (*tabernae*), the whole making up a commercial centre of a new kind. And the Column, while it found imitators, remained without a peer. Its reliefs immortalize perhaps the finest of all Roman armies, which under its imperial commander removed the Dacian menace from the northern frontiers, and opened up for Roman settlement new lands beyond the Danube. The glory Trajan won in war was matched by his generosity in peace (see p. 89). When the Senate hailed him as 'Optimus Princeps' it was not using words lightly; there was deliberate choice of a superlative hitherto reserved, in official usage, for Jupiter himself. Only in the light of this concept can we understand the magnificence of the Forum of Trajan. What Virgil, Horace, and Livy did for Augustus through literature, Apollodorus intended to do for Trajan through architecture. As, indeed, he did. The comments of observers, such as Constantius (see p. 29) and Cassiodorus, establish that for late antiquity, the Forum of Trajan reigned unchallenged as the finest thing in Rome. A more lasting compliment was paid by the architects of the fourth-century Basilica of S. Paolo fuori le Mura, who reproduced the dimensions of Basilica Ulpia in the nave of their great church. And even the destructive zeal of the Middle Ages halted before Trajan's Column, which had a preservation-order applied to it by a decree of the Roman Senate in 1162. This was so enlightened, be it noted, as to provide death as the penalty for any destroyer. Of the inscriptions quoted, CIL, VI. 959, is from the Basilica Ulpia, and is dated A.D. 112. A fragment of the Fasti Ostienses gives the date of dedication of the column—and presumably of the Forum, as May 12th, A.D. 113. CIL, VI. 960 is the dedicatory inscription of the Column; its superb lettering (Plate 41) is composed of the finest Roman capitals ever cut. Unfortunately, the wording is less clear. What is meant by the *mons et locus* whose dimensions are to be demonstrated by the height of the column (128 Roman, 100 English feet?) Round this problem has raged a long and spirited controversy. Dio's notion of a ridge connecting the Quirinal and the Capitol has won support, but geology and archaeology are emphatic against it. Another view is that the *mons* is the pile of precious stones and marbles accumulated for the building. Another—which at present seems to hold the field—is that the inscription refers to the height cut away from the flanks of the Quirinal hill for the Mercatus. That the inscription did not mention Trajan must rule out Dio's suggestion that the Column was originally intended as a burial place for that Emperor. It seems to be due to Hadrian that the urns containing his ashes and those of Plotina were eventually placed in the pedestal of the Column.

CIL, VI. 966 is the dedicatory inscription of the Temple of Divus Traianus, which should be more properly known as that of Trajan and Plotina, by analogy with the other imperial pair, Antoninus and Faustina, commemorated in the Forum.

Several inscriptions survive from the statues of famous men set up *in foro Traiani*. That quoted here honours the poet Claudian (*c.* A.D. 400), and is composed in the inflated style of late imperial panegyric. It is now to be seen in the Naples Museum.

No literary source describes, or even mentions, the reliefs on Trajan's Column. Yet they constitute a document in themselves—a book, indeed, as is emphasized by the siting of the Column between the two libraries, and by the spiral which carries them, as on the unrolled scroll of an ancient *liber*. The analogy can be carried further, if one recalls the Roman view that history is akin to poetry. It is not fanciful, then, to regard the sculptures as the expression in art of a prose epic. And, like all great epics, it moves on more than one level. On the factual, it narrates Trajan's victories in the two Dacian wars. On the symbolic, it represents the *ratio* and *disciplina* that made a Roman army superior to the undisciplined valour of the barbarians, and also the *labor* and *virtus* required from them and from their commander before victory can be won. By a happy concomitance, the high mark of Roman military achievement has been matched by the high mark of Roman art.

Juvenal's lines probably, but not certainly, refer to the transport of building materials for Trajan's Forum. Note the same word—*mons*—for the load on the lorry. Note too that the feeling of individual helplessness before the brute mass of heavy traffic is not peculiar to modern times.

THE ARCH OF CONSTANTINE

IMP. CAES. FL. CONSTANTINO MAXIMO P.F. AVGVSTO. S.P.Q.R. QVOD. INSTINCTV. DIVINITATIS. MENTIS. MAGNITVDINE. CVM EXERCITV. SVO. TAM. DE. TYRANNO. QVAM. DE. OMNI. EIVS. FACTIONE. VNO. TEMPORE. IVSTIS. REMPVBLICAM. VLTVS. EST. ARMIS. ARCVM. TRIVMPHIS. INSIGNEM. DICAVIT.

To the Emperor Caesar Flavius Constantinus Maximus, Pius, Felix, Augustus—since through the inspiration of the Deity, and in the greatness of his own mind, he with his army avenged the Commonwealth with arms rightly taken up, and at a single time defeated the Tyrant and all his Faction—the Senate and People of Rome dedicated this Arch adorned with Triumphs.

CIL, VI. 1139

The famous inscription is itself the only source for the Arch of Constantine, set up in A.D. 315 (or 316?) to commemorate the victory over Maxentius at the Battle of the Milvian Bridge in 312. Much care went into its wording, whose assonance and balance seem to echo that inscription which stood in the Circus Maximus in honour of Titus' conquest of Jerusalem (see p. 115). The veiled reference to the Vision of the Cross (instinctu divinitatis), and the appearance in the reliefs of Sol Invictus and Mithras as divine protectors of his army, catch perfectly the religious equivocations of the times. The message of the earlier triumphal reliefs—taken from monuments of Domitian, Trajan, Hadrian, and Marcus Aurelius—is less ambiguous. They bring Constantine into association with the greatest days of the Empire, and, especially, with Trajan. The *decennalia* of Constantine coincided, closely if not exactly, with the bicentenary of the dedication of Trajan's Forum. See Plates 43–44.

THE GOLDEN HOUSE OF NERO

Vestibulum eius fuit, in quo colossus CXX pedum staret ipsius effigie; tanta laxitas, ut porticus triplices miliarias haberet; item stagnum maris instar, circumsaeptum aedificiis ad urbium speciem; rura insuper, arvis atque vinetis et pascuis silvisque varia, cum multitudine omnis generis pecudum ac ferarum. In ceteris partibus cuncta auro lita, distincta gemmis unionumque conchis erant: cenationes laqueatae tabulis eburneis versatilibus, ut flores fistulatis, et unguenta desuper spargerentur; praecipua cenationum rotunda, quae perpetuo diebus ac noctibus vice mundi circumageretur; balineae marinis et albulis fluentes aquis. eiusmodi domum cum absolutum dedicaret, hactenus comprobavit, ut se diceret quasi hominem tandem habitare coepisse.

The entrance hall was designed for a colossal statue, 120 feet high, bearing Nero's head. So vast were the grounds, that triple colonnades ran for a mile. There was, too, an enormous lake, surrounded by buildings made to look like cities. The parklands contained fields, vineyards, pastures and woodlands; there were a great variety of animals, domestic and wild. Some parts of the palace were overlaid with gold, and studded with jewels and mother-of-pearl. The dining rooms had ceilings of ivory, with sliding panels to allow flowers and perfumes to be showered down upon the guests. The main dining room was a rotunda, which revolved slowly, day and night, like the vault of heaven itself. There were baths with a lavish supply of both sea-water and sulphur water. When the palace was completed on this sumptuous scale, Nero's approval as he dedicated it was confined to the remark 'At last I can begin to live like a human being!'

SUETONIUS, *Nero*, 31

Ceterum Nero usus est patriae ruinis extruxitque domum in qua haud perinde gemmae et aurum miraculo essent, solita pridem et luxu vulgata, quam arva et stagna et in modum solitudinum hinc silvae inde aperta spatia et prospectus, magistris et machinatoribus Severo et Celere. . . .

Nero made good use of this disaster to his country. For he built himself a palace, remarkable not so much for its gold and jewels—these are the usual trappings of luxury and have become commonplace—as for its meadows, its lakes, its artificial wilderness, now of woods and now of open spaces, and its vistas. Severus and Celer were the architects and engineers.

TACITUS, *Annals*, XV. 42

Piso . . . refused to allow Nero's murder (in his villa), however evil he might be. It would be an outrage against the laws of hospitality. The deed was better done in that hateful palace which had been spawned on the loot extracted from Roman citizens.

id. ib. 52

Roma domus fiet: Veios migrate Quirites,
si non et Veios occupat iste domus!

Rome will become a palace: Roman citizens, migrate to Veii! Unless that hated palace has reached Veii too!

Anon. in SUETONIUS, *Nero*, 39

Hic ubi sidereus propius videt astra colossus,
et crescunt media pegmata celsa via,
invidiosa feri radiabant atria regis,
unaque iam tota stabat in urbe domus.

Hic ubi conspicui venerabilis amphitheatri
  erigitur moles, stagna Neronis erant.
Hic ubi miramur velocia munera thermas,
  abstulerat miseris tecta superbus ager.
Claudia diffusas ubi porticus explicit umbras
  ultima pars aulae deficientis erat.
Reddita Roma sibi est, et sunt te praeside Caesar
  deliciae populi quae fuerant domini.

Here, where the glistening colossus views the stars at short range, where the scaffolding rises in the middle of the Sacred Way—here stretched wide the haughty entrance halls of the cruel tyrant, and a single great estate stood in the whole of Rome. Here, where the noble mass of the great amphitheatre is being built, was the lake of Nero. Here, where we admire the Thermae of Titus—that gift so quickly given—Nero's proud park had swallowed the cottages of the poor. Where the colonnade of Claudius' (temple) spreads its spacious shades, were the furthest bounds of that unfinished palace. Rome is restored to herself, and under your rule, Caesar, the people's pleasure is what once belonged to their lord and master.

MARTIAL, *Spectacula*, I. 2

Vespasian (restarted) a temple of the deified Claudius on the Caelian Hill, which had been begun by Agrippina, but almost destroyed by Nero.

SUETONIUS, *Vespasian*, 9

A recent artist was Famulus, grand and dignified, but also ornate and baroque. . . . He would paint for a few hours each day, and that in the most formal manner, always dressed in a toga, even on the scaffolding. The Golden House was the prison of his art, which is why no other important examples are extant.

PLINY, *Natural History*, XXXV. 120

(The reputation of some artists suffers because they have worked with others). . . . Such is the case of the Laocoon, in the palace of the Emperor Titus, a work to be ranked above any painting or bronze. From a single block of stone were carved Laocoon, his children, and the wonderful coils of the serpents, on an agreed plan by those supreme artists Hagesander, Polydorus, and Athenodorus of Rhodes.

Id. Ib. XXXVI. 37

Romae aurea domus incendio conflagravit.

At Rome the Golden House was destroyed by fire.

ST. JEROME, *Chornicle*, entry for A.D. 104

The splendours of the Domus Aurea have vanished as irretrievably as those of Nonesuch Palace of Henry VIII. It seems impossible to associate the sophisticated elegance described in the literary sources with the actual remains, enclosed like gloomy cellars by Apollodorus for the substructures of the Thermae of Trajan. Their frescoes and stuccoes—the only decorations to survive (Plate 45)—do not move us to the admiration they evoked from the artists of the Renaissance. It is possible to find something remarkable in the octagonal room with the domed roof and the artificial waterfall, but that is all. The only resource is to pay careful attention to the texts, to what they say and do not say. First, they make it plain that the envy and resentment caused by Nero's project were due, primarily, to the fact that it took up so much room (125 acres is the best modern estimate) in the heart of Rome. Horace had objected to luxury villas that evicted the peasants and sterilized good Italian agricultural land (*Odes*, III. 1. 33f.). Here, *a fortiori*, the objection was to the eviction of the urban poor, already rendered homeless by the Great Fire of A.D. 64 (see pp. 17 ff.). Second, as one might expect, Nero's combination of wealth and taste made the whole estate (*domus*) a *non-pareil*. New standards were set in landscape gardening, in the building of 'follies' in the park, in the luxury and decoration of the principal rooms, and in the ingenious devices with which they were fitted. The *subsellia*, the rooms which opened on to the colonnades where Nero displayed the works of art looted from Greece, and the *cenationes* or dining-rooms, were the most important of these. Two generations later, Hadrian's villa at Tivoli was conceived on the same scale of imaginative prodigality. Beyond this it is unsafe to go. The *cenatio rotunda*, in particular, has inspired some wild flights of solar and astrological symbolism. It is true that the passage of Suetonius does suggest some astronomical purpose, but Boethius has pointed out that this need not be more exotic than the planetarium or orrery—whichever it was—which Varro describes from his villa at Casino. It may, indeed, have anticipated those restaurants that revolve to allow for changing vistas—like those at Top o' the Mark in San Francisco, or now in the Post Office Tower in London.

Martial's poem shows how Vespasian and Titus won favour by converting features of the Domus Aurea for the pleasure of the Roman people. The thermae of Titus were constructed in great haste (*thermis celeriter extructis*, Suetonius *Titus* 7), perhaps incorporating the *balnea* of the palace. The lake was filled in to become the site of the *amphitheatrum Flavianum* (see p. 140). The Colossus now bore the features of the Sun God, not of Nero (see p. 117). The Temple of Claudius was completed, and its colonnade thrown open to the public. But Vespasian and Titus continued to live in the palace proper; although most of the works of

Greek art were transferred to the Temple of Peace (p. 130), Titus did not part with that *tour-de-force*, the Laocoon. Either it was lost after the fire of A.D. 104, or else it was transferred to the Baths of Trajan. Its discovery in 1506 moved the artists of the day to the same extravagant estimate as that of Pliny, and launched the long and ambivalent influence it has since wielded on the taste of Europe. The work of Famulus enjoyed a shorter vogue, though it influenced Raphael in decorating the *Stanze* of the Vatican: thus his elaborate, contrived art did, in a sense, emerge at last from its prison.

AMPHITHEATRUM FLAVIUM OR COLOSSEUM

Vespasian began work on the Flavian Amphitheatre, centrally placed in the city; this had been a favourite project of Augustus.

SUETONIUS, *Vespasian*, 9

None of Titus' predecessors ever displayed such generosity. At the time of the dedication of the Flavian Amphitheatre and the adjacent Thermae, he provided a most lavish display of gladiators. He also staged sea-battles on the artificial lake (built by Augustus): after the water had been let out, the basin was used for yet other gladiatorial contests and for a wild-beast hunt (*venatio*), in which 5,000 animals of different kinds were despatched in a single day. Titus was naturally kind-hearted. . . .

SUETONIUS, *Titus*, 17

At gladiatorial shows Commodus would come to watch and stay to fight, throwing a purple cloth over his bare shoulders. All his exploits, whether as gladiator or pimp, were publicized in the *Acta Diurna*. . . . The people would applaud his frequent exploits as though he were a god, but he thought they were mocking him, and ordered the marines who were handling the awnings to butcher the Roman people in the Amphitheatre.

HISTORIA AUGUSTA, *Commodus*, 15

Alexander Severus ordered that the taxes paid by bawds and prostitutes, male and female, should no longer go the public treasury, but be used for the restorations to the theatre of Marcellus, the Circus Maximus, the Amphitheatre, and the Stadium of Domitian.

HISTORIA AUGUSTA, *Alexander Severus*, 24

On another day Probus produced in the Amphitheatre one hundred male lions at a single performance: their roaring brought on a thunderstorm. Every one was despatched as he came from his den, a method of slaughter which produced nothing much for the spectators. For there were none of those charges which wild beasts habitually make when loosed out of cages: moreover, many refused to come out and had to be despatched with arrows. Then he displayed one hundred leopards from Libya: then one hundred from Syria: then one hundred lionesses together with three hundred bears. Displays on such a scale were lavish rather than enjoyable. He further displayed three hundred pairs of gladiators, among whom were many of the Blemmyae who had been prisoners in his triumph, also Germans, Sarmatians, and brigands from Isauria.

HISTORIA AUGUSTA, *Probus*, 19

Alypius . . . went ahead of me to Rome to study law, and there became obsessed with a strange enthusiasm for gladiatorial displays. He began by hating them, and refused to attend. But one day during the season for this savage and bloodthirsty sport he met a group of friends and fellow-students coming back from dinner. They brushed aside his protests and demurs and carried him off to the Arena. 'Well,' he said, 'you may get me here by force, but don't think that you can force me to watch the show, or give it my attention. I shall be there, but I shall behave as though I were not: so I shall prove myself superior to you and the games!' . . . They arrived, and the place was seething with bloodlust and cruelty. They found their seats. Alypius shut his eyes, resolved to detach himself from these atrocities. Unfortunately, he did not close his ears as well. For an incident in the fight provoked the crowds to a great roar, and this so startled him that could not contain his curiosity. But still he was confident that, be it what it might, it would be so disgusting that he would be able to control himself. So he opened his eyes. At once he was stabbed, and with a far more deadly wound than that which the gladiator he was trying to see had received in his body. He fell, and fell far more miserably than the man who had caused the crowd to bay with excitement. . . . For at the moment he saw blood, it was as though he had drunk a full draught of savage passion. Far from turning away, he riveted his gaze on the scene and took in all its frightfulness, unaware of what he was doing. The cruelty of the fighting delighted him, the thrill of seeing blood shed was an intoxication. No longer was he the man who had been dragged to the Arena, he was part of that vile crowd, fit companion for those who had brought him.

Why go on? He watched, he cheered, he sweated with excitement: when he left the Arena, his mind was so contaminated that he had no peace till he could go again . . . now leading his friends, fresh sheep for the slaughter. But from this madness, most merciful Lord, you rescued him . . . though much later.

ST. AUGUSTINE, *Confessions*, VI. 8

. . . LOCA ADSIGNATA IN AMPHITHEATRO L. AELIO PLAVTIO LAMIA, Q. PACTVMIO FRONTONE CONSVLIBVS ACCEPTVM AB LABERIO MAXIMO PROCVRATORE PRAEFECTO ANNONAE L. VENVLEIO APRONIANO MAGISTRO, CVRATORE THYRSO LIBERTO, FRATRIBVS ARVALIBVS MAENIANO I CVNEO XII GRADIBVS MARMOREIS VIII PEDES V . . . ET MAENIANO SVMMO II CVNEO . . . ET MAENIANO SVMMO IN LIGNEIS TABVLATIONE LIII . . . SVMMA PEDES CENTVM DVODETRIGINTA DEVNX SEMIVNCIA.

ARVAL BRETHREN.

Allocation of seats in the Amphitheatre: in the consulship of L. Aelius Plautus Lamia and Q. Pactumius Fronto: received from Laberius Maximus, prefect of the Annona, imperial agent, through L. Venuleius Apronianus, Master (of the college) and Thyrsus, clerk-in-charge, for the Arval Brethren:—In the First Storey, Wedge XII, on the eight marble rows, five feet . . . and in Second Storey, Wedge II . . . and in the Top Storey, on the wooden rows, on Row 53, . . . A total of 128 feet 11½ inches.

Acta Fratrum Arvalium, CIL, VI. 2059

SALVIS DOMINIS NOSTRIS THEODOSIO ET PLACIDO VALENTINIANO AVGVSTIS RVFVS CAECINA FELIX LAMPADIVS VIR CLARISSIMVS ET INLVSTRIS PRAEFECTVS VRBI HARENAM AMPHITHEATRI A NOVO VNA CVM PODIO ET PORTIS POSTICIIS, SED ET REPARATIS SPECTACVLI GRADIBVS RESTITVIT.

In the reign of the Emperors Theodosius and Placidus Valentinianus, Rufus Caecina Felix Lampadius . . . City Prefect, completely restored the Arena of the Amphitheatre and the Imperial Box, and the gateways on the outer face, also repairing the rows of seats of the amphitheatre.

(after A.D. 422) CIL, VI. 1763

The great amphitheatre with which the Flavians superseded the far more civilized project of Nero (see p. 140), is usually known by its later synonym, the Colosseum. An enormity, in every sense of the word, the admiration which it has been so oddly accorded over the centuries stems from the refusal to discriminate between means and ends. Its designers expended a good deal of technical ingenuity to enable some 50,000 people to glut by proxy their sadistic instincts, and to prevent them, while so engaged, from getting out of hand in a riot. Since the problem of handling large and vicious crowds is acute in the modern world, a certain interest attaches to the means they devised—the separate entrances to the different levels (*maeniana*), themselves divided into isolated *cunei* or wedges, within which the spectator gained access to a numbered seat (*locus*) in a numbered row (*gradus*): the broad *vomitoria* or passageways making for the quick filling and clearing of the stands: the ingenuity of the elevators for the animals, the awning or *velum* handled by marines, and so on. Apart from this, the passage of Augustine says all that is really worth saying about the Flavian Amphitheatre.

The first two passages refer to the commencement of the Amphitheatre, under Vespasian, and to its dedication by Titus in A.D. 80 (see also p. 140). The third describes the alarming—for the spectators—

exploits of the Emperor Commodus as a gladiator. The imperial nerves were touchy, and applause apt to be taken the wrong way. The two principal types of entertainment provided were *ludi* or gladiatorial shows and *venationes* or animal hunts. The passage of the *Confessions* describes the former: the great *venationes* staged under Probus are described in the passage from the Historia Augusta. The *ludi* were discontinued in 404 (to the disgust of the populace): the *venationes* lasted until 523.

The inscription assigning seats to the Arval Brethren (p. 143) is important and controversial. Note the exactitude with which the space at their disposal is measured, also that it was 'in all parts of the house', thus enabling them to give tickets to clients or servants. Note too that the distribution of reserved seats—no doubt an invidious task—was carried out by the *praefectus annonae*, one of the highest imperial officials in Rome.

Two of the many known restorations are represented—those carried out by Alexander Severus, after damage done by lightning in 217, and that by Rufus Caecina, the City Prefect, presumably after damage by the earthquake of 422. At this later period the building was used for *venationes* only.

THE PALATINE

Hoc quodcumque vides, hospes, qua maxima Roma est,
ante Phrygem Aeneam collis et herba fuit.
Atque ubi Navali stant sacra Palatia Phoebo
Evandri profugae procubuere boves.

All that you see, stranger, where mighty Rome lies spread to view, was once but grass and hill before Phrygian Aeneas came: where now the Palatine stands, sacred to Apollo who gave the Naval victory, there once Evander's wandering cattle lay at rest.

PROPERTIUS, *Elegies*, IV. I. 1–4

PAR—ROMA CONDITA.

Festival of Pales—Foundation of Rome. (April 21)

Fasti Caeretani, CIL, 1^2, p. 213

Palilia dicta a Pale, quod ei feriae.

The Palilia are named from Pales, whose festival they are.

VARRO, *De lingua Latina*, VI. 15

Who does not know that the Roman people sprang from shepherds? . . . And must it not be certain that they were shepherds themselves, since they founded their city by choice on the Parilia? . . .

VARRO, *De re rustica*, II. I. 9

Alma Pales, faveas pastoria sacra canenti
prosequor officio si tua festa meo.
certe ego de vitulo cinerem stipulasque fabalis
saepe tuli plena, februa casta, manu:
certe ego transilui positas ter in ordine flammas
udaque roratas laurea misit aquas . . .

pastor, oves saturas ad prima crepuscula lustra:
unda prius spargat, virgaque verrat humum,
frondibus et fixis decorentur ovilia ramis
et tegat ornatas longa corona fores.
caerulei fiant puro de sulpure fumi,
tactaque fumanti sulpure balet ovis.

Kindly Pales, be gracious as I sing the shepherds rites, as I pay you my respects on your holy day. Often have I brought in handfuls the ashes of the calf and the beanstalks, the things for expiation. Certain is it that I have jumped through the triple row of flames, and have been sprinkled from the wet olive-branch. . . . Shepherd, when twilight falls, purify the full-fed sheep: sprinkle water on the ground, and sweep it with a broom. Fix leaves and branches over the fold: cover the door with a trailing garland. Make blue smoke from live sulphur, let the sheep bleat when the sulphur touches them.

OVID, *Fasti*, IV. 723–8; 735–40

contrahere agrestes et moenia ponere utrique
convenit, ambigitur, moenia ponat uter.
'Nil opus est' dixit 'certamine' Romulus 'ullo:
magna fides avium est: experiamur aves.'
Res placet: alter init nemorosi saxa Palati
alter Aventinum mane cacumen init.
Sex Remus, hic volucres bis sex videt ordine: pacto
statur, et arbitrium Romulus urbis habet.

The Twins had agreed to gather the country people together and found a walled city: it was still in doubt which of the two should be the founder. Then Romulus spoke, 'No need for great contention. Much trust is put in the birds: let us try them.' So it was agreed. Romulus went to the rocks of the wooded Palatine—Remus, at morning, to the top of the Aventine. Remus saw six birds, Romulus, twelve—one after the other. They observed their pact, and Romulus was given rule over the city.

OVID, *Fasti*, IV. 811–18

Propertius' lines contain the essence of the story of the Palatine—*collis et herba*—the hill with the grassy plateau must have attracted early pastoralists. Then comes the link with Aeneas, and the legendary founders of Rome: at once the poet takes his visitor to the Temple of Apollo, first of the great buildings of the imperial age. The modern visitor to the Palatine is confronted by this same juxtaposition of early and late, often puzzling because there is so much yet for archaeology to do.

Somewhere about 800 B.C. a band of shepherds from the Alban Hills must have brought their flocks across the Campagna to this hill. The rich grazing tempted them to stay. They built the timber huts whose postholes can be seen on the archaic site close to the House of Augustus. Their dead were buried in the cemetery in the Roman Forum (see Plate 1). This shepherd's village attracted to itself the legends of Evander and his Arcadians, of the coming of Aeneas, of Romulus and Remus, and the ritual foundation of the city of Rome. Today, as in ancient times, the birthday of Rome is celebrated on 21st April, the festival of Pales, the divinity (sex uncertain—a goddess in Ovid) who looks after flocks and herds. Ovid's description of the Parilia (*Fasti*, IV. 721–862) should be read as a whole. The simple language in which he describes the country rites of the shepherds take on graver tones as the theme passes to the foundation of the city, and the burden of its imperial destiny.

SOME EARLY PALATINE SITES

Scalae Caci

There is a passage on the Palatine Hill which slopes downward and has a stone stairway: it is called after him the Stairs of Cacius, and is near the site of what once was Cacius' house.

DIODORUS SICULUS, *Bibliotheca*, IV. 21

Romulus lived beside the steps called "the steps of the Fair Shore", which are those by which you go down from the Palatine to the Circus Maximus.

PLUTARCH, *Romulus*, 20. 5–6

Ficus Ruminalis and Lupercal

Amulius made his brother's daughter, Rhea Silvia, a Vestal Virgin, outwardly an honour, really that her perpetual virginity should deprive her of the hope of children. But I suppose that the Fates were resolved on the founding of this great city, and of the mightiest of all Empires, next to that of Heaven. The Vestal was seduced: she gave birth to twins: she named Mars as their father, either really believing it so, or thinking it better to ascribe her fault to the gods. But neither gods nor men could protect the mother and her babes from the King's cruelty: he ordered the priestess to be chained and put in prison, and the babes to be thrown into the river. But by singular good fortune the Tiber happened to be in flood, and because of the stagnant pools there was no access to the regular channel of the river. This made the men bearing the babes think that they might be drowned there, although the flow of the river was slight. So they carried out the King's orders by putting the babes down at the highest point of the flood . . . where the fig-tree Ruminalis stands now. This was a wild and lonely district at the time. Now the story goes that, when the basket in which the babies had been placed was left high and dry when the floods went down, a thirsty she-wolf came down from the hills, and made towards the sounds of the infant's cries. So gently did she bend her teats towards them and give them suck that the shepherd of the royal flock—Faustulus was his name—actually found her licking them with her tongue. The story goes on that he took them to his hut and gave them to his wife, Larentia, to bring up.

LIVY, I. III. 11–IV. 7

Now there was a wild fig-tree near by, which they called the Ruminalis. . . . Here the babies lay, and the fabled she-wolf gave them suck, and a woodpecker came to share in feeding and watching over them. Now these two animals are considered sacred to Mars: as for the woodpecker, the Latins give it special respect and veneration—so when the mother declared that Mars was the father of her children, this was all the more convincing. And yet some say she was tricked into it: she was really deflowered by Aemulius himself, who came to her in armour and ravished her. And others again say that the name of the children's nurse was ambiguous, and this has introduced the element of myth into the story. For in Latin *Lupae* means not only she-wolves but also prostitutes, a class to which belonged Acca Larentia, wife of Faustulus, who reared the infants.

PLUTARCH, *Romulus*, 4

The basket floated for a little while, then it struck a rock and overturned, and there lay the babies, whimpering and wallowing in the mud. At this a she-wolf appeared. She had just whelped, and her udders were swollen. So she gave them her teats to suck and with her tongue licked the mud off them. In the meantime a shepherd driving his sheep . . . saw the wolf licking the children, and for a while could not believe what he saw. Then he went for his followers and called them together: they could not believe him, so he brought them to see for themselves. When they saw . . . the wolf fondling the babes as though they were her own cubs and the babes clinging to her as their own mother, they thought they were looking at something supernatural. They advanced on her in a body, shouting to drive her away. But the wolf took little notice of the shepherds, but quietly left the children and went away. . . . Now there was a holy place not far away, covered over by dense trees, with a hollow rock from which a spring issued . . . there the wolf went to hide herself. The trees have gone now, to be sure, but they still point out the cave from which the spring flows; it is built up against the slope of the Palatine hill on the path to the Circus. A sacred precinct is near it, with a group of statues to commemorate the incident: it shows a she-wolf suckling two children, the figures being ancient workmanship in bronze. They say this was a holy spot of the Arcadians, who once settled there with Evander.

DIONYSIUS HALICARNASSUS, *Roman Antiquities*, I. 79. 7–8

Hinc lucum ingentem, quem Romulus acer asylum
rettulit, et gelida monstrat sub rupe Lupercal
Parrhasio dictum Panos de more Lycaei.

Next he showed him the mighty grove, where warlike Romulus founded an asylum: also the Lupercal, under its cold rock, named in the Arcadian fashion for Pan of Lycaeus.

VIRGIL, *Aeneid*, VIII. 342–4.

LVPERCALIA.

The festival of the Lupercalia (15th February).

Fasti Caeretani, CIL, I^2, p. 212

Lupercis nudis lustratur antiquum oppidum Palatinum.

The ancient town on the Palatine is purified by the naked Luperci. . . .

VARRO, *De lingua Latina*, VI. 34

. . . TEMPLVM APOLLINIS IN PALATIO . . . LVPERCAL . . . FECI

I built the Temple of Apollo on the Palatine, and the Lupercal.

AUGUSTUS, *Res gestae*, 19

. . . EQVESTRIS QVOQVE ORDINIS DECRETO FACTO, QVO INCREDIBILEM DOLOREM PVBLICVM DECLARANDI CAVSA VVLTVSQVE EIVS RETINENDI PLVRIMOS ET MAXIMOS HONORES EI TRIBVIT, IN HIS AD MEMORIAM DRVSI CAESARIS CONSERVANDAM. . . . DRVSI CAESARIS IN LVPERCALI PONERETVR

The order of the Knights also passed a decree, to emphasize the extreme public grief, to retain the memory of his features, and to pay him the greatest possible marks of respect, that a statue of Drusus Caesar should be set up among these statues at the Lupercal, in order to preserve his memory.

CIL, VI. 912

CASA ROMULI

(Romulus and Remus)
They lived the life of shepherds, depending on the labour of their hands, and building the mountain huts made—roof and all—out of sticks and reeds. Now there was one of these, even in my own times, on the slope of the Palatine hill towards the Circus. Those in charge of it maintain it as a holy place: they must not embellish it at all: but if by weather or lapse of time it is damaged in any way, they repair it and restore it as closely as possible to the original condition.

DIONYSIUS HALICARNASSUS, *Roman Antiquities*, I. 79. 11

On the Capitol the Hut of Romulus, and other temples on the Citadel with roofs of thatch, can remind us of the ancient customs of Rome.

VITRUVIUS, *On Architecture*, II. I. 5

Ancient legends gathered thickly around the south-west corner of the Palatine Hill, looking towards the Circus Maximus and the Velabrum. Many of these were commemorated by monuments to which Augustus and later writers refer: unfortunately it is no longer possible to determine their site with certainty. The old stairway called the Scalae Caci must have been one of the approaches to the Palatine village. It will be seen that our sources do not agree about Cacus himself—was he a certain 'Cacius', as Diodorus thought, or the fire-breathing monster brought so dramatically by Virgil into the Eighth Book of the Aeneid? The second would be more likely. Cacius, son of Vulcan, was an ancient fire-god, and his consort Caca had a shrine on the Palatine. But above all this part of the hill was associated with the second and, for the Roman people, the more popular legend of Rome. The story and the characters, Rhea Silvia, Mars, Amulius, the Twins, the Wolf, Faustulus, and Acca are best known through the passage of Livy here quoted. But the two Greek authors add some details. Plutarch's sacred woodpecker, honoured by the Latins, links with Virgil's story of Picus, the woodpecker-King of Laurentum (*Aeneid*, VII. 170 ff.), and suggests totemism among the early Latins. Plutarch also shows how by his time higher criticism had been at work on the old Roman legends, with its inevitable result: the degradation of the she-wolf was perhaps even more painful than that of Rhea Silvia. Dionysius' description of the Lupercal in his day is invaluable. The figures of the wolf and twins are perhaps to be identified with those mentioned by Livy (X. 23, 11–12) as being placed in the year 295 B.C. *ad ficum Ruminalem*, and depicted on coins of the republic. They must not be confused with the famous—and much older—Wolf of the Capitol.

From these antiquarian speculations we return to the realities of the age of Augustus. He rebuilds the Lupercal as part of his programme for the restoration of temples: doubtless most of the statues Dionysius saw there are of his time. Among them the order of the Knights dedicates a statue to his adopted son Drusus, who died so tragically in Germany in 9 B.C. and who is commemorated by the great sepulchre at Mainz.

The Hut of Romulus (Casa Romuli) was clearly built like those *capanne* made of sticks and reeds even now by Italian shepherds. It was carefully maintained as a state monument, as Dionysius says, and stood near the house of Augustus. A reconstruction was made for the bimillenary exhibition of 1938 (see Plate 2). We know nothing of the second hut on the Capitol.

THE TEMPLE OF MAGNA MATER

It was found to be written in the Sibylline books that the Romans must set up a temple to Magna Mater, and see to the bringing of the sacred objects from Pessinus in Asia. (204 B.C.)

DIODORUS SICULUS, *Bibliotheca*, XXXIV. 33. 2

Publius Cornelius Scipio, with all the matrons, was sent to Ostia to meet the goddess. They all prayed that she would enter Rome freely and with goodwill, and they carried the goddess to the Temple of Victory on the Palatine. . . .

LIVY, XXIX. 14. 2–14

They say that, in the year when Magna Mater was brought, the yield of the harvest was greater than in the ten preceding years.

PLINY, *Natural History*, XVIII. 3. 16

Meanwhile, at Rome, the censors placed contracts for the road from the Forum Boarium to the Temple of Venus . . . and also for the building of a Temple of Magna Mater on the Palatine. (204 B.C.)

LIVY, XXIX. 37. 1–2

. . . Thirteen years after the contract was placed, the Temple was dedicated by M. Junius Brutus, and games were given to honour the dedication. Antias Valerius says that these were the first to be accompanied by stage-plays, and they were called the Megalesia. (191 B.C.)

LIVY, XXXVI. 36. 3–4

(for April 11th) LVDI IN CIRCO MATRI DEVM MAGNAE IDAEAE IN PALATIO QVOD EO DIE AEDIS EI DEDICATA EST.

Games in the Circus for Magna Mater, the Mother of the Gods, the Lady of Ida, who has her temple on the Palatine, because on that day her temple was dedicated.

Calendar of Praeneste, CIL, 1^2, p. 235

The statue of Claudia Quintia, dedicated by our ancestors in the Temple of the Mother of the Gods, had twice escaped the flames. This showed that the Claudii were sacrosanct and dear to the gods: additional solemnity was due to a place where the gods had shown such a signal mark of honour to the Emperor.

TACITUS, *Annals*, IV, 64

AEDEM MATRIS MAGNAE IN PALATIO FECI.

I restored the Temple of Magna Mater on the Palatine.

AUGUSTUS, *Res gestae*, 19

ONESIMVS, OLYMPIAS, LIVIA BRISEIS AVGVSTAE LIB. SACERDOTES MATRI DEVM MAGNAE IDAEAE.

Onesimus, Olympias, Livia Briseis, freed slaves of Augusta (Livia?) and priests, dedicated this to Magna Mater, Mother of the Gods, Lady of Ida.

CIL, VI. 496

The Temple of Magna Mater stood just to the west of the House of Augustus. Hers was the most important of the foreign cults brought to Rome in the emotional atmosphere of the closing years of the Second Punic War. The black stone from Pessinus in which the *numen* of the goddess was vested came by ship in 204 B.C. and reached Ostia on 4th April: it was met by the matrons of Rome and by the young Scipio Nasica, whom the oracle at Delphi had declared the person most suited to receive it. Then it was escorted to the Temple of Victory on the Palatine. A tradition that Scipio gave it lodging in his house for thirteen years while a Temple of Magna Mater was under construction is mentioned by Juvenal and Valerius Maximus, but may rest on a confusion.

From 191 B.C. the cult of the goddess and her young lover Attis was installed in Rome, with all its paraphernalia of eunuch priests, the *galli*, and ecstatic rites. It yielded dividends at once—not only the record harvest of 204 B.C. mentioned by Pliny, but in the more important fact that Hannibal left Italy for ever the next year. The association with Victory had been opportune. But under the Republic its observance was restricted. A procession was allowed to go to the Almo on 27th March for the *lavatio* or washing of the sacred image in the river: there followed the popular celebrations, gradually extended, of the Megalesia in early April, with its games and stage performances. Otherwise the cult was confined to quarters on the Palatine, and Roman citizens debarred from the priesthood. There are two famous descriptions of the rites of the Great Mother in republican literature—the *Attis* of Catullus, and Lucretius, II, 600–630. How far either poet was influenced by Roman observance of the cult is questionable—Catullus could of course have seen it in its Asian homelands while he was in Bithynia.

Under the Empire Cybele was shown more indulgence. Augustus rebuilt her temple after the fire of A.D. 3 mentioned by Tacitus: this is the building shown on the relief of Plate 49. Claudius, by making it a State cult, opened the priesthood to Roman citizens and promoted the full development of the ritual in its Asiatic forms.

Plate 50 shows the fragments of statues of the goddess and her lion discovered in 1872. More recently numerous votive offerings have been found. The association of the goddess with *ludi* led to the building of a temple for her in the Circus Maximus.

THE TEMPLE OF APOLLO

He built the Temple of Apollo in that part of his property on the Palatine where the soothsayers declared the god had signified his choice by striking it with lightning. To it he added colonnades, and a Greek and Latin library: here, in his old age, he would often summon meetings of the Senate, or approve panels of judges.

SUETONIUS, *Augustus*, 29

CVRIAM ET CONTINENS EI CHALCIDICVM . . . TEMPLVMQVE APOLLINIS IN PALATIO FECI.

I built the Curia, and the Chalcidicum which adjoins it . . . and the Temple of Apollo on the Palatine.

AUGUSTUS, *Res gestae*, 19

In this year (28 B.C.) Augustus completed and dedicated the Temple of Apollo on the Palatine, together with the sacred area around it, and the two libraries.

DIO CASSIUS, *Roman History*, LIII. 13

Actius haec cernens arcum intendebat Apollo
desuper: omnis eo terrore Aegyptus et Indi
omnis Arabs omnes vertebant terga Sabaei.

Actian Apollo, looking on, levelled his bow at them from high heaven: fear struck them, and they all turned their backs, every Egyptian and Indian, every Arab and Sabaean.

VIRGIL, *Aeneid*, VIII. 704–6

Ipse sedens niveo candentis limine Phoebi
dona recognoscit populorum aptatque superbis
postibus . . .

Augustus himself seated at the gleaming threshold of bright Phoebus, receives the gifts of nations and hangs them on the temple's splendid portals. . . .

VIRGIL, *Aeneid*, VIII. 720–2

'Candentis limine Phoebi' . . . on the Temple of Apollo on the Palatine, which was made of solid marble from Luna (Carrara), which is on the borders of Tuscany and Liguria. . . .

SERVIUS on *Aeneid* VIII. 720

quidquid fatidicorum librorum Graeci Latinique generis nullis vel parum idoneis auctoribus vulgo ferebatur undique cremavit ac solos retinuit Sibyllinos . . . Libros Sibyllinos condidit Augustus duobus forulis auratis sub Palatini Apollinis basi. . . .

All the prophetic writings, Greek and Latin, that were current but were the work of anonymous or untrustworthy authors, he collected together and burned to the number of more than two thousand; retaining only the Sibylline books, and even these only in selection. These Sibylline prophecies he placed in two golden bookcases under the pedestal of the statue of Apollo.

SUETONIUS, *Augustus*, 31. I

Quaeris cur veniam tibi tardior? aurea Phoebi
porticus a magno Caesare aperta fuit.
tanta erat in speciem Poenis digesta columnis
inter quas Danai femina turba senis,
tum medium claro surgebat marmore templum,
et patria Phoebo carius Ortygia;
in quo Solis erat super fastigia currus;
et valvae, Libyci nobile dentis opus,
altera deiectos Parnasi vertice Gallos,
altera maerebat funera Tantalidos,
deinde inter matrem deus ipse interque sororem
Pythius in longa carmina veste sonat.
hic equidem Phoebo visus mihi pulcrior ipso
marmoreus tacita carmen hiare lyra.
atque aram circum steterant armenta Myronis
quattuor artifices, vivida signa, boves.

Why, you ask, do I come so late? Mighty Caesar has opened the golden colonnades of Apollo's Temple. A glorious sight it was, as it lay open to view with its columns of African marble, and set between them statues of the many daughters of old Danaus. Then, in the midst, the temple with its shining marble rose up high, which Apollo loves even more than his home in Ortygia. On its roof were two chariots of the Sun, the doors were of Libyan ivory, marvellously wrought. On one was the story of the Gauls hurled down from Parnassus' height; the other told the death of the daughter of Tantalus. Then, at last, there stood the god himself, between his mother and sister—Pythian Apollo, clad in a long robe, and chanting song. The marble statue seemed to me fairer than the god himself, as he stood with parted lips and silent lyre. Round the altar stood the cattle of Myron, four oxen that seemed to live.

PROPERTIUS, *Elegies*, II. XXXI

quid dedicatum poscit Apollinem
vates? quid orat de patera novum
fundens liquorem?

What should the poet ask of Apollo in his new-built temple? What is his prayer as he pours forth the new wine from the bowl?

HORACE, *Odes*, I. 31. 1–3

... SACRIFICIOQVE PERFECTO PVERI XXVII QVIBVS DENVNTIATVM ERAT PATRIMI ET MATRIMI, ET PVELLAE TOTIDEM CARMEN CECINERVNT: EODEMQVE MODO IN CAPITOLIO. CARMEN COMPOSVIT Q. HORATIVS FLACCVS.

When the rites were over, a choir of 27 boys, whose fathers and mothers were certified as being alive, and an equal number of girls, sang the Hymn. The Hymn was written by Q. Horatius Flaccus. (See Plate 52.)

(3 June, 17 B.C.) CIL, VI. 32323

Phoebe silvarumque potens Diana,
lucidum caeli decus, o colendi
semper et culti, date quae precamur
tempore sacro,
quo Sibyllini monuere versus
virgines lectas puerosque castos
dis, quibus septem placuere colles,
dicere carmen.
alme Sol, curru nitido diem qui
promis et celas, aliusque et idem
nasceris, possis nihil urbe Roma
visere maius.

augur et fulgente decorus arcu
Phoebus acceptusque novem Camenis,
qui salutari levat arte fessos
corporis artus,
si Palatinas videt aequus aras,
remque Romanam Latiumque felix
alterum in lustrum meliusque semper
prorogat aevum.

Phoebus, and Diana Queen of the forests, shining glory of the heavens, divinities worshipped and to be worshipped for ever, grant our prayers on this holy festival, when the verses of the Sibyl have bidden chosen maids and spotless boys to sing this hymn to the gods who love the Seven Hills.

Kindly Sun, who in your bright chariot brings forth the day and takes it home, born ever new and always the same, may you never look on any greater thing than the city of Rome. . . .

May Phoebus the prophet, with his shining bow, dear to the nine muses of Latin verse, he whose healing arts relieve our weary limbs—may he, if he looks with favour on his altars on the Palatine, prolong Rome's empire and the happiness of Latium new and better from age to age!

HORACE, *Carmen Saeculare*, 1–12, 61–69

While Julian was asleep, his mind was disturbed by nightmares, foreboding some dire calamity. So both he and the interpreters of dreams decided that careful watch should be kept on the next day, being the 18th of March. And, as they discovered later, that was the very night when, during the prefecture of Apronianus, the Temple of Apollo on the Palatine was destroyed by fire in the Eternal City. If help had not come from all sides, the violence of the flames would have consumed even the prophecies of the Sibyl of Cumae.

(A.D. 363) AMMIANUS MARCELLINUS, XXIII. 33

THE PALATINE LIBRARY

Come now, and please bestow a little care on those who would rather put themselves in a reader's hands than endure the contempt of the haughty spectator—if you wish to fill with books that gift worthy of Apollo, and to spur on Roman poets to seek Helicon with greater zeal.

HORACE, *Epistles* II, I. 214–8

What is Celsus doing now? He was warned, and it must be repeated, to look for his own treasure, and forebear to touch the writings Apollo has received into the Palatine Library. One day the flock of birds will come to reclaim their feathers; then the poor crow will be stripped of his stolen plumes and look ridiculous.

HORACE, *Epistles* I, III. 15–20

Scholiast *ad loc.*: Augustus set up in the library a statue of himself in the guise and habit of Apollo.

All that the learned minds of ancient or of modern authors have produced, lies there open for the readers to consult. . . .

OVID, *Tristia*, III. 1. 63–64

(Marcus Hortalus) stood at the bar of the Senate, waiting permission to speak. The Senate was meeting in the Palatine (Library), and looking, now at the statue of his ancestor Hortensius among those of the orators, now at that of Augustus, he spoke as follows. . . .

TACITUS, *Annals*, II. 37

C. Julius Hyginus . . . freedman of Augustus, a Spaniard by birth . . . was Librarian of the Palatine Library, and taught many pupils.

SUETONIUS, *De grammaticis*, 20

D.M. TIBERIO IVLIO ZOILI F. FABIA TRIBV PAPPO, COMITI TIBERI CAESARIS AVGVSTI, IDEMQVE SVPRA BYBLIOTHECAS OMNES AVGVSTORVM AB TIBERIO CAESARE VSQVE AD TIBERIVM CLAVDIVM CAESAREM. PER TIBERIVM IVLIVM NICONEM HEREDEM IN PARTE QVARTA ET IVLIAM FORTVNATAM.

To the departed spirits of Tiberius Julius Pappus, son of Zoilus, of the Fabian Tribe, *comes* of the Emperor Tiberius, superintendent of all the imperial libraries from the time of the Emperor Tiberius to that of the Emperor Claudius. Set up by his heir Tiberius Julius Nico, also inheritor of one quarter of the estate, and by Julia Fortunata.

American Journal of Archaeology, LXIII (1959), p. 384

ALEXANDER C. CAESARIS AVGVSTI GERMANICI SERVVS PYLAEMENIANVS AB BYBLIOTHECE GRAECA TEMPLI APOLLINIS, VIXIT ANNIS XXX.

Alexander, slave of C. Caesar Augustus Germanicus, a Paphlagonian, clerk in the Greek Library of the Temple of Apollo. Aged 30.

CIL, VI. 5188

SVLPICIAE THALLVSAE ANTIOCHVS TI CLAVDII CAESARIS (servus) A BYBLIOTHECE LATINA APOLLINIS, CONIVGAE SVAE BENE MERITAE.

Antiochus, slave of Ti. Claudius Caesar, clerk of the Latin Library in the Temple of Apollo, to his dear wife Sulpicia Thallusa.

CIL, VI. 5884

There is now a fair consensus among archaeologists that the temple whose remains are to be seen immediately to the south-east of the 'house of Livia', and which used to be assigned to Jupiter Victor, is that of Apollo Palatinus. This agrees best with what is known of the temple's position from ancient sources. But in what can now be seen there is no sign whatever that here was a *chef d'oeuvre* of Augustan art and architecture, one of the most splendid temples in Rome. Fortunately, the literary sources are unusually full; the poem of Propertius, especially, describes not only its chief works of art, but also the reactions of contemporary taste.

The Temple was vowed during the campaigns against Sextus Pompeius, but it would seem that Apollo's claim was really based on his help at the battle of Actium in 31 B.C. It was dedicated on 9th October, 28 B.C.: Virgil, Horace and Propertius all allude to the opening ceremony. The stress is on the brilliance of the white Carrara marble—*candentis limine Phoebi*—then used for the first time in Rome, and highly suitable for the god of light himself. (Another response may be evoked from a generation that has seen too much of the Victor Emmanuel Monument.) Within the great colonnades, Propertius stresses the contrast between the coloured African marbles—*giallo antico*—and the pure white of the temple. The myths portrayed are chosen to symbolize the punishment of impiety and the power of Apollo. The ivory door with its two panels should be noted: the Celts are those driven back from Delphi by the god in 278 B.C. Later these same Celts settled in Asia under the name of 'Galatae': their defeat was commemorated on the great Altar of Pergamum: the parallel is no doubt deliberate. Myron (430 B.C.) was famous for his animal statues: the oxen were appropriate to Apollo's role as protector of herds. Pliny tells us the names of the artists of the three cult statues: Apollo, by Scopas (420 B.C.), Diana by Timotheus (fourth century B.C.), and Latona by Cephisodotus, the son of Praxiteles (296 B.C.).

Two passages show that the Temple was a focal point in the celebrations of the Secular Games (3rd June, 17 B.C.). Horace's *Carmen Saeculare* was sung by a choir of boys from Apollo on the Palatine and by one of girls from Diana on the Aventine. (See also Plate 52.)

The placing in the Temple of Sibylline books, after their recension and the suppression of spurious versions, meant that Apollo was now guarding the secrets of Rome's future, as he had formerly inspired the Sibyl of Cumae herself.

Like that of its dedication, we know the precise date of the Temple's destruction—18th March, A.D. 363. Julian had restored the temple as part of the revival of pagan cults: he was on campaign against Persia that year, and on the night of his terrible dreams was encamped at Carrae, 'a town notorious for the disaster of Crassus and the Roman army' (*Ammianus* XXIII. 3. 1). A few months later he was dead.

As patron of music and poetry, it was proper that Apollo should preside over the Palatine library. It could well be called a royal foundation. There Roman authors had free access to all the works of Greek and Latin literature; there they gave their own recitals, or, like Celsus, strung together other men's pearls. Among these surroundings, with the busts of poets and orators looking on, a meeting of the Senate could suitably be held. Marcus Hortalus, descendant of Hortensius, thought it apt for his plea to Tiberius for a grant from public funds for the proper support of his four sons (A.D. 19). It failed. The Librarian (*praepositus bibliothecae*) was an imperial appointment: the Hyginus mentioned (not the writer on mythology), evidently found time for his own research and teaching. Tiberius Julius Pappus must have been a near—perhaps immediate—successor. Probably one of the learned Greeks in whose company Tiberius took pleasure, his authority 'over all the imperial libraries' must have included that established by Tiberius in the Temple of Augustus, as well as the Greek and Latin Libraries on the Palatine. The inscription, discovered in 1958, shows that his long tenure extended into three reigns. (Cajard, 1959, 384.) The epitaphs of the two library clerks—one from the Greek and one from the Latin Library—show that they were appointed from the slaves of the imperial household.

PRIVATE HOUSES OF THE REPUBLIC

Marcus Livius Drusus

When M. Livius Drusus was building a house on the Palatine . . . the architect promised him that he would build it in such a way that it would not be seen by the public, be inaccessible to prying eyes, and that it would not be overlooked by any neighbour: "No" said Drusus "if you have the skill for it, please build my house so that whatever I do is clearly seen by all." (91 B.C.)

VELLEIUS PATERCULUS, *Roman Histories*, II. 14. 3

Then, since what had been well begun was turning out badly, Drusus' mind began to turn to giving the citizenship to the Italians. Returning from the Forum and working on this plan—and accompanied as usual by the large disorderly crowd which invariably followed him—he was struck by a butcher's knife in the courtyard of his house. It was left in his side, and a few hours later he was dead. (91 B.C.)

Ib. 45. 3

L. Licinius Crassus

Crassus, one of the great orators of the day, had a fine house, but an even finer one on the Palatine was owned by Quintus Catulus, victor with Marius over the Cimbri. . . . (His colleague) Gn. Domitius, a man of quick temper, and fired with that carping hatred that springs from rivalry, severely rebuked Crassus for living in such a grand manner at the time that he was censor. He repeatedly offered one million sesterces for the house, but Crassus, always ready of wit and quick in repartee, replied 'The offer is accepted, but I withdraw six trees from the sale'. Domitius declined to give even one denarius for the house on that condition. To which Crassus replied, 'Tell me, Domitius, who deserves a mark of censure from my office? I myself, who live quietly in the house I have inherited, or you, who would value six trees at a million sesterces?' . . . Let no one suppose that the house of Crassus was a poor affair in other respects, or that there was nothing but the six trees to attract Domitius' offer. Indeed, he had already erected in the courtyard six columns of marble from Mount Hymettus, which as aedile he had bought to embellish the stage of the theatre, at a time when no public building had any marble pillars. So recent a growth is opulence in Rome! (92 B.C.)

PLINY, *Natural History*, XVII. I. 6–7

Cicero

It was on your motion, Lentulus, that a full senate decreed that whoever damaged my house should be guilty of an act harmful to the state. I maintain that no public work, no historical monument, no temple, has ever had so many decrees of the Senate passed about it as has my house. Indeed, since the foundation of Rome, it is the only house which the Senate has ordered to be erected at the cost of the public Treasury, released from the supervision of the pontiffs, protected by the magistrates and vindicated in the courts.

CICERO, *De Haruspicum responso*, VIII. 15

M. Scaurus

When M. Scaurus was aedile (52 B.C.), the laws were silent when 360 marble columns were taken to decorate a temporary theatre, intended for no more than a single month's use. . . . Very well, that was indulgence to the pleasures of the public. Yet the laws were still silent when the largest of them, each 38 ft. high and made of Lucullan marble, were placed in the hall of Scaurus' house. And there was no secrecy about it. The contractor for the sewers forced Scaurus to give him insurance against any risk of damage when the columns were being hauled to the Palatine. Would it not have been wiser, at so bad a precedent, to insure against damage to our morals? And the laws were still silent when these huge masses of marble, to adorn a private house, were dragged past the terracotta pediments of the temples of the gods!

PLINY, *Natural History* XXXVI. ii. 5. 6

Chrysogonus

Now you have Chrysogonus coming down from his fine house on the Palatine: for his recreation he has a pleasant villa in the country, a number of good farms, all close to Rome. . . . His town house is crammed with gold and silver vessels from Delos and Corinth, among them the famous automatic cooker, which he bought at so high a price that those who were passing the auction and heard the bid thought an estate was up for sale. What about the embossed silver, coverlets, pictures, statues, marble, that you must suppose he owns? Precisely the amount that could be gathered into a single house from the plunder and ruin of many noble families! . . . When a man lives on this scale, gentlemen, what must his expenditure be, on display, on dinner parties? Reasonable, I suppose, for such a house—if you can call a house what is the source of wickedness and a common lodging-house for crime! (80 B.C.)

CICERO, *Pro Roscio*, XLVI. 133

Mark Antony

What will Antony not do as victor, when without gaining any victory he has committed such crimes after Caesar's death? He has gutted his house, pillaged his gardens, transferred all their fittings to his own house. . . .

CICERO, *Philippics*, III. 12. 30

Again, are we to tolerate these immense profits which the entire household of Antony has absorbed? He has sold false decrees, and taken money to have bronze inscriptions of immunity from taxation made out. All this he says he has done from Caesar's notebooks—which he wrote himself. And in the inner part of the house there was conducted a veritable hiring-fair in the interests of the state: his wife—luckier than her two first husbands—sold provinces and kingdoms . . . unless these things are rescinded by the Senate, all trace of a free republic will have disappeared. (44 B.C.)

CICERO, *Philippics*, V. IV. ii

From about 150 B.C. the Palatine developed as a fashionable residential district, until by the time of Augustus it was the most favoured in Rome. Hortensius, Sulla, Cicero, Crassus, Clodius, Antony and Milo are known to have had houses there, as did Gaius Gracchus until for political reasons he moved "to be closer to where the poor and humble had to live" (Plutarch, *Gaius Gracchus* 33. 1). Most of these republican houses were destroyed in the building of the imperial palaces—incorporated in their substructures or pounded into rubble. Sometimes excavators discover at their lowest levels rooms with frescoes or mosaics of this period, but the owners of the houses to which they belong cannot be identified. We must rely on the literary sources for an idea of what the *domus* or town houses of the late Republic were like. Here Cicero is especially important, though it must always be kept in mind that he speaks as an advocate. About the vicissitudes of his own house Cicero tells us a great deal,—how it was bought by a private mortgage in 62 B.C., destroyed, in his absence, by Clodius four years later, and levelled to the ground as a site for a temple. In 57 B.C. Cicero, back from exile, complains of the inadequate compensation offered to him by the consuls, and his difficulty in persuading the pontiffs to allow the site to be restored to private use. It would take too much space to give the texts with all the details of this affair: but the passage quoted is his comment on the fourfold record established at its triumphant conclusion. The other passages cover about fifty years of the late Republic. The architect of Drusus' house clearly expects that a gentleman planning to build on the Palatine will need privacy and seclusion. Drusus, a tribune of the people, chose to live *in conspectu*: the result was fatal. For other nobles with less public spirit, *opulentia* had already set in. The quarrel between Domitius and Crassus reads like the rivalries of eighteenth-century bucks over their town-houses in Dublin. Before long such pastimes were no longer the preserve of the nobles. L. Cornelius Chrysogonus, the freedman of Sulla, gross with the fattest pickings of the civil wars and the proscriptions, showed that new men could set new standards: he foreshadows the enormous wealth of the freedman of Claudius and Nero. In the months after the assassination of Caesar, Antony had a similar opportunity for personal enrichment, but combined, now, with political power. The Roman world and its perquisites are up for sale from a private house on the Palatine.

THE 'CASA LIVIAE' OR HOUSE OF AUGUSTUS

After his victory Octavian returned to Rome, and announced that he meant to reserve for public use several houses which he had purchased through agents, to allow for more space round his own dwelling. He also promised to build a Temple of Apollo with a colonnade surrounding it, a work which he carried out with princely generosity. (36 B.C.)

VELLEIUS PATERCULUS, *Roman Histories*, II. 81. 3

Phoebus habet partem, Vestae pars altera cessit:
  quod superest illis, tertius ipse tenet.
State Palatinae laurus, praetextaque quercu
  stet domus! aeternos tres habet una deos.

Part of the site is given to Phoebus: Venus has the second part: the third, left over by the gods, Augustus holds himself. Flourish, laurels of the Palatine: stand fast for ever, house with the oak-leaf garland! A single home, it is the abode of three immortal gods.

OVID, *Fasti*, IV. 951–4

Augustus lived first close to the Roman Forum, at the top of the Scalae Anulariae, in a house which had once belonged to the orator Calvus. Later he lived on the Palatine, but even so, in a modest house which had been that of Hortensius. It was not particularly large or elaborate: there were short colonnades, with columns of Alban stone, no marble, nor any elaborate floor mosaics. For more than forty years he used the same bedroom, winter and summer, although he found the winter climate of Rome particularly trying, and although he persistently spent the winter in the city. If he had some particularly secret business on hand, and needed to be free from interruption, there was a private study at the top of the house, which he used to call 'Syracuse' or 'the workshop': there he would go, or also to the suburban villa of one of his freedman. When he was ill, he would take to bed in the house of Maecenas. His simple taste in fittings and furniture is apparent in the couches and tables that are still preserved, most of which hardly reach the standard of elegance to be expected from a private person.

SUETONIUS, *Augustus*, 72. 1–2

TERTIVM DECIMVM CONSVLATVM CVM GEREBAM, SENATVS ET EQVESTER ORDO POPVLVSQVE ROMANVS VNIVERSVS APPELLAVIT ME PATREM PATRIAE, IDQUE IN VESTIBVLO AEDIVM MEARVM ET IN CVRIA IVLIA ET IN FORO AVGVSTO SVB QVADRIGIS QVAE TVM EX SENATVS CONSVLTO POSITAE SVNT CENSVIT.

In my thirteenth consulship, the Senate, the Order of Knights, and the entire Roman people, hailed me with the title 'Father of My Country'. It was decreed that this title should be inscribed at the entrance to my house, in the Curia Julia, and on the quadriga which had been set up in my honour in the Forum of Augustus. (A.D. 2)

AUGUSTUS, *Res gestae*, 35

To restore his house on the Palatine after its destruction by fire, the veterans, the *decuriae* and tribes, and indeed other individuals, all gladly offered contributions according to their means. But he would only take a token contribution from each group, and not more than one denarius from any single person.

SUETONIUS, *Augustus*, 57 (A.D. 3)

CORONA QVERNA VTI SVPER IANVAM DOMVS IMP. CAESARIS AVGVSTI PONERETVR SENATVS DECREVIT QVOD REM PVBLICAM POPVLO ROMANO RESTITVIT.

The Senate decreed that a garland of oak-leaves should be placed on the house of the Emperor Caesar Augustus, because he restored the commonwealth to the Roman People. (A.D. 6–10)

Calendar of Praeneste for January 13th, CIL I^2, p. 231

Then the funeral procession of Augustus took place. The bier was of ivory and gold . . . the corpse within it was covered with a pall, but a wax likeness, in triumphal attire, was displayed. So it was conducted from the Palatine by those newly come to power. . . .

DIO CASSIUS, *History of Rome*, LVI. 34. 1–2 (A.D. 14)

By contrast with the *opulentia* of the great nobles, *parsimonia* or simplicity was carefully cultivated in one house on the Palatine—that of Augustus himself. It has long been identified with some confidence with the house first excavated in 1869 and called the 'Casa Liviae', whose three main rooms, with their frescoes of mythological and Egyptian scenes (Plate 51), are now on display. Recently, however, the discovery (1961) of another house with frescoed rooms on an adjacent site has re-opened the question.

In Augustus' time great care had been taken over the siting of the house and its associations. Augustus had been born on the Palatine: he was returning to the scenes of his boyhood. But also to the origins of the Roman race, for not far away stood the *Casa Romuli*. Virgil fostered the belief that the palace of Evander had once stood on this spot, and that there Aeneas had spent his first night in Rome. Now Augustus would share it with Vesta—brought up to a second temple on the Palatine—and with Apollo, who had given him victory at Actium. The symbolism is characteristic and effective. The *parsimonia* of furnishings and amenities seem to have been from personal choice as much as policy. Short colonnades, of the native Alban stone, accord with the simple clothes Augustus habitually wore. He mentions the house only in terms of the display of public honours granted to him, the laurelled door-posts and the *clupeus aureus* (see p. 164), the garland of oak, the inscription PATER PATRIAE. There is, however, some reason to think that after the fire of A.D. 3 the house was restored more elaborately. We do not know why the private study was called Syracuse. but it is to be noted that another part of the house—used as a sunning-place—was called Sicilia. After Augustus' death the house was preserved as a national monument, together with its furniture, to judge from the comment of Suetonius. No-one else lived there. With Tiberius began the building of the vast series of imperial palaces, which his successors extended to cover almost the whole surface of the Palatine.

THE IMPERIAL PALACES

TIBERIUS

They waited for a night when the false Agrippa was off his guard: then with a suitable force they dragged him, bound and gagged, to the Palace. . . . Tiberius did not dare to punish him openly, but ordered him to be put to death in the private part of the Palace, and the body to be carried away in secret.

TACITUS, *Annals*, II. 40 (A.D. 16)

Next came the death of Drusus: he had kept himself alive for eight days by the pitiful expedient of gnawing his mattress. There is one account that Macro had written instructions that, if Sejanus took up arms, Drusus was to be released (he was under arrest in the Palace), and placed at the head of the people.

TACITUS, *Annals*, VI. 23 (A.D. 33)

CALIGULA

Caligula extended part of the Palace towards the Forum, and converted the Temple of Castor and Pollux into an entrance-hall. He would often sit between the Divine Brethren, offering himself for the adoration of visitors to the Temple.

SUETONIUS, *Caligula*, 22. 2

In the daytime Caligula would have confidential talks with Jupiter Capitolinus, now whispering, now putting his ear to the mouth of the god. Sometimes he would raise his voice and shout, and once he was heard threatening 'You raise me up, or I'll——.' But finally he reported that he had allowed himself to be won over, and that the god freely invited him to lodge with him. So he built a bridge over the Temple of Augustus, and so joined the Palace and the Capitol.

SUETONIUS, *Caligula*, 22. 4

Interfectus Caligula in Palatio est anno aetatis vicesimo nono: imperii tertio, mense decimo, dieque octavo.

Caligula was murdered in the Palace in the twenty-ninth year of his life, after a reign of three years, ten months, eight days.

EUTROPIUS, *Breviarium*, VII. 12. 4

CLAUDIUS

Claudius became Emperor in his fiftieth year by a remarkable piece of luck. The assassins of Caligula had locked out the crowd on the plea that the Emperor wanted privacy. Claudius was excluded with the rest, and went to a pavilion called the Hermaeum. A little later, terrified at the news of the murder, he crawled to a balcony, and hid himself among the curtains hung over the door. A common soldier, idly prowling about, saw his feet sticking out, dragged him forth for investigation, and saw who he was. Claudius fell at his feet in panic: the soldier saluted him as Emperor. Then he took him to his fellow-soldiers, who were in a state of uncertainty and hysteria. They put him on a litter and . . . carried him to the Castra Praetoria . . .. Passers-by pitied him as an innocent man going to his death.

SUETONIUS, *Claudius*, 10. 1

Among the spoils taken from the Britons, Claudius fixed a naval crown on the gable of the Palace, next to the civic crown of Augustus, as a sign of the crossing and, as it were, the conquest of the Ocean.

SUETONIUS, *Claudius*, 17. 3

MESSALINA

Now hear what Claudius had to endure. When she knew her husband was asleep, the Imperial Harlot would take her night-cloak, and leave with a single maid. She preferred a common mat to the bedroom in the palace for the couch of love. So, hiding her dark hair under a blond wig, she entered the brothel, reeking with the stained coverlets, and the empty cell reserved for her. . . .

JUVENAL, *Satires*, VI. 115–22

Claudius died in the Palace, in the 64th year of his age.

ST. JEROME, *Chronicle*, 2070

There is general agreement that Claudius died by poison, but where, and by whom, it was given is in dispute. Some say that it was given by his taster, the eunuch Halotus, as he was dining with the priests on the Capitol: others, that Agrippina herself gave him a poisoned *boletus* mushroom, a dish for which he had a passion. Many say that as soon as he swallowed the poison he lost his power of speech, and after a night of excruciating agony died just before dawn. . . .

SUETONIUS, *Claudius*, 24. 2

VESPASIAN

Vespasian spent very little time in the Palace, but lived mostly in the Gardens of Sallust. The gates of the Palace were open throughout the day, and no guard was posted.

DIO CASSIUS, *Roman History*, LXVI. 10. 54

It is said of Vespasian that he once dreamed that he saw a balance set up in the middle of the Palace forecourt. In one pan were Claudius and Nero, in the other himself and his two sons; and the beam was level. The dream came true, since both lines reigned for the same space of time—i.e. 27 years.

SUETONIUS, *Vespasian*, 25

TITUS

At this time Berenice was at the height of her power. She came to Rome with her brother, the younger Herod Agrippa. He was given the honorary rank of praetor: she lived in the Palace as the mistress of Titus.

(A.D. 75) DIO CASSIUS, *Roman History*, LXV. 16. 3.

Domus Augustiana (*or Augustana*)

DOMITIAN

Astra polumque pie cepisti mente, Rabiri,
  Parrhasiam mira qui struis arte domum.
Phidiaco si digna Iovi dare templa parabit
  Has petet a nostro Pisa tonante manus.

With a pious mind, Rabirius, have you conceived the heavens and their stars, when you built the mansion on the Palatine with marvellous skill. If ever Elis wishes to build a temple worthy of the Jove of Pheidias, she will beg our Thunderer to let her use your hands.

(A.D. 92) MARTIAL, *Epigrams*, VII. 56

Ad cenam si me diversa vocaret in astra
  hinc invitator Caesaris, inde Iovis,
astra licet propius, Palatia longius essent
  responsa ad superos haec referenda darem:
'Quaerite qui malit fieri conviva Tonantis,
  me meus in terris Iupiter ecce tenet.'

If I received invitations to dinner in two different parts of Heaven, one from Caesar, the other from Jove: And if the stars were near, and the Palace farther away: my reply to the gods would be in these words: please look for those who would rather be Heaven's guests, my Jupiter detains me here, on earth.

(A.D. 94) MARTIAL, *Epigrams*, IX. 91

quidquid Parrhasia nitebat aula
donatum est oculis deisque nostris.
miratur Scythicas virentis auri
flammas Iupiter et stupet superbi
regis delicias gravesque luxus.
haec sunt pocula quae decent Tonantem,
haec sunt quae Phrygium decent ministrum,
omnes cum Iove nunc sumus beati;
at nuper (pudet a pudet fateri)
omnes cum Iove pauperes eramus.

All that glitters in the Palatine hall has been given to the gods of Rome, and for us to see. Jupiter himself marvels at the gleaming gold set with Russian emeralds: he is amazed at the toys and burdensome luxury of the haughty king. Here are cups worthy of Jove himself, cups too worthy his Phrygian cupbearer. Now all of us together with Jupiter are rich: formerly (ah, shame to confess) all together with Jupiter were poor.

MARTIAL, *Epigrams*, XII. 15 (A.D. 102)

If anyone marvels at the extravagant expenditure on the Capitol, let him look at a single feature of Domitian's Palace—the Basilica, the Baths, the pavilion for his concubines. Then he will recall Epicharmus' line on conspicuous waste: 'Beneficent—no, not that. You have a disease: a mania for giving things away.' Something of this kind would apply to Domitian. 'It is neither pity,' he would say, 'nor magnificence. You have a craze for building: like Midas, you change everything into gold or stone.'

PLUTARCH, *Publicola*, 15

But as the time of the danger he anticipated grew close, Domitian became more nervous every day. He had the walls of the colonnades in which he used to walk lined with the translucent stone *phengites*, so that he could see in its bright surface the reflections of all that went on behind his back.

SUETONIUS, *Domitian*, XIV. 4

DOMVS AVGVSTANAE, SVCCVRA EVHODAE AVGVSTI LIBERTI PROCVRATORIS.

Belonging to the Domus Augustana, under the care of Euhodes, freedman of the Emperor and procurator (on two lead water-pipes).

CIL, XV. 7246

Meanwhile Agricola handed over to his successor a province of Britain that was orderly and peaceful. He did not wish to make any public stir by the number and rank of those who came to greet him on entering Rome. So, as his instructions went, by night he entered Rome, by night he went to the Palace. There he was greeted with a cursory embrace: no words were spoken: and he mingled with the crowd of slaves.

TACITUS, *Agricola*, XL (A.D. 84)

Domitian was killed in the Palace, in the 35th year of his age.

PROSPER, *Chronicles*

ANTONINUS PIUS, MARCUS AURELIUS, COMMODUS

When Antoninus summoned Apollonius (whom he had brought to Rome from Chalcis), to the Domus Tiberiana to take charge of Marcus Antoninus, Apollonius said "The master should not go to the pupil, but the pupil to the master." Antoninus laughed at him and said, 'So, it was easier for him to come to Rome from Chalcis than from his home to the Palace'. . . . Later, when Marcus mourned the death of his tutor and the palace officials tried to restrain his grief, Antoninus said, 'Let him be a natural man: neither philosophy nor empire take away the affections.'

HISTORIA AUGUSTA, *Antoninus*, 10. 4–5

From my Tutor I learned not to support either the Greens or the Blues at the Circus, nor the Lightshields or the Heavies in the Arena. And to bear toil and want little: to do my own work and look after my own business: to pay little heed to slanders. . . .

MARCUS AURELIUS, *Meditations*, 1. 5

From Apollonius I learned to rely on myself, and be resolute in trusting nothing to chance: to look to nothing but Reason, even for a minute: to remain the same, in moments of acute pain, at the loss of a child, in long illnesses: to see, too, from a living example, that the same man can be very resolute and yet very gentle: not to be impatient in giving instruction to others: to see in him a man who clearly considered his long experience and great skill in teaching philosophy as the least of his gifts. I learned also how to accept apparent favours from friends, not being lessened by such things, nor accepting them insensitively as a matter of course.

MARCUS AURELIUS, *Meditations*, 17. 8

At this time (A.D. 140) . . . Antoninus made Marcus consul with him, and gave him the title of Caesar . . . and bade him take up residence in the Domus Tiberiana with all the splendour of a court.

HISTORIA AUGUSTA, *Marcus*, 6. 3

Verus had a golden statue of the horse "Flyer", which belonged to the Greens, and always took it round with him. Indeed he used to put nuts and raisins in the horse's manger instead of barley: he ordered him to be brought to him in the Domus Tiberiana, covered in with a purple horse-blanket: when he died he built a tomb for him on the Vatican hill.

HISTORIA AUGUSTA, *Verus*, 6. 3–4

Before the death of Commodus . . . a fire that began in some dwelling house at night spread to the Temple of Peace, and after that to the storehouses of Egyptian and Arabian goods. From there the flames rose up to enter the Palace, and burned down a very great part of it, and virtually all the state archives were destroyed.

DIO CASSIUS, *Roman History*, LXXIII. 24. 2 (A.D. 192)

SEPTIMIUS SEVERUS

Then Severus entered Rome, armed and with armed guards, and ascended the Capitol. Thence, still under arms, he went to the Palace, bearing the standards he had seized from the Praetorians reversed and not erect. Then soldiers were billeted through the whole city, in temples, in colonnades, in houses on the Palatine, and lived there as though in barracks. The entry of Severus aroused fear and hatred, for the soldiers seized goods without payment, and threatened to sack the city.

HISTORIA AUGUSTA, *Severus*, 7. 1–3

Severus' most notable public works were the Thermae Severianae and the Septizonium.

HISTORIA AUGUSTA, *Severus*, 19. 5

When he built the Septizonium his only intention was that his own building should meet the eyes of travellers from Africa. He would have made the main entrance to the Palace—the royal residence—on that side, and might have done so, had not the City Prefect set up his statue there while he was away.

HISTORIA AUGUSTA, *Severus*, 24. 3

C. IVLIO AVG. L. EVTYCHO MEDICO DOMVVM PALATINARVM . . .

To C. Julius Eutychus, freedman of Augustus, doctor at the Palace, attached to the Palace buildings.

CIL, VI. 8656

IVLIA GEMELLA ISIDORI VXOR VIXIT ANNOS XXV. ALBANVS CAESARIS SERVVS A SVPPELECTILE DE DOMV TIBERIANA VIXIT ANNOS XLV.

Julia Gemella wife of Isidorus, aged 25. Albanus slave of Caesar, attached to the care of the furnishings of the Domus Tiberiana. Aged 45.

CIL, VI. 8654

DIS MANIBVS TI. CLAVDIVS THALLVS, PRAEPOSITVS VELARIORVM DOMVS AVGVSTIANAE, FECIT SIBI ET FILIIS SVIS. . . .

To the departed spirits, Ti. Claudius Thallus, controller of the awnings in the Domus Augustiana, made this sepulchre for himself and his sons. . . .

CIL, VI. 8649

IMPERATORI. CAESARI.
M. AVRELIO ANTONINO.
AVG (vsto).
L. SEPTIMI. SEVERI. PII.
PERTINACIS. AVG (vsti). FILIO.
DOMINO. INDVLGENTISSIMO.
PAEDAGOGI. PVERORVM. A CAPITE.
AFRICAE. QVORVM. NOMINA. INFRA.
SCRIPTA. SVNT.

TRYFERVS. VER. LIV.	PETIZACES. LIB.
EVPERILEMPTVS. LIV.	ZOILLVS. LIB.
EVTYFRON. LIV.	FREQVENS LIB.
TROPHIMVS. VER. LIB.	MODESTVS LIB.
POLLVX. VER. LIB.	PATROCLVS LIB.
CHRYSTOMALLVS. LIB.	HERMES LIB.
PHILETERVS. VER. LIB.	NICOMACHVS. VER. LIB.
EVTYCHES. LIB.	PAEDICVS. LIB.
SPENDON. LIB.	HERMOGENES. LIB.
PERSEVS. LIB.	NEON. VER. LIB.
HERMES. LIB.	ANEMVRIVS. VER.
FELIXS. LIB.	EVTYCHES LIB.

PROCVRANTIBVS. SATVRNINO. ET EVMENIANO
DEDIC (at-). IDIB (vs). OCT (obribvs). SATVRNINO. ET. GALLO CO (n) S (vlibus).

To the Imperial Caesar, M. Aurelius Antoninus Augustus (Caracalla) son of Lucius Septimius Severus, etc. etc., a most indulgent ruler, set up by the schoolmasters of the pages' school at the *Caput Africae* whose names are written below: TRYFERUS, born in the household, freedman, etc. (there follow a further 23 names), carried out by Saturninus and Eumenianus and dedicated on the Ides of October in the consulship of Saturninus and Gallus (15th October, A.D. 198).

CIL, vi. 1052

The building of the Imperial palaces spread over two centuries from Tiberius to Septimius Severus. The best architects of the day must have been employed on such a commission, but the only name we know is that of Rabirius. The building Emperors were Tiberius, Caligula, Domitian, especially, and Septimius Severus, with Hadrian making some extensions. Nero's interests were, in the main, directed to the Domus Aurea. Nerva and Trajan made a virtue of not adding to imperial luxury, and thereby won popularity. But there was more to it than the housing of the Emperor. It was necessary to provide for state receptions, distinguished visitors, the imperial bureaus, and for the ceremonial of an increasingly elaborate court. Many thousand of courtiers, clerks, and technicians must have been employed on the Palatine, and were known collectively as the Palatini. Their pleasure and amusements had to have special provision, so as not to overcrowd the amenities enjoyed by the common people.

So it was that the Palatine became virtually a Palace Quarter. Huge buildings covered almost the whole plateau, obliterating its natural features with artificial levels and terraces, and indeed extending beyond it on the vast substructures to be seen on the Forum side. In their final form, they were grouped in two great building complexes—the Domus Tiberiana on the north-west of the hill, overlooking the Forum, and the Domus Augustiana (whose name is vouched for on lead water-pipes, see p. 169) in the centre and south-east. The latter, the work of Domitian's great architect Rabirius, was in itself a double palace, with a Basilica and State Rooms for official use (to which the modern name of Domus Flavia is sometimes given), and a separate block of buildings on two main levels for the private residence of the imperial family.

The various building stages cannot be fully documented from literary sources, which are all too often more interested in the foibles and eccentricities of emperors than in their serious activities. Archaeologically, too, much is still to be done on the Palatine; in any case much has been lost by the neglect of the Middle Ages, and the subsequent building of the Villa Palatina and the Farnese Gardens. Yet where Byron at the beginning of the nineteenth century could complain

> 'all that learning reaped
> From her research hath been, that these are walls'

there is today a much richer harvest and learning can say a good deal more.

Tiberius, as always in Tacitus, is remembered for his crimes. But if passages on the deaths of Clemens, the 'false Agrippa', and of Drusus make it clear that there was already a private part of the palace, we should not think in terms of an imperial prison.

Caligula's building plans are interpreted as the megalomania always attached to that Emperor. But the bridge from the Palatine to the Capitol, making use of existing buildings, is not in architectural terms more extravagant than the covered gallery connecting the Vatican and the Castle of Sant' Angelo—or that linking the Pitti Palace to the Uffizi in Florence.

The passage on Claudius' humiliating discovery by the soldier has some interesting details. The Hermaeum sounds like a separate building or pavilion (*diaeta*) in the Palace grounds, which also accords better with the straying soldier. The *velaria* under which Claudius tried to hide are those elaborate awnings over doorways which were a feature of Roman palaces: note the *velarii* of the last inscription. There is a fine example of such *velaria* in the mosaic of the Palace of Theoderic in S. Apollinare in Ravenna.

The naval crown 'for the conquest of Ocean'—and of Britain—was Claudius' most valued trophy: the civic crown must have been moved from the House of Augustus (p. 165) to keep it company.

Juvenal's famous and terrible passage on the nymphomaniac Empress Messalina—*meretrix Augusta*—begins with her slipping away in disguise from the Domus Tiberiana for her nightly debauch. This palace is also the setting for Claudius' death by the poisoned mushroom.

The Palace had become associated in the public mind with the vices of the later Julio-Claudians, and Vespasian at first made little use of it. And when Titus tried to use it for his *liaison* with Berenice, public opinion made him give her up—*dimisit invitus invitam.*

It is with Domitian, above all, that the Domus Augustiana is associated. Its grandiose construction represents his *folie de bâtir* and his inflated conception of what a Roman emperor should be: it was the scene of some of his worst atrocities, and finally of his death. The three poems of Martial form an amusing sequence. The first two are nauseating in their flattery of Domitian—*noster Tonans, noster Jupiter*. But by A.D. 102 when the third was written, Domitian was dead, and the austere Trajan had dedicated the Palace treasure to Jupiter and the gods, and thrown them open to public view. Martial's repetition of *pudet* does not seem enough to excuse the impudent *volte-face*. But the poem is important for the architecture of the Palace. Martial speaks of Rabirius as building '*Parrhasiam domum*', and '*Parrhasia*' has a double sense: of Evander and his Arcadians (and from his palace we have come a long way), and of the northern constellations and the Pole. This last meaning, linked with '*astra polumque*', might suggest that Rabirius built for Domitian one of those vaults, symbolic of the vault of Heaven, that we meet elsewhere at the Domus Aurea and the Pantheon. This does not seem to have been so: and from a poem of Statius we can get a better idea of what is meant. Whether Martial got his invitation to dinner with the Emperor we do not know. Statius did, and has left a highly obsequious poem (Silvae, IV. 2) as a letter of thanks. He speaks of a banquet set out at a thousand tables, in a huge hall supported on countless columns:

> quantae superos caelumque Atlante remisso
> sustentare queant

(as many as would support the heavens, if Atlas were to tire).

This suggests the Basilica, not the Triclinium of the Domus Flavia: this Basilica is known to have had a barrel vault 'more than a hundred feet wide, which is wider than that of the nave of St. Pauls'. After describing the coloured marbles from Africa and the Troad, from Syene and Greece, Statius looks up to the ceiling

> 'longa supra species: fessis vix culmina prendas
> visibus auratique putes laquearia caeli.'

'Far upward mounts the gaze: the eyes tire before they reach the roof, and you would think the ceiling the golden canopy of the sky.' This is clearly the barrel-vault, and on it—perhaps on an apse or half-dome, or else in a canopy on the barrel itself—a painting of the starry sky. The lines describing Domitian

> 'tranquillum vultus et maiestate serena
> mulcentem radios. . . .'

'his face unclouded, his calm majesty tempering his rays', suggest that this cosmos had its Sun-King. Juvenal's satire on the Great Turbot is an apt comment on such extravaganzas.

The translucent stone (*phengites lapis*) of the Colonnades (p. 169) is syenite from Cappadocia. The next passage is Tacitus' well-known description of Agricola's frigid reception on his return from Britain. Note the contempt of the historian for the Palatini—they are '*turba servientium*'.

Reaction and reform began with Nerva, and the passages quoted show a very different atmosphere in the age of Antonines—except for Commodus. Marcus Aurelius' tribute to his tutor, the Stoic Apollonius, is moving and eloquent: Apollonius must have had his share in the moulding of the philosopher emperor. Lucius Verus, it would seem, had a high degree of resistance to education. Note the use of the Domus Tiberiana by Marcus as heir-apparent. The passage on the great fire under Commodus is of topographical interest. Beginning at the Temple of Peace, it spreads to the warehouses for luxury goods, then occupying the site of the Basilica of Constantine, and to the Horrea Margaritaria, between the Temple of Vesta and the Arch of Titus. From there, fanned presumably by a strong north wind, the flames reach the Palace buildings that overlook the Forum.

Septimius Severus, a military emperor and an African, was feared and hated by the Senate: this comes out in the comment on his buildings. We owe to him the belvedere with the view across to the Alban Hills. The Septizonium survived until 1588, and seems to have been designed as a monumental approach to the city for travellers from the south. It might be compared with Bernini's Porta del Popolo, designed for the welcome to Rome of Queen Christina of Sweden.

It appears from inscriptions that the Domus Tiberiana and Augustiana each had its own staff, though doubtless the authority of some of the higher officials extended over the whole Palace Quarter. Their organization must have been complex and highly specialized. Lugli's collection of inscriptions includes valets-de-chambre (*diaetarchi*), footmen (*pedisequi*), a clerk of works (*praepositus opificibus*), bath-attendants (*balnearii*), caretakers of mirrors (*speclarii*), and cooks (*coci*), who are now organized in a college under the presidency of an *archimagirus* or chef. There is also evidence of a School of Heralds, and a School of Imperial Pages, who have their own training-school (*paedagogium*, see p. 172). Inscriptions relating to higher officials all fall outside our chronological limits, but those on p. 171 refer respectively to a Palace doctor, a caretaker of furniture, and a *velarius* or caretaker of awnings—a class of domestic for whom Claudius must have had a warm regard.

PORTICUS OF OCTAVIA

He built certain buildings to bear the names of other persons, such as his grandsons, wife, or sister: for example, the Porticus of Octavia and that of Livia, and the Theatre of Marcellus.

SUETONIUS, *Augustus*, 29

IMP. CAES. L. SEPTIMIVS SEVERVS PERTINAX AVG. ARABIC . . . TRIB. POT XI. IMP. XI. CAES. AVRELIVS ANTONINVS PIVS . . . INCENDIO CORRVPTAM REST.

The Emperor L. Septimius Severus . . . and M. Aurelius Antoninus Pius (Caracalla) restored this (building) after its destruction by fire.

CIL, VI. 1034

We must not forget Saura and Batrachus, who built the temples surrounded by the Porticus of Octavia. They were Spartans, but some consider that they were very wealthy and built the temples at their proper charge, hoping to have the honour of an inscription. This was refused, but, it is said, they attained their object in another way: indeed, on the bases of the columns there are carved a lizard (*saura*) and a frog (*batrachus*), attesting their names.

PLINY, *Natural History*, XXXVI. 42

. . . AEDITVVS DE AEDE IOVIS PORTICVS OCTAVIAE.

Temple attendant of the Temple of Jupiter in the Porticus of Octavia.

CIL, VI. 8708

PHILOXENVS IVLIAN. PVBLIC. DE PORTICV OCTAVIAE A BIBLIOTHECA GRAECA.

Philoxenus Julianus Publicus, from the Greek Library in the Porticus of Octavia.

CIL, VI, 2348

D.M.S. SOTERICHI PVBLICI VESTRICIANI A BVBLIOTHECE PORTICVS OCTAVIAE STATILIA HELPIS CONIVGI B.M.F.V.D. XX. VIII.

To the departed spirit of Soterichus Publicius Vestricianus, from the Library in the Porticus of Octavia. Set up by Statilia Helpis to her dear husband, who lived 28 years.

CIL, VI. 5192

The Porticus of Octavia was built by Augustus in 27 B.C., to replace the Porticus of Metellus. He enclosed the temples of Jupiter Stator and Juno Regina, which were no doubt included in Augustus' programme of temple-restoration (see p. 15). What lies behind the story of Saura and Batrachus it is now impossible to say; Pliny, the only source, relates it in a tone of scepticism. The colonnades and temples were, however, only part of a complex or buildings, known collectively as the *opera Octaviae*. These included the Greek and Latin libraries (CIL, VI. 4431 refers to a decurio . . . a bibliotheca Latina), we hear of a *schola* or lecture-hall, which may be identical with the *curia* in which the Senate occasionally met. In this group of buildings was assembled one of the finest collections of paintings and sculpture in Rome, in part no doubt inherited from the republican buildings, but mostly collected or commissioned by Augustus. Pliny, who refers to it frequently, mentions especially an Aphrodite by Phidias and the Cupid of Praxiteles, which was taken from Thespiae, and other works attributed either to Scopas or to Praxiteles. Velleius is the authority for the great equestrian group of Lysippus.

The Porticus was damaged in the great fire of A.D. 80, and restored by Domitian. Another restoration was carried out by Septimius Severus, to whom belongs the inscription (see Plate 53) on the monumental gateway or *propylaea* which is the most striking feature of what now survives of the buildings.

THE THEATRE OF MARCELLUS

Julius Caesar was always undertaking great new works to embellish Rome. . . . His two first projects were for a temple of Mars, to be the biggest in the world, (for which he would have had to fill in and pave the lake where the *naumachiae* were held) and for a huge theatre, built into the side of the Tarpeian rock.

SUETONIUS, *Caesar*, 44

THEATRVM AD AEDEM APOLLINIS IN SOLO MAGNA EX PARTE A PRIVATIS EMPTO FECI, QVOD SVB NOMINE M. MARCELLI GENERI MEI ESSET.

I built the Theatre by the Temple of Apollo, on a site most of which was purchased from private owners, intending that it should bear the name of my nephew Marcus Marcellus.

AUGUSTUS, *Res gestae*, 21

When Augustus opened the Games at the dedication of the Theatre of Marcellus, his chair collapsed and sent him sprawling backwards. At a special performance in the Theatre in honour of Gaius and Lucius Caesar, there was a panic among the audience, who thought the walls were going to collapse. Augustus tried in vain to pacify them, but in the end left his private box and sat down in what seemed the most dangerous part.

SUETONIUS, *Augustus*, 43

At the games when the stage-buildings of the Theatre of Marcellus were dedicated after being restored, Vespasian revived the ancient stage contests (*acroamata*). He gave 400,000 sesterces to the tragic actor Apollinaris, 200,000 to the lyre-players Terpnus and Diodorus. Several others received 100,000: 400 was the minimum: there were also many gold crowns awarded.

SUETONIUS, *Vespasian*, 19

Sed nec Marcelli Pompeianumque, nec illic
  sunt triplices thermae nec fora iuncta quater,
nec Capitolini summum penetrale Tonantis
  quaeque nitent caelo proxima templa suo.

But there is no theatre of Marcellus nor of Pompey (at Ravenna): nor the three thermae and the four *fora* joined together: no august shrine of Capitoline Jupiter, gleaming bright near the sky he rules.

MARTIAL, *Epigrams*, X. 51. 11–14

SIG. DIVO AVGVSTO PATRI AD THEATRVM MARCELLI IVLIA AVGVSTA ET TI. AVGVSTVS DEDICARVNT.

Julia Augusta and Tiberius Augustus dedicated a statue to their father Augustus at the Theatre of Marcellus.

ILS, 8844a

Q. CORNELIVS Q. L. PHILOMVSVS SAGARIVS A THEATRO MARCELLI FECIT SIBI ET SVIS. . . .

Q. Cornelius . . . Philomusus, dealer in mantles from the Theatre of Marcellus, made this burial-place for himself and his descendants. . . .

CIL, VI. 9868

The theatre owed its origin to Julius Caesar's wish to outbid Pompey: Suetonius' phrase that he planned it *accubans Tarpeio monti* suggests that it was to have been hollowed out of the rock like the Theatre of Dionysus at Athens. But, like so many of Caesar's projects, it was carried out by Augustus much later, and in another form. That Emperor built it by the river *ad aedem Apollinis*,—that is, the temple of Apollo Sosianus.

To the design of the theatre was linked that of the Porticus of Octavia (see p. 177), so that the god presided, as it were, over a new centre of the arts, commemorating the family of Augustus. Although it was used for the *ludi saeculares* of 17 B.C., the theatre was not dedicated till 13 B.C. Damaged in the Great Fire of A.D. 64, it was restored by Vespasian. In size and seating capacity it was much the same as the Theatre of Pompey, but it did not displace the earlier theatre in the affections of the Roman people. Both theatres fell into disrepair and neglect in the later Empire: but while the stones from the *cavea* of the Theatre of Marcellus were used to repair the Pons Cestius in 375, thus bringing to an end its life as a theatre, the Theatre of Pompey was restored at the end of the fourth century (see p. 182), and yet again under Theoderic (see Plate 54). The statue of Augustus dedicated by Julia and Tiberius presumably stood over the central doorway of the *scaena*, like that in the theatre at Orange. The *sagarius* who sold his mantles *a theatro Marcello* anticipated those shops to be seen around the façade of the theatre in older photographs, before the archaeological scourings of 1927–32.

THE THEATRE OF POMPEY

All Italy hates you (Piso) . . . try to test this bitter, universal hatred if you dare. We are approaching the most gorgeous and magnificent games ever known in the memory of man—not merely unparalleled in the past, but, I suspect, such that the future can never rival. Trust yourself to the people: appear at these games. . . .

CICERO, *In Pisonem*, 65

At Mitylene . . . Pompey was delighted with the theatre, and had sketches and plans of it made, so that he could build one like it at Rome, but larger and more magnificent.

PLUTARCH, *Pompey*, 42

When Pompey was building the large and splendid theatre which bears his name, he built close to it—like a small boat towed by a ship—a finer house than he had before. Even this was not so large as to provoke envy: when the next owner entered it, he asked in surprise, 'But where did Pompey the Great eat his dinner?'

PLUTARCH, *Pompey*, 50. 5

Pompey opened his theatre, and gave gymnastic and literary shows at its dedication. There were also combats of wild beasts, in which five hundred lions were killed. To crown all, there was the terrifying spectacle of an elephant fight.

PLUTARCH, *Pompey*, 52

If only Pompey had died two years before the Civil War broke out, but after the completion of the theatre and the other public buildings around it, at the time when he was smitten with serious illness in Campania, and all Italy prayed for his safety as her first citizen, then Fortune would never have had the chance to overthrow him, and he would have taken to the grave unimpaired all those high qualities he had borne throughout his life.

VELLEIUS PATERCULUS, *Roman Histories*, II. 48

So far, things may have happened of their own accord. . . . But the place of the struggle and the assassination, where the Senate was then assembled, contained a statue of Pompey, and Pompey had dedicated it as an embellishment to his theatre. This made it obvious that some divine power was guiding and summoning the event to a consummation in that place. . . . In the end, when Caesar saw that Brutus had drawn his dagger, he pulled his toga over his head and sank down, whether by chance, or pushed there by the assassins—against the pedestal of Pompey's statue. The pedestal was drenched with his blood, and it might be thought that Pompey himself was presiding over the vengeance on his enemy, who lay stretched at his feet, quivering from his many wounds. For he is said to have received twenty-three wounds: and many of the conspirators, too, were wounded as they struggled among each other to get in their blows on the body of one man.

PLUTARCH, *Caesar*, 66

CAPITOLIVM ET POMPEIVM THEATRVM VTRVMQVE OPVS IMPENSA GRANDI REFECI SINE VLLA RESCRIPTIONE NOMINIS MEI.

The Capitol and the Theatre of Pompey, both works costing very large sums, I repaired without any inscription of my own name.

AUGUSTUS, *Res gestae*, 20

Augustus also placed the statue of Pompey over the Royal Door of his theatre.

SUETONIUS, *Augustus*, 31

LVDOS COMMITTIMVS . . . NONIS IVN. GRAECOS THYMELICOS IN THEATRO POMPEII H. III.

June 5th. Performances of Greek plays in the Theatre of Pompey for three hours.

ILS, 5050 (*Ludi Saeculares*, 17 B.C.)

A command performance in the Theatre was also decreed. In the theatre not only was the stage gilded, but also the whole interior of the theatre around it: every property used was decked with gold, so that people named the occasion 'The Golden Day'. The curtains stretched above them to keep off the sun were of purple, adorned with a gold-embroidered figure of Nero driving a chariot, surrounded by golden stars. Such were the arrangements: there was, of course, a great banquet to follow.

DIO CASSIUS, *Roman History*, LXII. 6. 2–4 (A.D. 66)

Q. ACILIO C. FILIO PAPIRIO FVSCO V.E. PROC. ANNON. AVGG. NN. OSTIENSIVM PROC. OPERIS THEATRI POMPEIANI . . . RESPVBLICA THIB. BVRE CIVI ET PATRONO.

Q. Acilius Papirius Fuscus, imperial procurator for the corn-supply at Ostia, procurator of the buildings of the Theatre of Pompey, set up by the city of Bure to their patron and fellow citizen.

ILS, 1430 (A.D. 209–211)

DD. NN. ARCADIVS ET HONORIVS INVICTI ET PERPETVI AVGVSTI THEATRVM POMPEIVM COLLAPSO EXTERIORE AMBITV, MAGNA ETIAM EX PARTE INTERIORE RVENTE CONVVLSVM RVDERIBVS SVBDVCTIS ET EX-CITATIS INVICEM FABRICIS NOVIS RESTITVERVNT.
(Copies by Einsied.)

Our Lords, the invincible Augusti Arcadius and Honorius, restored the Theatre of Pompey, which had collapsed on its outer periphery, and was in a dangerous condition in much of its interior. All damaged material was withdrawn and replaced in every case with new construction.

ILS, 793 (393–402)

VENERIS VICTRICIS.

Temple of Venus Victrix. (See Plate 55.)

Colonnades should be built behind the scaena of a theatre, so that, when the play is suddenly interrupted by rain, the crowd will have somewhere to go from the theatre: also, so as to provide room for the preparation of all the stage sets. Such, for example, is the Porticus of Pompey. . . .

VITRUVIUS, *On Architecture*, v. 9

Scilicet umbrosis sordet Pompeia columnis
  Porticus, aulaeis nobilis Attalicis,
et platanis creber pariter surgentibus ordo,
  flumina sopito quaeque Marone cadunt,
et leviter Nymphis tota crepitantibus urbe
  cum subito Triton ore recondit aquam.

You care nothing for Pompey's Porticus, or its shady columns, splendid with curtains from Pergamum: nothing for the avenue of matched plane-tress: nothing for the streams that flow from the sleeping Silenus, whose plashing waters are heard through the whole city, until suddenly the Triton swallows them again in his mouth.

PROPERTIUS, *Elegies*, II. 32. 11–16

The site of the Theatre can readily be seen from the air (see Plate 56): some of the buildings around Piazza di Grottapinta contain parts of its substructure: it is shown, together with a part of the Porticus of Pompey, in the best preserved fragment of the Marble Plan (see Plate 55). Apart from this, we depend on the literary sources to form some idea of the magnificence of this, the earliest and always the most important theatre in Rome. It was begun in 55 B.C., a date by which the great days of the Roman drama were over by a century. Yet even Pompey at the height of his prestige had trouble in overcoming the residual puritanism in the minds of the Roman Senate at the idea of a permanent theatre. This he did by including the theatre in a kind of art-centre—the *opera Pompeii*—comprising a colonnade surrounding a garden, the Curia Pompeii for meetings of the Senate or other public occasions, and, above all, the Temple of Venus Victrix at the summit of the *cavea*.

In the first passage, Cicero challenges Piso to test the feelings of the great crowd expected for the opening ceremonies. These are described in the other passages from Plutarch; Velleius reflects that this was the zenith of Pompey's fame: had he died then, he would have been *felix opportunitate mortis*. From Plutarch, too, comes the description of Caesar's murder in the Curia of Pompey, and how he fell at the last 'at the foot of Pompey's *statua*'. It seems to have been this statue which Augustus placed over the 'Royal Door'—the centre entrance—when he magnanimously repaired the theatre. Two passages refer to performances in the theatre—one the Greek plays staged at the Secular Games in 17 B.C. (see p. 181), the other, the gala performance on the Golden Day when Nero received Tiridates, King of Armenia, in A.D. 66. Propertius describes the Porticus of Pompey with its shady colonnades, trees, and fountains: the details of the last are uncertain, but we must think of something splendid, like the fountain of Trevi, or Piazza Esedra. Pliny, speaking of the many works of art in this porticus, mentions a Cadmus and Europa by Callicles, a painting by Pausias of the Sacrifice of the Oxen, and an Alexander and a Calypso by the younger Nicias (all artists of the first century B.C.). The inscription of the reign of Severus shows the whole complex in charge of an official called *procurator operis theatri Pompeiani*. This man, Q. Acilius Papirius Fuscus, was a citizen of Bure in Africa, and was presumably one of the many Africans who followed Severus to Rome. The next inscription (recorded from an earlier source, now lost) is evidence for a full-scale restoration which can be dated to the years 393–402. The last inscription (also lost) was found '*anno MDXXV post aedem D.M. in Cripta*', and must have belonged to the Temple of Venus Victrix.

THE STADIUM OF DOMITIAN

Of Domitian's new buildings . . . there were the Temple of the Flavian House, the Stadium, the Odeum. . . .

SUETONIUS, *Domitian*, 5

At this time (A.D. 200) there was a gymnastic contest, at which such a throng of athletes had been compulsorily assembled that we wondered how the stadium could hold them. In this contest women also took part, and the competition between them was exceedingly fierce. As a result derisory remarks were passed about certain other ladies of very distinguished position: this led to a total prohibition on any woman entering a single combat, whatever her social position.

DIO CASSIUS, *Roman History*, LXXV. 16.

The Colosseum was struck by lightning on the very day of the Volcanalia (Aug. 23rd, A.D. 217): such was the conflagration that the entire upper floors and all the arena were reduced to ruins: then the rest of the structure was destroyed. Because of this disaster the gladiatorial shows were held in the Stadium for many years afterwards.

DIO CASSIUS, *Roman History*, LXXIX. 25. 1

Elagabalus gathered together in a public building all the harlots from the Circus, the Theatre, the Stadium, the baths, and other sites, and delivered to them a public address, as to troops, calling them 'fellow-soldiers . . .'.

HISTORIA AUGUSTA, *Elagabalus*, 26

Alexander Severus ordered that the taxes on bawds, prostitutes, and homosexuals should not go into the public treasury, but should be employed to meet the State's expenditure on the restoration of the theatre, the Circus, the Amphitheatre, and the Stadium.

HISTORIA AUGUSTA, *Alexander Severus*, 24

A Stadium in the Campus Martius for athletic contests, seating 15,000, was the chief contribution made by the third Flavian Emperor to the amusement of the Roman People. It ranked as one of the marvels of Rome (see p. 29); none the less, athletes had little appeal as a public spectacle, and it seems to have been valued chiefly because it could provide spare capacity for gladiatorial shows. For some years, indeed, it replaced the Colosseum after fire had put the latter out of action: when Alexander Severus repaired it he did so—on impeccable economic principles—from taxes levied on the brothels functioning in its arcades. Here is the link with St. Agnes, traditionally martyred in one of these brothels. In an air-photograph the outline of the Stadium comes startlingly to life (see Plate 57). This is because the great houses and churches of Piazza Navona stand round its perimeter, thus providing one of the most striking examples of continuity in Rome. Substantial remains of the Stadium still exist on the foundations of these houses, and a number of rooms are preserved under the church of S. Agnese in Agone.

THE ARCH OF CLAUDIUS

TI. CLAVDIO. DRVSI. F. CAESARI. AVGVSTO GERMANICO PONTIFIC. MAXIM. TRIB. POTESTAT. XI. COS V. IMP. XXII. CENS. PATRI. PATRIAI. SENATVS. POPVLVSQVE. ROMANVS. QVOD. REGES. BRITANNORVM. XI. DEVICTOS. SINE VLLA. IACTVRA. IN DEDITIONEM. ACCEPERIT. GENTESQVE. BARBARAS. TRANS. OCEANVM. PRIMVS. IN. DICIONEM. POPVLI. ROMANI. REDEGERIT.

To the Emperor Tiberius Claudius, son of Drusus, Caesar Augustus Germanicus, Pontifex Maximus, Tribunician power for the eleventh time, consul for the fifth time, saluted as Imperator twenty-two (?) times, Censor, Father of his country. Set up by the Senate and People of Rome because he received the formal submission of eleven Kings of the Britons, overcome without any loss, and because he was the first to bring barbarian peoples across the Ocean under the sway of the Roman People.

CIL, VI. 920 (restored)

On hearing of Claudius' achievement (in Britain) the Senate voted him the title of Britannicus, and gave permission for him to celebrate a triumph. They further approved an annual festival of commemoration and the erection of two triumphal arches, one in Rome, and one at the place where he had crossed over to Britain.

DIO CASSIUS, *Roman History*, LX. 22

The triumph of Claudius was held in A.D. 44, but the Arch was not dedicated until 52. Nothing of it survives except the substantial part of the dedicatory inscription now in the courtyard of the Conservatori Museum, and some fragments of sculpture (see Plates 58–59). The site (the modern Piazza Sciarra, on the Corso) of the arch was carefully chosen: it stood in the Via Lata, bridging the great artery leading from the Forum and Capitol to the Porta Flaminia and the road to the North, to Gaul and to Britain itself. This part of the Campus Martius had been developed by Augustus and his great ministers—it contained the Ara Pacis, the Mausoleum of Augustus, the Pantheon and the Thermae of Agrippa. The Arch was also designed to carry to these Thermae a branch of the Aqua Virgo, which Claudius had restored after the neglect of Gaius. Thus the siting of the Arch of Claudius proclaimed his British conquests *Urbi et Orbi*, and brought him into association with Augustus. The eleven British Kings of the inscription must be all those who, whether after defeat or negotiation, made their surrender in person to Claudius at Colchester. Note the stress laid on 'the conquest of the Ocean': a point also made by Claudius in his famous 'Speech to the Gauls' recorded on the bronze tablet at Lyons. Nothing is known of the other arch mentioned by Dio, which presumably stood at Gesoriacum (Boulogne).

HADRIANEUM

(Antoninus Pius) constructed the following buildings, which still remain: in Rome, the Temple of Hadrian. . . .

HISTORIA AUGUSTA, *Antoninus*, 8

On the day when Lucius Verus assumed the *toga virilis*, Antoninus, who on the same occasion dedicated a temple to his father, distributed bounty to the people.

HISTORIA AUGUSTA, *Verus*, 3

The substantial remains of the Hadrianeum, or Temple of Hadrian, now incorporated in a modern building in Piazza di Pietra, deserve to be better known. The passages from the Historia Augusta enable us to place its dedication in A.D. 145, under Antoninus Pius, but it is possible that the building was designed by Hadrian—or at least, that he selected the site, in the Campus Martius close to the Pantheon. It is noted for the splendid figure of provinces which—together with trophies of arms—formed the decoration of the *cella*. Sixteen of these survive: that illustrated (see Plate 61) has been identified as Hispania. They were an appropriate choice for the man who knew more of the provinces of the Roman world at first-hand than any other Emperor.

THE PANTHEON

M. AGRIPPA. L. F. COS. TERTIVM FECIT.

M. Agrippa, son of Lucius, built this when Consul for the third time.

IMP. CAES. L. SEPTIMIVS SEVERVS. PIVS. PERTINAX. AVG. . . . TRIB POTEST X . . . ET IMP. CAESAR. M. AVRELIVS ANTONINVS PIVS FELIX . . . PANTHEVM VETVSTATE CORRVPTVM CVM OMNI CVLTV RESTITVERVNT.

The Emperor Severus . . . and the Caesar M. Aurelius Antoninus (Caracalla) . . . restored the Pantheon, dilapidated by old age, in all sumptuousness. (A.D. 202).

CIL, vi. 896

IS. CONS. PR. IDVS IANVAR. IN PANTHEO . . . ASTANTIBVS . . . FRATRIBVS ARVALIBVS . . . SACRIFICIVM DEAE DIAE INDIXIT L. CALPVRNIVS L. F. PISO MAGISTER. . . .

On the last day of December, as consul in the Pantheon, in the presence of the Arval Brethren, L. Calpurnius Piso paid sacrifice to the goddess Dia.

ILS, 229 (A.D. 59)

Meanwhile (27 B.C.) Agrippa beautified Rome at his own expense. . . . He completed the building which is called the Pantheon. Perhaps it has this name because it had many statues of the gods among its images, notably those of Venus and Mars: in my opinion, however, it is because with its circular shape it resembles the vault of Heaven. Agrippa also wished to place a statue of Augustus there and to give him the honour of naming the building after him. Augustus refused both compliments: but Agrippa placed in the temple proper a statue of Julius Caesar, and in the *pronaos*, statues of Augustus and of himself. This was done, not out of rivalry for Augustus nor from a wish to share his honours, but from a genuine loyalty towards him, and a constant desire for the common good. Not merely did Augustus not reproach him for it: he actually honoured him the more.

DIO CASSIUS, *Roman History*, LIII. 27

With this story (that of Cleopatra's pearls), goes the following story also. When the queen who had won this famous wager was captured, the second of the two pearls was cut in half, so that a half of her banquet might be in each of the ears of the Venus in the Pantheon! That trophy, at least, they will not carry away, and they will be robbed of the record for luxury!

PLINY, *Natural History*, IX. 121

Hadrian built countless public buildings everywhere, but never inscribed his own name, save on the temple of Trajan. At Rome, he restored the Pantheon, the Saepta, etc. etc., and dedicated them all in the names of their proper builders.

HISTORIA AUGUSTA, *Hadrian*, 19

Hadrian conducted all the most urgent and important business with the aid of the Senate. He sat in judgment, with the assistance of the leading men of the day, sometimes in the Palace, at others in the Forum or the Pantheon or elsewhere: always he sat on a tribunal, so that all that was done was done in public.

DIO CASSIUS, *Roman History*, LXIX. 7. 1

When Hadrian tried lawsuits, he had among his advisors not merely his friends and members of his staff, but also jurists, especially Juventius Celsus, Salvius Julianus, and Neratius Priscus, and others—but always such as had been unanimously approved by the Senate.

HISTORIA AUGUSTA, *Hadrian*, 18

Among the public works of Antoninus were . . . the restoration of the temple of Agrippa.

HISTORIA AUGUSTA, *Antoninus*, 8

Brick-stamps

ROSCIANI DOMITI AGATHOBVLI DOLIARE DE LICINI.

. . . by Agathobulus from the kilns of Licinius.

CIL, XV. 276

DOL. EX. PRAE. CAESA N. CAQVILI. APRILIS.

. . . by Aprilis (from the kilns) on the estates of Caesar.

CIL, XV. 360 (A.D. 123–125)

The Pantheon of Agrippa was embellished by Diogenes of Athens: his Caryatids, among the columns of the Temple, are works of the highest quality: so too are the other groups on the gable, though less well-known owing to their lofty position.

PLINY, *Natural History*, XXXVI. 38

It will be seen that the ancient evidence does not contribute much towards an understanding of the Pantheon and its problems. Even the famous inscription of Agrippa cannot be taken at its face value. Agrippa's Pantheon was part of a complex that included the Basilica Neptuni and the Thermae Agrippae, the first Thermae in Rome; it must have invited comparison with the *opera Pompeii* which stood close by. That the *templum Agrippae* was intended for the *gens Julia* seems likely enough from what Dio says of the cult statues of Venus and Mars, and indeed from those of Augustus and Agrippa in the *pronaos*. The Basilica Neptuni, moreover, would seem to be a tribute to one of the gods who favoured the naval victory won by Augustus and Agrippa at Actium. None the less, it is odd that we hear nothing of such a project from the Augustan poets. This first Pantheon was destroyed in the great fire under Titus in A.D. 80, and rebuilt by Domitian. We know nothing of this restored building, itself destroyed in 110. Hadrian carried out a thorough reconstruction of the entire group between 118 and 128; the brick-stamps show that the rotunda and the dome are entirely of this period. The next question is whether they had any predecessors in Agrippa's building. Here it is to be noted that Pliny's references to the Pantheon comment on certain statues, but not on any remarkable architectural feature of the building itself, which does not figure in his list of the *miracula urbis nostrae* in Book XXXVI. Arguments from silence are notoriously untrustworthy, but there is the weightier consideration that the technical virtuosity and brilliantly original concept of the dome, the rotunda, and the *oculus* belong most naturally to the reign of Hadrian—indeed, to the imperial architect himself.

The impression of the interior of the Pantheon is overwhelming; one is bound to ask what it means.

Here there is little doubt that Dio was right—*θολοειδὲς ὂν τῷ οὐρανῷ προσέοικεν*—'with its circular shape it resembles the vault of heaven'. This is what Shelley put in better words—'it is, as it were, the visible image of the universe'. It is indeed, and with its seven niches (for the seven planetary gods, the *cosmocratores* or lords of the universe of ancient astrology) it forms a microcosm, linked with the macrocosm by the great eye in the roof. The *oculus* itself is the central of seven rings: the others being the plain surrounding ring and the five coffered rings of the vault. The outlines of this symbolism seem fairly clear; its details must elude us. The dimensions of the 'circle within a circle' (140 ft. diameter of the vault at its base: 140 ft. from the floor to the *oculus*) cannot be accidental, but they stem from a religious and mathematical symbolism to which we do not have the key. (See Plate 60.)

The reference to Antoninus Pius need mean no more than that he completed Hadrian's building. More puzzling is the restoration by Septimius Severus, attested by an inscription. It is odd that Hadrian's building should be *vetustate corruptum* in little over seventy years: does the phrase cover damage done by Severus' notoriously undisciplined soldiers when they entered Rome?

Two passages deal with the use of the building. The Arval Brethren sacrifice there to Diana in A.D. 59. Hadrian sits in judgment, employing as assessors the great jurists who were a distinction to his reign—though one suspects that the Basilica Neptuni—also restored by Hadrian—is a more likely setting for the Emperor's court than the Pantheon itself.

THE COLUMN OF MARCUS AURELIUS

For his victories against the Germans and Sarmatians, the Senate and People of Rome voted Marcus Aurelius temples, columns, priesthoods, and many other honours.

AURELIUS VICTOR, *The Caesars*, 16

TEMPLVM ANTONINI ET COLVMNAM COCHLIDEM ALTA PEDES CLXXV SEMIS GRADVS INTVS HABET CCIII FENESTRAS LVI.

The Temple of Antoninus and the spiral column, 175½ ft. high, with 203 steps and 56 windows.

Regionary Catalogue IX

AELIVS ACHILLES CL. PERPETVVS FLAVIANVS EVTYCHVS EPAPHRODITO SVO SALVTEM. TEGVLAS OMNES ET INPENSA DE CASVLIS ITEM CANABIS ET AEDIFICIIS IDONEIS ADSIGNA ADRASTO PROCVRATORI COLVMNAE DIVI MARCI VT AD VOLVPTATEM SVAM HOSPITIVM SIBI EXSTRVAT QVOD VT HABEAT SVI IVRIS ET AD HEREDES TRANSMITTAT LITTERAE DATAE VIII IDVS AVG. ROMAE FALCONE ET CLARO COS.

Aelius Achilles and Claudius Perpetuus Flavianus Eutychus to Epaphroditus: greetings. Grant to Adrastus, guardian of the Column of the deified Marcus, all the tiles and materials from suitable cottages huts and buildings to build himself a lodge to his own satisfaction. These letters dated from Rome on August 6th in the consulship of Falco and Clarus (A.D. 193) testify that this is to be his own property and may be made over to his heirs.

Part of CIL, VI. 1585

Marcus fought a great war against the Quadi, and won a most unexpected victory—or rather, it was granted him by God. . . . For the Quadi had encircled the Romans at a place chosen for that purpose . . . the Romans were fighting bravely, their shields fastened together. The barbarians broke off the fight, expecting to capture the Romans because they were suffering from heat and thirst. So they posted guards everywhere to prevent the Romans from reaching any water. The Romans now were in extreme distress from fatigue, wounds, the heat of the sun, and thirst. They could neither fight nor retreat, but simply stood in line at their posts. Suddenly, many storm-clouds gathered together and a prodigious rain burst over them—not without the help of the gods. There is indeed a story that Arnuphis, a magician from Egypt, who accompanied Marcus, had used his enchantments to invoke certain spirits, notably Hermes, god of the air, and had thus produced the rainstorm. . . . When the rain came, first they turned their faces up to catch it in their mouths, then they held up their shields and their helmets, and not only took huge draughts themselves, but also gave drinks to their horses. Then the barbarians charged them, and they drank and fought at the same time: some of the wounded actually drank the blood that flowed down into their helmets, along with the water. And they were so intent on drinking that they would have received a severe setback from this enemy charge, if a violent storm of hail and lightning had not fallen on the barbarians. So water and fire could be seen descending from the sky simultaneously: one side was being drenched and drinking, the other struck by lightning and dying. For the fires did not touch the Romans, but were immediately extinguished, if they fell among them: yet the rain did the barbarians no good, but actually fed the flames destroying them, like so much oil. . . .

DIO CASSIUS, *Roman History*, LXXI. 8–10

By his prayers, Marcus summoned a thunderbolt from heaven to destroy an enemy engine of war, and he obtained rain for his men when they were in distress from thirst.

HISTORIA AUGUSTA, *Marcus*, 24

When the army of Antoninus, who bore the cognomen Pius, was dying of thirst, the Emperor raised his two hands to heaven and said, 'With this hand, which has never taken life, I beseech Thee, O Giver of Life.' And he prevailed on God, so that out of a clear sky clouds came up to bring his soldiers rain.

THEMISTIUS, *Orations*, 15. 196

This book I wrote among the Quadi on the Gran.

MARCUS AURELIUS, *Meditations*, I. 17

A spider is proud of catching a fly; so one man prides himself on catching a hare, another on netting a sprat, another on taking wild boars or bears—another on catching Sarmatians. If you look at their principles, are they not all of them robbers?

MARCUS AURELIUS, *Meditations*, X. 10

Inspired by the Column of Trajan, the Column erected by the Senate and People to honour Marcus Aurelius was also an assertion that his work on the Danube frontiers was complementary to that of Trajan. So indeed it might have been, had its achievement not been cast away by the folly of Commodus. The Column was sited in the Campus Martius, between the Ara Pacis, the Temple of Hadrian, and the Pantheon. Despite the air of precision, the details given in the Regionary Catalogue are inaccurate, for the column is a 'columna centenaria'—base and shaft measuring 100 Roman feet. It was erected between the death of Marcus in A.D. 180 and 193, when we find the completed monument in charge of a *procurator*, who applies for permission to build himself a lodge. That quoted is one of three letters about the Adrastus affair preserved in the inscription: it is written by the two Treasury clerks (*rationales*) Aelius Achilles and Claudius Perpetuus to Epaphroditus, Master of Works, who would have in his charge the building materials needed.

Much has recently been made of the contrasts, artistic and psychological, between the sculptures on the two Columns. While those on the Column of Trajan stand for the grandeurs of war and victory, on that of Marcus Aurelius, with its concentration on atrocity and death, the emphasis is certainly on misery and disaster. Under Trajan the Roman Army reached the peak of its offensive power; under Marcus Aurelius it was fighting a desperate struggle in which, in retrospect, the balance of advantage can be seen to have swung over to the northern barbarians. There is some truth in this, but it must not be pushed too far. The contrast is accentuated because the reliefs on Trajan's Column are in a classicizing style, whereas on that of Marcus they are in the graphic 'realistic' vein that probably derived from popular paintings of triumphs. The same contrast is to be found between the reliefs on the Column of Marcus Aurelius and the sculptures now incorporated in the Arch of Constantine, which undoubtedly belong to his reign. On the Arch of Severus, indeed, it is to be seen in one and the same monument. It is therefore wrong to explain the contrast between the prevailing moods of the sculptures on the two great columns on grounds of history alone.

The finest scene on the Column of Marcus depicts the Miracle of the Rain (see Plate 62 and p. 190). Its details tally fairly closely with those recorded in the passage of Dio Cassius. This battle, when the weather intervened so startlingly on the Roman side, took place in Moravia, probably in A.D. 172. Later, the Roman victory was ascribed to the prayers of Christian soldiers, fighting in the Legion 'Fulminata', hence the Christian story, for which Eusebius is responsible, of the 'Miracle of the Thundering Legion'—an archetype as it were of the 'Christian miracle' of Constantine's victory at the Milvian Bridge. Note that the passage from the *Historia Augusta* attributes two 'miracles' to the prayers of Marcus himself: in fact, the destruction of a siege-engine by lightning is shown as a separate episode on the Column.

The last two passages are a reminder that, amid all the stresses of these campaigns, Marcus Aurelius composed the 'Meditations'; they show too how he viewed such activities from the high peaks of stoic detachment.

ARA PACIS AUGUSTAE

CVM EX HISPANIA GALLIAQVE, REBVS IN IIS PROVINCIIS PROSPERE GESTIS, ROMAM REDII TI. NERONE ET P. QVINTILIO CONSVLIBVS, ARAM PACIS AVGVSTAE SENATVS PRO REDITV MEO CONSACRANDAM CENSVIT AD CAMPVM MARTIVM, IN QVA MAGISTRATVS ET SACERDOTES VIRGINESQVE VESTALES ANNIVERSARIVM SACRIFICIVM FACERE IVSSIT.

When I returned to Rome from Spain and Gaul, after the successful conduct of affairs in those provinces, in the consulship of Ti. Nero and P. Quintilius (13 B.C.), the Senate decreed that an Altar of Peace should be set up in the Campus Martius in honour of my safe return, and ordered that the magistrates, pontiffs, and Vestal Virgins, should there offer an annual sacrifice.

AUGUSTUS, *Res gestae*, 12

FER. EX S.C. Q.E.D. ARA PACIS AVG. IN CAMP. MART. CONSTITVTA EST NERONE ET VARO CONSVLIBVS.

Public holiday by decree of the Senate because on that day the Altar of the Peace of Augustus was set up in the Campus Martius in the consulship of Nero and Varus (4 July, 13 B.C.).

Fasti Amiterni, CIL, 1^2, p. 324

FERIAE EX. S.C. QVOD EO DIE ARA PACIS AVGVSTAE IN CAMP. MARTIO DEDICATA EST DRVSO ET CRISPINO COS.

Public holiday, because on that day the Altar of the Peace of Augustus in the Campus Martius was dedicated in the consulship of Drusus and Crispinus (30th January, 9 B.C.).

Fasti Praenestini, CIL, 1^2, p. 313

Ipsum nos carmen Pacis deduxit ad aram
  haec erit a mensis fine secunda dies . . .
utque domus, quae praestat eam, cum pace perennet
  ad pia propensos vota rogate deos.

My song itself has led me to the Altar of Peace. The day will be the second from the end of the month. . . .

Pray that the House which secures our peace may itself flourish in peace, and pray to the gods who are ready to answer righteous prayers.

OVID, *Fasti*, I. 709–10, 721–2

Concines laetosque dies et Urbis
publicum ludum super impetrato
fortis Augusti reditu forumque
 litibus orbum.

tum meae, si quid loquar audiendum,
vocis accedat bona pars, et, O Sol
pulcher! o laudande! canam recepto
 Caesare felix.

You shall sing of days of rejoicing, of public games in Rome, granted the return of brave Augustus, for which she prayed, and of the courts free from legal business. Then, if I am to speak something worth hearing, let my voice join in its happier tones, and 'O noble Sun, praise to you!' I shall cry, happy that Caesar is back again.

HORACE, *Odes*, IV. 2. 41–48

Sed gravidae fruges et Bacchi Massicus umor
implevere: tenent oleae armentaque laeta. . . .

adde tot egregias urbes operumque laborem,
tot congesta manu praeruptis oppida saxis

fluminaque antiquos subterlabentia muros. . . .
salve magna parens frugum, Saturnia tellus,
magna virum.

But heavy crops, and the juice of the Massic grape dear to Bacchus, fill the land of Italy, olives and fine cattle hold it as their own. . . . Add, too, all those noble cities, and the masterpieces wrought by human toil—all the towns piled by human hands on their steep cliffs, with rivers gliding past their ancient walls. . . . Hail, mighty mother of crops and men: land of Saturn, hail!

VIRGIL, *Georgics*, II. 143–4, 155–7, 173–4

ecce autem subitum atque oculis mirabile monstrum,
candida per silvam cum fetu concolor albo
procubuit viridique in litore conspicitur sus.
quam pius Aeneas tibi enim, tibi, maxima Iuno,
mactat sacra ferens et cum grege sistit ad aram.

But, look, a sudden portent, wonderful to see. A white sow, with all her litter white, lay stretched out, easy to see on the grassy shore. To you, to you there, great Juno, did dutiful Aeneas sacrifice her, bearing the sacred offering, and placed her with all her flock besides your altar.

VIRGIL, *Aeneid*, VIII. 81–5

The Ara Pacis, the supreme achievement of Augustan art, is also an expression of the ideals of the Augustan Principate. Its recovery for the bimillenary of 1938 was a *tour-de-force* of modern archaeology.

The more disappointing, then, that the ancient references are meagre. The *Res Gestae* itself authenticates context, occasion, and place. Augustus had been away from Rome for three years, setting in order the affairs of the western provinces. As Horace says, his return was eagerly awaited; it was made the occasion of great public ceremonies, the lasting memorial of which was to be the Ara Pacis, set up in the Campus Martius by the road on which he had entered the City from Via Flaminia and the north. The evidence of the Fasti give 4th July, 13 B.C., as the date of the ceremony depicted on the Altar, 30th January, 9 B.C., for the dedication of the Altar in its monumental form. This last date was perhaps chosen as the birthday of the Empress Livia.

The Altar was enclosed in a precinct wall, round the outside of which ran the most important sculptures. On the two long sides are shown two parts of the procession—the Senate and People of Rome, the magistrates, the Imperial Family, and at their head, though only *primus inter pares*, Augustus, occupying the place which was his both as *princeps* and as *pontifex maximus*. Ovid does well to stress the emphasis on the Imperial Family. This is the high noon of the Principate, and Augustus is shown with his family, his friends, and his grandchildren. The death of Marcellus is, so far, his only personal loss; death had not touched his friends Agrippa and Maecenas, nor scandal his daughter Julia. The succession seemed amply provided for: who could guess that it would eventually fall on the uncongenial Tiberius? These realistic sculptures are balanced, on the two short sides, by four panels of myth and allegory. The White Sow of Lavinium and the Wolf and Twins juxtapose the Trojan and the Latin origins of Rome: Dea Roma balances Terra Mater or Italia. Here, the sculptures of the Ara Pacis derive from literature, rather than the reverse. The portrayal of the miracle at Lavinium could well be an illustration of Virgil's lines: the venerable Aeneas and the faithful Achates, the Penates in their little shrine, derive from the *Aeneid* (Plate 64). More doubt surrounds the allegorical relief shown on Plate 63. The case for Terra Mater as the noble matron on the rock does not lack grounds. But the specific claims of Italia seem stronger, when they are taken point by point with the *laudes Italiae* of the second Georgic, and in view of the balance with Dea Roma.

The Acts of the Arval Brethren attest a performance of the annual ceremony in A.D. 38: the coin of Nero (see Plate 96) was one of an issue struck to commemorate the 75th anniversary. After that, nothing more is known till 1568, when fragments of the sculptures came to light while foundations were being dug for Palazzo Fiano. Others were added in 1859 and 1903; they were dispersed between several museums. The excavators of 1937–8, under the direction of Moretti, were able to recover the rest of the Altar from beneath Palazzo Fiano, to reassemble most of the sculptures, and to place the restored monument in its present site—on the banks of the Tiber hard by the Mausoleum of Augustus.

THE MAUSOLEUM OF AUGUSTUS

MARCELLVS. C. F.
GENER
AVGVSTI CAESARIS.

OCTAVIA. C. F.
SOROR
AVGVSTI CAESARIS.

Marcellus, son of Gaius, son-in-law of Augustus Caesar. Octavia, daughter of Gaius, sister of Augustus Caesar.

L'Année Epigraphique 1928, no. 2

quantos ille virum magnam Mavortis ad urbem
campus aget gemitus! Vel quae, Tiberine, videbis
funera, cum tumulum praeterlabere recentem!

heu miserande puer, si qua fata aspera rumpas,
tu Marcellus eris! manibus date lilia plenis,
purpureos spargam flores. . . .

What laments will the Campus Martius bring to Mars' city! What funeral rites will you behold, Father Tiber, as you glide by the new-raised mound! Unhappy boy—if you might only break free from your tragic destiny!—You shall be Marcellus. . . . Come, give lilies with full hands: I shall scatter their purple flowers. . . .

VIRGIL, *Aeneid*, VI. 872–5, 882–4 (23 B.C.)

Condidit Agrippam quo te, Marcelle, sepulcro,
  et cepit generos iam locus ille duos;
Vix posito Agrippa tumuli bene ianua clausa est,
  percipit officium funeris ecce soror.

Ecce ter ante datis iactura novissima Drusus
a magno lacrimas Caesare quartus habet.
Claudite iam, Parcae, nimium reserata sepulcra,
claudite: plus iusto iam domus ista patet.

(Augustus) buried Agrippa in your sepulchre, Marcellus, and already that place held his two sons-in-law. Hardly was the door well closed on Agrippa, when his sister (Octavia) received the funeral rites. Three times, now, has the tribute been paid, now Drusus comes as the fourth to draw tears from great Caesar. Now, Fates, close that tomb, too often unbarred: a hateful house, it has been opened already more than is just.

Consolatio ad Liviam, 67–74

The Senate demanded emphatically that the body of Augustus should be carried to the grave on the shoulders of their members. Tiberius excused them, by a haughty moderation: further, he warned the people by edict not to repeat the excesses which had led to disturbances at the funeral of Julius Caesar (see p. 100), by asking that Augustus should be cremated in the Forum Romanum rather than the Campus Martius, which had been appointed as his place of burial.

On the day of the ceremony, troops were drawn up as though on guard. This occasioned comment from those who had seen for themselves—or heard from their fathers—the day when slavery was still new, when an unsuccessful attempt had been made to recapture freedom by the assassination of the Dictator Caesar—the best of deeds to some, the worst to others. 'Here we have an aged prince; after a long reign, he has even provided his heirs with the means to oppress the state: does he need the protection of soldiers to get himself quietly to the grave?'

TACITUS, *Annals*, I. 8

Although a limit was set on the honours paid to him, Augustus received two eulogies: once before the Temple of Divus Julius, by Tiberius, and again from the old Rostra, by Drusus, and he was carried on the shoulders of senators to be cremated on the Campus Martius. An ex-praetor was not lacking to swear on oath that he saw the form of the Emperor going up to Heaven after his cremation. The remains were gathered up by leaders of the equestrian order, bare of foot and with unfastened tunics, and buried in the Mausoleum. This work he had built, in his sixth consulship (28 B.C.), between Via Flaminia and the Tiber Bank: at the same time, he had thrown open to the public the surrounding groves and footpaths. . . . (Augustus) left instructions that the two Julias, his daughter and his granddaughter, should not be buried in the Mausoleum, should anything happen to them.

SUETONIUS, *Augustus*, 100–1

OSSA TIBERII CAESARIS DIVI AVG. F. AVGVSTI PONTIFICIS MAXIMI TRIB. POT. XXXIIX, IMP. VIII. COS. V.

The bones of Tiberius Caesar, son of the deified Augustus, Pontifex Maximus, Tribunician Power 38 times, hailed as Imperator eight times, Consul five times.

CIL, VI. 887 (lost)

OSSA AGRIPPINAE. M. AGRIPPAE. F. DIVI. AVG. NEPTIS. VXORIS. GERMANICI. CAESARIS. MATRIS. C. CAESARIS. AVG. GERMANICI. PRINCIPIS.

The bones of Agrippina, daughter of Agrippa, granddaughter of Augustus, wife of Germanicus Caesar, mother of Gaius Caesar Augustus Germanicus, the Emperor (Gaius).

CIL, VI. 886

As early as 28 B.C., Augustus had built in the Campus Martius a great mausoleum for himself and his family. The tumulus perhaps derives from Etruscan burial mounds, the enclosing wall and its architectural treatment parallel such elaborate Roman tombs as that of Caecilia Metella, but the scale places it beside the great monuments of Hellenistic and oriental kings. Strabo (see p. 4) gives a good idea of its original appearance. It was surrounded by a park which Augustus threw open to the public.

Never robust in health, Augustus may have expected to be one of its first occupants: his serious illness in 23 B.C. nearly brought this about. In fact, he still had thirty-seven years to live—and to suffer a series of tragic blows to his dynastic plans. The first was the death of Marcellus, at the age of 19, in 23 B.C. Virgil's famous and moving lines were added as a finale to Anchises' prophetic vision of the future of Rome, and recited by the poet in the presence of Augustus and Octavia. In 11 B.C. Octavia was laid beside her son: their funeral inscriptions (Plate 65) were found in the excavations of 1927. Agrippa had been buried in 12 B.C. In 9 B.C. came Drusus, aged 29: his death was not merely a blow to Augustus but the effective end of a forward policy in Germany. He is commemorated by the Cenotaph at Mainz, and also by the (rather commonplace) poem *Consolatio ad Liviam*. The young princes Lucius and Gaius Caesar died in A.D. 2 and 4. The Fates did not relent.

The burial of Augustus himself took place in A.D. 14. His niche is empty, and no inscription has been discovered. A year or so before his death, the original of the *Res Gestae* had been inscribed on pillars at the entrance to the Mausoleum. Livia survived him for fifteen years—the most formidable of dowager Empresses. The Julias, mother and daughter, had been expressly deprived by Augustus of their claim to a place in the family monument. Germanicus died in Asia: his ashes were brought back to Rome by his wife Agrippina in A.D. 19; she died in exile, and it was only in A.D. 37, four years later, that her bones were placed in the Mausoleum by her son Gaius (Plate 66). Tiberius' funeral inscription, extant in the sixteenth century, is now lost. Other Emperors buried here were Gaius, probably Claudius, and certainly Nerva (in A.D. 98). Then came a change. Trajan was buried at the foot of his column: Hadrian built a new and yet more grandiose mausoleum for himself and his heirs.

Known in the Middle Ages as Monte Augusto, the Mausoleum was used in turn as a fortress, a pasture, a garden, a bull-ring and a concert-hall. Finally it was excavated and restored to its present state for the bimillenary of Augustus in 1938.

See Plates 65 and 66.

THE MAUSOLEUM OF HADRIAN

IMP. CAESARI. DIVI. TRAIANI. PARTHICI. FILIO. DIVI. NERVAE. NEPOTI. TRAIANO. HADRIANO. AVGVSTO PONT. MAX. TRIB. POT. XXII. IMP. II. COS. III. P.P. ET. DIVAE. SABINAE. IMP. CAESAR. T. AELIVS. HADRIANVS. ANTONINVS. AVGVSTVS. PIVS. PONTIFEX. MAX. TRIB. POTEST. II. COS. II. DESIGN. III. P.P. PARENTIBVS SVIS.

To the Emperor Trajanus Hadrianus Augustus, son of the deified Trajan . . . grandson of the deified Nerva . . . and to the deified Sabina. Set up by the Emperor T. Aelius Hadrianus Antoninus Augustus Pius . . . to his parents.

CIL, VI. 984

He was buried hard by the Tiber, by the Aelian Bridge, where his monument had been prepared.

DIO CASSIUS, *Roman History*, LXIX. 23

IMP. CAESARI. TITO AELIO HADRIANO. ANTONINO. AVGVSTO. PIO. PONTIFICI. MAXIMO. TRIBVNIC. POT. XXIIII IMP. II. COS. III. P.P

To the Emperor Titus Aelius Hadrianus Antoninus Augustus Pius, Pontifex Maximus, Tribunician power 24 times, hailed as Imperator twice, consul three times, Father of his Country.

CIL, VI. 986

DIVAE. FAVSTINAE. AVGVSTAE. IMP. CAESARIS. T. AELII. HADRIANI. ANTONINI. AVGVSTI. PII. P.P.

To the deified Faustina, wife of the Emperor Titus Aelius Hadrianus Antoninus...

CIL, VI. 987

IMP. CAESARI. L. AVRELIO. VERO. AVG. ARMENIAC. MED. PARTHIC. PONTIFIC. TRIBVNIC. POT. VIIII. IMP. V. COS. III. P.P.

To the Emperor Lucius Aurelius Verus Augustus, Armeniacus, Medicus, Parthicus, Pontifex Maximus. Tribunician power nine times, five times hailed imperator, thrice consul, Father of his Country.

CIL, VI. 991 (A.D. 169)

IMPERATORI. CAESARI. DIVI. MARCI. ANTONINI. PII. GERMANICI. SARMATICI. FILIO. DIVI. PII. NEPOTI. DIVI. HADRIANI. PRONEPOTI. DIVI. TRAIANI. PARTHICI. ABNEPOTI. DIVI. NERVAE. ADNEPOTI. L. AELIO COMMODO. AVGVSTO. SARMATICO. GERMANICO. MAXIMO. BRITANNICO. PONTIFICI. MAXIMO. TRIBVNICIAE. POTEST. XVIII. IMPERAT. VIII. CONSVLI. VII. PATRI. PATRIAE.

To the Emperor Lucius Aelius Commodus Augustus, son of the deified Marcus Antoninus Pius, Germanicus, Sarmaticus, grandson of the deified Pius, great-grandson of the deified Hadrian, great-great-grandson of the deified Trajan . . . great-great-great-grandson of the deified Nerva. Germanicus Maximus, Britannicus, Pontifex Maximus, Tribunician power 18 times, hailed as Imperator 8 times, Consul 7 times, Father of his Country.

CIL, VI. 992 (A.D. 198)

fecit et sui nominis et pontem et sepulchrum iuxta Tiberim . . .

He built a bridge and a mausoleum bearing his own name by the banks of the Tiber.

HISTORIA AUGUSTA, *Hadrian*, 19

Periit Eboraci in Britannia . . . inlatus sepulchro Marci Antonini quem ex omnibus imperatoribus tantum coluit . . . ut et Commodum in divos referret et Antonini nomen omnibus quasi Augusti deinceps putaret, ipse a senatu agentibus liberis, qui ei funus amplissimum exhibuerunt, inter divos est relatus. . . .

Corpus eius a Britannia Romam usque cum magna provincialium reverentia susceptum est: quamvis aliqui urnulam auream tantum fuisse dicant Severi reliquias continentem eandemque Antoninorum sepulchro inlatam, cum Septimius illic ubi vita functus est esset incensus.

(4th February, A.D. 211)

(Septimius Severus) died in Britain, at York . . . he was buried in the tomb of Marcus (Aurelius) Antoninus, whom he esteemed as the greatest of the Caesars:

so much so, that he even arranged for the deification of Commodus, and thought that all future emperors should bear the name of Antoninus, like that of Augustus. He himself was deified by the Senate at the instance of his sons, who gave him a magnificent funeral.

His body was conveyed from Britain, and everywhere met with the greatest respect by the provincials. Some say, however, that only a small golden urn containing the ashes of Severus was deposited in the tomb of the Antonini, and that he was cremated in the place where he died.

HISTORIA AUGUSTA, *Severus*, 19. XXIV

In the meanwhile, another Gothic assault was under way against the Porta Aurelia (Cornelia). The tomb of the Emperor Hadrian stands outside this gate, about a stone's throw away. It is a most notable sight, for it is made of Parian marble, and the stones fit together so closely that there are no joins visible. It has four equal sides (each a stone's throw, 300 ft., in length, while their height is greater than that of the city wall). Above this, there are statues of men and horses, of the same marble, superb pieces of craftsmanship. Since this tomb seemed a fortress which could threaten the city, it had been enclosed by two covering-walls from the Wall (of Aurelian), thus incorporating it in the city defence. . . . Constantinus had been appointed by Belisarius to command the garrison at the Mausoleum, and also on the flanking walls, which were very lightly held. . . . The Goths began an assault on the Gate and the Mausoleum: they lacked siege engines, but brought up a large number of scaling-ladders, and thought that by discharging huge quantities of arrows they could easily overpower the small garrison. Holding shields before them . . . they managed to get to close quarters before the Romans saw them, for they were under the cover of the colonnade which goes to the church of the Apostle Peter. From this shelter they launched their attack, and the defenders could not fire their *ballistae*, which can only fire straight in front of them, nor repel them by ladders. . . . The Goths were on the point of placing their scaling-ladders on the wall, and had surrounded the defenders of the Mausoleum. . . . For a short time the Romans were in panic, unable to decide how to save themselves. Then, by common agreement, they broke up most of the statues, which were very large, and used the great number of stones thus provided to hurl down on the heads of the enemy, who gave way before them. . . then the Romans brought their siege engines into play, and reduced their opponents to dismay, so that the assault was soon abandoned. . . . So was the position restored at the Aurelian Gate.

PROCOPIUS, *Gothic War*, I. XXII (11th March, A.D. 537)

The Mausoleum was set in the Gardens of Domitia on the opposite bank of the Tiber to that of Augustus. Together with the Pantheon, it has been the most enduring of Hadrian's buildings in Rome. Brick stamps show that its construction had begun in A.D. 134. The first to be buried there was Hadrian himself: the dedicatory inscription (CIL, VI.

984) was set up by Antoninus Pius in 139. Recorded by earlier observers, it is now lost, as are those of Antoninus Pius (d. 161), Faustina the Elder (d. 140/1), Lucius Verus (d. 169), whose titles record the triumphs won for him by Avidius Cassius, and Commodus (d. 198). It is ironic that the grandiloquent epitaph of Commodus proudly records the ancestors he had disgraced, and whose work on the northern frontier he had largely rejected. By this time the monument had become commonly known as the *Antoninianum* or *Antonini sepulcrum*, as is shown in the passage on Septimius Severus. There may have been a cenotaph to that Emperor at York, but no trace of it has been found.

The second use of the monument—fortress, as well as Mausoleum—began with the building of the Aurelian Wall in 270–275. With its huge concrete drum, it was seen to be admirably fitted as a bridgehead defence: the passage from Procopius shows it successfully filling that role when Belisarius defended Rome against the Gothic King Vitigis in 537. Note that its famous statues had survived until that date, when those that could be broken up were used as missiles by the defenders. Some of the bronze statues, however, were later taken to the *atrium* of Old St. Peter's.

The miracle which gave it the name of Castel St. Angelo is said to have occurred in 590. The building formed the nucleus of the Civitas Leonina, built between 845 and 847, later it entered on its long life as the chief fortress of the Popes. This lasted, in effect, until the entry into Rome of the troops of United Italy in 1870.

THE THERMAE OF DIOCLETIAN

D.D. N.N. DIOCLETIANVS. ET. MAXIMIANVS. INVICTI. SENIORES. AVGVSTI. PATRES. IMPP. ET. CAESS. ET. D.D. N.N. CONSTANTIVS. ET. MAXIMIANVS. INVICTI. AVGG. ET. SEVERVS. ET. MAXIMINVS. NOBILISSIMI. CAESARES. THERMAS. FELICES. DIOCLETIANAS. QVAS. MAXIMIANVS. AVG. REDIENS. EX. AFRICA. PRAESENTIA. MAIESTATIS. DISPOSVIT. AC. FIERI. IVSSIT. ET. DIOCLETIANI. AVG. FRATRIS. SVI. NOMINE. CONSACRAVIT. COEMPTIS. AEDIFICIIS. PRO. TANTI. OPERIS. MAGNITVDINE. OMNI. CVLTV. PERFECTAS. ROMANIS. SVIS. DEDICAVERVNT.

Our Lords Diocletian and Maximian, the elder and invincible Augusti, fathers of the Emperors, and the Caesars, our Lords Constantius and Maximian, and Severus and Maximin, noblest Caesars, dedicated these auspicious Baths of Diocletian to their beloved Romans—Baths which Maximian, present in majesty on his return from Africa, ordered to be built and consecrated in the name of his brother Diocletian, having purchased the premises required for so huge and mighty a work, and furnishing them with every sumptuous refinement.

CIL, vi. 1130 (restored from eight fragments and completed from a copy made in the eighth century)

The building of these, the most sumptuous and splendid of the imperial thermae, may be deduced from the inscription. Maximian returned from Africa in A.D. 298: Diocletian and Maximian abdicated on the 1st of May 305: Constantius Chlorus died on 25th July 306. The buildings must therefore have been dedicated between the last two dates. Another inscription (CIL, vi. 1131) refers to a restoration at an unknown but much later date. The Baths presumably remained in use until the cutting of the aqueducts during the Gothic Wars of the sixth century. See Plate 71.

Everything about them is on a colossal scale: a labour force of 40,000 is said to have worked on them: 3,000 bathers could be accommodated at a time, and could find within their walls all the amusements of a major spa. Various parts of the buildings have been put to a fantastic range of uses at later periods—besides Michelangelo's Church of S. Maria degli Angeli, they have housed a convent, granaries, an asylum, a planetarium, stables, wine, coal and oil cellars, and a physical training centre. Disengaged and restored by the devoted labours of Italian archaeologists over a period of sixty years, they now form an incomparable setting for the treasures of the Museo Nazionale Romano.

THE THERMAE OF CARACALLA (ANTONINIANAE)

Opera Romae reliquit thermas nominis sui eximias, quarum cellam solearem[1] architecti negant posse ulla imitatione, qualis facta est, fieri, nam et ex aere vel cupro cancelli sub[2] positi esse dicuntur, quibus cameratio tota concredita est, et tantum est spatii ut id ipsum fieri negant potuisse docti mechanici.

Among the public works Caracalla left at Rome were the splendid Thermae named after himself. Architects declare that the *cella solearis*, as built by him, defies imitation. For the whole vaulting is said to rest on gratings of copper or bronze, placed underneath it[3]; but its size is such that those skilled in mechanics say that it could not have been made in that way.

HISTORIA AUGUSTA, *Caracalla*, 9

Antoninus Romae thermas sui nominis aedificavit.

[1] soliarem? [2] super? [3] or over it?

Antoninus (i.e. Caracalla) built at Rome the Baths that bear his name.

St. Jerome, ad Eusebius a. 2231 (A.D. 216)

CVCVMIO ET VICTORIA SE VIVOS FECERVNT CAPSARIVS DE ANTONINIANAS.

Cucumius and Victoria made this monument for themselves during their own lifetime. He was a cloak-room attendant at the Antoninianae.

CIL, vi. 9232

OPVS DOLIARE EX PRAEDIS DVORVM AVGVSTORVM NOSTRORVM FIGLINIS C. TER. TIT.

Pottery made at the workshops on the estate of our lords the Augusti (Geta and Caracalla) G. Terentius Titus (overseer).

CIL, xv. 769

Here is another instance of a major Roman building for which the literary and epigraphic evidence is exiguous. The names of an illiterate cloakroom attendant and his wife are no substitute for the loss of all building inscriptions, except for restorations undertaken in the time of Theoderic. And, as so often, the *Historia Augusta* creates problems rather than solves them. The *cella soliaris*—if that is the correct reading—would seem to have been a sun-lounge or sun-deck, but the text also leaves it in doubt whether the *cancelli* (beams or plates?) supported or rested on the vaulting, and much controversy has failed to establish the purpose which they served. But at least the passage of Jerome gives A.D. 216 as a firm date for the dedication of the building, and the brick-stamp with its AUGG—two G's, neither one nor three—refers to Caracalla and Geta as Augusti, and shows building in progress between February 211 and February 212. It is likely that it began under Septimius Severus, and was not completed until 221 or later.

There is also a contemporary list of sculptures, for which the baths were famous: they include the Bull, the Hercules, and the Flora now in the Naples Museum, all discovered in the sixteenth century.

For the rest, we must study the remains themselves, as has been done by a distinguished line of architects and archaeologists, from Palladio to Blouet, Ivanoff and Rostovtzev. As a result at least the main features are known, and are well seen in the model reconstruction made for the *plastico* of Rome (see Plate 72). The baths proper are set on a large platform, 20 ft. high, which enclosed service-corridors giving access to all rooms. They are axially planned around the great hall or concourse, seen in the centre, with its three huge bays: behind it rises the dome of the *caldarium* or hot bath. The *frigidarium* is in front and is here shown open to the sky, a point on which there has been much controversy. To left and right of this were the main *apodyteria* or dressing-rooms, where our *capsarius* and his fellows were employed. The open courtyards seen to the left and right of the central block were *palaestrae* or exercise-grounds. Besides these, there must have been smaller baths of various temperatures, some of them for medicinal treatment, also lecture-rooms, restaurants, etc., but identification is uncertain.

These buildings are surrounded by gardens and walks, and enclosed by a *peribolus* or peripheral series of colonnades and buildings, symmetrically planned. To left and right are *exedrae* each with an identical set of three rooms; these include the *nymphaea* with their famous octagonal domes. The long side to the rear has as its central feature a stadium, above which rise the cisterns for the water-supply, derived from an arm of Aqua Marcia. The pavilion-like buildings to the left and right of the stadium are probably libraries. The two tiers of small apartments on the front or street façade were perhaps let off for shops, offices and brothels.

Such in brief, were the features of the Thermae of Imperial Rome—capable of providing amusement for 1,600 people simultaneously—buildings unparalleled in any other age. Nor must we forget the power even their ruins have had to speak for themselves. They inspired Shelley to write *Prometheus Unbound*, and McKim to design the great hall of Pennsylvania Station in New York. And among the thousands who go on summer nights to the Baths of Caracalla to see the open-air opera, some at least will respond to the grand effects of mass and space that are the attributes of late Roman architecture.

THE TOMB OF THE SCIPIOS

CORNELIVS LVCIVS SCIPIO BARBATVS GNAIVOD PATRE PROGNATVS, FORTIS VIR SAPIENSQVE, QVOIVS FORMA VIRTVTEI PARISVMA FVIT; CONSOL, CENSOR, AIDILIS QVEI FVIT APVD VOS; TAVRASIA CISAVNA SAMNIO CEPIT, SVBIGIT OMNE LOVCANAM OPSIDESQVE ABDOVCIT. (See Plate 74).

Lucius Cornelius Scipio Barbatus, son of Gnaius, a brave man and a wise: his beauty matched his character: consul, censor, aedile among you: He captured Taurasia and Cisauna in Samnium; he subdued the whole of Lucania and took hostages from it.

CIL, VI. 1284

HONC OINO PLOIRVME COSENTIONT R(OMAI) DVONORO OPTVMO FVISE VIRO, LVCIOM SCIPIONE. FILIOS BARBATI, CONSOL, CENSOR, AIDILIS HIC FVET A(PVD VOS). HEC CEPIT CORSICA ALERIAQVE VRBE, DEDET TEMPESTATEBVS AIDE MERETO. (See Plate 73.)

Most men at Rome agree that this was the best of all good men—Lucius Scipio, son of Barbatus. Consul, censor, aedile among you: He captured Corsica and took the city of Aleria in battle: He dedicated a temple to the storms which they had earned. . . .

CIL, VI. 1287

QVE APICE INSIGNE DIAL(IS FL)AMINIS GESISTEI, MORS PERFE(CIT) TVA VT ESSENT OMNIA BREVIA, HONOS FAMA VIRTVSQVE GLORIA ATQVE INGENIVM, QVIBVS SEI IN LONGA LICV(I)SET TIBE VTIER VITA, FACILE FACTEIS SVPERASES GLORIAM MAIORVM. QVARE LVBENS TE IN GREMIV, SCIPIO, RECIP(I)T TERRA, PVBLI, PROGNATVM PVBLIO, CORNELI.

You who bore on your head the insignia of Flamen Dialis—Your death has made all ephemeral—honour, reputation, character, glory, intellect. Had you been able to use these in a long life, your deeds would easily have surpassed the glory of our ancestors. So, Publius Cornelius Scipio, son of Publius, earth receives you gladly in her bosom.

CIL, VI. 1288

CN. CORNELIVS CN. F. SCIPIO HISPANVS
PR., AID. CVR., Q., TRI. MIL. II, XVIR SL. IVDIK.,
XVVIR SACR. FAC.

VIRTVTES GENERIS MIEIS MORIBVS ACCVMVLAVI,
PROGENIEM GENVI, FACTA PATRIS PETIEI.
MAIORVM OPTENVI LAVDEM, VT SIBEI ME ESSE CREATVM
LAETENTVR; STIRPEM NOBILITAVIT HONOR.

Cn. Cornelius Scipio Hispanus, son of Gnaius, praetor, aedile, quaestor, military tribune, decemvir, etc. etc.

I enriched the qualities of my race with my own character:
bore offspring: followed the deeds of my father.
I won praise from my ancestors, so that they are glad
I was born to them: the honour I won has ennobled my line.

CIL, VI. 1293

L. CORNELIVS CN. F. CN. N. SCIPIO. MAGNA SAPIENTIA MVLTASQVE VIRTVTES AETATE QVOM PARVA POSIDET HOC SAXSVM. QVOIEI VITA DEFECIT, NON HONOS, HONORE. IS HIC SITVS, QVEI NVNQVAM VICTVS EST VIRTVTEI. ANNOS GNATVS XX IS L..EIS MANDATVS: NE QVAIRATIS HONORE QVEI MINVS SIT MANDATVS.

L. Cornelius Scipio, son of Gnaius, grandson of Gnaius. Great wisdom, many virtues, this stone holds—how short a span! Life, not character, deprived him of honours. Here he lies, whose worth was never surpassed. At the age of 20, he is committed to this place: Ask not for his honours, without them he lies here.

CIL, VI. 1289

An tu regressus Porta Capena, cum Calatini, Scipionum, Serviliorum, Metellorum sepulcra vides, miseros putas illos?

When you leave Porta Capena, and see the tombs of Calatinus, of the Scipios, the Servilii, the Metelli, do you consider those mighty dead 'unhappy'?

CICERO, *Tusculan Disputations*, I. VII

Carus fuit Africano superiori noster Ennius, itaque etiam in sepulcro Scipionum putatur is esse constitutus ex marmore. At iis laudibus certe non solum ipse qui laudatur, sed etiam populi Romani nomen ornatur.

Our great poet Ennius was dear to Scipio Africanus the Elder—so much so, that a marble statue of him is said to have been placed in the tomb of the Scipios. Certainly the praises Ennius bestowed redounded not merely on Scipio, but also on the name of the Roman People.

CICERO, *Pro Archia*, IX

Morientem rure eo ipso loco sepeliri se iussisse ferunt monumentumque ibi aedificari, ne funus sibi in ingrata patria fieret.

When Scipio lay dying, he is said to have ordered that he should be buried in that very place (Liternum), and that there his monument should be built, lest his funeral should be held in his ungrateful country.

LIVY, XXXVIII. 53

At both Rome and Liternum tombs and statues of Scipio Africanus are shown—At Liternum is a tomb, with a statue on it, which I recently saw, badly damaged by weather: at Rome, outside Porta Capena, and in the sepulchre of the Scipios, are three statues, two of which are said to be Publius and Lucius Scipio, the third, the poet Ennius.

LIVY, XXXVIII. 56

But let us also review the glory of our own countrymen. The elder Africanus gave orders for a statue of Ennius to be placed on his tomb, and for that famous name, a trophy won over the spoils of a third of the world, to be read over his ashes, together with the name of a poet.

PLINY, *Natural History*, VIII. 114

The tomb of the Scipios, on the Appian Way outside Porta Capena, is by far the finest extant example of the family tomb of a great Roman house. It would have been better, no doubt, had its discovery not been made before the days of scientific archaeology. Even so, eight epitaphs have survived, covering between them more than a century and a half, from the L. Cornelius Scipio Barbatus, who was consul in 298 B.C., to a Paulla Cornelia who died later than 150 B.C. They are documents of unique importance. Linguistically, they are in archaic Latin, although the earliest does not seem to have been composed before the end of the Second Punic War. For the history of Latin literature, the change from the Saturnian to the elegiac metre is significant. Yet perhaps their chief interest is social. They speak for the collective personality of a great Roman aristocratic *gens*: the belief in inherited virtues, the obligation of public service as the first duty, the insistence on *virtus*, *gloria*, *honos*, *fama*. Early death may be accepted, if these exist in potential: not to disgrace your ancestors is the supreme praise. Of the epitaphs quoted, the first is L. Cornelius Scipio Barbatus, who won victories in Lucania and Samnium, the second, his son L. Cornelius Scipio, conqueror of Corsica (259 B.C.), who triumphed over the Sardinians, Corsicans, and Carthaginians, the third, perhaps the elder son of Africanus, who died young, the fourth Gn. Cornelius Scipio Hispanus, who took part in the Third Punic War, the last may be his younger brother.

The confusion about the burial of the greatest of the line, Scipio Africanus, is noteworthy. The memorial at Liternum was clearly no longer maintained in Livy's day, but perhaps the three statues in the Roman family monument—Africanus, his brother, and Ennius—argue that Africanus was not buried at Rome.

All the sarcophagi now to be seen *in situ* are copies.

STATIO ANNONAE

L · IVLIO · VEH*il*IO GR*ato*
IVLIANO PRA*ef*. PR . PRAEF

ANN · Á RATIONIB′ · PRAEF · *classis p*RAET · MISENAT · PRA*ef*
CLASSIS · PRAET · RAVEN*nat. proc.* AVG · ET · PRAEP · VEXIL*la*
TION · TEMPORE BELLI *britannici pr*ŏC · AVG · PROVIN*ciae*
LVSIT*aniae* ET . VETT*oniae proc. a*VG · ET · PRAEPOSIT
VEXILLATIONIS · PER . . . . PRŎC · AV́G ·
ET · PRAEF · CLASSIS · P*ontic*AE *proc. augg. e*T PRA*ep*
VEXILLATIONIS · PER ACHAIAM · ET · MACEDONIM
ET · IN · HISPANIAS · ADVERSVS · CASTABOCAS · ET

MAVROS · REBELLES · PRAEPOSITO · VEXILLATIO
NIBVS · TEMPORE · BELLI · GERMANICI · ET · SARMAT ·
PRAEF · ALAE · TAMPIANAE · PRAEF · ALAE · HER
CVLANAE · TRIB′ · COHORT · PRIMAE · VLPIAE · PAN
NONIORVM · PRAEF · COHORT · TERTIAE · AVGVST ·
THRACVM · DONIS MILITARIBVS · DONATO AB IMPE
*rato*RIBVS · ANTONINO · ET · VERO · OB VICTORIAM
*belli parthi*CI · ITEM · AB · ANTONINO · ET ·
*commodo ob uic*TOR · BELLI · GERM*a*NIC
et sarmatici . . . . .

To Lucius Julius Vehilius Gratus Julianus, Prefect of the Praetorian Guard, Prefect of the Annona, Prefect of the Fleet at Misenum, Prefect of the Fleet at Ravenna, Procurator of Augustus and Commander of a Field Force at the time of the war in Britain, Procurator of Augustus in the Province of Lusitania and Vettonia, and Commander of a Field Force in . . . Procurator of Augustus and Prefect of the Black Sea Fleet, Commander of a Field Force in Achaea and Macedonia, also in the Spanish provinces against the rebellious Castabocae and Mauri, Commander of Field Forces in the wars against the Germans and Sarmatians, Commander of the Ala Tampiana, also the Ala Herculana, Military Tribune in the First Ulpian Cohort of Pannonians, Prefect of the Third Augustan Cohort of Thracians, decorated by the Emperors Antoninus and Verus for a victory won in the Parthian War, also by the Emperors Antoninus and Commodus for a victory in the German and Sarmatian Wars.

CIL, VI. 31856

DIVO AC VENERABILI PRINCIPI CONSTANTINO PATRI PRINCIPVM MAXIMORVM FL. CREPEREIVS MADALIANVS VC. PRAEF. ANN. CVM. IVRE. GLAD.

To the deified and venerable Emperor, Constantine, Father of our mighty emperors, Flavius Crepereius Madalianus, Praefectus Annonae. . . .

CIL, VI. 1151 (A.D. 337–341)

. . . CIVS AVGG. ANNONA (TRAJANVS DECIVS ET ALII AVGVSTI ANNONA)

The Annona . . . under Trajanus Decius and his sons.

The ancient arches and columns to be seen in the church of S. Maria in Cosmedin are those of the *statio annonae*, the headquarters of the great organization which had charge of the corn supply (Plate 75). They formed part of a *porticus* which appears to have been built on to the Temple of Ceres (?) in the Forum Boarium, and is dated to the third century A.D.

The office of *Praefectus Annonae* was an important equestrian post. A number of inscriptions referring to these officials have been found. The two quoted belong to the second and fourth centuries A.D. Note the remarkable career of Vehilius (?) Gratus Julianus, with its extraordinary range of offices held in all branches of the armed forces and all parts of the empire. This much-employed soldier—whose career is given in descending order of dignity, with the office of *Praefectus Annonae* second only to that of *Praefectus Praetorio*—may perhaps be the praetorian prefect who, 'in formal dress and in the presence of his staff' was pushed into a fishpond by the Emperor Commodus.

Several *sigilla*, lead or bronze stamps for merchandise, have been found with the mark ANNONA (CIL, XV. 7952–7999).

THE ARCH OF THE ARGENTARII

IMP. CAES. L. SEPTIMIO SEVERO PIO PERTINACI AVG. ARABIC(O), ADIABENIC(O), PARTH(ICO) MAX(IMO), FORTISSIMO, FELICISSIMO, PONTIF(ICI) MAX(IMO), TRIB(VNICIA) POTEST(ATE) XII, IMP. XI, COS. III, PATRI PATRIAE, ET / IMP. CAES. M. AVRELIO ANTONINO PIO FELICI AVG., TRIB(VNICIA) POTEST(ATE) VII, COS. III, P(ATRI) *p(atriae)*, *procos.*, *fortissimo felicissimoque principi* ET / IVLIAE AVG. MATRI AVG(VSTI) *n(ostri)* ET CASTRORVM ET *senatus et patriae, et* IMP. CAES. M. AVRELI ANTONINI PII FELICIS AVG. / *Parthici Maximi, Brittannici Maximi* / ARGENTARII ET NEGOTIANTES BOARI HVIVS *loci qui invehent,* DEVOTI NVMINI EORVM.

To the Emperor L. Septimius Severus etc., etc.
Pontifex Maximus, tribunician power for the 12th time . . . (A.D. 204) consul for the 3rd time . . . and to the Imperial Caesar M. Aurelius Antoninus Pius etc. (Caracalla) tribunician power for the 7th time . . . most brave and fortunate of princes . . . and to Julia Augusta, mother of the Armies, the Senate and People, and of the Imperial Caesar . . . (Caracalla). The money lenders and merchants dealing in the Forum Boarium, set up this from respect to their divine powers.

CIL, VI. 1035

The little Arch of the Argentarii was built in honour of the house of Septimius Severus by the money-lenders and cattle-dealers of the Forum Boarium, to which it served as a monumental entrance. The inscription and its history illustrate the crimes and scandals of the dynasty. Geta's name and titles were erased, as elsewhere (see p. 85). Plautilla, wife of Caracalla, suffered indignity twice; after the fall of her father Plautianus in A.D. 205 the words *filiae P. Fulvi Plautiani pontificis praefecti praetorio* were erased: after her own murder in 211 her figure was chiselled out.

CIRCUS MAXIMUS

Tarquin also built the largest of the Circuses, which lies between the Aventine and the Palatine Hills. He was the first to surround it with covered seats—previously the spectators had stood—the wooden stands resting on beams. Dividing up the place among the thirty *curiae*, he assigned to each *curia* its own section, so that each spectator was sitting in the enclosure proper to him. In the course of time this work was to become one of the most beautiful and remarkable buildings in Rome: the Circus being 3½ stades long (2,100 ft. Greek) and four plethra wide (400 ft.). There is a canal around it on the two long sides, and on one of the shorter ones: this is ten feet wide and ten feet deep. Behind this are three tiers making up the porticoes: the lowest of stone, the upper two of wood: they rise above each other like tiers in the theatre. The two larger porticoes are made continuous by being linked by the shorter one, which is crescent-shaped: this gives a single portico resembling that of an amphitheatre, 8 stades in circuit (4,800 ft.) and seating 150,000 persons. The other short side is not covered, but contains the roofed starting-boxes for horses, which are started simultaneously at the one signal. On the outside of the Circus there is another portico of one storey, which has shops with apartments over them. These have entries and stairways for the spectators at each shop, so that many thousands of people may enter or leave without congestion.

DIONYSIUS HALICARNASSUS, *Roman Antiquities*, III. 68

At the Ludi Romani in that year (187 B.C.) . . . a badly-fixed mast fell down on the statue of Pollentia and destroyed it. Disturbed by this omen, the Senate voted first, to add a day to the Games, second, to set up two statues in place of one, the new one to be gilded.

LIVY, XXXIX. vii. 8

(Julius Caesar) gave races for which the Circus was lengthened at either end and a channel (euripus) dug around it. Then young men of the best families drove two-horse and four-horse chariots, and rode horses yoked in pairs, vaulting from one to the other. The Ludus Troiae or Game of Troy was performed by two teams, one of younger and one of older boys. For five successive days there were combats of wild beasts: finally, there was a battle between two opposing armies, each of which had 500 men, 20 elephants, and 30 cavalry. To give room for the fighting, the *metae* were taken down, and in their places two camps were built facing each other.

SUETONIUS, *Caesar*, 30

Suppose we omit from our great achievements the Circus Maximus, built by Julius Caesar, three stades long and one broad, but covering three acres of buildings and with seating for 250,000. . . .

PLINY, *Natural History*, XXXVI. 102

Seeing that the groundsmen made mistakes about the number of laps completed in the races, Agrippa set up the Dolphins and Eggs, so that they should serve to indicate clearly the number of laps completed.

DIO CASSIUS, *Roman History*, XLIX. 43. 2

PVLVINAR AD CIRCVM MAXIMVM . . . FECI

I built the Imperial Box in the Circus Maximus.

AUGUSTUS, *Res gestae*, 19

SENATVS POPVLVSQVE ROMANVS . . . IMP. TITO CAESARI. DIVI. VESPASIANI F. AVGVSTO. TRIB. X . . . PRINCIPI SVO QVOD PRAECEPTIS PATRIS CONSILIISQ. ET AVSPICIIS GENTEM IVDAEORVM DOMVIT ET VRBEM HIERVSOLYMAM OMNIBVS ANTE SE DVCIBVS REGIBVS GENTIBVS AVT FRVSTRA PETITAM AVT OMNINO INTEMPTATAM DELEVIT.

The Senate and People of Rome . . . to the Emperor Titus Caesar, son of Vespasian . . . tribunician power for the tenth time (A.D. 81), their princeps . . . because, following his father's advice and policy, and under his auspices, he conquered the Jewish people and captured the city of Jerusalem, which all kings, generals, or peoples before his time had assailed in vain or left unassailed.

CIL, vi. 944; ILS, 264

IMP. CAESARI. DIVI NERVAE F. NERVAE TRAIANO AVGVSTO GERMANICO DACICO . . . TRIB. POT. VII. TRIBVS XXXV QVOD LIBERALITATE OPTIMI PRINCIPIS COMMODA EARVM ETIAM LOCORVM ADIECTIONE AMPLIATA SINT.

To the Emperor Trajan Augustus . . . son of the deified Nerva, tribunician power for the seventh time (A.D. 103). Set up by the Thirty-Five Tribes because by the generosity of that best of princes their amenities have been improved by an addition to the number of seats.

CIL, vi. 955

Iam pridem, ex quo suffragia nulli
vendimus, effudit curas: nam qui dabat olim
imperium fasces legiones omnia, nunc se
continet atque duas tantum res anxius optat,
panem et circenses.

The people have long shed their anxieties—since we stopped selling our votes. That sovereign people, who once disposed of everything—power, fasces, the legions—now restrains itself to two objects of prayer—the corn dole and the shows in the circus.

JUVENAL, *Satires*, x.77–81

Si potes avelli circensibus . . .

If you can tear yourself away from the circus shows . . .

JUVENAL, *Satires*, III. 223

interea Megalesiacae spectacula mappae
Idaeum sollemne colunt, similisque triumpho
praeda caballorum praetor sedet, ac mihi pace
immensae nimiaeque licet si dicere plebis,
totam hodie Romam circus capit, et fragor aurem
percutit, eventum viridis quo colligo panni.
nam si deficeret, maestam attonitamque videres
hanc urbem veluti Cannarum in pulvere victis
consulibus. spectent iuvenes, quos clamor et audax
sponsio, quos cultae decet adsedisse puellae.

Meanwhile, they observe the festival of the Goddess of Ida, the spectacle marked by Cybele's handkerchief. There sits the praetor, as at a triumph, but he's only the nags' booty. If the enormous, the superfluous, population of the city will let me say so, all Rome is today in the Circus. Its roar beats on the ear: I deduce that the Green has won the race. For, had it lost, you'd have seen the whole city depressed and appalled, as when the consuls were defeated in the dust of Cannae. Well, let the young men watch, who like the noise, and bold bets, and sitting beside a pretty girl.

JUVENAL, *Satires*, XI. 193–202

The Circus is a model of the vault of Heaven. The wisdom of the ancients gave it the shape and mathematical proportions of the starry realm. For the twelve gates represent the twelve months, and all the signs of the zodiac through which the golden chariot of the sun takes his course. The four horses match the four seasons, the colours of the factions, the four elements. The barriers enclose the chariots in their proper courses, and Janus bids them go when he raises his flag. When the starting-gates are open and spill forth the chariots, one tries to gain a lead on all the others. They strive to round the circuit marked out by the *metae*: these twin axes mark the rising and the setting of the sun. Then the canal, like the mighty ocean, lies between: the highest obelisk is in the middle of the central *spina*. Again, seven laps complete the course for the prize, even so do the seven zones bind together the heavens. A two-horse chariot is sacred to the Moon, a four-horse to the Sun, single horses are dedicated to Castor and Pollux. Our circus shows are in harmony with the divine order of the world: their great popularity increases to the honour of the gods.

Anthologia Latina, I. 197, 1–20

[*C. Appu*]LEIVS DIOCLES, AGITATOR FACTIONIS RVSSATAE, / [*nat*]IONE HISPANVS LVSITANVS, ANNORVM XXXXII MENS. VII D. XXIII. / [*Pri*]MVM AGITAVIT IN FACTIONE ALB. ACILIO AVIOLA ET CORELLIO PANSA COS. / [*Primu*]M VICIT IN FACTIONE EADEM M'. ACILIO GLABRIONE C. BELLICIO TORQVATO COS. / [*P*]RIMVM AGITAVIT IN FACTIONE PRASINA TORQVATO ASPRENATE II ET ANNIO LIBONE COS. PRIMVM VICIT / [*in faction*]E RVSSATA LAENATE PONTIANO ET ANTONIO RVFINO COS. SVMMA: QVADRIGA AGITAVIT ANNIS XXIIII, MISSVS OSTIO $\overline{IIII}$ CCLVII, / [*vicit MCCC*]CLXII, A POMPA CX. SINGVLARVM VICIT ∞LXIIII, INDE PRAEMIA MAIORA VICIT LXXXXII, $\overline{XXX}$ XXXII, EX HIS SEIVGES III, $\overline{XXXX}$ XXVIII, / [*ex his seiuge*]S II, $\overline{L}$ XXVIIII INDE SEPTEIVGE I; $\overline{LX}$ III. BINARVM VICIT CCCXXXXVII, TRIGAS AD HS $\overline{XV}$ IIII. TERNARVM VICIT LI. AD HONOREM VENIT ∞ / . . . . [*tulit s*]ECVNDAS ĐCCCLXI, TERTIAS ĐLXXVI. QVARTAS AD HS ∞ I, FRVSTRA EXIT ∞CCCLI. AD VENETVM VICIT X, AD ALBATVM VICIT LXXXXI, INDE AD HS $\overline{XXX}$ II. [*Rettulit quaest*]VM HS $\overline{CCCLVIII}$ $\overline{LXIII}$ CXX. PRAETEREA BIGAS M' VICIT III, AD ALBATV / AD PRASINV II. OCCVPAVIT ET VICIT ĐCCCXV, SVCCESSIT ET VICIT LXVII. / [*praemisit et vici*]T XXXVI, VARIIS GENERIBVS VIC. XXXXII, ERIPVIT ET VICIT ĐII PRASINIS CCXVI VENETIS CCV ALBATIS LXXXI. EQVOS CENTENARIOS FECIT N. VIIII ET DVCENAR. I /

Gaius Appuleius Diocles,[1] charioteer of the Red Stable, a Lusitanian Spaniard by birth, aged 42 years 7 months 23 days. He drove his first chariot in the White Stable, in the consulship of Acilius Aviola and Corellius Pansa. He won his first victory in the same stable, in the consulship of Manius Acilius Glabrio and Gaius Bellicius Torquatus. He drove for the first time in the Green Stable in the consulship of Torquatus Asprenas (for the second time) and Annius Libo. He won his first victory in the Red Stable in the consulship of Laenas Pontianus and Antonius Rufinus.

Grand totals: He drove chariots for 24 years, ran 4,257 starts, and won 1,462 victories, 110 in opening races. In single-entry races he won 1,064 victories, winning 92 major purses, 32 of them (including three with six-horse teams) at 30,000 sesterces, 28 (including two with six-horse teams) at 40,000 sesterces, 29 (including 1 with a seven-horse team) at 50,000 sesterces, and 3 at 60,000 sesterces; in two-entry races he won 347 victories, including four with three-horse teams at 15,000 sesterces; in three-entry races he won 51 victories. He won or

[1] Born 104, died A.D. 146.

placed 2,900 times, taking 861 second places, 576 third places, and 1 fourth place at 1,000 sesterces; he failed to place 1,351 times. He tied a Blue for first place 10 times and a White 91 times, twice for 30,000 sesterces. He won a total of 35,863,120 sesterces. In addition, in races with two-horse teams for 1,000 sesterces he won three times, and tied a White once and a Green twice. He took the lead and won 815 times, came from behind to win 67 times, won under handicap 36 times, won in various styles 42 times, and won in a final dash 502 times (216 over the Greens, 205 over the Blues, 81 over the Whites). He made nine horses 100-time winners, and one a 200-time winner.

CIL, XIV. 2884 (translation by N. Lewis and M. Reinhold).

. . . ADIVRO TE DEMON QVICVMQVE ES ET DEMANDO TIBI EX ANC DIE EX AC ORA EX OC MOMENTO VT EQVOS PRASINI ET ALBI CRVCIES ET AGITATORES CLARVM ET FELICEM ET PRIMVLVM ET ROMANVM OCIDAS COLLIDAS NEQVE SPIRITVM ILLIS LERINQVAS; ADIVRO TE PER EVM QVI TE RESOLVIT TEMPORIBVS DEVM PELAGI CVM AERIVM IAW LASDAW

I adjure you, demon, whoever you are, and I demand of you, from this hour from this day from this moment, that you torture the horses of the Greens and the Whites and destroy and destroy and smash their drivers Clarus and Felix and Primulus and Romanus and leave no breath in them. I adjure you by that god of the sea who has released you in due season and by the god of the air, Iaw etc. etc.

From a lead tablet

The *spectacula* of the Circus Maximus, and especially the chariot-racing, were a ruling passion of the Roman people for at least four centuries. The references to them are very numerous, and those quoted above no more than a representative selection.

The *Vallis Murcia* between the Palatine and the Aventine, was well adapted for public festivals and sports: legend placed there that first of Roman athletic contests, the upshot of which was the Rape of the Sabine Women. The evolution of permanent buildings, adapted in their final form to the highly professionalized chariot-racing of the Empire, was a gradual process whose stages are not known in detail. It is as though the same piece of ground had been in continuous use for cricket from the earliest times to the modern Lords. Clearly the work of Julius Caesar and of Augustus was important, and theirs is the Circus described by Dionysius, writing in 7 B.C. There were additions by Nero, Vespasian (after the fire of A.D. 64; see p. 17) and Trajan, under whom the Circus Maximus reached its final form. A multi-purpose arena under Caesar, it could be reserved for chariot-racing after the opening of the Colosseum in A.D. 81. When Juvenal wrote, it may have been able to seat as many as

350,000 spectators, or perhaps one third of the population of Rome. Few race-tracks or football grounds of modern times can match that figure. The track proper was 550 metres long and 80 wide; down the middle ran the *spina*, with its symbolic obelisks and the *ova* and *delphines* used to mark the number of laps completed.

There were four *factiones* or racing-stables, the Reds, the Whites, the Greens, and the Blues. Each maintained its own training-school for drivers, and bred and reared its own horses. The champion drivers are here represented by the portrait shown in Plate 82, and by the epitaph of Diocles, the Bradman or Babe Ruth of his profession (whose career is set out in more detail that that of a Senator), the man in the crowd, by the curse or *defixio* quoted. The cosmic analogies drawn in the poem from the Anthologia Latina may be seem odd: the modern devotee does not read such symbolism into his favourite sport. Yet these displays did, after all, originate from religious festivals, and when the Circus passed to Constantinople as one of the chief legacies from Rome, support for the *factiones* followed the lines of current controversy in theology.

SECTION III

PRAISES OF ROME

PRAISES OF ROME

Iuli iugera pauca Martialis
hortis Hesperidum beatiora
longo Ianiculi iugo recumbunt:
lati collibus imminent recessus
et planus modico tumore vertex
caelo perfruitur sereniore,
et curvas nebula tegente valles
solus luce nitet peculiari:
puris leniter admoventur astris
celsae culmina delicata villae.
hinc septem dominos videre montes
et totam licet aestimare Romam,
Albanos quoque Tusculosque colles,
et quodcunque iacet sub urbe frigus,
Fidenas veteres brevesque Rubras
et quod virgineo cruore gaudet
Annae pomiferum nemus Perennae.
illinc Flaminiae Salariaeque
gestator patet essedo tacente;
ne blando rota sit molesta somno,
quem nec rumpere nauticum celeuma,
nec clamor valet helciariorum
cum sit tam prope Mulvius, sacrumque
lapsae per Tiberim volent carinae.

The few acres of Julius Martialis—a retreat more blessed than the Garden of the Hesperides—lie on the long ridge of the Janiculum. A wide sheltered plain looks out over the neighbouring hills; the flat summit with its gentle swell enjoys to the full a sunnier sky, for when mist clings to the winding valleys, this alone is bright with sunshine of its own. The fine roofs of the lofty villa rise gently to the pure stars. From here you can see the seven lordly hills, and measure the whole of Rome—the Alban Hills, too, and those of Tusculum, and every cool retreat outside the city walls, ancient Fidenae, little Saxa Rubra, and the apple orchard of Anna Perenna, where the maiden's blood is shed. From there the traveller is seen on the Flaminian and Salarian Roads, though you cannot hear his chariot wheels. No sound of traffic comes to disturb easy sleep, which is unbroken by the sound of oars on the river, and the bargeman's cries: although the Milvian Bridge is so near, and the ships glide down Tiber's sacred stream. . . .

MARTIAL, *Epigrams*, IV. 64

In classical times the Janiculum was largely given over to gardens and villas, some of them luxurious, the true predecessors of the Villa Doria Pamfili or the Farnesina. The villa of Martial's cousin Julius Martialis does not seem to have been of this kind, but it enjoyed all the natural advantages that make the Janiculum so delightful today, a micro-climate of sunshine above the river-mists, freedom from the noise of traffic, and, above all, the wonderful view over the city towards the Alban Hills and the *castelli Romani*. The exact site has not been determined, but it must have been near the northern end of the ridge, if the Milvian Bridge seemed close, and travellers could be seen on the Via Flaminia and Via Salaria. Note the references to traffic on the river, busy then but dead today. The *helciarii* were the bargemen who pulled boats up against the current. Not only was there heavy traffic between Rome and Ostia, but also upstream from the city, while several ferries plied across the river.

Sed dum tota domus raeda componitur una
substitit ad veteres arcus madidamque Capenam.
hic ubi nocturnae Numa constituebat amicae—
nunc sacri fontis nemus et delubra locantur
Iudaeis quorum cophinus faenumque supellex—
omnis enim populo mercedem pendere iussa est
arbor et eiectis mendicat silva Camenis—
in vallem Egeriae descendimus et speluncas
dissimiles veris. quanto praesentius esset
numen aquis, viridi si margine cluderet undas
herba nec ingenuum violarent marmora tofum.
hic tunc Umbricius 'quando artibus' inquit 'honestis
nullus in urbe locus. . . .'

But while his whole household is being loaded on a single cart, he stops at the old aqueduct and dripping Porta Capena. Here, where Numa once kept assignations with his mistress at night, today the sacred spring, the grove, and all the shrines are hired out to Jews, whose belongings consist of a basket and some hay. For every tree now has to pay rent to the people, and the whole grove has become a beggar, and the Camenae are driven away. We went down to Egeria's Vale and the caves, all artificial now. How much nearer the water-nymph's presence would be felt if green grass bordered the water, instead of marble slabs that insult our native rock! Then said Umbricius 'Since there's no place for honest occupations in Rome. . . .'

JUVENAL, *Satires*, III. 10–22

Few passages in Latin convey so intense a feeling of locality as these lines from the Third Satire of Juvenal. Umbricius—*Romano di Roma*—is leaving the polyglot and corrupt city he has come to loathe. His tirade is delivered outside Porta Capena in the Servian Wall, where the Via Appia left Rome for Capua, and over which passed the Aqua Marcia. What he sees around him symbolizes his mood. The grove of the Camenae and the Valley of Egeria, with their ancient associations, are crowded with destitute Jewish refugees, end-product of Titus' Jewish wars. The caves are a travesty of nature, instead of turf, vulgar marble surrounds the pool. Everything is foreign, imported, meretricious. In the rest of the Satire Umbricius develops his famous assault on Rome as the savage Megalopolis, hostile to her native children, and favouring only the unscrupulous immigrant.

Ἡ γὰρ δὴ πρώτη λόγου δύναμιν ἐξελέγξασα οὐκ ἐπὶ πᾶν ἀφικνουμένην ἥδε ἐστί· περὶ ἧς μὴ ὅτι εἰπεῖν κατὰ τὴν ἀξίαν ἔστιν, ἀλλ' οὐδ' ἰδεῖν ἀξίως αὐτήν, ἀλλ' ὡς ἀληθῶς Ἄργου τινὸς πανόπτου, μᾶλλον δὲ τοῦ κατέχοντος αὐτὴν πανόπτου θεοῦ δεῖ. Τίς γὰρ ἂν τοσάσδε ὁρῶν κορυφὰς κατειλημμένας ἢ πεδίων νομοὺς ἐκπεπολισμένους ἢ γῆν τοσήνδε εἰς μιᾶς πόλεως ὄνομα συνηγμένην, εἶτα ἀκριβῶς κατεθεάσατο; Ἀπὸ ποίας τοιαύτης σκοπιᾶς; ὅπερ γὰρ ἐπὶ τῆς χιόνος Ὅμηρος ἔφη, χυθεῖσαν αὐτὴν «ὑψηλῶν ὀρέων κορυφὰς καὶ πρώονας ἄκρους» καλύπτειν «καὶ πεδία λωτεῦντα καὶ ἀνδρῶν πίονα ἔργα, καὶ τ' ἐφ' ἁλὸς πολιῆς», φησί, «κέχυται λιμέσιν τε καὶ ἀκταῖς», τοῦτο ἄρα καὶ ἥδ' ἡ πόλις· καλύπτει μὲν ἄκρους πρώονας, καλύπτει δὲ τὴν ἐν μέσῳ γῆν, καταβαίνει δὲ καὶ μέχρι θαλάττης, οὗ τὸ κοινὸν ἀνθρώπων ἐμπόριον καὶ ἡ κοινὴ τῶν ἐν γῇ φυομένων διοίκησις· ὅπου δέ τις αὐτῆς γίγνοιτο, οὐδέν ἐστι τὸ κωλῦον ὁμοίως εἶναι ἐν μέσῳ. Καὶ μὲν δὴ οὐδ' ἐπιπολῆς γε κέχυται, ἀλλ' ἀτεχνῶς πολὺ ὑπὲρ τὸ παράδειγμα ἐπὶ πλεῖστον ἄνω ἥκει τοῦ ἀέρος, ὡς εἶναι μὴ χιόνος καταλήψει τὸ ὕψος προσεικάσαι, ἀλλὰ μᾶλλον αὐτοῖς τοῖς πρώοσι. Καὶ ὥσπερ τις ἀνὴρ πολὺ νικῶν τοὺς ἄλλους μεγέθει τε καὶ ῥώμῃ οὐκ ἀγαπᾷ μὴ καὶ ἄλλους ὑπὲρ αὑτὸν ἀράμενος [[φέρειν]], ὣς δὲ καὶ ἥδε ἐπὶ τοσαύτης γῆς ᾠκισμένη οὐκ ἀγαπᾷ, ἀλλ' ἑτέρας ἰσομετρήτους ὑπὲρ αὐτὴν ἀραμένη φέρει ἄλλας ἐπ' ἄλλαις. Ὡς ἄρα ἐπώνυμον αὐτῇ τοὔνομα καὶ οὐδὲν ἀλλ' ἢ ῥώμη τὰ τῆσδε. Ὥστ' εἴ τις αὐτὴν ἐθελήσειε καθαρῶς ἀναπτύξαι καὶ τὰς νῦν μετεώρους πόλεις ἐπὶ γῆς ἐρείσας θεῖναι ἄλλην παρ' ἄλλην, ὅσον νῦν Ἰταλίας διαλεῖπόν ἐστιν, ἀναπληρωθῆναι τοῦτο πᾶν ἄν μοι δοκεῖ καὶ γενέσθαι πόλις συνεχὴς μία ἐπὶ τὸν Ἰόνιον τείνουσα. Τοσαύτη δὲ οὖσα, ὅσην ἐγὼ μὲν οὐδὲ νῦν ἴσως ἀρκούντως ἐνεδειξάμην, ὀφθαλμοὶ δὲ ἄμεινον μαρτυροῦσιν, οὐχ ὥσπερ ἐπὶ τῶν ἄλλων εἰπεῖν ἔστιν, ἐνταῦθα ἕστηκεν, οὐδ' ὅ τις εἶπεν περὶ τῆς Ἀθηναίων καὶ Λακεδαιμονίων πόλεως, λέγων τῶν μὲν τὸ μέγεθος διπλάσιον ἢ κατὰ τὴν δύναμιν, τῶν δὲ πολὺ τῆς δυνάμεως ἔλαττον ἂν φανῆναι τὸ μέγεθος—ἀπείη δὲ τὸ βλάσφημον τοῦ παραδείγματος—, τοῦτο ἄν τις φαίη καὶ περὶ τῆσδε τῆς πάντα μεγάλης, ὡς ἄρα οὐκ ἀκόλουθον τὴν δύναμιν τῷ τοσούτῳ μεγέθει κατεσκευάσατο· ἀλλ' ἔστιν εἰς μὲν τὴν ὅλην ἀρχὴν βλέψαντα [[μηκέτι]] τὴν πόλιν θαυμάζειν, πολλοστὸν μέρος τῆς ἁπάσης ἄρχειν νομίσαντα γῆς, εἰς δ' αὐτὴν τὴν πόλιν καὶ τοὺς τῆς πόλεως ὅρους ἰδόντα μηκέτι θαυμάζειν, εἰ ὑπὸ τοσαύτης ἄρχεται πᾶσα ἡ οἰκουμένη.

Ὅπερ δὲ πόλις τοῖς αὐτῆς ὁρίοις καὶ χώραις ἐστίν, τοῦθ' ἥδε ἡ πόλις τῆς πάσης οἰκουμένης, ὥσπερ αὐτῆς χώρας ἄστυ κοινὸν ἀποδεδειγμένη· φαίης ἂν περιοίκους ἅπαντας ἢ κατὰ δῆμον οἰκοῦντας ἄλλον χῶρον, εἰς μίαν ταύτην ἀκρόπολιν συνέρχεσθαι. ἡ δὲ οὐδεπώποτε ἀπεῖπεν, ἀλλ' ὥσπερ τὸ τῆς γῆς ἔδαφος, φέρει πάντας· ὥσπερ δὲ ἡ τοῖς κόλποις δεχομένη τοὺς ποταμοὺς θάλαττα πάντα τοσούτους κρύψασα ἔχει, ἐξιόντων καὶ εἰσιόντων ἴση οὖσα καὶ φαινομένη, οὕτω καὶ ἥδε δέχεται μὲν ἐξ ἁπάσης γῆς, κοινὸν δ' αὐτῇ καὶ τοῦτο, πρὸς τὴν θάλαττάν ἐστιν· οὔτε γὰρ ἐκείνη μείζων ὑπὸ τῆς ἐμβολῆς τῶν ποταμῶν γίγνεται, ὡς συνειμαρμένου τούτου σὺν αὐτοῖς εἰσροῦσι αὐτὴν ἔχειν τὸ μέγεθος. τῇδε ὑπὸ μεγέθους οὐδὲν ἐπίδηλον.

For it is she (Rome) who first proved that oratory cannot reach every goal. About her not only is it impossible to speak properly, but it is impossible even to see her properly. In truth it requires some all-seeing Argos—rather, the all-seeing god who dwells in the city. For beholding so many hills occupied by buildings, or on plains so many meadows completely urbanized, or so much land brought under the name of one city, who could survey her accurately? And from what point of observation?

Homer says of snow that, as it falls, it covers 'the crest of the range and the mountain peaks and the flowering fields and the rich acres of men, and,' he says, 'it is poured out over the white sea, the harbors and the shores.' So also of this city. Like the snow, she covers mountain peaks, she covers the land intervening, and she goes down to the sea, where the commerce of all mankind has its common exchange and all the produce of the earth has its common market. Wherever one may go in Rome, there is no vacancy to keep one from being, there also, in mid-city. And indeed she is poured out, not just over the level ground, but in a manner with which the simile cannot begin to keep pace, she rises great distances into the air, so that her height is not to be compared to a covering of snow but rather to the peaks themselves. And as a man who far surpasses others in size and strength likes to show his strength by carrying others on his back, so this city, which is built over so much land, is not satisfied with her extent, but raising upon her shoulders others of equal size, one over the other, she carries them. It is from this that she gets her name, and strength (*rômé*) is the mark of all that is hers. Therefore, if one chose to unfold, as it were, and lay flat on the ground the cities which now she carries high in air, and place them side by side, all that part of Italy which intervenes would, I think, be filled and become one continuous city stretching to the Strait of Otranto.

Though she is so vast as perhaps even now I have not sufficiently shown, but as the eye attests more clearly, it is not possible to say of her as of other cities, 'There she stands'. Again it has been said of the capital cities of the Athenians and the Lacedaemonians—and may no ill omen attend the comparison—that the first would in size appear twice as great as in its intrinsic power, the second far inferior in size to its intrinsic power.

What another city is to its own boundaries and territory, this city is to the boundaries and territory of the entire civilized world, as if the latter were a country district and she had been appointed the common town. It might be said that this one citadel is the refuge and assembly place of all *perioeci* or of all who dwell in outside demes.

She has never failed them, but like the soil of the earth, she supports all men; and as the sea, which receives with its gulfs all the many rivers, hides them and holds them all and still, with what goes in and out, is and seems ever the same, so actually this city receives those who flow in from all the earth and has even sameness in common with the sea. The latter is not made greater by the influx of rivers, for it has been ordained by fate that with the waters flowing in, the sea maintain its volume; here no change is visible because the city is so great.

But of this city, great in every respect, no one could say that she has not created power in keeping with her magnitude. No, if one looks at the whole empire and reflects how small a fraction rules the whole world, he may be amazed at the city, but when he has beheld the city herself and the boundaries of the city, he can no longer be amazed that the entire civilized world is ruled by one so great.

AELIUS ARISTIDES, *Orationes*, XXVI (*Speech to Rome*), 6–9; 61–62 (translation by James H. Oliver).

'The Greeks', wrote Tacitus in a well-known passage, 'care only for their own affairs.' In general, the censure is just. But there were Greeks who addressed themselves to the theme of Rome and what she stood for in the history of the world. Polybius is the most eminent in a list which includes Dionysius of Halicarnassus, Plutarch, Dio Cassius, and Appian. Among these works the Roman Oration of Aelius Aristides holds a modest but distinctive place. Modest, because Aristides lacked any very profound insight into history or politics: his gifts were those of a famous orator of the Second Sophistic, with a wide but superficial knowledge of Greek literature and philosophy. Distinctive, because the Oration was delivered during the golden age of the Antonine Peace, when the benefits of the Roman Empire as the bringer of a common citizenship, law, and civilization on a world-wide scale were at their most apparent.

Aristides, then a young man of twenty-seven, visited Rome for the celebration of the Parilia or Birthday of Rome (21st April) in the year A.D. 143. Presumably on the invitation of the emperor Antoninus Pius, he gave a public address on the theme of Rome. This is thought to have been delivered in the Athenaeum or public lecture hall, which perhaps was included in the *peribolus* of the newly-consecrated Temple of Venus and Rome.

The passages quoted are those which refer to the city itself. They are best left to speak for themselves in testimony of the impressions made by Rome on an educated Greek who knew Alexandria and Antioch, the other two 'great cities' of the Empire. The 'cities which Rome bears on her back' must be the *insulae* or blocks of flats which housed the vast bulk of the population. In the fourth century there were more than 46,000 of these, many of them 'high-rise' buildings. It is of these that Aristides says that if laid flat and placed end-to-end, they would reach from Rome to the Strait of Otranto.

Non alium certe decuit rectoribus orbis
esse larem, nulloque magis se colle potestas
aestimat et summi sentit fastigia iuris.
attollens apicem subiectis regia rostris
tot circum delubra videt tantisque deorum
cingitur excubiis! Iuvat infra tecta Tonantis
cernere Tarpeia pendentes rupe Gigantas
caelatasque fores mediisque volantia signa
nubibus et densum stipantibus aethera templis
arvaque vestitis numerosa puppe columnis
consita subnixasque iugis inmanibus aedes,
naturam cumulante manu, spoliisque micantes
innumeros arcus.

For sure, no other place could so justly be the home of the rulers of the world, on no other hill but the Palatine could power rank itself so high, and feel that here is the peak of authority. The Imperial Palace raises its roofs above the rostra it has overthrown, and sees around it so many shrines, and is encircled by so many mighty abodes of the gods. It is a fair sight to see the Giants on the Tarpeian rock, below the roofs of Jove's Temple, the embossed doorways, the bright sky thick set with crowding temples, the fields with their crop of columns bearing many a ship's prow, the houses set on the huge ridges, where the work of man is piled on that of nature, the many triumphal arches gleaming with trophies won . .

CLAUDIAN, *On the Sixth Consulship of Honorius*, 39–51

. . . Septem circumspice montes,
qui solis radios auri fulgore lacessunt,
indutosque arcus spoliis aequataque templa
nubibus et quidquid tanti struxere triumphi.
Quantum profueris, quantam servaveris urbem,
attonitis metire oculis. . . .
Proxime dis consul, tantae qui prospicis urbi,
qua nihil in terris complectitur altius aether,
cuius nec spatium visus nec corda decorem
nec laudem vox ulla capit; quae luce metalli
aemula vicinis fastigia conserit astris;
quae septem scopulis zonas imitatur Olympi;
armorum legumque parens quae fundit in omnes
imperium primique dedit cunabula iuris.

Look round on the Seven Hills, whose gleaming gold challenges the sun's rays, on the arches carved with trophies, the temples that rise to the clouds, and all the Rome's many triumphs have built upon high. Measure with astonished gaze how great the service you have done, how noble, the city you have saved! . . . Great consul, you are next to the gods, as you gaze over this great city, for no loftier on earth does the heaven encompass! Eye cannot match her extent, nor mind her glory, nor voice her praise: with the gleam of previous metal she has decked her peaks to match the neighbouring stars: with her seven hills she matches the seven zones of Olympus. Mother of arms and laws, she has spread her rule over all peoples, she has been the cradle of human rights.

CLAUDIAN, *On the Consulship of Stilicho*, III. 65–70, 130–7

Porrigis ingentem spatiosis moenibus urbem,
quam tamen angustam populus facit; itur in aequor
molibus et veteres tellus nova contrahit undas;
namque Dicarcheae translatus pulvis harenae
intratis solidatur aquis durataque massa
sustinet advectos peregrino in gurgite campos.
Sic te dispositam spectantemque undique portus
vallatam pelago terrarum commoda cingunt.

Rome, you extend as a huge city within ample walls, yet your population makes you too small. So moles are built over the sea, and a new land constricts the old realm of the waves. Dust brought from the sands of Dicarchaea is made solid in the waters it has invaded; when its mass has hardened it supports fields imported to the alien deep. So the fruits of every land surround you, thus laid out, looking towards your harbours on all sides, and fortified by the sea.

SIDONIUS APOLLINARIS, *Carmina* II. 56–63

Postquam vere clarissimum terrarum omnium lumen exstinctum est, immo Romani imperii truncatum caput: et ut verius dicam, in una Urbe totus orbis interiit, 'obmutui et humiliatus sum, et silui a bonis, et dolor meus renovatus est: concaluit cor meum intra me, et in meditatione mea exarsit ignis'.

After that the brightest of earthly lights went out, when, truly, the very head of the Roman Empire was cut off, when, to speak yet more truly, the whole world perished along with a single city then I fell silent and was abashed, and spoke not, and my sorrow was renewed: my heart within me was afire, a flame broke through my meditations (Psal. XXXVIII, 4).

ST. JEROME, *Commentary to Ezechiel*, I, 3

Ezechielis volumen olim adgredi volui et sponsionem creberrimam studiosis lectoribus reddere, sed in ipso dictandi exordio ita animus meus occidentalium provinciarum et maxime urbis Romae vastatione confusus est, ut iuxta vulgare proverbium proprium quoque ignorarem vocabulum, diuque tacui sciens tempus esse lacrimarum.

Once when I wished to take up the book of Ezekiel and to give a commentary I had promised to eager readers, I was so distracted with the affairs of the western provinces, and especially with the catastrophe at Rome, that as I began my speech it was as in the proverb 'I could not even find the proper word'. For long I kept silent, knowing that this was the time for tears.

St. Jerome, ap. Augustinum, *Epistulae*, clxv. 2

Horrenda nobis nuntiata sunt; strages facta, incendia, rapinae, interfectiones, excruciationes hominum. Verum est, multa audivimus, omnia gemuimus, saepe flevimus. . . .

We hear of atrocious news: slaughter, fires, rape, murder, torturing. It is all true. We have heard much, and sorrowed for all, often we have fallen to weeping. . . .

St. Augustine, *De wibis excidio*, ii, 3

exaudi, regina tui pulcerrima mundi
inter sidereos Roma recepta polos,
exaudi, nutrix hominum genetrixque deorum
(non procul a caelo per tua templa sumus)

percensere labor densis decora alta tropaeis
ut si qui stellas pernumerare velit,
confunduntque vagos delubra micantia visus;
ipsos crediderim sic habitare deos.
quid loquar aerio pendentes fornice rivos
qua vix imbriferas tolleret Iris aquas?

intercepta tuis conduntur flumina muris
consumunt totos celsa lavacra lacus.

Hear me, fairest Queen of the world you rule, Rome, received into the starry heavens. Hear me, nurse of men and mother of gods (for in your Temples we are not far from heaven). . . .
To number the lofty arches set with trophies would be a task like counting the stars, your glittering shrines dazzle the eyes that turn to them—thus, I think, the gods must live! What, too, of the water-courses, hung high in air on lofty archways—even Iris could scarce raise the rainbow's arch so high!
Rivers are caught within your walls and buried underground: whole lakes are swallowed up by your mighty baths!

Rutilius Namatianus, *De reditu*, i. 46–50, 93–98, 102–3

The last group of passages belong to the late fourth and early fifth centuries. Rome's political power is nearly gone: her physical presence still dazzles. The passage from Sidonius speaks of the use of *pozzolana* to build vast platforms over the sea, like the luxury villas of Baiae that Horace deplored in the time of Augustus. In Claudian's poem hopes are pinned on a feeble Emperor and an unreliable mercenary (Stilicho) to save the city. Alaric and his Goths captured it in A.D. 410. Jerome in Palestine and Augustine in Africa voice the shock heard round the world. Yet only six years later Rutilius is writing of the city's beauty and serenity, from which he tears himself unwillingly away to return to his plundered estates in Gaul. This was on September 21st, A.D. 416: the sounds of the Ludi Romani faintly reach his ears as he takes ship at Ostia.

Rutilius had held the office of *praefectus urbi*, and his poem was meant as no more than a personal farewell. Because of the date, and its apt summing-up of the mission that Rome had discharged—

dumque offers victis proprii consortia iuris
Urbem fecisti, quod prius orbis erat.

(Because you offered the conquered equal rights under your laws, you have made a city out of what was once a world)—it is often taken as a valedictory to the Roman Empire. But there are other lines that should not be forgotten.

iam tempus laceris post saeva incendia fundis
vel pastorales aedificare casas.

(it is time now, after these fearful fires, to build on my ravaged estates, even if only cottages for shepherds.)

For, when empires and cities fall, that is where they must start again.

NOTES ON THE TEXT

The serious student of ancient Rome is remarkably fortunate in the works of reference at his disposal. First, there is S. B. Platner and T. Ashby, *A Topographical Dictionary of Ancient Rome,* 2 volumes (1929). This indispensable work discusses all major monuments and sites, listed in alphabetical order, and gives a full bibliography up to the date of publication. It has long been out of print, but is to be found in most large libraries: fortunately a new and revised edition is now being prepared. Ernest Nash, *A Pictorial Dictionary of Ancient Rome,* 2 volumes (1961) concentrates no less successfully on the visual side; the entries are enhanced by up-to-date bibliographies. By far the most authoritative guide-book is G. Lugli, *Roma Antica, Il Centro Monumentale* (1946), which covers the Capitol, Forum Romanum, Imperial Fora, Velia, Palatine and Forum Boarium. Nothing comparable exists for the rest of the city. A complete collection of all the ancient evidence—literary, epigraphic, numismatic—is now in progress, under the editorship of G. Lugli and the title *Fontes ad Topographiam Veteris Urbis Romae Pertinentes* (1952–), which already covers many of the most important regions of the city. To the same scholar we owe the most complete map of the ancient city, *Forma Urbis Romae Imperatorum Aetate.* To these authoritative sources the student should refer first.

The Notes that follow are intended to do no more than amplify certain points in the text, and to suggest books and articles for further reading. I have tried to give English books where possible, but much of the best work in this field is published in French, German and, of course, Italian.

ABBREVIATIONS

A.A.	*Archäologischer Anzeiger.* Berlin, 1889–
B. Arte	*Bollettino d'Arte del Ministero della Pubblica Istruzione,* Rome 1907–
B. Com.	*Bullettino della Commissione Archeologica Comunale di Roma,* 1872–
B.S.R.	*Papers of the British School at Rome,* 1902–
C.R.A.I.	*Comptes-rendus des séances de l'Académie des Inscriptions et Belles-Lettres,* Paris 1857–
Crema.	L. Crema. *L'Architettura Romana.* 1959.
J.R.S.	*The Journal of Roman Studies.* London, 1911–
L.R.	R. Lanciani, *The Ruins and Excavations of Ancient Rome,* 1897.
M.A.A. Rome	*Memoirs of the American Academy in Rome.* Rome, 1917–
O.C.D.	*Oxford Classical Dictionary.*
R.M.	*Mitteilungen des Deutschen Archäologischen Instituts, Römische Abteilung.* 1886–

Pages 3–6.

For speculations on geography and climate see J. O. Thomson, *History of Ancient Geography* (1948).

For Vitruvius see *Vitruvius and the Liberal Art of Architecture* by F. E. Brown, *Bucknell Review*, 11. 4 (1963), 99–107.

Pages 11–12.

The Lex Julia Municipalis was in fact passed by Antony, though it contained various provisions drafted by Julius Caesar for the administration of the city. These relate to the cleaning and paving of streets, control of traffic, regulations for public places, etc. Note that the terms apply to 'the city and within one mile of the city', showing that houses had already spread beyond the *pomoerium* (see E. G. Hardy, *Roman Laws and Charters*, pp. 136 ff.; C. Knapp, 'The Care of City Streets in Ancient Rome', in *Classical Weekly*, Vol. XIX).

Pages 14–17.

For the *Res Gestae* of Augustus see the edition by E. G. Hardy (1923). For the buildings of Augustus' time see M. Reinhold, *Marcus Agrippa* (1933); M. Nilsson, *Imperial Rome* (1926).

Pages 17–21.

For the Great Fire of A.D. 64 see A. Profumo, *Fonti e tempi dell'incendio neroniano* (1905). For the rebuilding A. Boethius, *The Neronian Nova Urbs* in Corolla archaeologica, pp. 84–97.

Pages 23–25.

For developments from Vespasian to Hadrian see William A. MacDonald, *The Architecture of the Roman Empire*, Vol. I (1965).

For the buildings of Trajan see R. Paribeni, *Optimus Princeps* (1926, 1927).

Pages 26–29.

The *Curiosum* and the *Notitia* are published with commentary in H. Jordan. *Topographie der Stadt Rom im Altertum* (1871), Vol. II.

Pages 31–33.

The *novella* of Majorian is published in Lugli, *Fontes*, Vol. I, p. 70: for other preservation orders see ib. pp. 66–67.

Pages 34–37.

On the 'Wall of Servius Tullius' see G. Saflund, *Le Mura di Roma Repubblicana* (1932).

On the Walls of Aurelian see I. A. Richmond, *The City Wall of Imperial Rome*—itself a classic of field-work.

Pages 38–42.

The two basic books on the aqueducts are E. B. van Deman, *The building of the Roman Aqueducts* (1934), and T. Ashby, *Aqueducts of Ancient Rome* (1935).

For a useful popular account see now E. M. Winslow, *A Libation to the Gods* (1963).

The figures given for volume, etc., are an attempt to translate Frontinus' figures

into modern terms. They contain a substantial margin of error, no doubt, but they give at least an order of magnitude.
Frontinus *De Aquis* is edited in the Loeb series by M. B. McElwain.

Pages 43–47.

For the Tiber, see J. Le Gall, *Le Tibre, fleuve de Rome* (1953).

Pages 51–54.

For the Capitol see T. Ashby and W. Dougill, *The Capitol* (1927); E. Rodocanachi, *The Roman Capitol in Ancient and Modern Times* (trans. F. Lawton, 1906); G. Lugli *Il Campidoglio nell' età classica* in Capitolium (1943), pp. 97 ff. For the legend of Tarpeia see E. Pais. *Ancient Legends of Roman History* (1950), pp. 96–127. The story of the Druids is in Tacitus *Histories*, IV. 54.

Pages 54–58.

For the Temple of Jupiter Optimus Maximus see A. Zadoks Jitta, *Iuppiter Capitollinus*, *JRS* (1938), pp. 50 ff.
For the cult, C. Koch, *Der Römische Juppiter* (1937).

Pages 58–68.

For Triumphs see E. Pais, *Fasti Triumphales populi Romani* (1920) and G. C. Picard, *Les Trophées Romaines* (1957).
For the Agon Capitolinus see L. Friedländer, *Roman Life*, Vol. IV, pp. 264 ff.

Pages 68–69.

For the Gallic siege see now R. Ogilvie, *A Commentary on Livy, Books* 1–5 (1965), p. 734.

Pages 70–71.

For the Carcer Mamertinus see Tenney Frank, *Roman Buildings of the Republic* (1924), pp. 39–47.

Pages 71–72.

On the Tabularium see Tenney Frank, *Roman Buildings of the Republic* (1924), pp. 49–51 and C. van Essen, *Précis de l'histoire de l'art*, (coll. Latomus XLII) (1960), pp. 60–62.

On the Temple at Palestrina see F. Fasolo and G. Gullini, *Il santuario della Fortuna Primigenia* 2 vols. (1953). There is a short account of the architectural innovations of these buildings in William L. MacDonald, *The Architecture of the Roman Empire*, I (1965), pp. 7–9.

Pages 73–78.

For the Forum see C. Huelsen, *The Forum and Palatine* (1928). E. Gjerstad, *Act. Inst. Sueciae*, XXI (1960), 84–88, E. B. Van Deman, *The Sullan Forum*, J.R.S. XII (1922), 1 ff. and R. Bloch, *The Origins* of Rome (1960), chs. iv and v.

Pages 78–81.

For the Temple of Saturn see Tenney Frank, *Roman Buildings of the Republic* (1924), pp. 51–53 and A. V. Gerkan, Die Datierung der Castortempels, *A.A.* 1964, p. 650.
For the cult see the article *Saturnus* by H. J. Rose, O.C.D.

Pages 81–82.

For the Milliarium Aureum see M. E. Blake, *Ancient Roman Construction in Italy* (1947) I. 340.

Pages 83–84.

For the Volcanal, see Tenney Frank, *Buildings*, p. 59. K. Latte, *Römische Religionsgeschichte* (1960), pp. 129 f.

Pages 84–85.

The reliefs on the Arch of Septimius Severus are discussed by G. Rodenwaldt in C.A.H. XII. 546 f.; see also P. G. Hamberg, *Studies in Roman Imperial Art* (1947), pp. 145–7.

Pages 85–87.

For the Basilica Julia see L.R. pp. 275–9, M. E. Blake, op. cit. I. pp. 151, 177.

Pages 87–88.

For the Curia Julia see A. Bartoli, *I lavori della Curia*, and *Studi Romani* (1954), pp. 129–37. For the *clupeus virtutis* see M. P. Charlesworth, 'The Virtues of a Roman Emperor' (*Proceedings of the British Academy*, 1937). For the debates on the Statue of Victory see Gibbon (ed. Bury). III. 201 f.

Page 89.

For the *Plutei Trajani* see M. Hammond, M.A.A. Rome, XXI (1953), 127–83. For the *alimenta* see R. Duncan-Jones B.R.S. XIX (n.s.) (1964), 123.

Pages 89–90.

For the Lapis Niger see A. Degrassi, I.L.L.R.P. I. (1957) pp. 4–6. G. Carettoni, J.R.S. I (1960), p. 198; F. G. Dumezil, 'L'Inscription archaïque du Forum' in *Recherches de Science religieuse* (1951–2), vol. XXXIX–XL. There is a useful short account in Paul MacKendrick, *The Mute Stones Speak* (1960), pp. 80 f.

Page 91.

For the Comitium see Tenney Frank, *Buildings*, pp. 61–66, L. Richardson, jr., *Archaeology*, X (1957), 49–55.

Pages 92–93.

For the Rostra see G. Carettoni, J.R.S. L (1960), 196.

Pages 93–94.

For the Column of C. Duilius and the inscription, see A. Degrassi, *Inscr. Italiae*, XIII. 3, pp. 44–49.

Pages 94–95.

For the Fig, Olive, and Vine see P. Romanelli, B. Arte. XI (1955), 349. For the statue of Marsyas and the reliefs see J. Paoli, in *Revue des études latines*, XXIII (1945) 150–67.

Pages 95–97.

For the Lacus Curtius see E. B. van Deman, J.R.S. XII (1922), 20 f.; Tenney

Frank, *Buildings*, p. 76. For the legend see R. Ogilvie, *A Commentary on Livy*, 1–5 (1965), pp. 75 f.

Pages 97–99.

For the Basilica Aemilia see A. M. Colini, B. Comm. (1939), pp. 193 f; G. Carettoni, J.R.S. L. (1960) 192 f.
For the historical reliefs A. Bartoli, *Il fregio figurato della Basilica Aemilia*, B. Arte, XXXV. 289 ff.

Page 100.

Antony's Funeral Speech is discussed by M. E. Deutsch (Univ. of California Publ. Class. Arch., 1928).
Terence Spencer, *The Elizabethan Romans*, is good on the influence of the Shakespearean picture of these events. (Shakespeare Survey 10.)

Pages 104–107.

For the Regia see F. E. Brown, M.A.A. Rome XII (1935), pp. 67–88.
For the *Annales Maximi* see the article 'Tabulae Pontificum', O.C.D.

Pages 107–110.

For the Atrium Vestae see E. B. van Deman, *The Atrium Vestae* (1909), also J.R.S. XII (1922), 29.
For the cult, see the article by Wissowa in Roscher's *Lexikon*.

Pages 110–111.

For the Lacus Juturnae see E. B. van Deman, J.R.S. XII (1922), 5; E. Nash, A.C. XI (1959), 227–31.

Pages 111–114.

For the legend of the Dioscuri see R. Ogilvie, *A Commentary on Livy 1–5* (1965), pp. 288 f.
For the Temple of Castor and Pollux see Tenney Frank, M.A.A. Rome V. (1925), pp. 79–102; J. B. Ward Perkins, Gnomon, XXXI (1959), 363 f.

Pages 114–115.

For the Temple of Antoninus and Faustina see R. Lanciani, *Ruins of Ancient Rome* (1897), pp. 216–19, Ch. Huelsen, *Le Chiese di Roma nel Medio Evo* (1927).

Pages 115–116.

For the reliefs on the Arch of Titus see J. M. C. Toynbee, J.R.S. XXXVII (1947), 190 f.; G. C. Picard, *Les trophées Romaines* (1955). For the spoils of the Temple, S. Reinach, *L'arc de Titus et les dépouilles du Temple de Jérusalem* (1920).

Pages 116–117.

For the Basilica of Constantine, see A. Minoprio, B.S.R. XII (1932), 1–25.

Pages 117–119.

For the Temple of Venus and Rome see H. Mattingly, J.R.S. XV (1925), 219 f.; A. Munoz, in *Capitolium*, XI (1935), 215–34; D. E. Strong, B.S.R. XXXI (1953),

122 f., 127–9. There is a good passage on Apollodorus and Hadrian in William A. MacDonald, *The Architecture of the Roman Empire,* I (1965), 129 f.

Pages 120–123.

On the imperial fora in general see R. Paribeni, *I Fori Imperiali* (1933), and on their inscriptions, id; 'Iscrizioni dei Fori Imperiali' in *Notizie Scavi* (1933), pp. 431 ff.

On the Forum of Caesar see C. Ricci, 'Il Foro di Cesare', in Capitolium (1932), pp. 157 ff. and O. Grossi, *The Forum of Julius Caesar and the Temple of Venus Genetrix* in M.A.A. Rome (1936), pp. 215 ff.

Pages 123–129.

For the Forum of Augustus see C. Ricci, *Capitolium,* VI (1930), 157–89; H. T. Rowell, *The Forum and funeral 'imagines' of Augustus* in M.A.A. Rome (1940), pp. 132 ff. For the Elogia see A. DeGrassi, *Ins. It.* XIII. (1937), 3; for the Fasti, Id. *Ins. It.* XIII (1947), I.

Pages 129–132.

For the Forum Pacis see A. M. Colini, *Forum Pacis,* B. Comm. (1937), pp. 7 ff.; F. Castagnoli, L. Cozza, B. Comm. LXXVI (1956/8), 119–42.

For the Forma Urbis Romae see G. Carretoni, A. M. Colini, etc., *La pianta marmorea di Roma antica, Forma Urbis Romae* (1960).

Pages 132–133.

For the Forum of Nerva see P. H. von Blanckenhagen, *Flavische Architektur etc. untersucht am Nervaforum* (1940).

Pages 133–137.

For Trajan's Forum see P. Ducati, *L'Arte classica* 3 (1948), pp. 619–28; R. Paribeni, *Optimus Princeps,* II (1927), 65 ff., and the short account in Paul MacKendrick, *The Mute Stones Speak* (1960), pp. 265–72. For the Mercatus Trajani see William A. MacDonald, *The Architecture of the Roman Empire* I. 75–90. On the Column, P. Romanelli, *La Colonna Traiana* (1942); G. Becatti, *La Colonna coclide istoriata* (1960), pp. 25–31. See also I. A. Richmond, *Trajan's Army on Trajan's Column,* B.S.R. XIII (1935), 1–40.

Page 138.

On the Arch of Constantine see P. G. Hamberg, *Studies in Roman Imperial Art* (1945), pp. 56–63, 78–103; A. Giuliano *Arco di Constantino* (1955).

For the Colossus see H. V. Canter, *Trans. Am. Ph. Ass.* LXI (1930), 150–64.

Pages 138–142.

For the Domus Aurea see A. Boethius, *The Golden House of Nero* (1960); J. B. Ward Perkins, *Antiquity,* XXX (1956), 209–19.

The Golden House is discussed in William MacDonald, *The Architecture of the Roman Empire,* I (1965), 20–41. For Severus and Celer id. ib. pp. 122 ff.

For the Laocoon and its discovery in 1506 see M. Scherer, *The Marvels of Ancient Rome* (1955), pp. 92 f; Margarete Bieber, *Laocoon* (1942); also R. Lanciani, *Storia degli Scavi,* I (1902), 139 ff.

Pages 142–145.

For the Colosseum see F. Colagrossi, *L'Anfiteatro Flavio nei suoi venti secoli di storia* (1913); H. V. Canter, *Trans. Am. Phil. Ass.* (1930), pp. 150–64; H. Kahler, R.M. LIV (1939), 252–65.
Ch. Huelsen discusses the seating of the Arval Brethren in B. Comm. (1894), pp. 312 ff.
On gladiatorial shows see L. Friedländer, *Roman Life and Manners* (1908), vol. II, ch. I.

Pages 146–151.

On the Palatine see F. G. Scott, *Early Roman Traditions in the Light of Archaeology*, M.A.A. Rome, (1929), pp. 3 ff.; P. Ducati, *Come nacque Roma* (1940).
Raymond Bloch, *The Origins of Rome 1960*, especially chs. iii and iv.
The archaeological story of the Palatine settlement is told in the article by S. M. Puglisi and others, 'Gli abitatori primitivi del Palatino', etc. in *Mon. Ant. dei Lincei*, XLI (1951), 1–146.
On the foundation legends see J. Hubaux, *Les grandes mythes de Rome* (1945); J. Carcopino, *La louve du Capitol* (1925); G. Dumezil, *Naissance de Rome, Jupiter, Mars, etc. Quirinus*, vol. II (1949).

Pages 151–153.

For the Temple of Magna Mater see K. Esdaile, R.M. XXIII (1908), 368–74; G. Carettoni, J.R.S. L (1960), 200 f.
For the cult see H. Graillot, *Le culte de Cybèle* (1912); F. Cumont, *Oriental Religions in Roman Paganism* (1911), pp. 46 f.

Pages 154–160.

For the Temple of Apollo see G. Lugli, *Le temple d'Apollon et les édifices d'Auguste sur le Palatin*, C.R.A.I. (1950), pp. 276–85.
For the cult see J. Gagé, *Apollon Romain* (1955).
For the Palatine library, and Roman libraries in general, see Crema, pp. 376 f.
For the Ludi Saeculares see J. Gagé, *Recherches sur les jeux seculaires* (1934).

Page 161.

The vicissitudes of the affair of Cicero's house are set out at length in his speech *De domo sua* (ed. R. G. Nisbet, 1936).

Page 161.

The speech *Pro Sextio Roscio Amerino*, exposing Chrysogonus, was delivered in 80 or 79 B.C.

Pages 161–162.

Antony's house was burned in 29 B.C.

Pages 163–165.

For the House of Augustus (Casa di Livia) see G. Carettoni, J.R.S. L (1960), 201; G. E. Rizzo, *Monumenti della Pittura Antica*, Roma III, *Le pitture della Casa di Livia* (1936).

Pages 165–166.

For the Domus Tiberiana see E. Nash *Antike Kunst*, I (1958), 24–28.

Pages 168–169.

For the Domus Augustiana see the standard work of A. Bartoli, *Domus Augustana* (1938); and now William MacDonald *The Architecture of the Roman Empire*, I (1965), 47–74: on Rabirius, id. ib. pp. 127 f.

On the Basilica see Karl Lehmann, 'The Dome of Heaven', *Art Bulletin* (1945), pp. 1–27.

On Claudius see A. Momigliano, *Claudius* (3rd edn. 1961). There is a good account of the education of the young Marcus in Anthony Birley, *Marcus Aurelius* (1966).

Pages 171, 175.

For the Septizonium see Th. Dombart, *Das palatinische Septizonium zu Rom* (1922).

Pages 177–178.

On the Porticus of Octavia see G. Gatti, *Capitolium*, xxxv (1960), 10.

Pages 178–184.

On Roman theatres in general see M. Bieber, *The History of the Greek and Roman theatre* (2) (1961) and W. Beare, *The Roman Stage* (3rd edn. 1964).

On the Theatre of Pompey see J. A. Hanson, *Roman Theatre Temples* (1959), pp. 43–55.

On the Theatre of Marcellus A. Calza Bini 'Il Teatro di Marcello' in *Boll. del centro per la storia dell' architettura*, 7 (1953).

For the murder of Caesar see R. E. Smith, 'The Conspiracy and the Conspirators' in *Greece and Rome*, IV, n. I (1957) 58 ff.

Pages 184–185.

For the Stadium of Domitian see A. M. Colini, *Stadium Domitiani* (1943); P. Romano-P. Partini, *Piazza Navona* (1953).

Page 186.

For the reliefs of the provinces, now in the courtyard of the Palazzo dei Conservatori, see J. M. C. Toynbee, *The Hadrianic School* (1934), pp. 152–9.

Pages 187–190.

On the Pantheon see R. Vighi, *Il Pantheon* (1955), English translation by J. B. Ward-Perkins.

Ch. v of William MacDonald's *Architecture of The Roman Empire*, vol. I is a brilliant account of the structure and symbolism of the building. See especially the section 'The Meaning of the Pantheon', pp. 118 f.

For its later history see C. Montani, 'Il Pantheon e i suoi recenti restauri' *Capitolium* (1932), pp. 417–26.

Pages 190–192.

There are two recent books on the Column of Marcus Aurelius: C. Caprino, A. M. Colini, etc., *La Colonna di Marco Aurelio* (1955) and G. Becatti, *Colonna di Marco Aurelio* (1957).

The battle of the Rain Miracle is discussed by Antony Birley, *Marcus Aurelius* (1966), pp. 237 ff.

Pages 193–196.

The most comprehensive study of the Ara Pacis is G. Moretti, *Ara Pacis Augustae* (1948). See also J. M. C. Toynbee, in *Proceedings of the British Academy*, XXIX (1953), 67–95.
There is a good discussion of the Ara Pacis and the ideals of the Augustan age in A. Grénier, *The Roman Spirit in Religion, Thought, and Art* (1926), pp. 348 f. It must be said that the ascription of the reliefs to the Ara Pacis has been challenged, see S. Weinstock, J.R.S. L (1960), 44–58. For a suggested identification of the *matrona* with Venus, see now G. Karl Galinsky in *American Journal of Archaeology*, Vol. 70. no. 3 (1966) pp. 223f.

Pages 196–199.

For the Mausoleum of Augustus see R. A. Cordingley and I. A. Richmond, B.R.S. X (1927), 23–25; A. Munoz, in *Capitolium*, XIII (1938), 491–508.

Pages 199–202.

For the Mausoleum of Hadrian see M. Borgatti. *Castel Sant'Angelo in Roma* (1931); D. E. Strong, B.R.S. XXI (1953), 129–47.

Pages 202–205.

On thermae in general see Anderson, Spiers and Ashley, *The Architecture of Ancient Rome*, edn. 3, (1927), ch. 6.
On the Thermae of Caracalla see L. Crema, *Arch. Rom.* pp. 531–9.
For their influence on the building of Pennsylvania Station in New York see Paul MacKendrick, *The Mute Stones Speak* (1960), pp. 309 ff. See further, L. Mumford, *The Disappearance of Pennsylvania Station*, New Yorker 34 (June 7, 1958), pp. 106–13.
For the Thermae of Diocletian see R. Paribeni, *Le Terme di Diocleziano e il Museo Nazionale Romano* (2), (1932); M. Sant'Angelo, *Quirinale*, pp. 192–203. For the Circus Maximus see P. Bigot, *Circus Maximus* in *Mélanges de l'Ecole Française*, 1908, pp. 229 ff.
F. W. Shipley, *Agrippa's building activities in Rome* 1933 (Washington University Studies, new series, language and literature, No. 4).

Pages 205–208.

For the tomb of the Scipios see E. Strong, *Art in Ancient Rome* (1928), pp. 45 f.; U. Scamuzzi, in *Rivista di studi classici*, V (1957), 248–68.
The epitaphs are in CIL, VI. 1284–94.
For the tomb of Eurysaces see I. A. Richmond, *The City Wall of Imperial Rome*, pp. 207 f.; H. Kahler, *Rom und seine Welt*, pp. 161 f.

Pages 208–210.

On the Statio Annonae see M. de Dominicis, *La Statio Annonae Urbis Romae* in B. Comm. (1924), pp. 134 ff.; G. B. Giovenale, *La basilica di S. Maria in Cosmedin* (1927).
For the institution of the *annona* see D. van Berchen, *Les distributions de blé et d'argent à la plèbe romaine sous l'empire* (1939).

Pages 211–216.

On the chariot-racing and its organization see L. Friedländer, *Roman Life and Manners*, Vol. II, ch. I. *The Spectacles*, pp. 493 ff., also id., *Three Inscriptions on Charioteers*, Vol. IV, Appendix XXIV.
The translation of the epitaph of Diocles is taken from N. Lewis and M. Reinhold, *Roman Civilization*, by permission of Columbia University Press, New York.

Pages 221–224.

For the Roman Oration of Aelius Aristides see J. H. Oliver, in *Transactions of the American Philosophical Society*, vol. XLIII (1953), Part 4 (text, translation, and commentary). I am grateful to Professor Oliver for giving me permission to quote from his translation.

Page 226–227.

Rutilius Namatianus' poem *De Reditu Suo* is published in the Loeb series: *Minor Latin Poets* by J. W. and A. M. Duff.

ILLUSTRATIONS

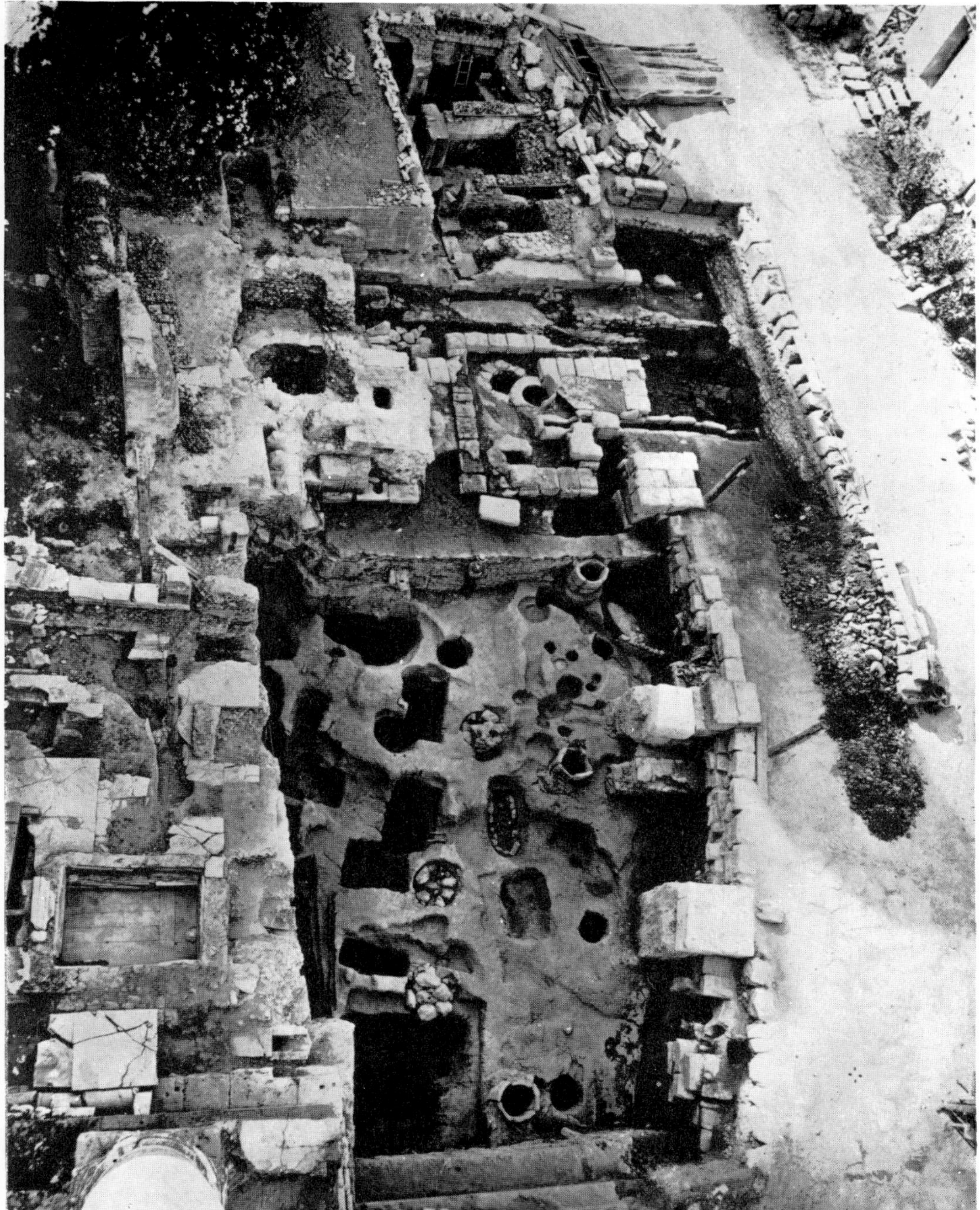

1. ARCHAIC CEMETERY by the Temple of Antoninus and Faustina in the Roman Forum as excavated by Boni. Both cremation and inhumation graves are visible: the circular wells marking the former, the oblong depressions the latter. The grave goods, now in the Antiquarium of the Forum, include models of huts like that shown in Plate 2. The cemetery was in use from the ninth to the sixth centuries B.C. See p. 147.

2. RE-CONSTRUCTION of a turf and timber hut, similar to those of the first settlement on the Palatine. The Casa Romuli and Evander's Palace were of this type, which persists today in the *capanne* built by shepherds in the summer pastures of Italy. See pp. 8, 109, 150.

3. PONS FABRICIUS. The inscription—L. FABRICIVS. C. F. CVR. VIARVM FACIVNDVM COERAVIT—records its building in 62 B.C. Another records a restoration by M. Lollius and Q. Lepidus in 21 B.C. See p. 47.

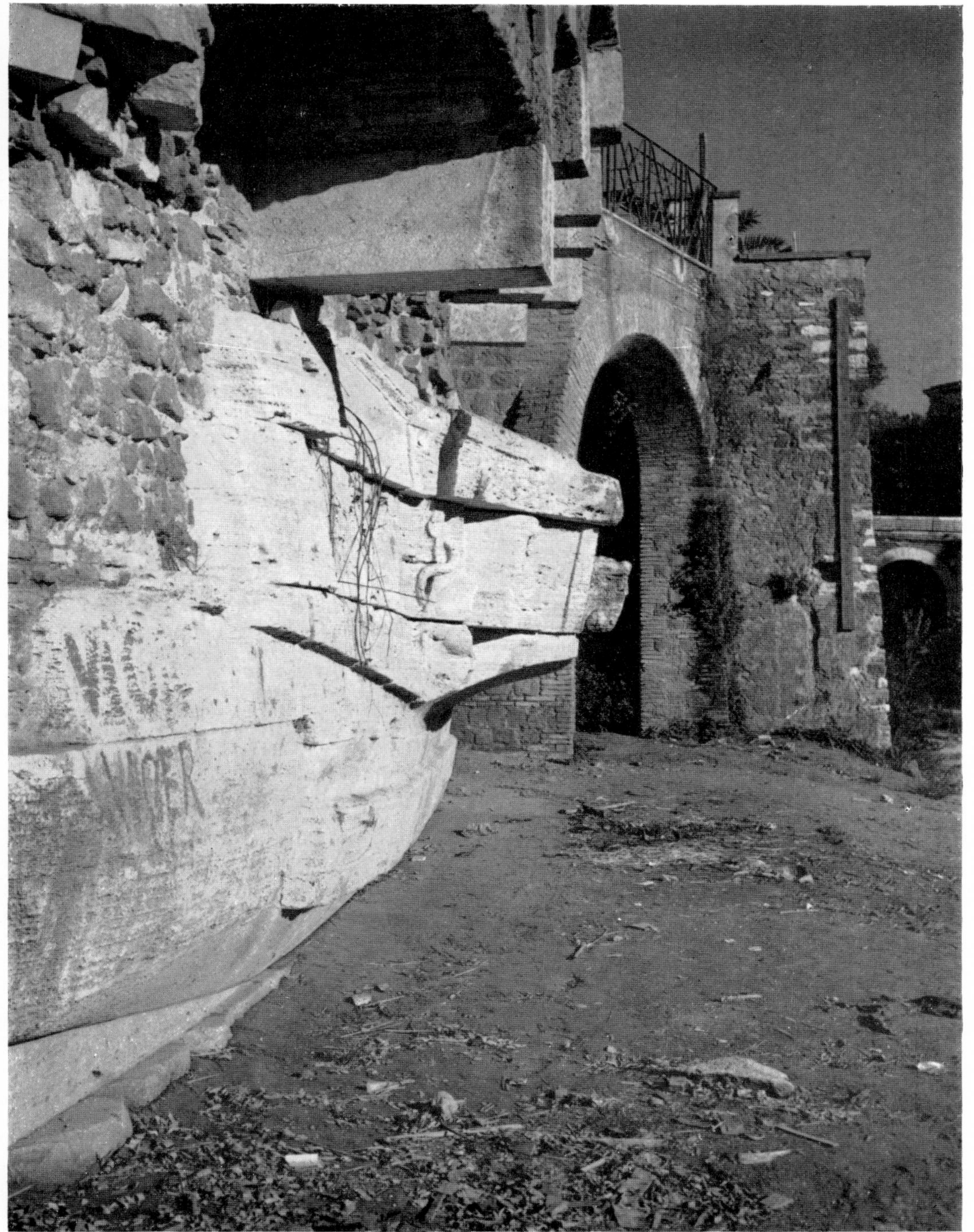

4. INSULA TIBERINA. Note the remains of the 'ship', with a bull's head, and the serpent and staff of Aesculapius, thought to date from the same period as the building of the Pons Fabricius (Plate 3). See p. 47.

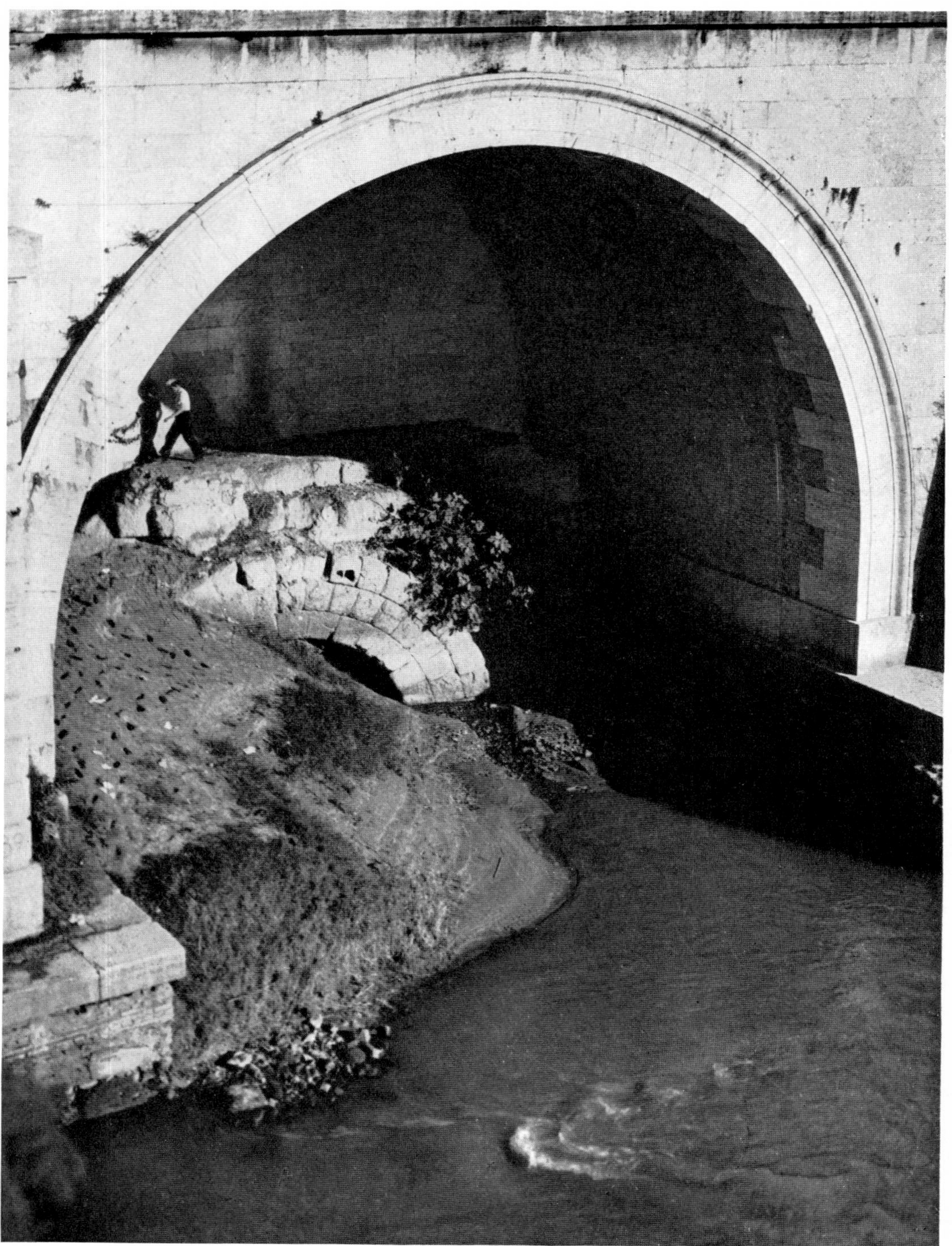

5. CLOACA MAXIMA. The ancient arches (c. 100 B.C.) are seen below the modern embankment. The *cloaca* still discharges into the river, but is no longer allowed to flood back towards the Forum. See p. 54.

6. THE WALL OF SERVIUS TULLIUS outside the modern Stazione Termini—a time-gap of at least 2,300 years. This section included the ancient Porta Viminalis. See p. 34.

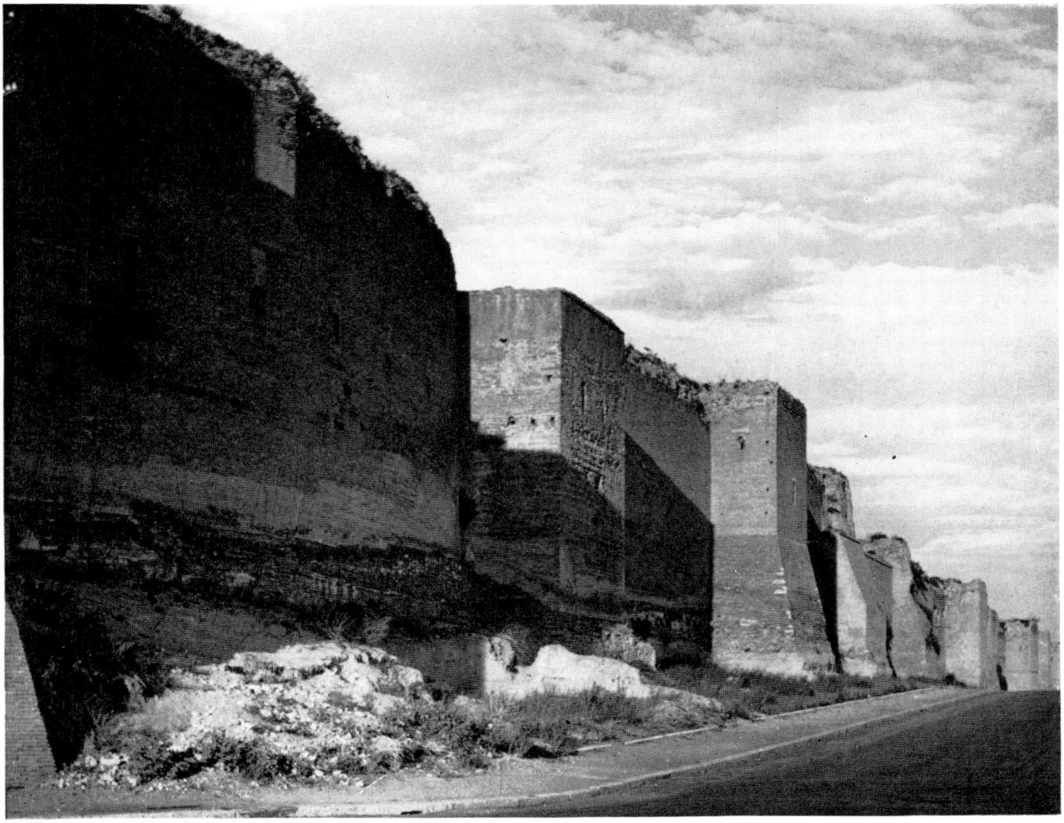

7. THE WALLS OF AURELIAN. One of the best preserved sections is that running east of Porta Appia, and followed on the outside by the modern Viale di Porta Ardeatina. The towers are at intervals of 100 Roman feet. See p. 35.

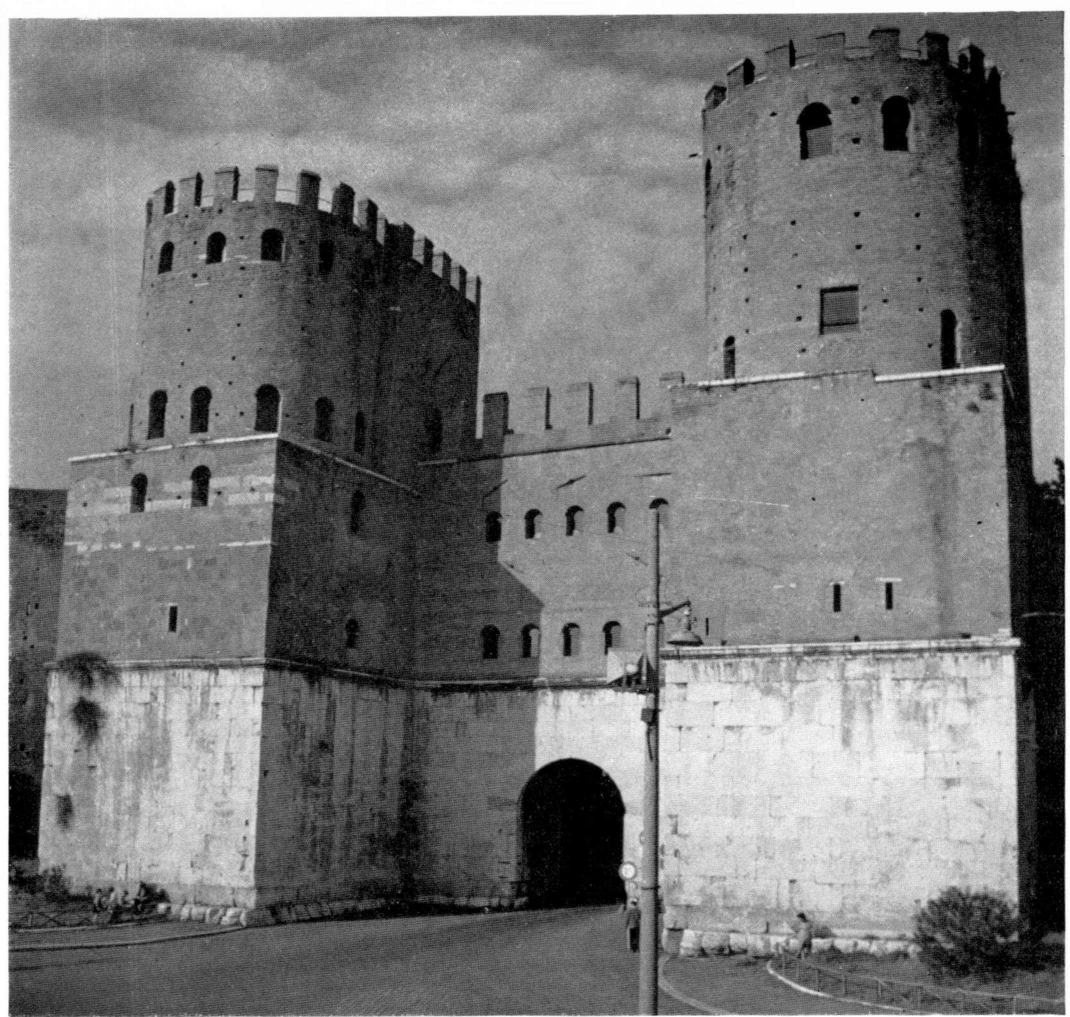

8. THE PORTA APPIA (the modern Porta San Sebastiano). The outer side is shown, with the Via Appia leaving the city. The original gateway had two entrances, and was flanked by semi-circular brick towers. The square towers now seen are of a later period. The crenellated semi-circular towers above were added at the restorations of Arcadius and Honorius (see p. 37), when the two lower storeys seem to have been remodelled and refaced.

9. THE PORTA PRAENESTINA (the modern Porta Maggiore) and its surrounds have a complicated building history. The oldest object seen is the Tomb of Eurysaces (see Plate 77), which stood between the Via Labicana (left) and the Via Praenestina (right). Claudius, bringing in the waters of the Aqua Claudia and the Anio Novus, built a large double archway across the two roads, over which he carried the channels of the aqueducts. This is recorded by an inscription of A.D. 52. Two other inscriptions record restorations by Vespasian and Titus. Then a double gateway was built for the wall of Aurelian over the tomb of Eurysaces, which provided a splendid core. Finally Arcadius and Honorius reconstructed this gateway and added towers and a vantage-court (see the inscription on p. 36). Pope Gregory XVI caused the destruction of the gateway in 1838–9, to reveal the tomb of Eurysaces and the aqueduct arches.

10. THE PORTA TIBURTINA (the modern Porta S. Lorenzo) has a similar building history. Here the aqueduct arch was built by Augustus in 5 B.C., as recorded in the highest of three inscriptions visible on the inner side of the gateway. The others record restorations of Vespasian and Septimius Severus (CIL, VI. 1244–6). Two towers were built in front of the archway for the Walls of Aurelian: the restorations of Arcadius and Honorius reconstructed this gateway, and added a vantage-court. A Honorian inscription (CIL, VI. 1190) survives on the curtain-wall. The vantage-court was destroyed in 1869.

9. THE PORTA PRAENESTINA. See facing page.

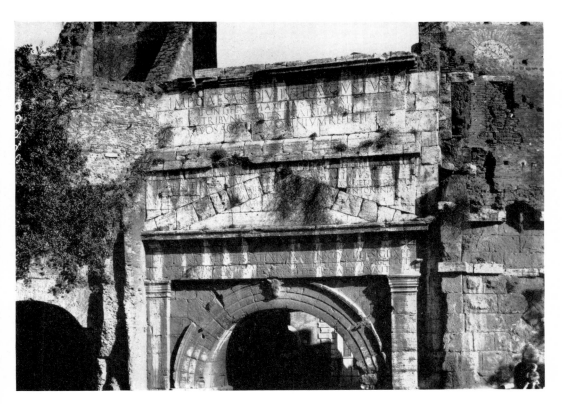

10. THE PORTA TIBURTINA. See facing page.

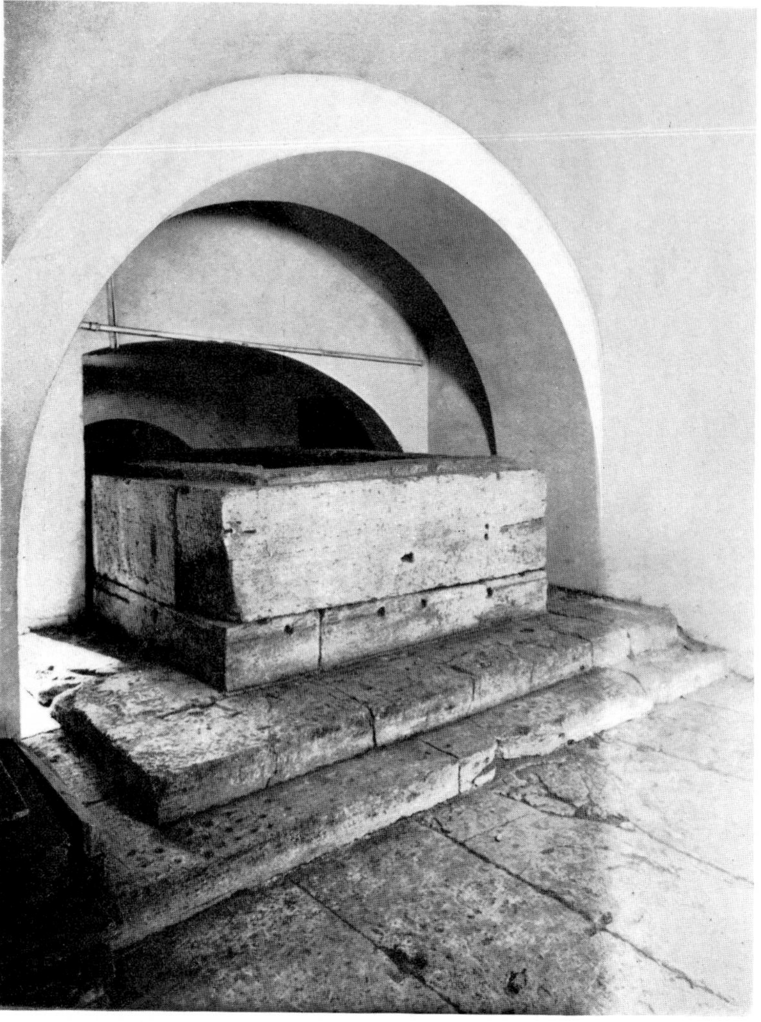

11. THE ALTAR OF THE FIRE OF NERO. See p. 20 f.

12. JUNO MONETA. Two fragments of a second-century relief from Ostia show a temple, below which geese flap their wings and honk in the most authentic manner. The conclusion that this is Juno Moneta at the time of the Gallic siege seems irresistible. See p. 68.

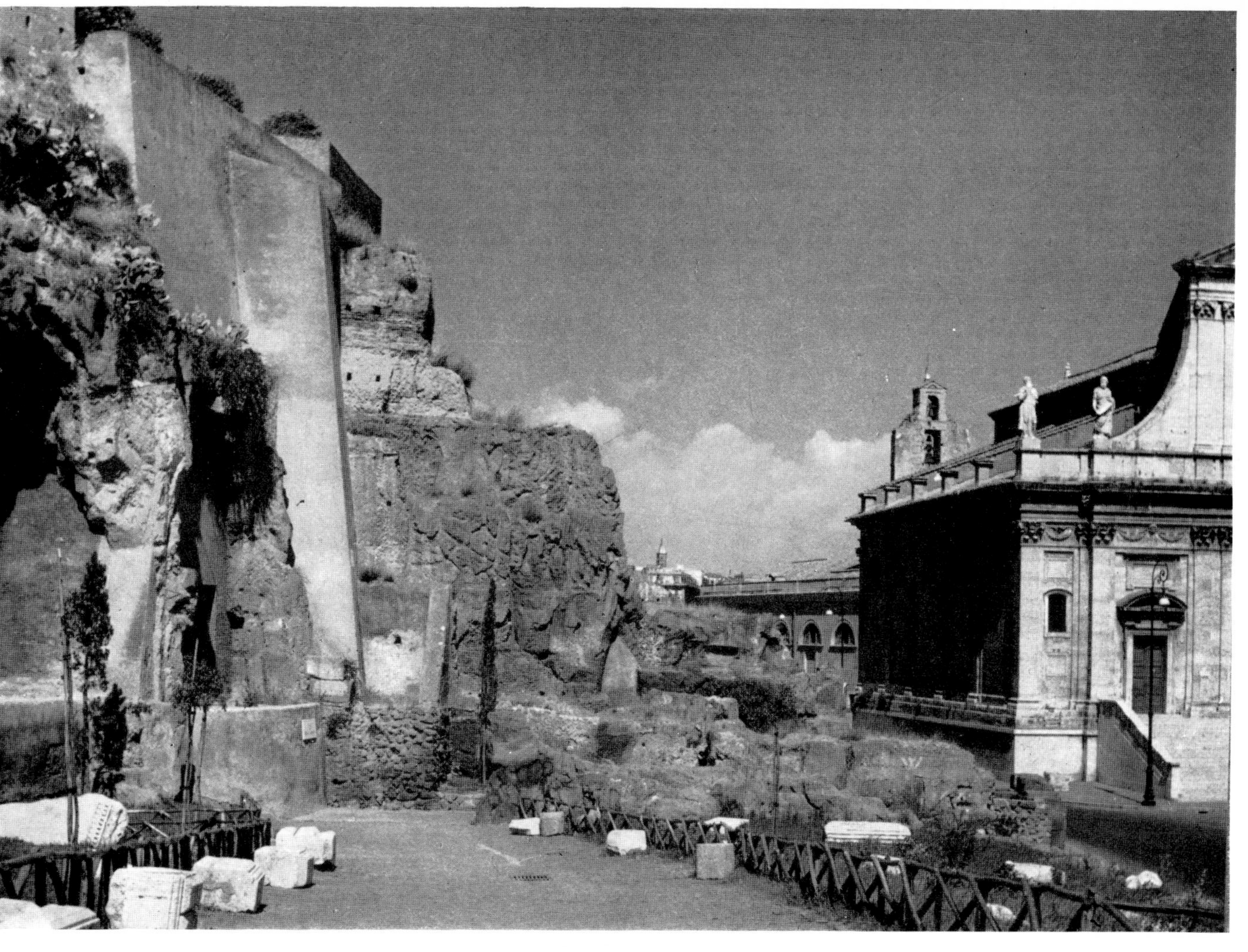

13. THE CAPITOL rises to the left; on the right is the modern Piazza della Consolazione. Excavations in 1931–2 removed the ancient houses which had covered the Saxum Tarpeium, and revealed the natural cliff over which criminals were thrown. See p. 51 f.

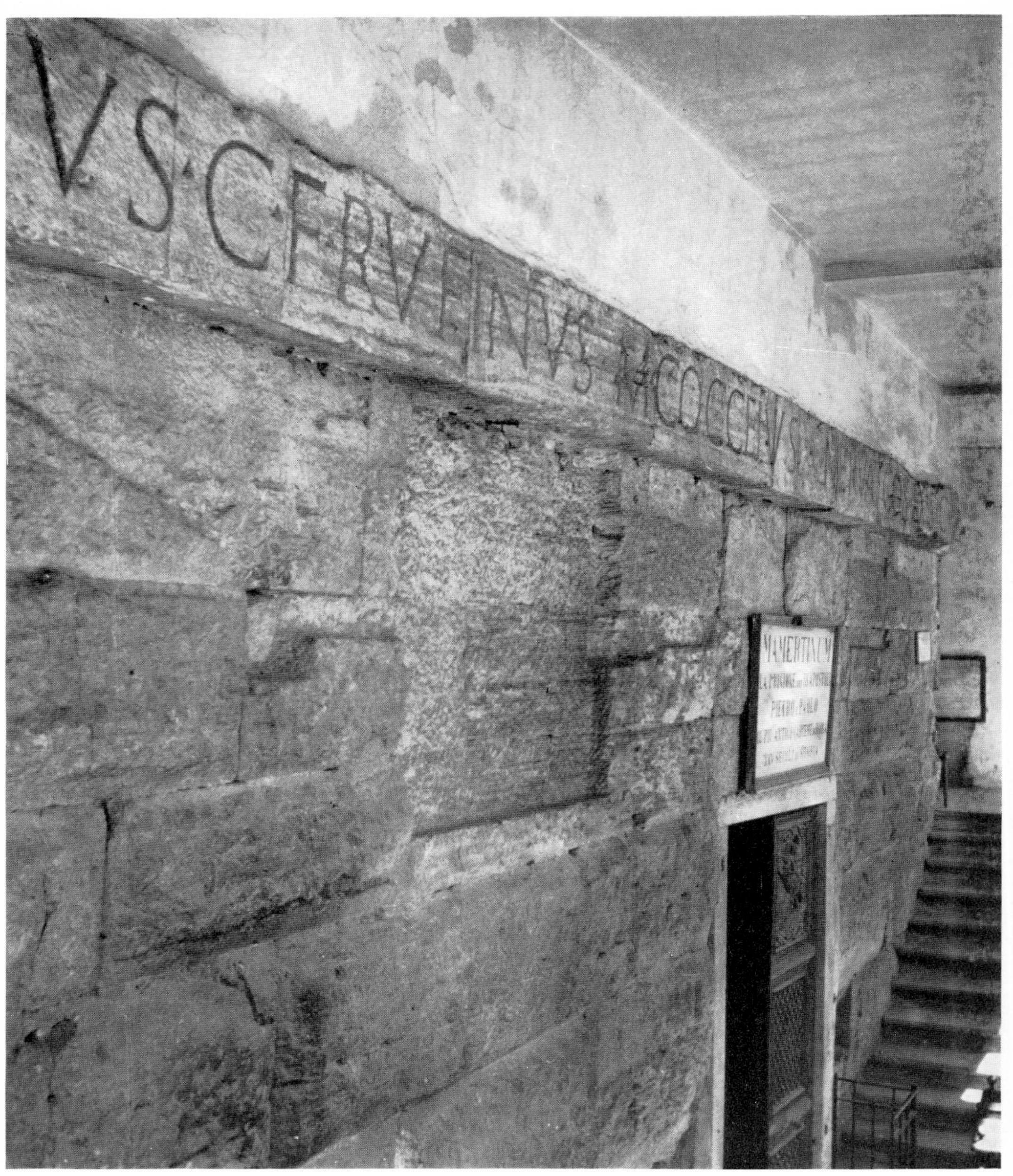

14. CARCER MAMERTINUS. Above the façade is seen the inscription recorded on p. 70.

15. CARCER MAMERTINUS. The Tullianum or death-cell, the only access to which was originally the hole in the archaic vault. The legend of St. Peter is recalled by the modern relief showing St. Peter baptizing his gaoler. See p. 71.

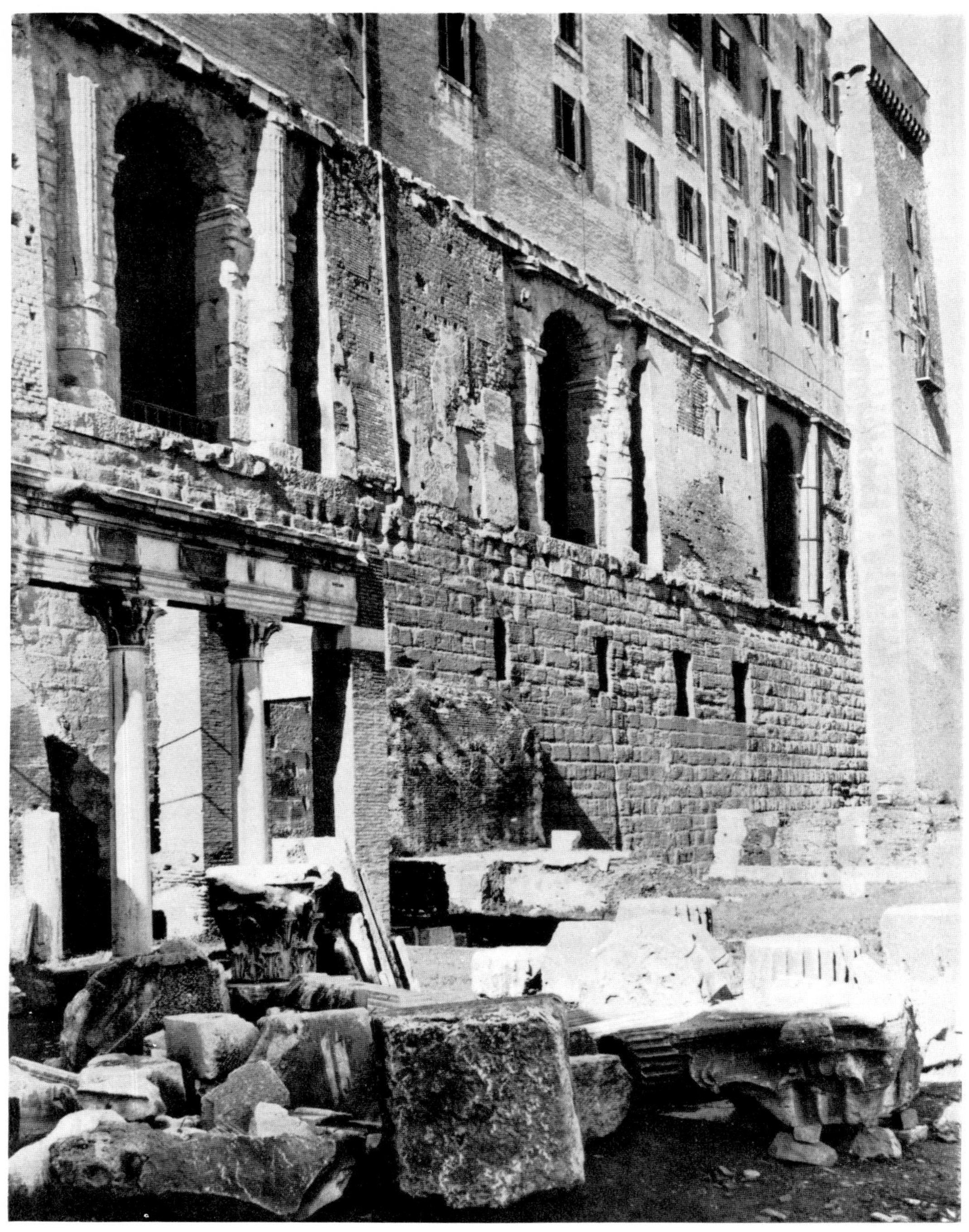

16. THE TABULARIUM, on the Forum side. The *substructio* is shown, above which rise the Doric arcades of Sulla's building, with the windows of Michelangelo's addition higher still. See p. 72.

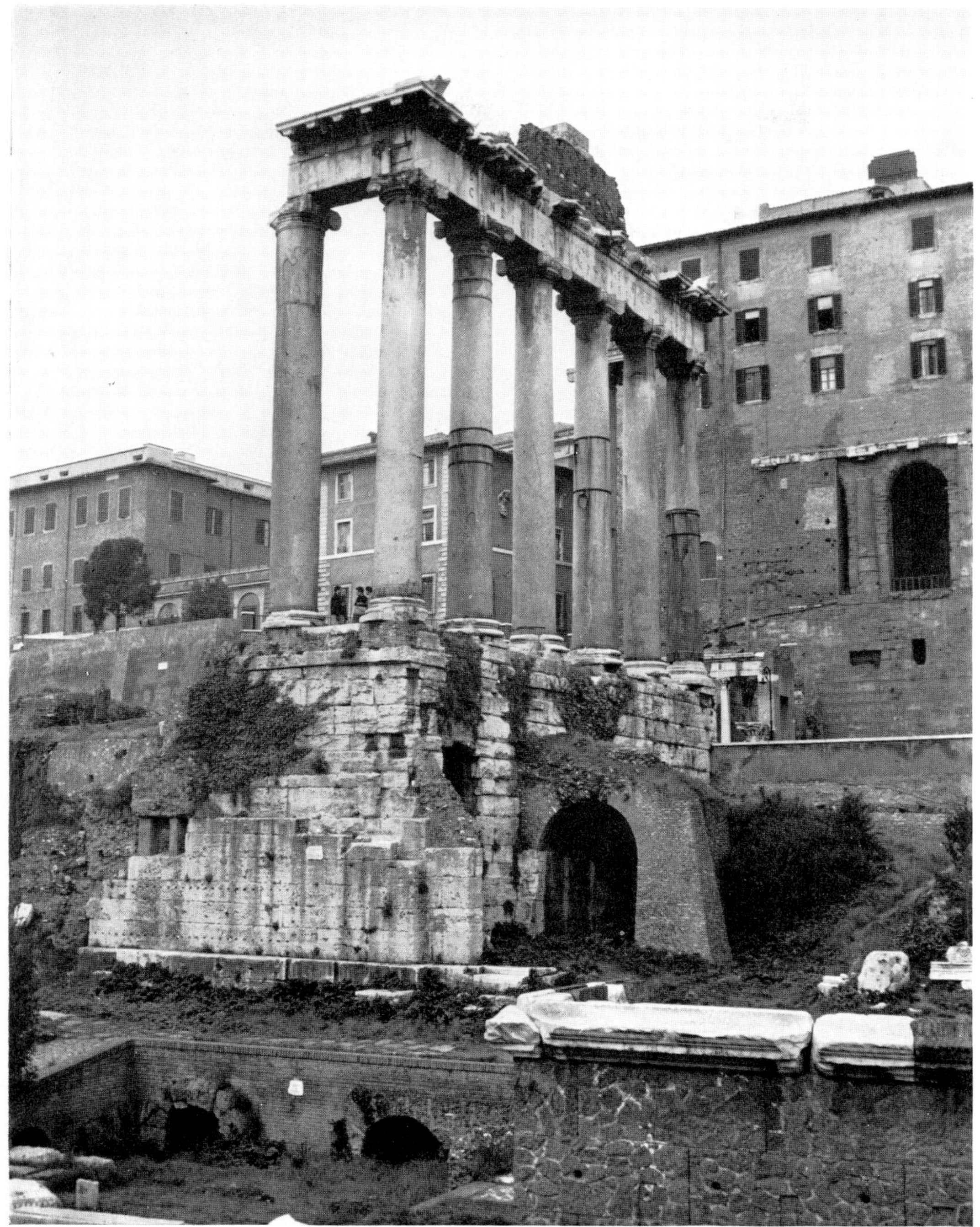

17. THE TEMPLE OF SATURN, showing on the right the entrance to the *aerarium Saturni*. See p. 81.

18. THE MILLIARIUM AUREUM. The column drum and the circular marble plinth above it are now attributed to this monument.

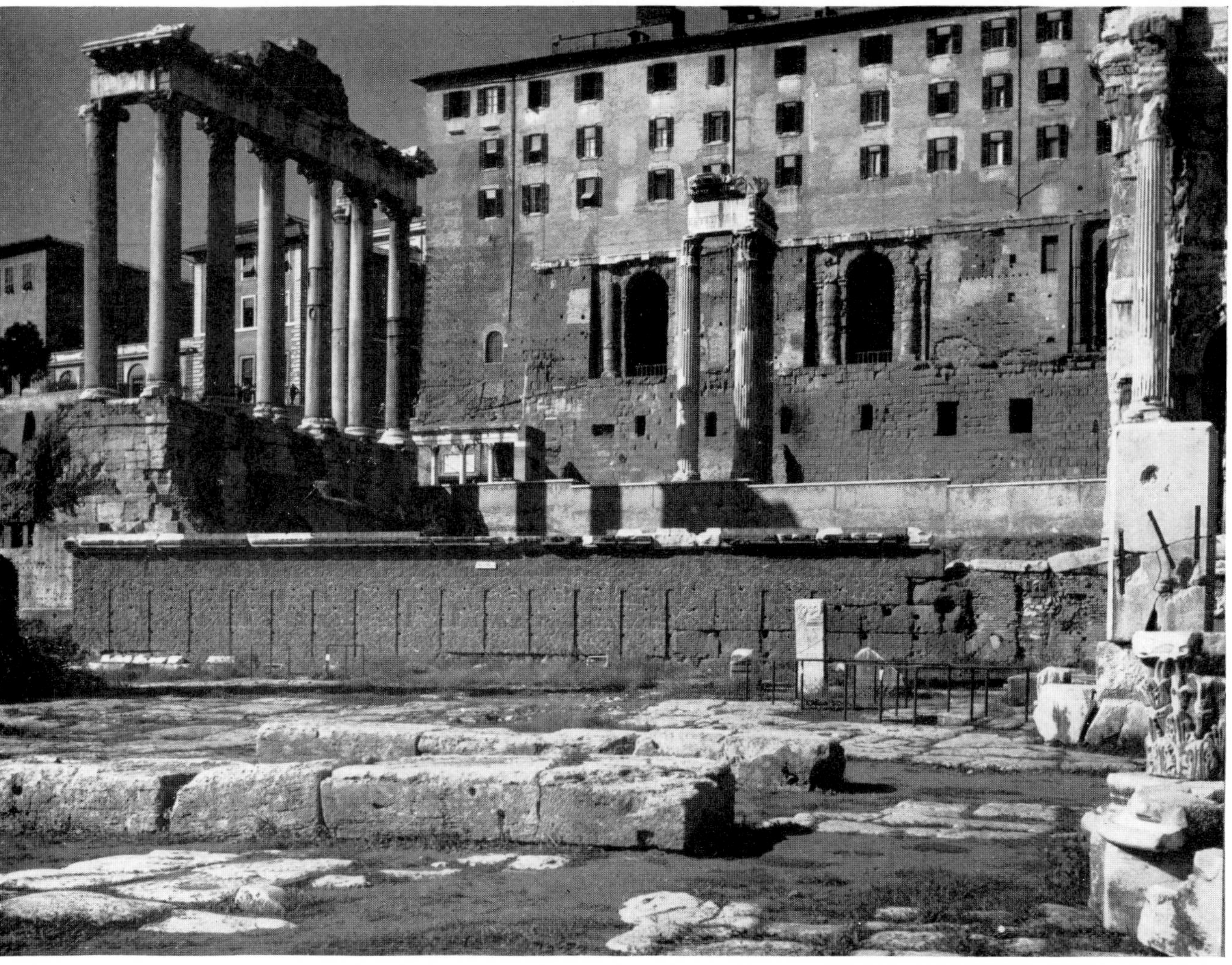

19. THE ROSTRA. The excavations of 1904 revealed them as replanned by Julius Caesar: a stone platform, with its front wall decorated with the beaks of ships. The dowel-holes for these are clearly seen. To the left, the Temple of Saturn, to the right, the Arch of Septimius Severus. See p. 92.

20. THE ARCH OF SEPTIMIUS SEVERUS. The relief shown is set above the left-hand arch (Capitol side). In three stages it records scenes from the Parthian Wars. Top: the capture of Seleuceia: middle, that of Ctesiphon: below, captives surrender to Dea Roma. In the spandrels, river gods (Tigris and Euphrates?). See p. 85.

21. LAPIS NIGER, south and west sides of the stele. The inscription is set out on p. 90.

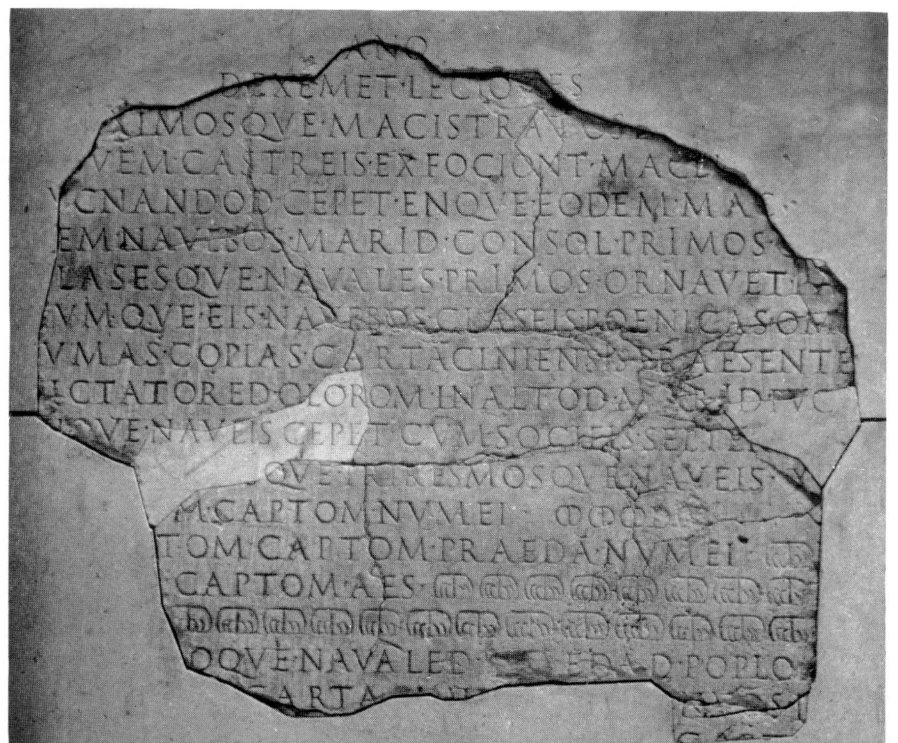

22. COLUMN OF C. DIULIUS. Inscription. See p. 93.

23. PLUTEI TRAIANI, right panel. The tax-clerks advance from the Tabularium with their records, which are piled for destruction. In the background, the buildings whose identification has aroused so much controversy. The most probable is (right to left): The Temple of Vespasian, an arch of the Tabularium (?), the Temple of Saturn, the arcades of the Basilica Julia, followed by the Statue of Marsyas and a fig-tree. This provides a link with the left panel shown in Plate 24. See p. 89.

24. PLUTEI TRAIANI, left panel. After Marsyas and the fig-tree, we see an Emperor (Trajan?) seated on a tribunal, receiving the thanks of a woman (Italia? a mother?). The four personages on the right would then be the *populus Romanus*. A more numerous group, facing left, look at an Emperor (Hadrian?) on the Rostra, who

25. AN EMPEROR (HADRIAN ?), FOUR ROMANS, THE STATUE OF MARSYAS AND THE SACRED FIG-TREE. Marsyas carries a wine-skin: the Ficus is shown as an ancient tree, but still bearing ripe fruit. Detail from Plate 24.

26. LACUS CURTIUS: RELIEF OF METTIUS CURTIUS. See pp. 95–97.

L NAEVIVS L F SVRDINVS
PR
INTER·CIVIS·ET·PEREGRINOS

27. LACUS CURTIUS: INSCRIPTION. See p. 96.

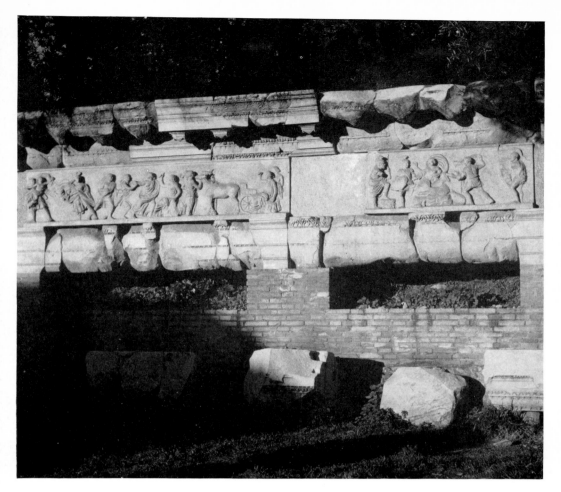

28. BASILICA AEMILIA. Plaster casts of the historical reliefs. On the right, the death of Tarpeia, on the left, the Rape of the Sabines. See p 99.

29. FASTI CONSULARES AND TRIUMPHALES, engraved on the Piers of the Arch of Augustus, which was voted by the Senate in 29 B.C. to commemorate the victory at Actium and stood beside the Temple of Divus Julius close to the Temple of Vesta.

30. THE TEMPLE OF VESTA. The famous relief in the Uffizi Gallery in Florence probably depicts this Temple after its restoration by Augustus. Note the Ionic capitals, the bronze roof with its circular louvre, and the oak tree, which represents the ancient Lucus Vestae. See p. 109.

31. VESTAL VIRGINS AT A BANQUET. Detail from a relief now attributed to the Ara Pietatis Augusti, a monument voted by the Senate in A.D. 22, when the aged Empress Livia, mother of Tiberius, recovered

32. AIR PHOTOGRAPH OF THE SITE OF THE REGIA. The marble blocks from the rebuilding by Calvinus (36 B.C.) are clearly distinguished from the tufa of earlier periods. Note the circular base of the large room at the top, perhaps the hearth of the early Regia. On the right, a triangular courtyard with two wells and a cistern. See pp. 106–7.

33. LACUS JUTURNAE. Aedicula. See p. 111.

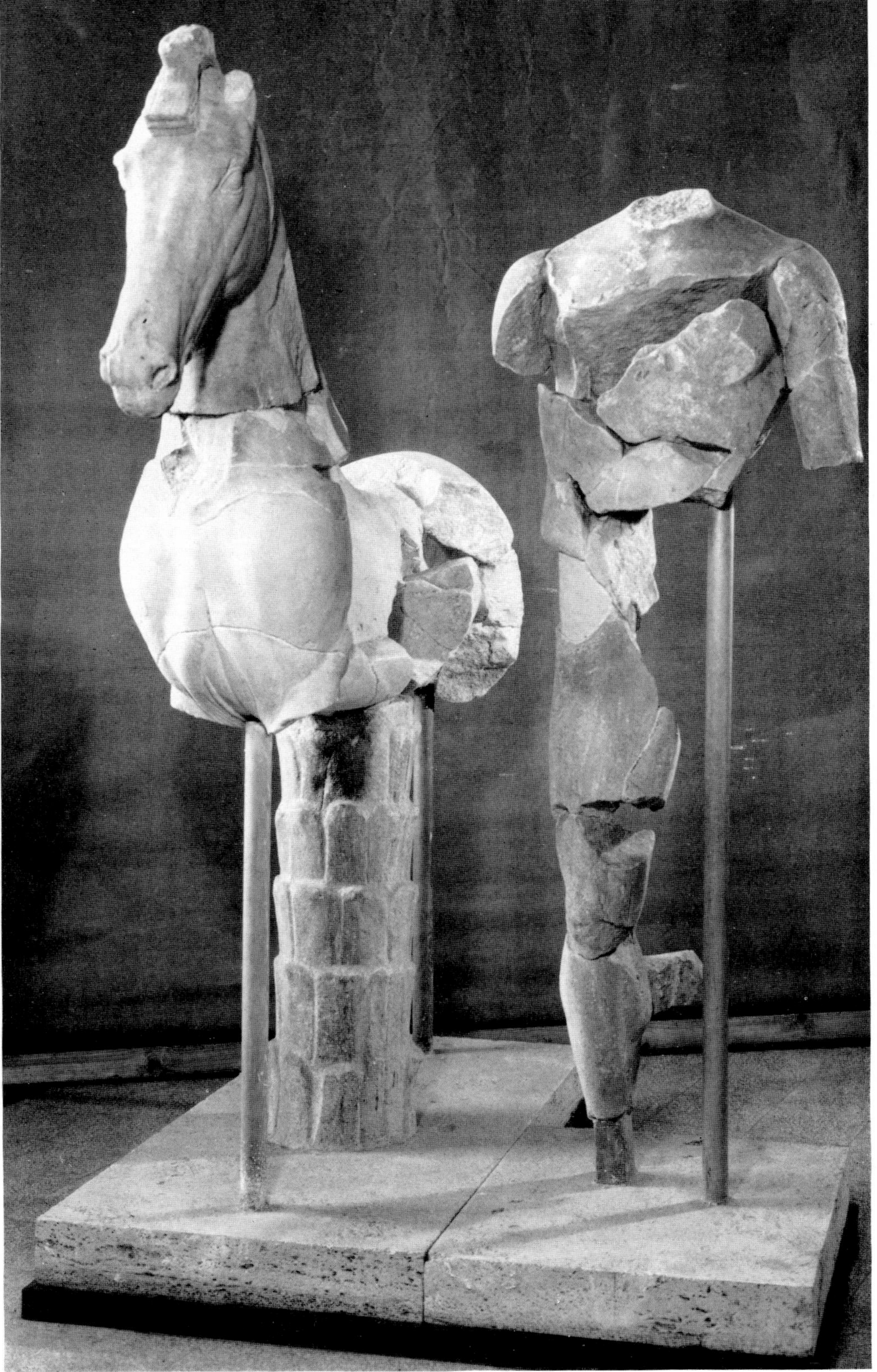

34. LACUS JUTURNAE: ARCHAIC STATUES OF THE DIOSCURI, found in the course of the excavations of 1900. They are probably South Italian, of the fifth century B.C. Now in the Antiquarium of the Forum. See p. 111.

35. TEMPLE OF ANTONINUS AND FAUSTINA Frieze See p. 115

36. APOTHEOSIS OF ANTONINUS PIUS AND FAUSTINA, on the relief from the base of the Column of Antoninus. The deified pair are borne upwards by a winged figure, bearing in his left hand the symbols of the vault of heaven and the serpent of Time. The two eagles accompanying the flight stand for the eagles actually released from the funeral pyre. Below, Dea Roma, her arms laid aside during the peace of Antoninus' reign, bids farewell to the imperial pair. The semi-nude figure left is the Genius of the Campus Martius, identified by the Column of Antoninus which he holds. This relief is now in the Cortile della Pigna in the Vatican. Cf. Plate 67 for the relief of the Apotheosis of Sabina.

37. ARCH OF TITUS. Relief from the south jamb of the passage-way. The *pompa*, about to pass under a triumphal arch, bears the sacred objects from the Temple at Jerusalem—the table for the shew-bread, the trumpets, and the seven-branched candlestick. The number of bearers, and the pillows on their shoulders, emphasize the

38. TEMPLE OF VENUS AND ROME. Part of the coffered ceiling is seen; the marble floor and columns belong to the restorations of Maxentius. Hadrian's gigantic statue of Dea Roma will have stood in this *cella*. See pp. 118–19.

39. TEMPLE OF ROMULUS. Bronze door and lock.

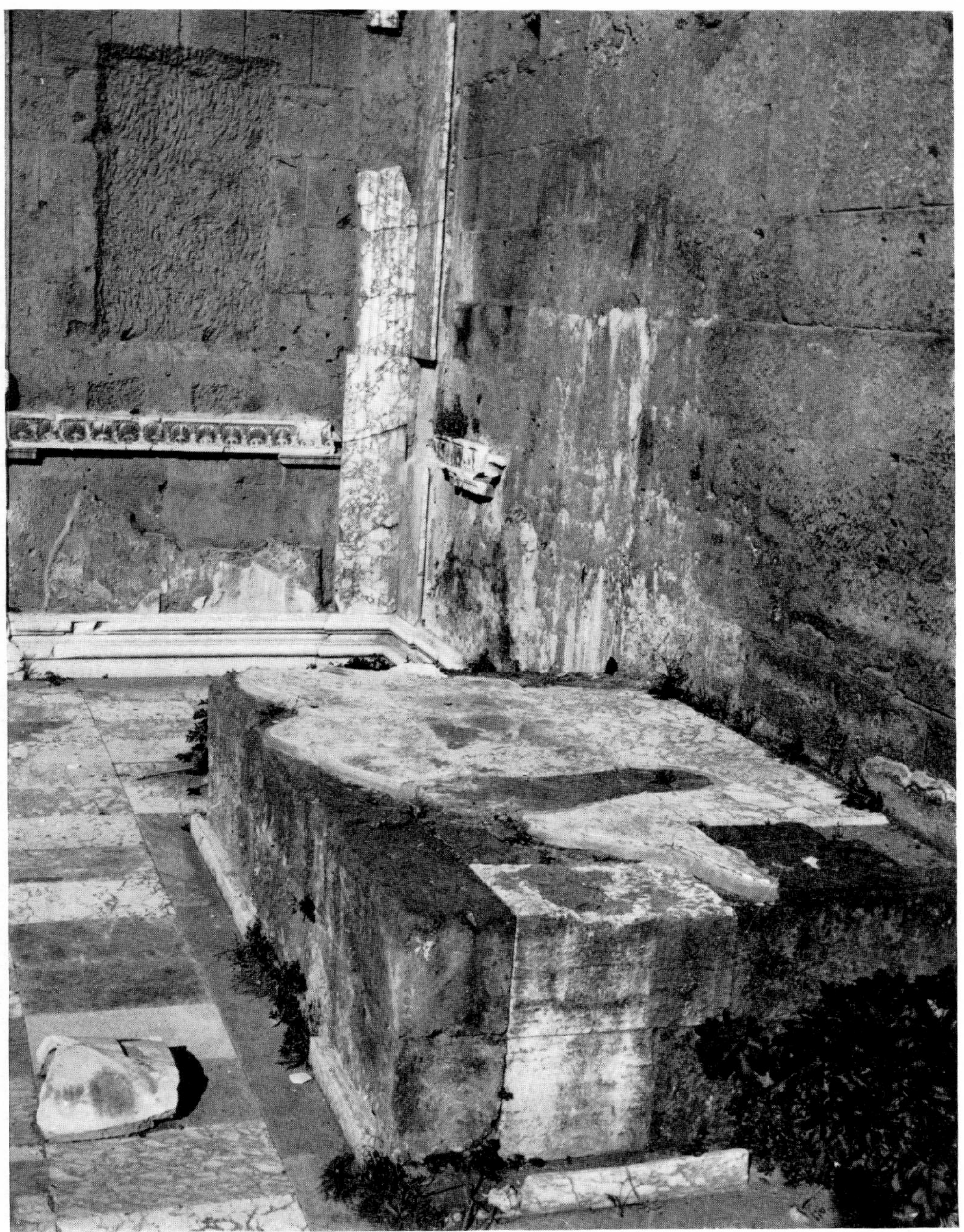

40. FORUM OF AUGUSTUS. Pedestal of colossal statue. See p. 129.

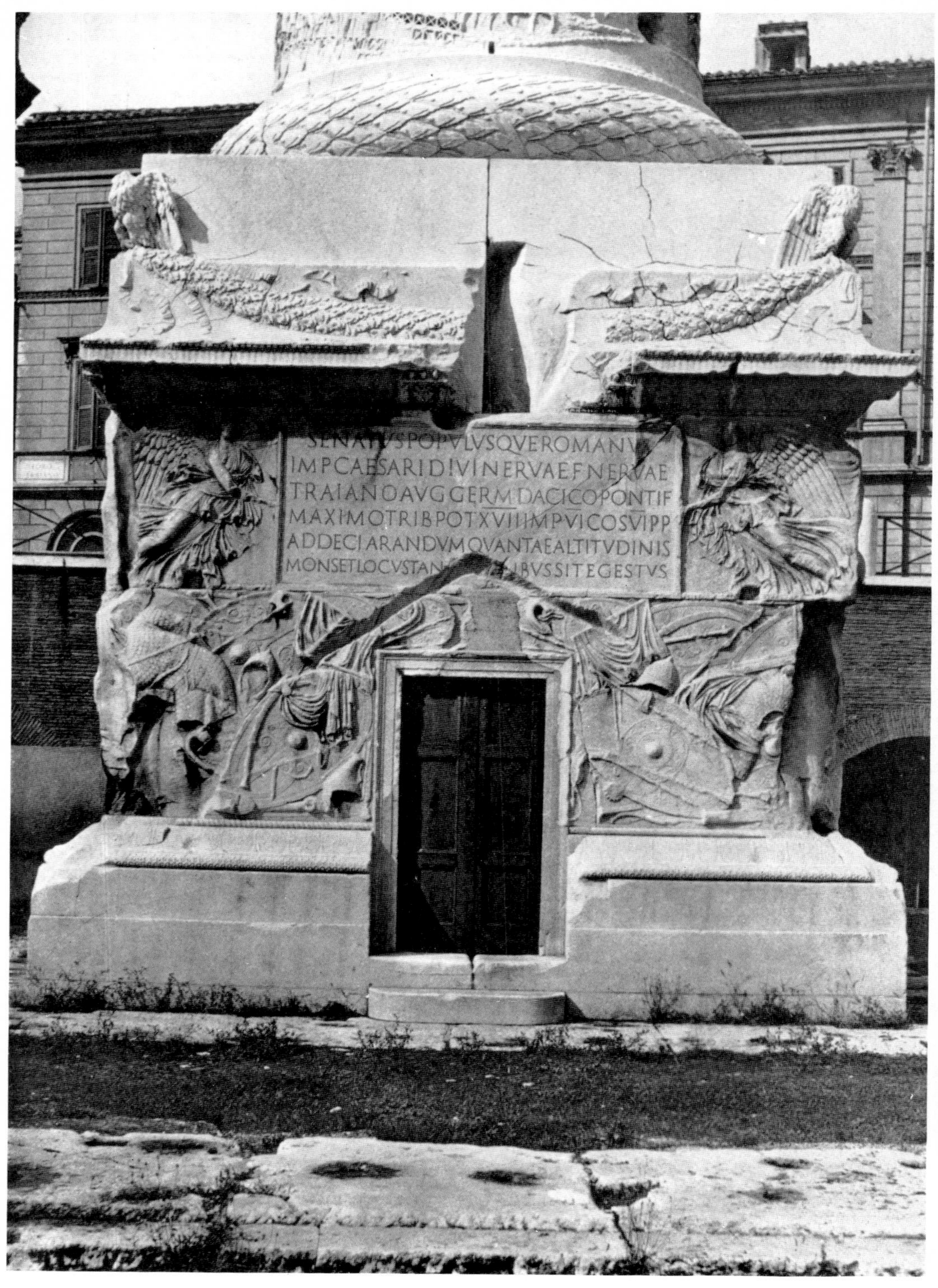

41. TRAJAN'S COLUMN. The trophy of Dacian arms, the Victories supporting the *titulus* with its magnificent lettering, the garlands, and the laurel wreath at the base of the column proper, all exemplify the art of triumphal monuments at its highest level. See p. 136.

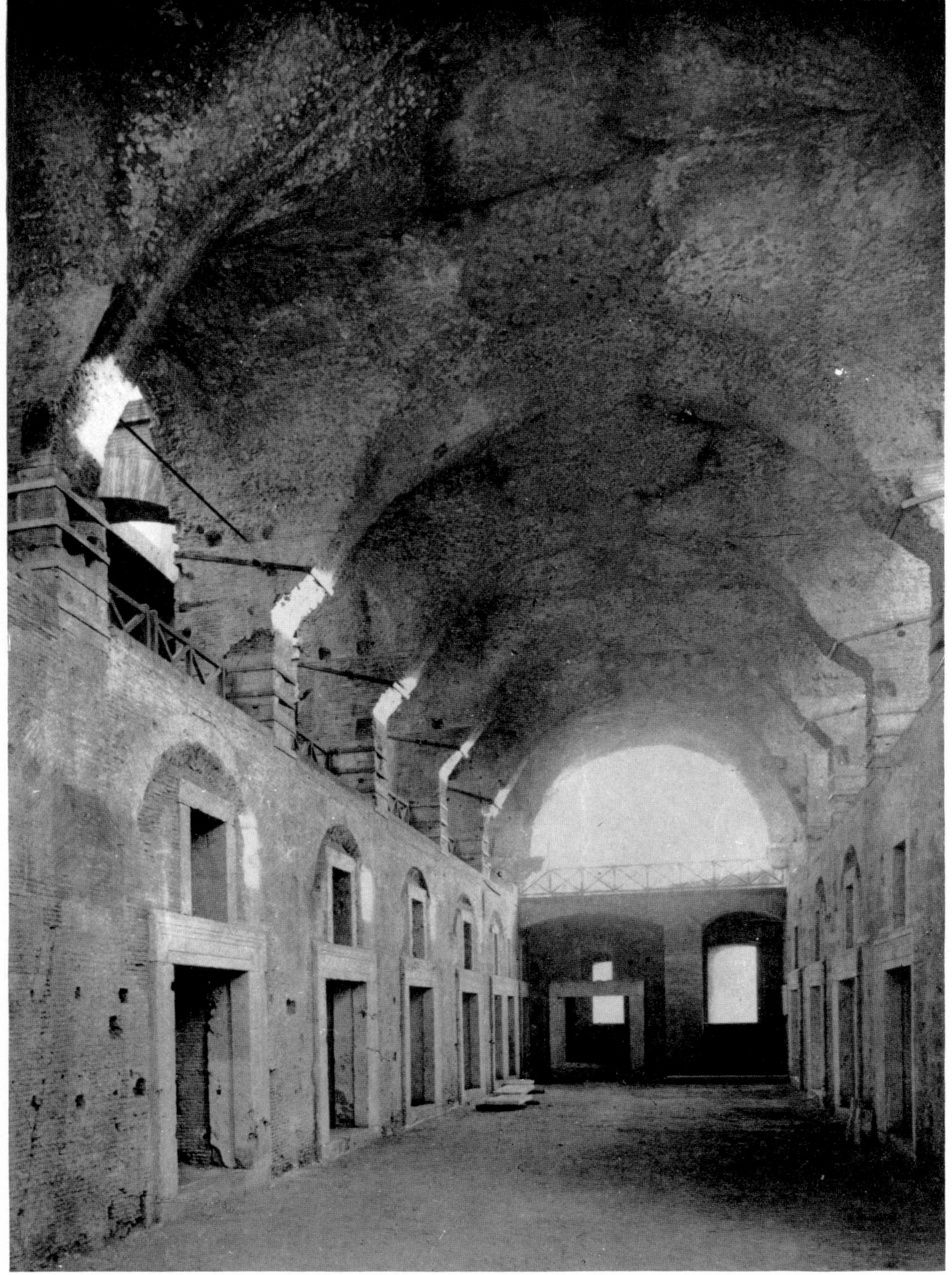

42. TRAJAN'S MARKETS. The great hall (aula Trajana) with its gallery and vaulted roof. The many original features of this building are discussed in William MacDonald's *The Architecture of the Roman Empire*, I, pp. 90ff. See p. 136.

43. ARCH OF CONSTANTINE: A relief of the period of Marcus Aurelius, generally interpreted as 'Reditus Augusti'. Roma and Mars conduct a returning Emperor, whose features have been reworked as Constantine, into a city bedecked in welcome. In the background, Vestal Virgins, a garlanded triumphal arch, and the Temple of Fortuna Redux(?). See p. 138.

44. ARCH OF CONSTANTINE: One of the eight Dacians probably taken from a monument in the Forum of Trajan. These are among the most noble portrayals of 'barbarians' in Roman art. See p. 138.

45. GOLDEN HOUSE. Reliefs from the main service corridor. See p. 141.

46. THE COLOSSEUM, in a relief from the Tomb of the Haterii, now in the Lateran Museum. It shows a building of three storeys, with an entrance crowned by a *quadriga*, and colossal statues in the arches of the arcades. Note the corbels for the *velarium* at the top. These features are reproduced in the model shown in Plate 47.

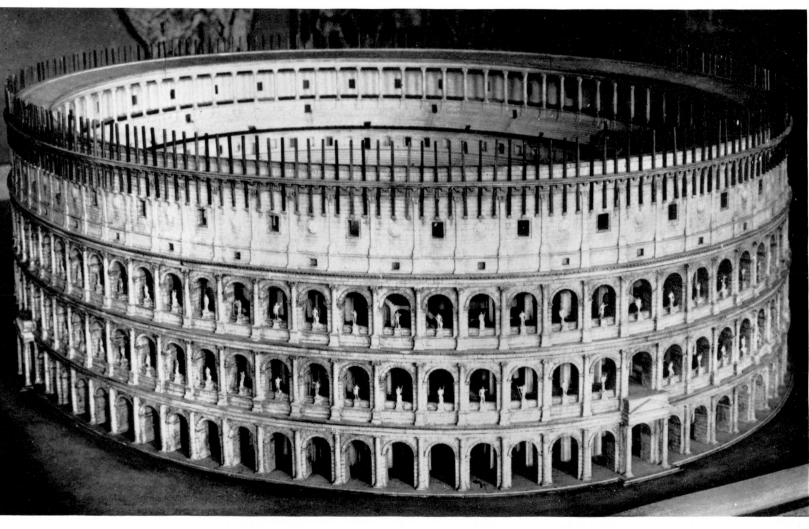

47. THE COLOSSEUM. Model in the Museo della Civiltà Romana. See p. 144.

48. SHIP'S PROW with a boar's head and sea monster, used for a fountain-decoration in the Temple of Claudius. The sea-monster motif would suit the 'Conquest of Ocean' implied by the British expedition of A.D. 43. See p. 186.

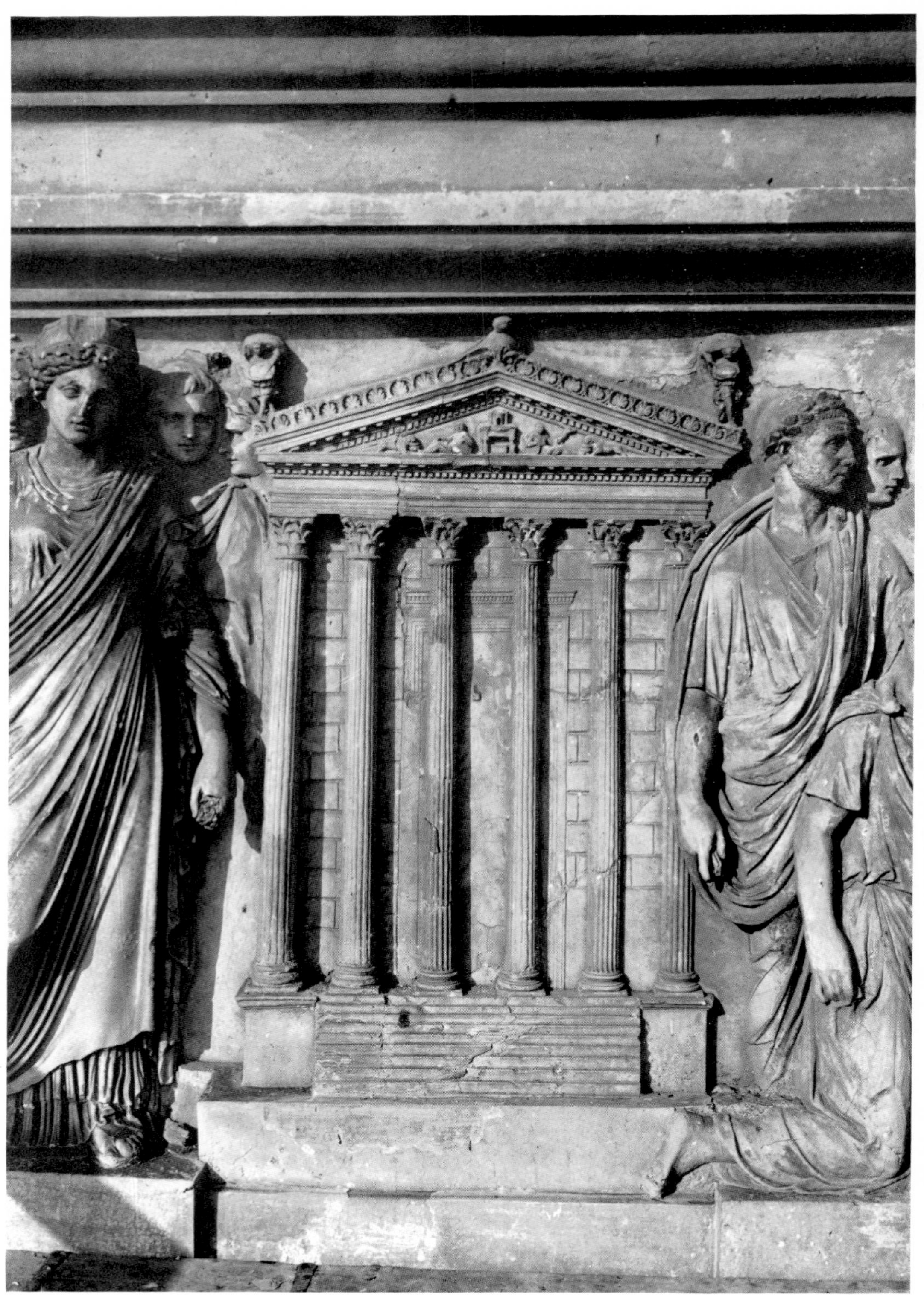

49. THE TEMPLE OF MAGNA MATER. Relief in the Villa Medici. See p. 153.

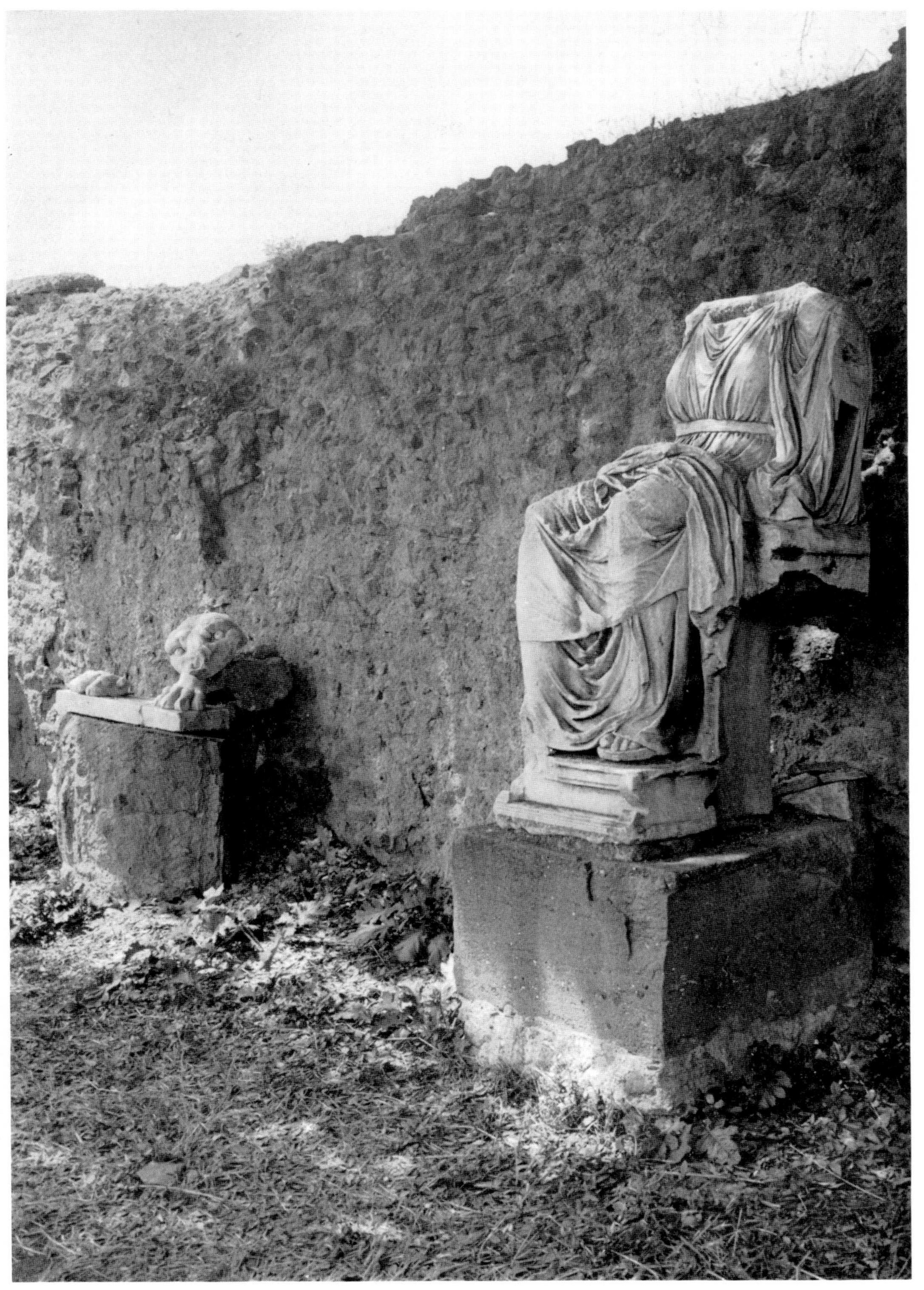

50. THE TEMPLE OF MAGNA MATER: Cybele and lion. See p. 153.

51. HOUSE OF AUGUSTUS: Room generally called the 'tablinum'. The relief in the centre of the right-hand wall shows Io, guarded by Argus (right) under a pillar capped by a statue of Juno. Her rescuer, Mercury, comes from the left. See p. 165.

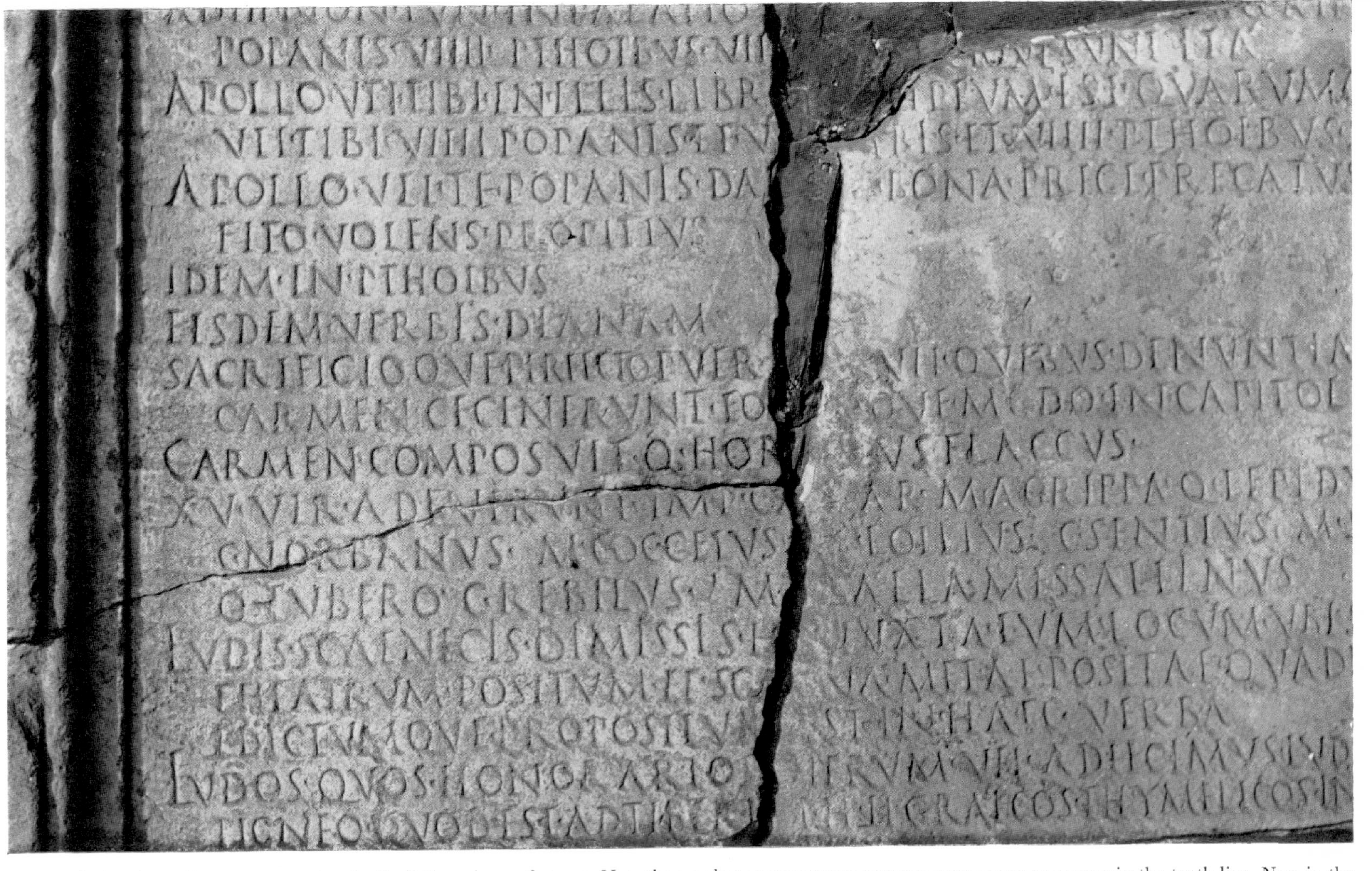

52. Inscription (p. 156) commemorating the Ludi Saeculares of 17 B.C. Note the words CARMEN COMPOSVIT Q HORATIVS FLACCVS in the tenth line. Now in the Museo Nazionale Romano. See p. 159.

53. PORTICUS OF OCTAVIA: The *propylaea* or main entrance; behind, the church of S. Angelo. See p. 177.

54. THE THEATRE OF MARCELLUS. See p. 179.

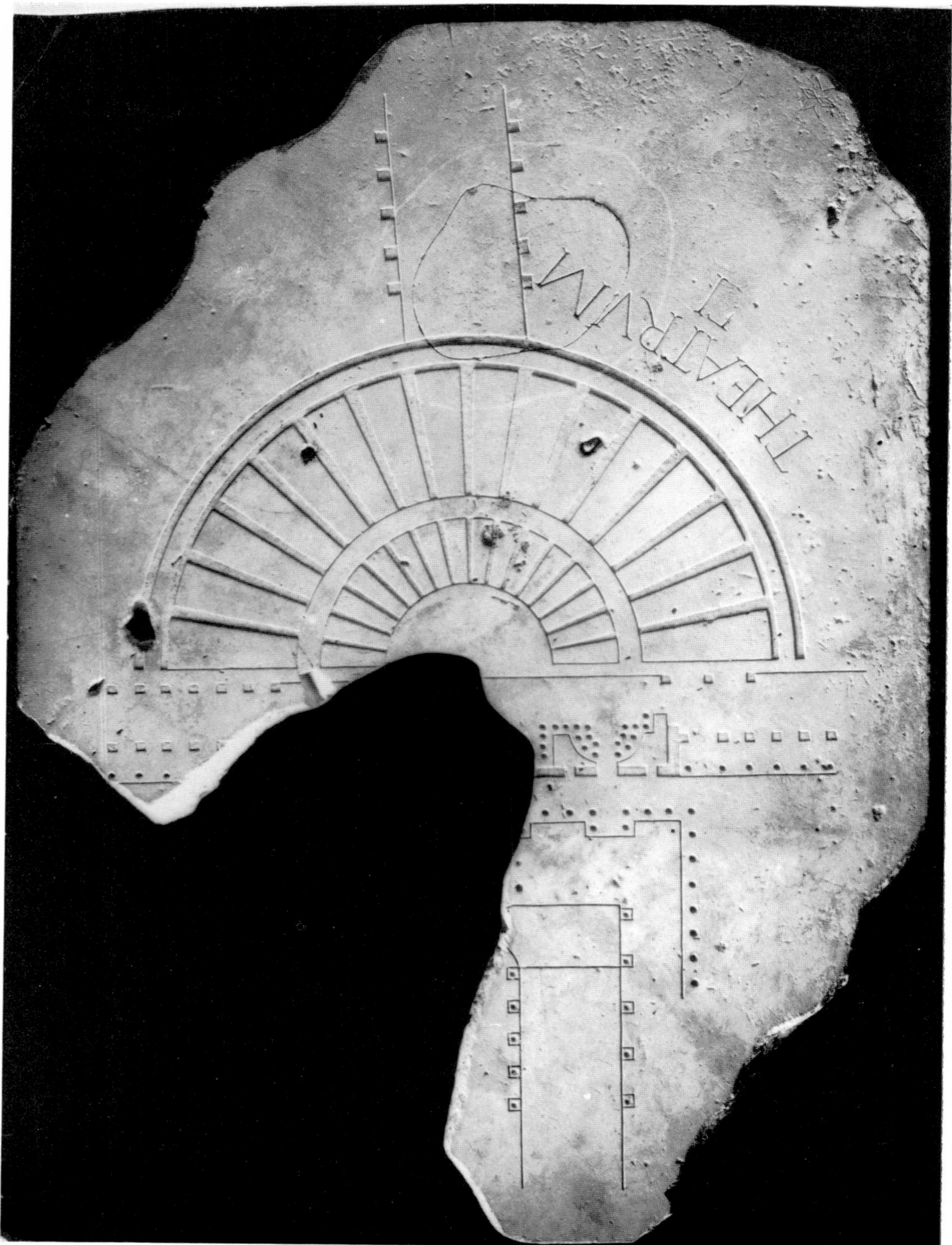

55. THE THEATRE OF POMPEY is shown in one of the best preserved fragments of the Forma Urbis. Note the Temple of Venus Victrix at the top of the *cavea*, and the *porticus* below. See p. 183.

56. AN AIR PHOTOGRAPH brings out clearly how the remains of the Theatre of Pompey have determined the lay-out of the modern streets and buildings. The outer curve of the *cavea* is followed by Via dei Giubbonari (left) and Piazza del Biscione (right): the inner, by Via di Grottapinta. The church of S. Andrea della Valle stands at the right hand corner of the *scaena*. The open space beyond the *cavea* and to the right is Campo di Fiori. See p. 183.

57. The outlines of the Stadium of Domitian are perfectly preserved in Piazza Navona. At the bottom left is Palazzo Braschi, immediately above it, the two courtyards of Palazzo Pamphili. It was the Pamphili family, especially the Pamphili pope Innocent X (1644–55), who transformed the area into the most splendid piece of baroque townscape in Rome. The church of S. Agnese in Agone (Borromini etc.) shows its dome and belfries halfway up the left-hand side: this is the traditional site of the martyrdom of St. Agnes. Opposite in the centre of the piazza, Bernini's *Fountain of the Four Rivers*, with the obelisk brought by Innocent X from the *Spina* of the Circus of Maxentius on Via Appia. But the piazza can show a still more splendid synthesis of the classical and the baroque in the wonderful Aeneas frescoes by Pietro da Cortona in the Pamphili Palace (now the Brazilian Embassy). No student of Virgil should fail to see them when they are open to public view. See p. 185.

58. Fragments from a relief found in Via del Corso, and attributed to the Arch of Claudius (see p. 185).

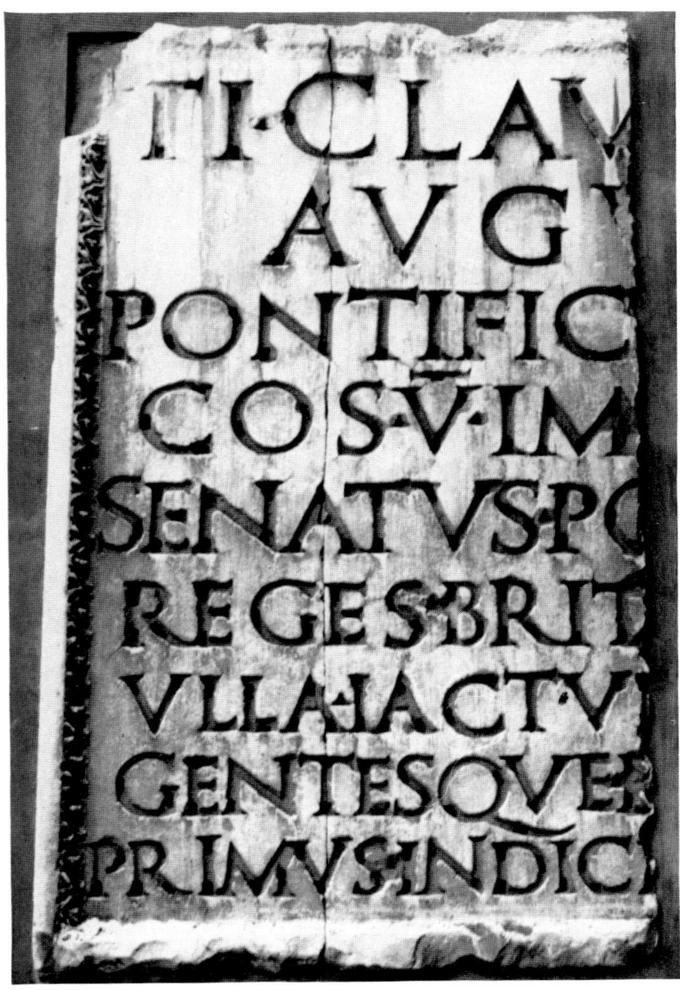

59. THE ARCH OF CLAUDIUS. Inscription. See pp. 185–186.
Reproduced by courtesy of Dr. Graham Webster.

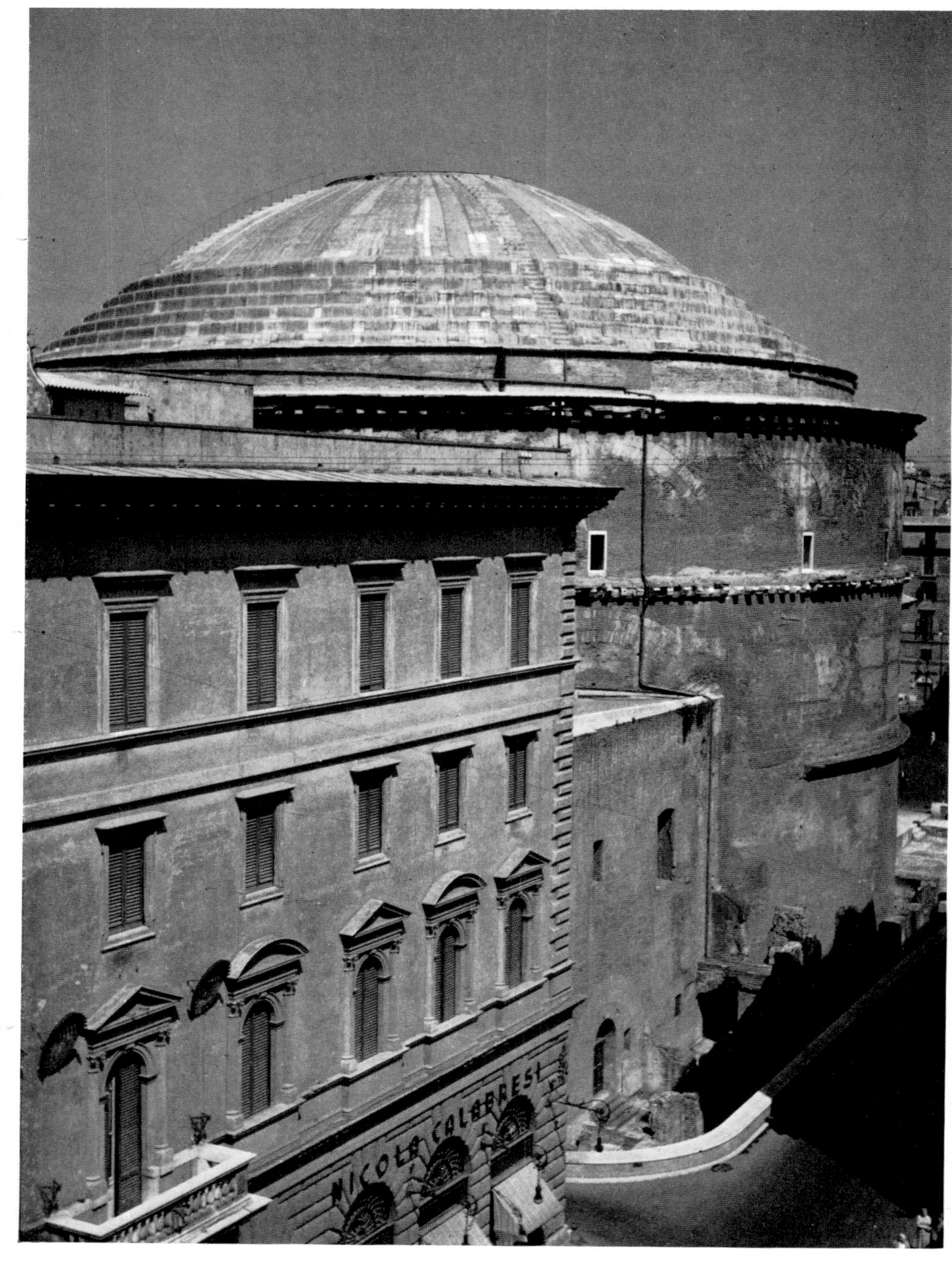

60. PANTHEON. Rotunda and dome. See pp. 187–190.

61. HADRIANEUM. Reliefs. See p. 186.

62. COLUMN OF MARCUS AURELIUS. The Miracle of the Rain. Note the stress on the different ways in which it affected the two armies. The rain falls gratefully on the tired Romans. One man puts up his shield as a kind of umbrella, his neighbour, to catch and drink the drops. But over the barbarians the Rain God sweeps as a terrible demon, bringing their cavalry charge to a halt, and sweeping away men and horses in the flood. It has understandably been called 'perhaps the most haunting and imaginative figure that a Roman artist ever conceived'. See p. 192.

63. ARA PACIS: A young matron is seated on a rock, with two babes seeking the breast. At her feet are a bull and a ram, flowers and corn grow behind her, at the bottom left birds come to drink among the reeds. The two figures with cloaks billowing over their heads are the *Aurae* or Winds. If the woman is Italia, all the other details correspond closely with the praises of Italy in the Second Georgic, as Grénier has well shown (see note on p. 236). See p. 195.

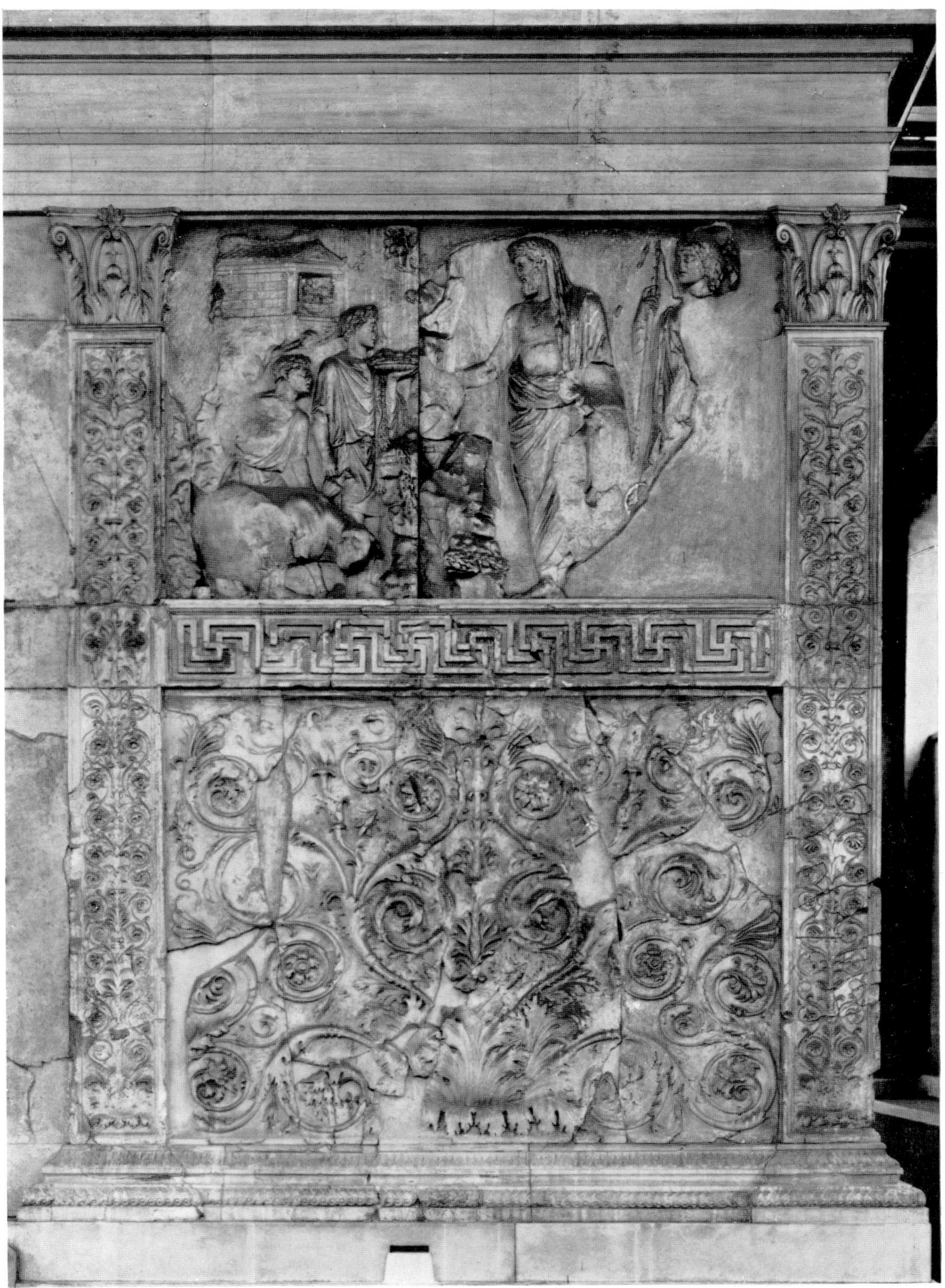

64. ARA PACIS: Aeneas, a grave bearded figure with the toga drawn over his head in the ceremonial *cinctu Gabino*, is about to sacrifice the White Sow. This is the finest portrayal of *pius Aeneas* in ancient art. Two young *camilli* reverently bear the sacrificial vessel. The figure behind Aeneas, with his spear, is *fidus Achates*. At the shrine in the background are two seated figures, semi-nude and carrying spears: these are the *Penates* brought by Aeneas from Troy and established in Lavinium. See p. 195.

65. MAUSOLEUM OF AUGUSTUS. Epitaphs of Marcellus and Octavia. See p. 196.

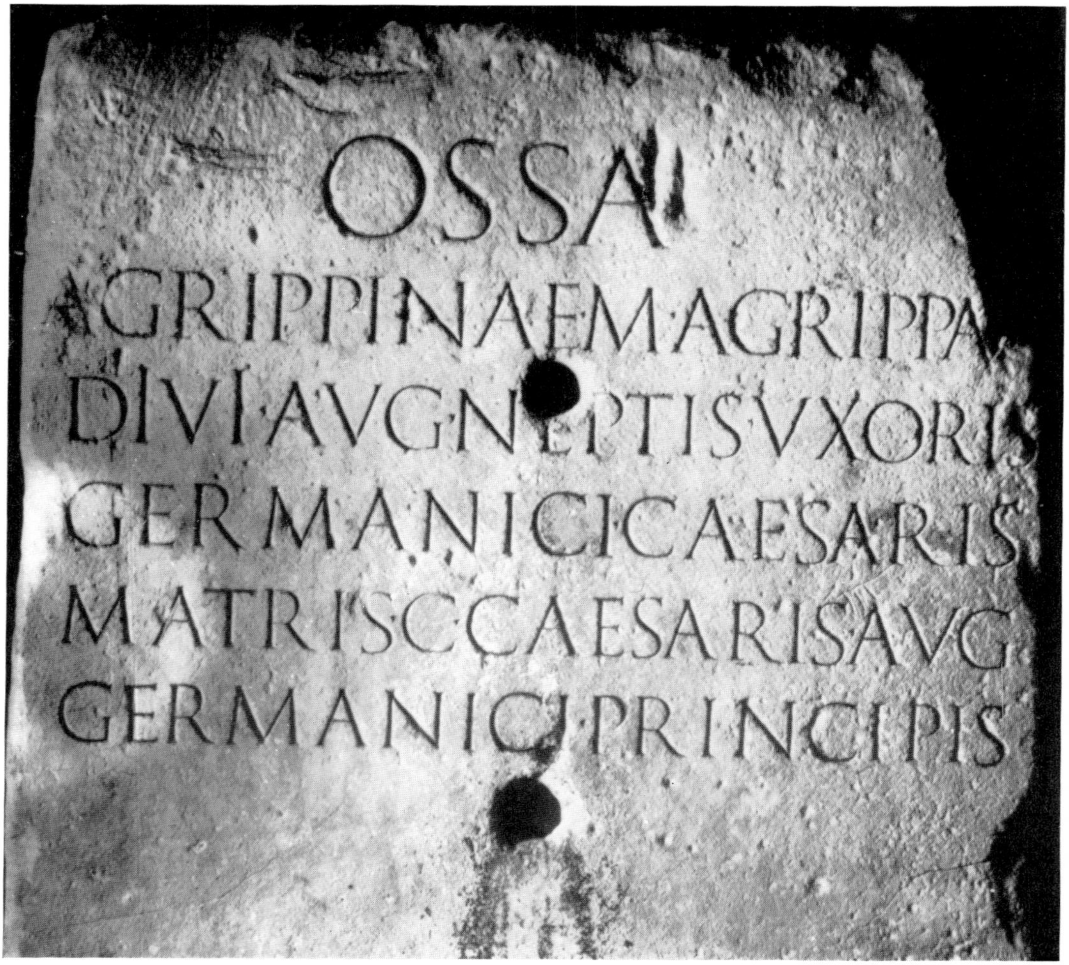

OSSA
AGRIPPINAE M AGRIPPAE F
DIVI AVG NEPTIS VXORIS
GERMANICI CAESARIS
MATRIS C CAESARIS AVG
GERMANICI PRINCIPIS

66. MAUSOLEUM OF AUGUSTUS. Epitaph of Agrippina. See p. 198.

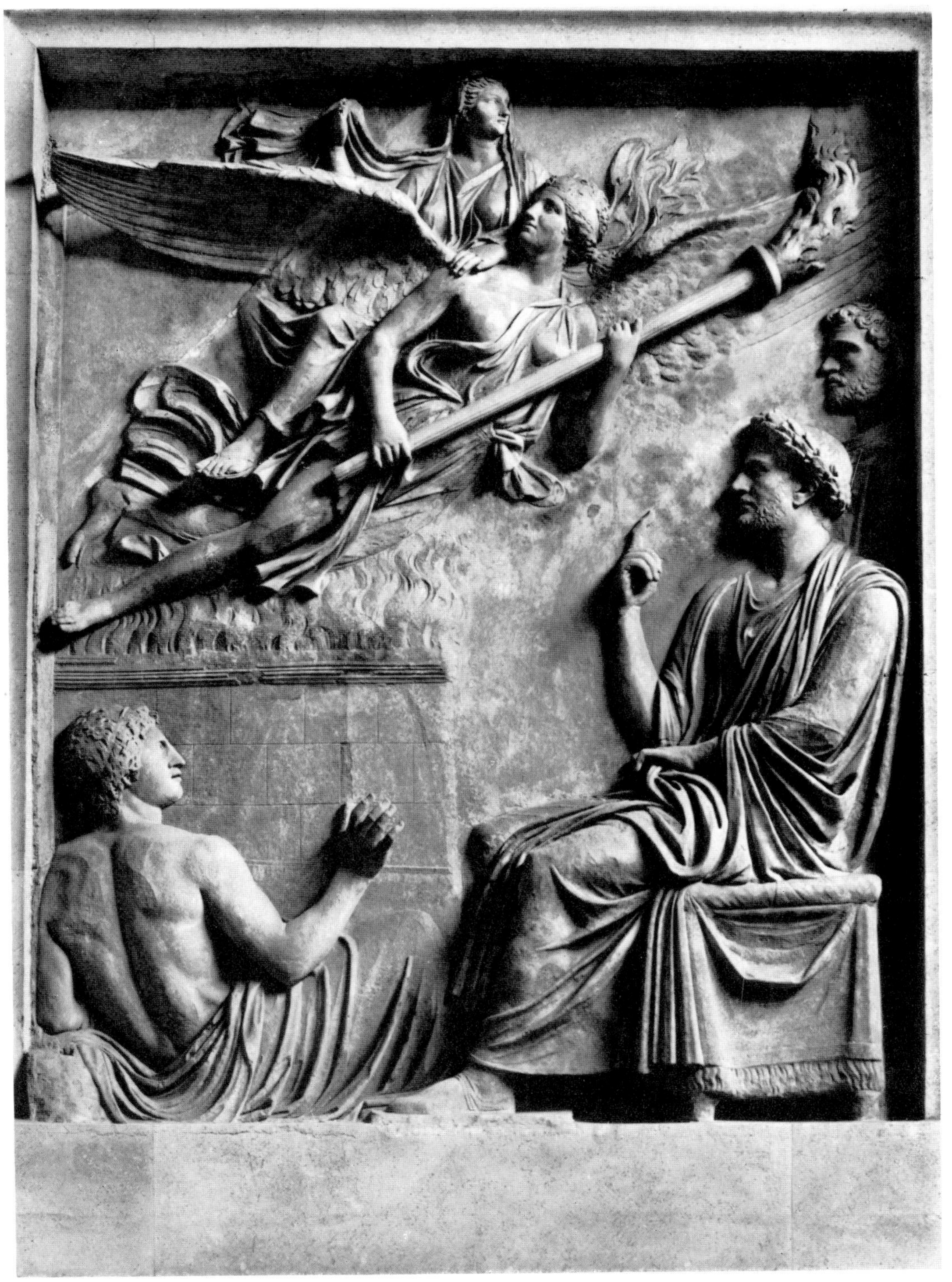

67. APOTHEOSIS OF SABINA, WIFE OF HADRIAN (Arco di Portogallo). See Plate 36.

COLLEGIO·LIBERI·PATRIS·ET·MERCVR
NEGOTIANTIVM·CELLARVM·VINA
RIARVM·NOVAE·ET·ARRVNTI
ANAE CAESARIS N
CINNAMVS·IMP·NERVAE·CAESARI
RAIANI·AVG·GERM·SERVOS·VER
NA·DISPENSATOR·OB·IMMVNITA
D·D·CVRA·AGENTIBVS·ANN·PRI
TI·CLAVDIO·ZOSIMO·ET·SEX·CAELIO

68. The inscription was found on a building on the banks of the Tiber by the Farnesina, which it shows to have been a wine-warehouse belonging to the Imperial house. It refers to the merchants of the *cellae vinariae*, who are organized, suitably enough, into a *collegium Liberi Patris et Mercurii*. The consuls named in the last line are those of the year A.D. 102.

ALVT·GENIVM·HORREOR
RIPPIANORVM·NEGOTIANTIB
L·ARRIVS· HERMES
C·VARIVS· POLYCARPVS
C·PACONIVS·CHRYSANTHVS
IMMVNES · · S · P · D · D

69. A parallel inscription to that of Plate 68, set up by the merchants trading in the Horrea Agrippiana to the Genius of that building. This warehouse was in the Forum Romanum.

70. THE OBELISK OF AUGUSTUS. Brought from Heliopolis by Augustus in 10 B.C., it was placed to serve as the gnomon for the *Horologium Augusti* in the Campus Martius. The inscription shows that it was 'set up as a gift to the Sun, after the conquest of Egypt for the Roman People'. The religious beliefs are here interfused, the Roman *evocatio* or bringing over the gods of a defeated enemy, and the Egyptian-Hellenistic idea of the obelisk of the Sun-God as a symbol of universal empire. The obelisk now stands in Piazza di Montecitorio, where it was set up in 1792.

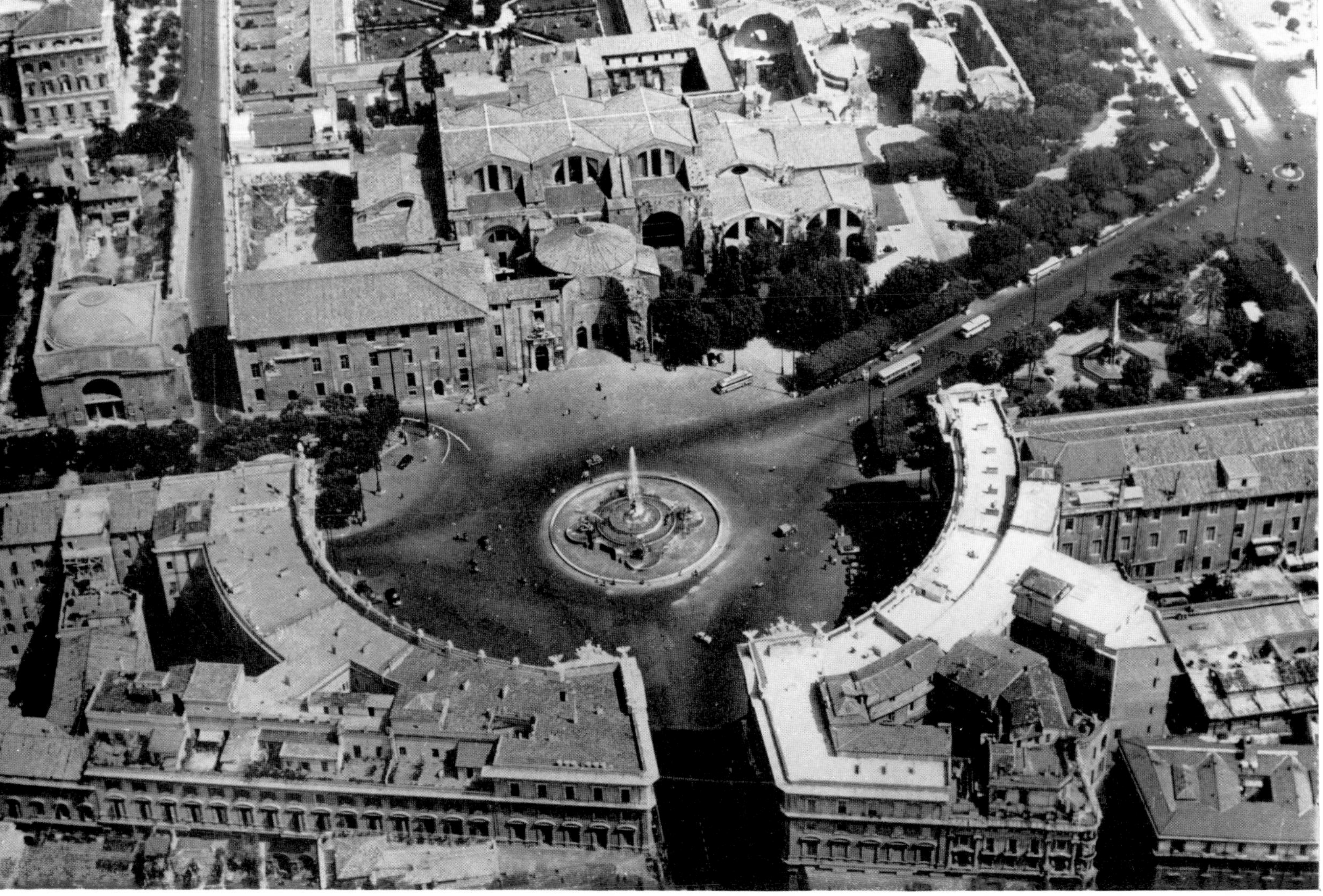

71. THERMAE OF DIOCLETIAN, air photograph. The modern Piazza dell' Esedra occupies the site of the former *exedra* of the Thermae: behind, note the three

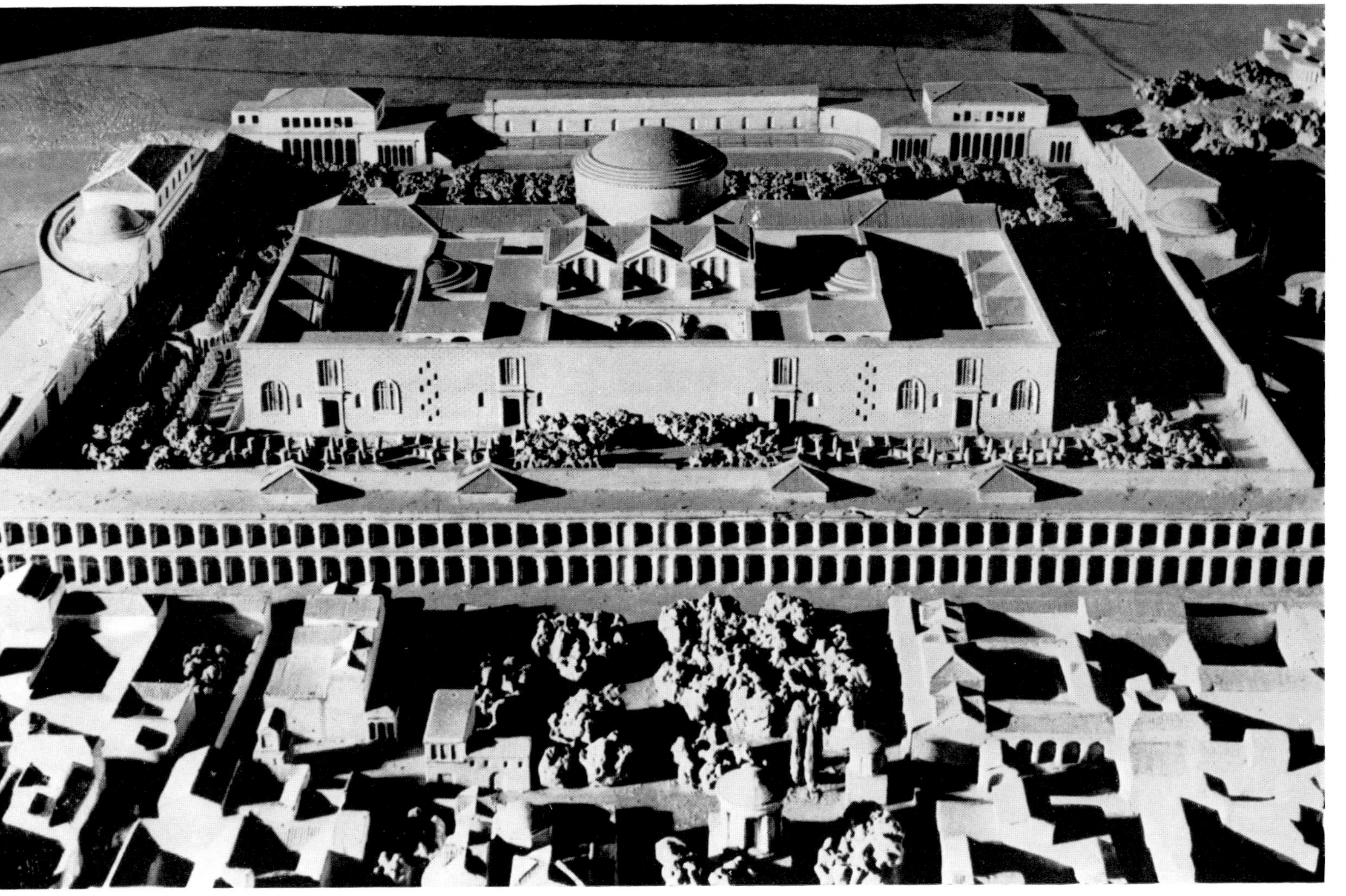

72. THERMAE OF CARACALLA, model. The features of this model are described on p. 204.

73. THE TOMB OF THE SCIPIOS. Epitaph of L. Scipio. See p. 206.

74. THE TOMB OF THE SCIPIOS. Sarcophagus of L. Cornelius Scipio Barbatus. See p. 205.

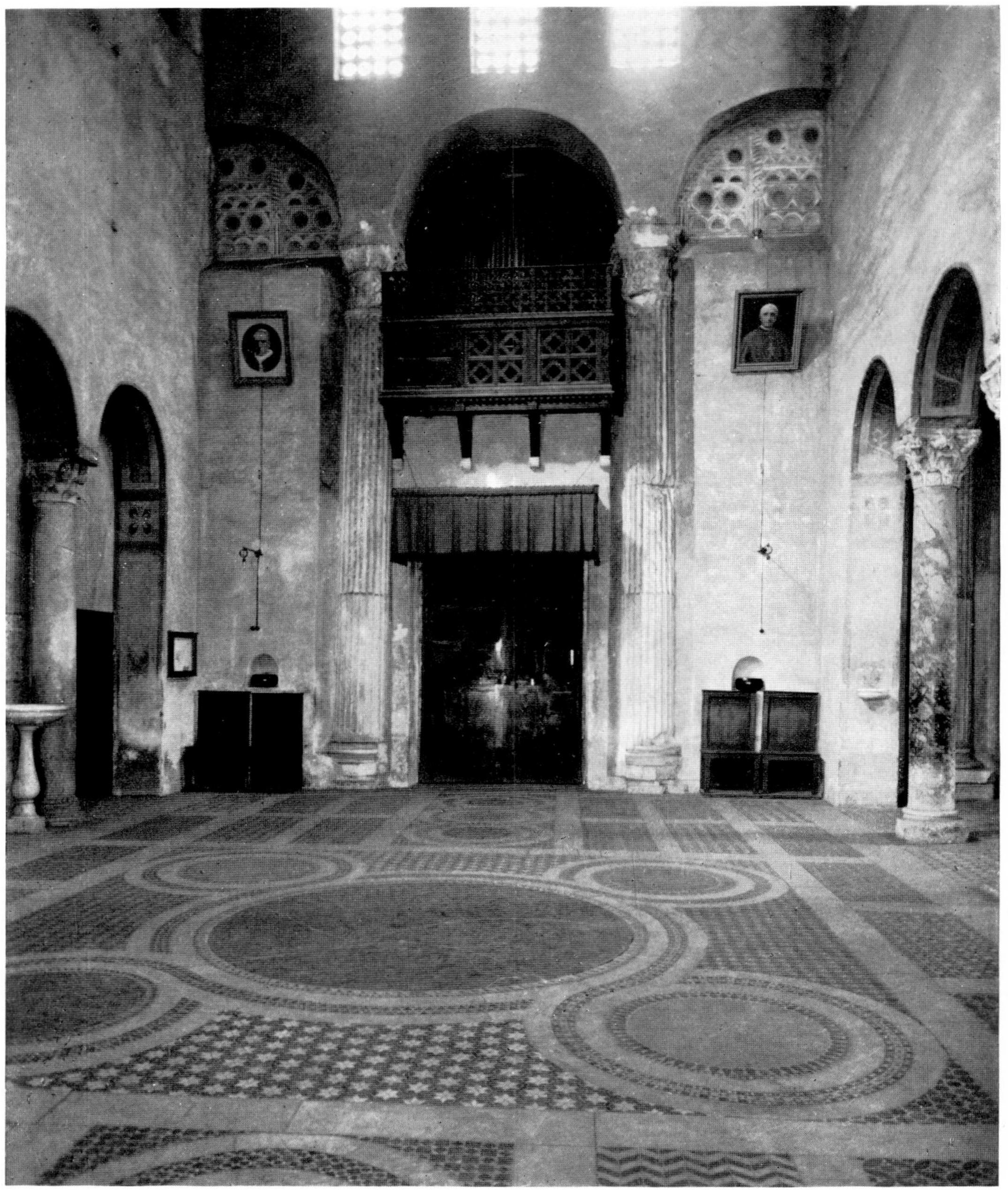

75. STATIO ANNONAE. The wall of S. Maria in Cosmedin, with columns and arches of the Statio Annonae. See pp. 208–210.

76. THE ARCH OF THE ARGENTARII. The Emperor Septimius Severus and his wife Julia Domna offer a sacrifice. See p. 210.

77–78. THE TOMB OF EURYSACES. The millionaire baker Marcus Vergilius Eurysaces was not ashamed of his trade. He built himself a conspicuous tomb at the junction of the Via Labicana and the Via Praenestina (See Plate 9), in which bakers' ovens form the leading motif. The inscription proclaims (EST HOC MONVMENTV)M MARCEI VERGILEI EVRYSACIS PISTORIS REDEMPTORIS ATPARET (ORIS . . .) 'This is the Tomb of Marcus Vergilius Eurysaces, Baker, Contractor, Public Servant' (CIL, VI. 1958). Presumably he contracted to bake for the *annona*. His wife Atistia—'that excellent woman'—FEMINA OPITVMA—was also buried IN HOC PANARIO (in this baker's oven). So was his friend Ogolnius, described as PISTOR SIMILAGINARIVS or pastrycook. The figures of Eurysaces and Atistia (Plate 78) are now lost.

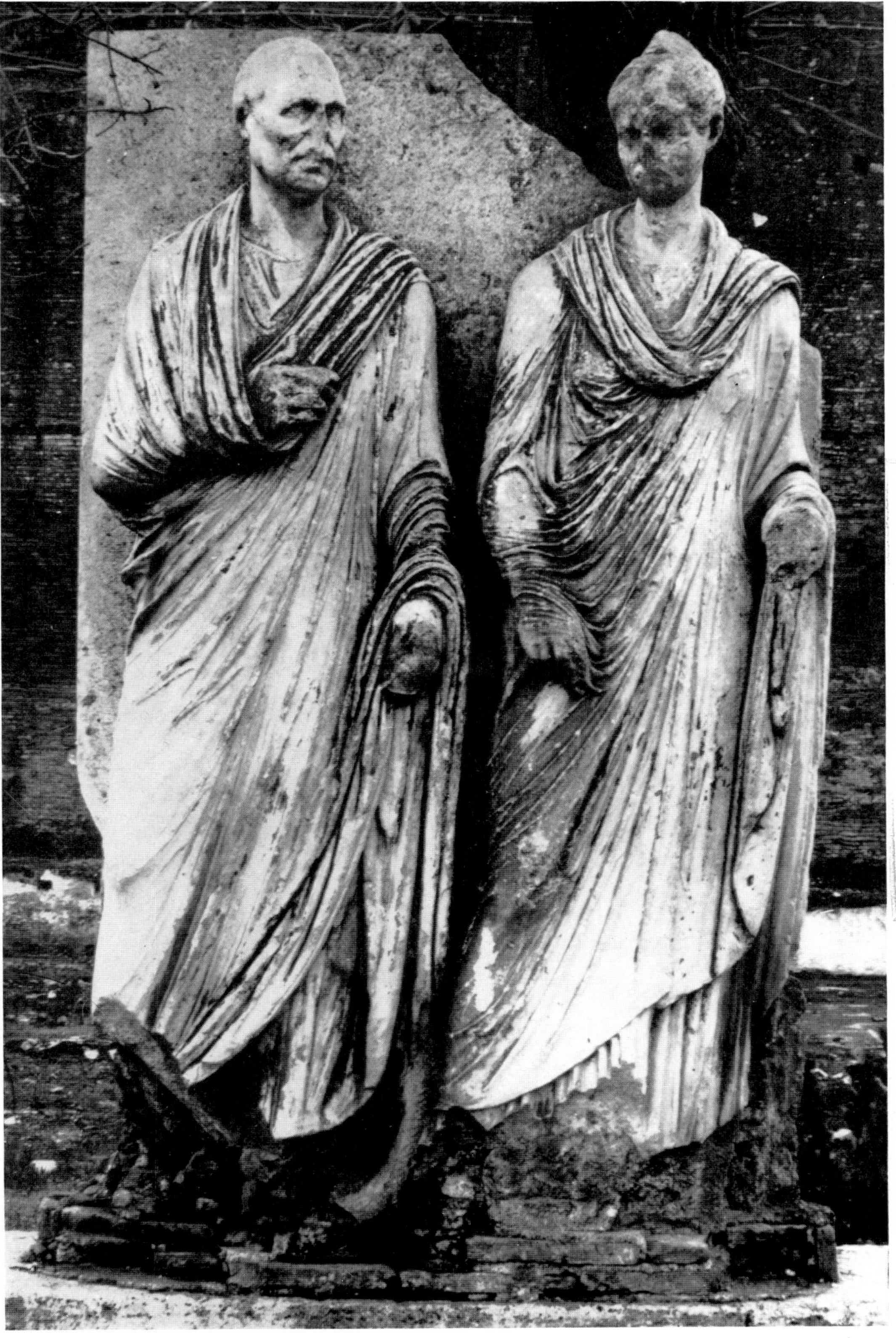

78. EURYSACES AND ATISTIA. See caption to Plate 77.

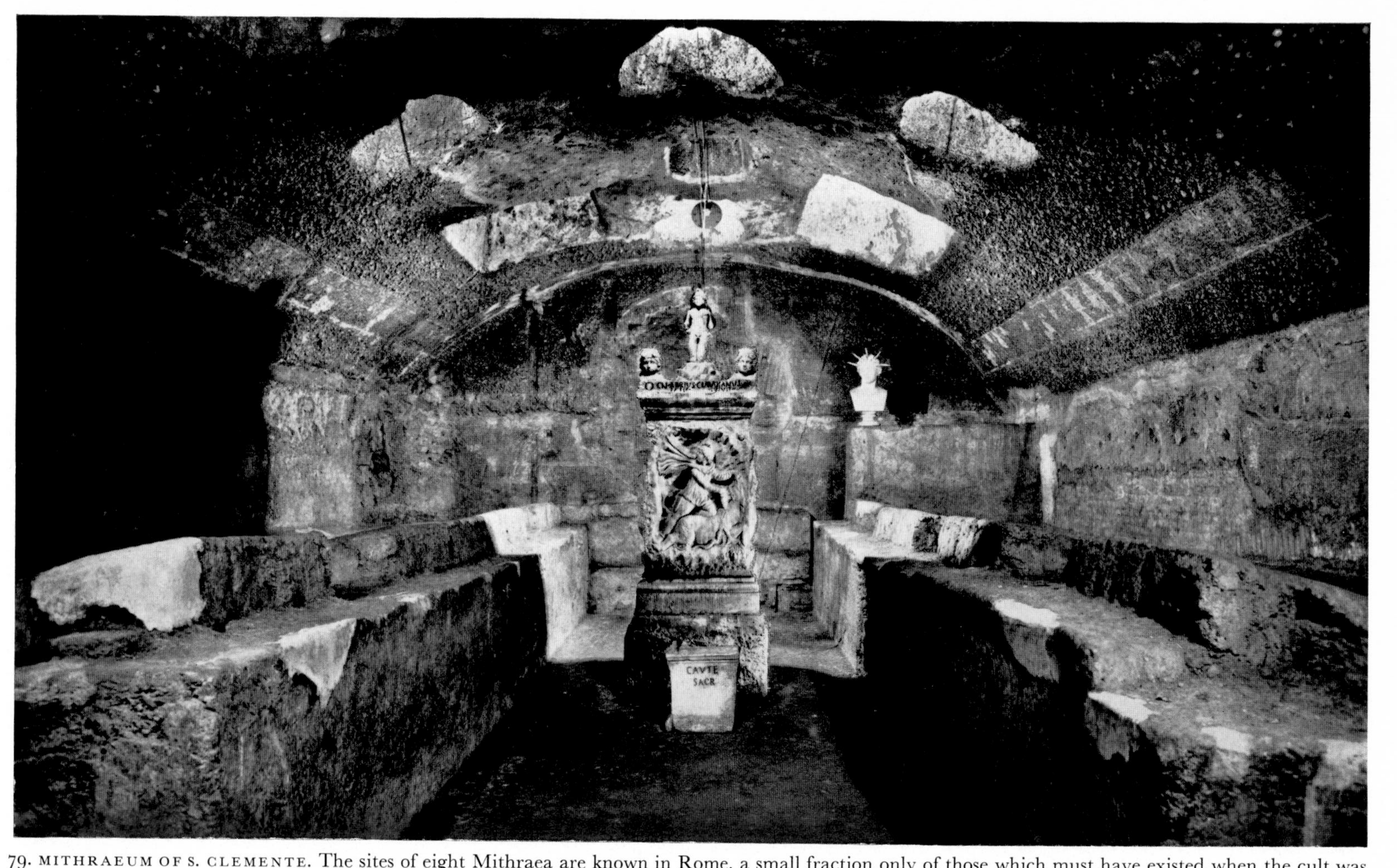

79. MITHRAEUM OF S. CLEMENTE. The sites of eight Mithraea are known in Rome, a small fraction only of those which must have existed when the cult was at its most popular in the second and third centuries A.D. Of these, the Mithraeum under the Basilica of S. Clemente is the best known and most impressive. The visitor descends through the level of three super-imposed Christian churches, his ears filled with the rushing noise of the copious springs under the Caelian Hill. The benches for the initiates are preserved, together with the main altar. This bears, on the front, the customary relief of Mithras killing the bull, on either side the attendants Cautes and Cautopates, on the back panel, the serpent. Note the altar with the dedication CAVTE PATER, and the radiate head (right) of Mithras

80. MITHRAEUM OF S. PRISCA. Tablet in which Mithras is addressed as Sol Invictus by an unknown donor 'whose prayers he has often heard'. For the cult of Mithras see F. Cumont, *Les religions orientales dans le paganisme romain*, 3rd ed. 1928.

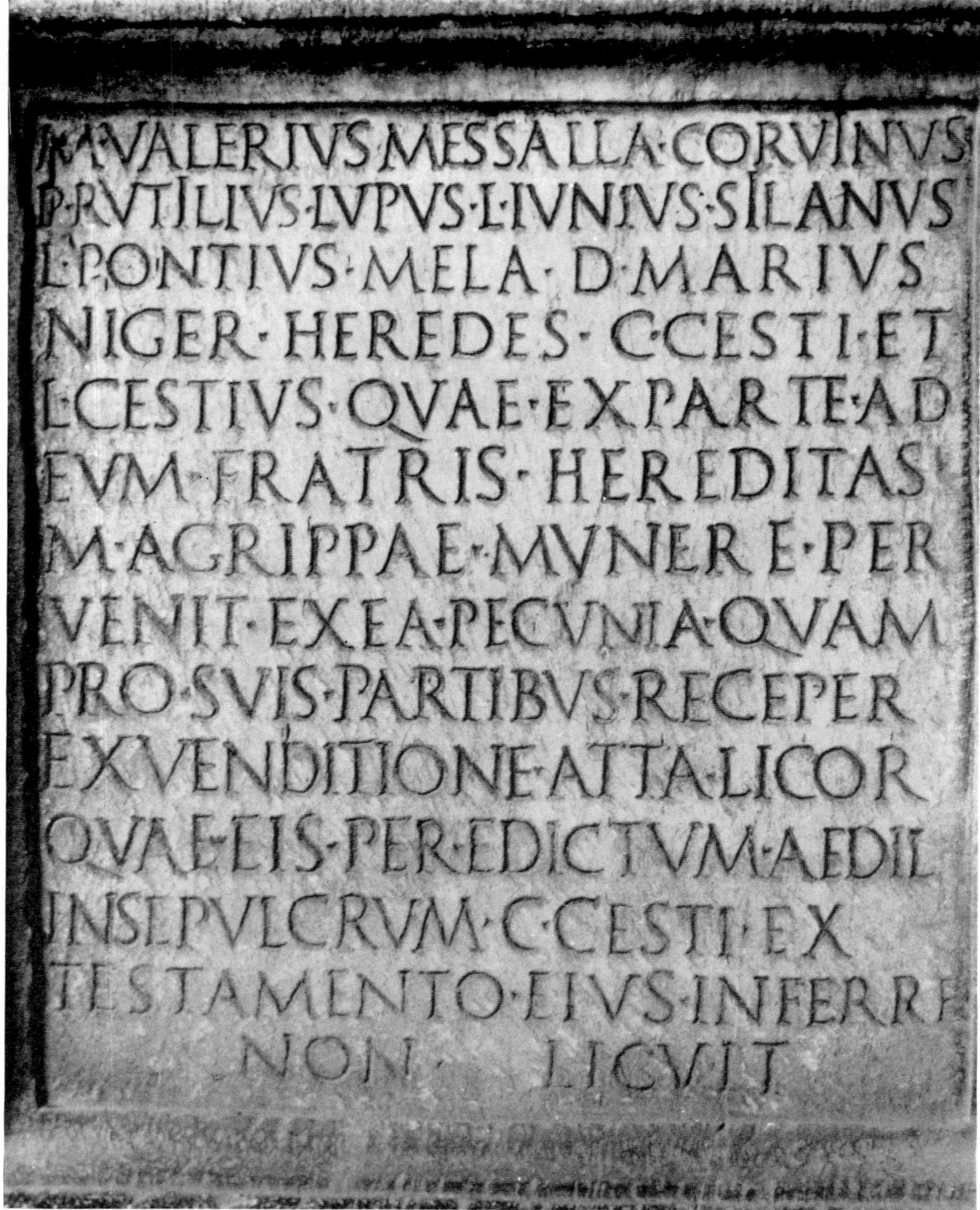
M·VALERIVS MESSALLA·CORVINVS
P·RVTILIVS·LVPVS·L·IVNIVS·SILANVS
L·PONTIVS·MELA·D·MARIVS
NIGER·HEREDES·C·CESTI·ET
L·CESTIVS·QVAE·EX PARTE·AD
EVM·FRATRIS·HEREDITAS
M·AGRIPPAE·MVNERE·PER
VENIT·EX EA·PECVNIA·QVAM
PRO·SVIS·PARTIBVS·RECEPER
EX VENDITIONE·ATTALICOR
QVAE·EIS·PER·EDICTVM·AEDIL
IN SEPVLCRVM·C·CESTI·EX
TESTAMENTO·EIVS·INFERRE
NON·LICVIT

81. THE HEIRS OF GAIUS CESTIUS. Five heirs are named, and M. Agrippa renounces his share to Lucius Cestius. Gaius Cestius had asked in his will to have precious fabrics (*attalica*) buried in his tomb—the Pyramid of Gaius Cestius. Since this was forbidden by the aediles, the heirs sold the fabrics and used the proceeds to set up statues of themselves (CIL, VI, 1375).

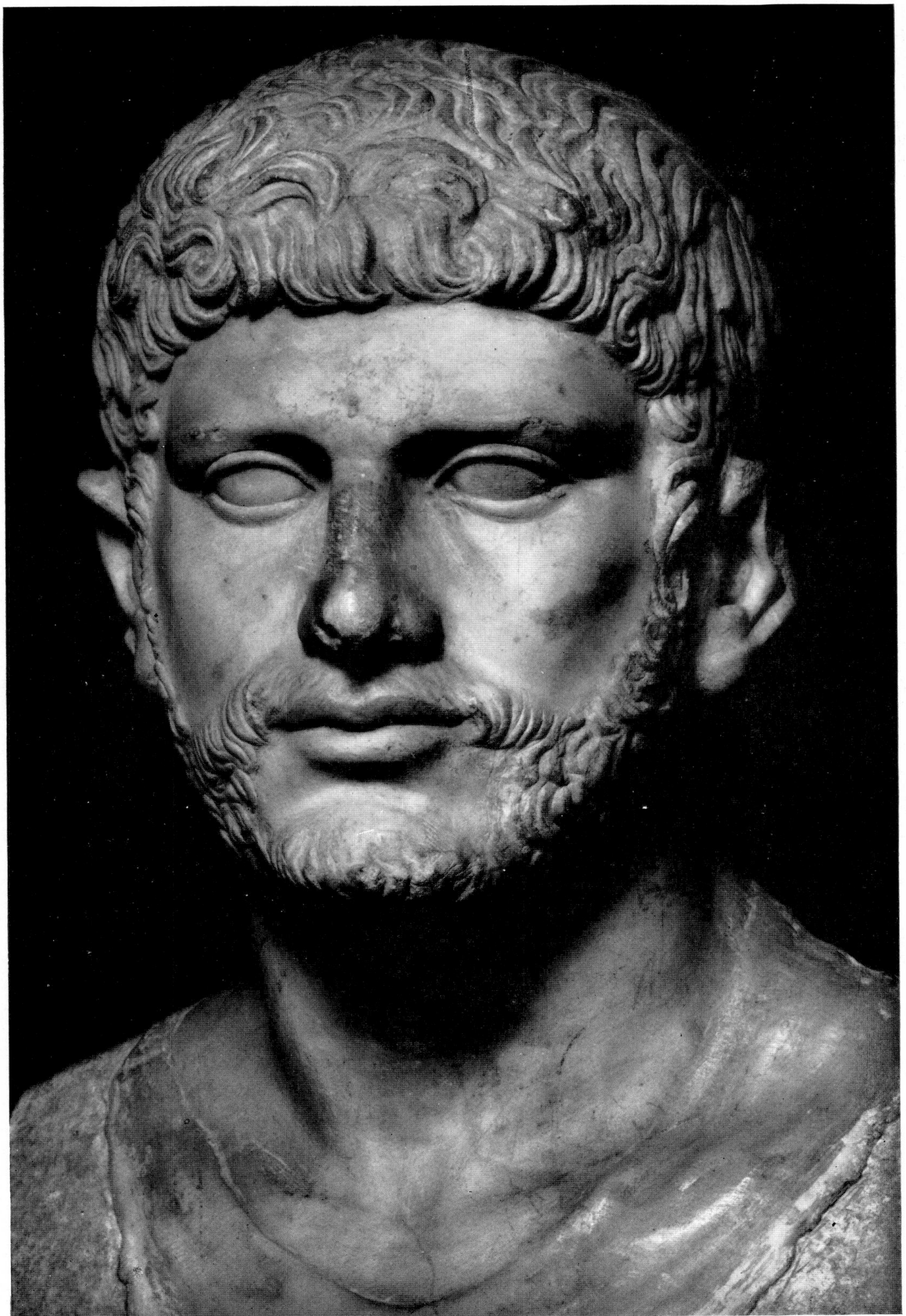

82. CHARIOTEER. A small sanctuary discovered in 1889 on the right bank of the river, close to Viale Trastevere, contained seven busts of charioteers, and a relief of the banqueting Hercules. The reliefs form a fine series of studies of the popular idols of the Circus Maximus. Now in the Museo Nazionale Romano. See p. 216.

83. Coin of M. Aemilius Lepidus (c. 65 B.C.) showing the interior of BASILICA AEMILIA with the shields mentioned on page 99.

84. Coin of L. Vinicius, 17–15 B.C.: The Parthian ARCH OF AUGUSTUS, voted by the Senate in 19 B.C.

85. Coin of Julia Domna, who restored the TEMPLE OF VESTA after the fire of A.D. 191. Six vestals at an altar outside a circular temple with a conical roof.

86. Coin of Antoninus Pius: THE TEMPLE OF VENUS AND ROME. See pp. 117–119.

87. Coin of Trajan: TEMPLE OF VENUS GENETRIX and Colonnades of the Forum Julium, restored A.D. 113. Front centre, the fountain of the Appiades (?) Legend.

88. Coin of Augustus, 29–27 B.C.: CURIA JULIA, with a statue of the Victory of Tarentum on the apex. A colonnade surrounds the building.

89. Sestertius of Domitian (A.D. 95–96): DOMUS TIBERIANA, Forum façade (?).

90. Sestertius of Nero: THE TEMPLE OF JANUS.

91. Coin of Nero: THE TEMPLE OF JANUS.

92. Coin of Gordian III (A.D. 238–244): COLOSSEUM, with beast-fight. Outside, the Colossus, with radiate head, as re-erected by Hadrian.

93. Coin of Titus: THE COLOSSEUM, shown as a building of four storeys.

94. Sestertius of Trajan (A.D. 103–111): CIRCUS MAXIMUS—represented by colonnades and arches, with obelisks on spina.

95. Aureus of Septimius Severus: THE STADIUM OF DOMITIAN.

96. Coin of Nero: ARA PACIS. (Struck to commemorate 75th anniversary.)

97. Coin of Antoninus Pius: THE TEMPLE OF FAUSTINA.

98. Coin of Vespasian: TEMPLE OF JUPITER OPTIMUS MAXIMUS with cult statues in the three *cellae*. Struck to commemorate the restoration by Vespasian.

99. Aemilius Paullus: TROPHY FOR PERSEUS.

100. Caesar: TROPHY FOR VERCINGETORIX.

101. Coin of Augustus: TEMPLE OF MARS ULTOR.

102. Coin of Claudius: CASTRA PRAETORIA.

103. Coin of Trajan: FORUM TRAJANI. Six columns on a podium, arched doorway and shrines, above a six-horse chariot.

104. MODEL OF ANCIENT ROME. Looking N.E. from above the Insula Tiberina, with the Capitol in the right foreground. In the foreground, left, the Theatre of Marcellus, behind it the Porticus of Octavia, enclosing two temples. The Circus Flaminius appears immediately above: in fact, its exact site and alignment are not determined. On the right (S.E.) flank of the Capitol, the crags of the Tarpeia Rupes. Above, the Temple of Jupiter Optimus Maximus, crowning the south-west of the twin summits, with the Temple of Juno Moneta on the Arx beyond.

105. MODEL OF ANCIENT ROME. Looking N.E. from the Aventine across the Circus Maximus to the Palatine. Note the obelisks and columns of the spina of the Circus, the Triumphal Arch at the rounded end, and the pulvinar or imperial box. Across the Circus, the long flank of the Domus Augustiana: below (right) the Septizonium, and the arches of Aquae Claudiae.

106. MODEL OF ANCIENT ROME. Looking N.E. from the Palatine across the Forum Romanum. In the foreground, bottom left, the Temple of Saturn, then the Temple of Divus Augustus in its courtyard, to the right, parts of the Domus Tiberiana. Behind (S.W. to N.E.) Basilica Julia, Temple of Castor and Pollux, Temple of Vesta, the Regia, Atrium Vestae, and buildings leading on to the Temple of Venus and Rome and the Colosseum. Parallel, but beyond the Forum, the Arch of Septimius Severus, the Curia, the Basilica Aemilia, Temple of

107. MODEL OF ANCIENT ROME. The Palatine, looking to the Colosseum. The Temple of Cybele is seen at the S.W. corner of the hill, with the Domus Tiberiana on the N.W. To the right of the Temple of Cybele is the Temple of Apollo. Immediately above, the Domus Flavia, with the nave of its great Basilica conspicuous. At the right-hand edge, the exedra of the imperial box above the stadium of the Domus Augustana. In the background, centre, the Colosseum, flanked on the left by the Temple of Venus and Rome, on the right, by that of Divus Claudius.

108. MODEL OF ANCIENT ROME. The Imperial Fora. From left to right: The Forum Pacis, the Forum of Nerva or Forum Transitorium, the Forum of Augustus with the Temple of Mars Ultor and the two hemicycles, beyond it the Forum of Caesar and Temple of Venus Genetrix, then the Forum of Trajan, Basilica Ulpia, and the Column of Trajan rising between the two libraries. In front the Mercatus Trajani. Behind (left to right) the Basilica of Constantine, the Forum Romanum, with the façade of Basilica Julia. Top right, the Capitol crowned by the Temple of Jupiter Optimus Maximus.

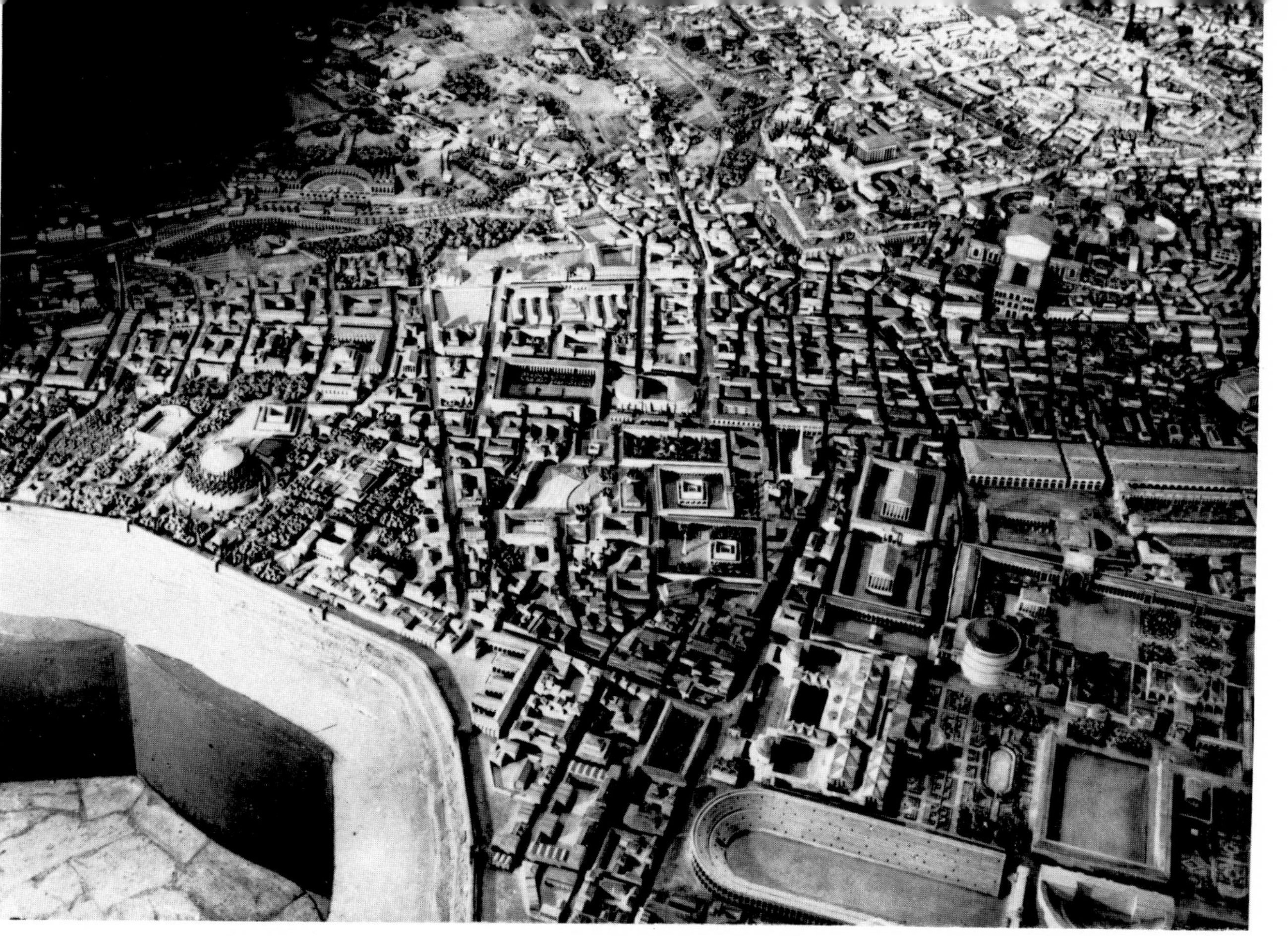

109. MODEL OF ANCIENT ROME. Looking East across the Campus Martius. In the foreground, the Stadium of Domitian. The Thermae of Nero are just above it. Beyond, the Pantheon, with the Thermae of Agrippa to its right, and the rectangle of the Saepta Julia behind. To its left, the Temple of Hadrian is the more distant of two temples enclosed in courtyards. Beyond them, and running directly across the picture, the line of Via Flaminia and Via Lata. Further north-east the large building with a white gable represents the little-known Temple of Serapis. Towards the left edge and across the river, the cypress-ringed mound of the Mausoleum of Augustus, with the *ustrinum domus Augustae* above. Behind it again, the great hemicycle of a building thought to be a luxurious villa in the Gardens of Lucullus, below which run the arches of the Aqua Virgo.

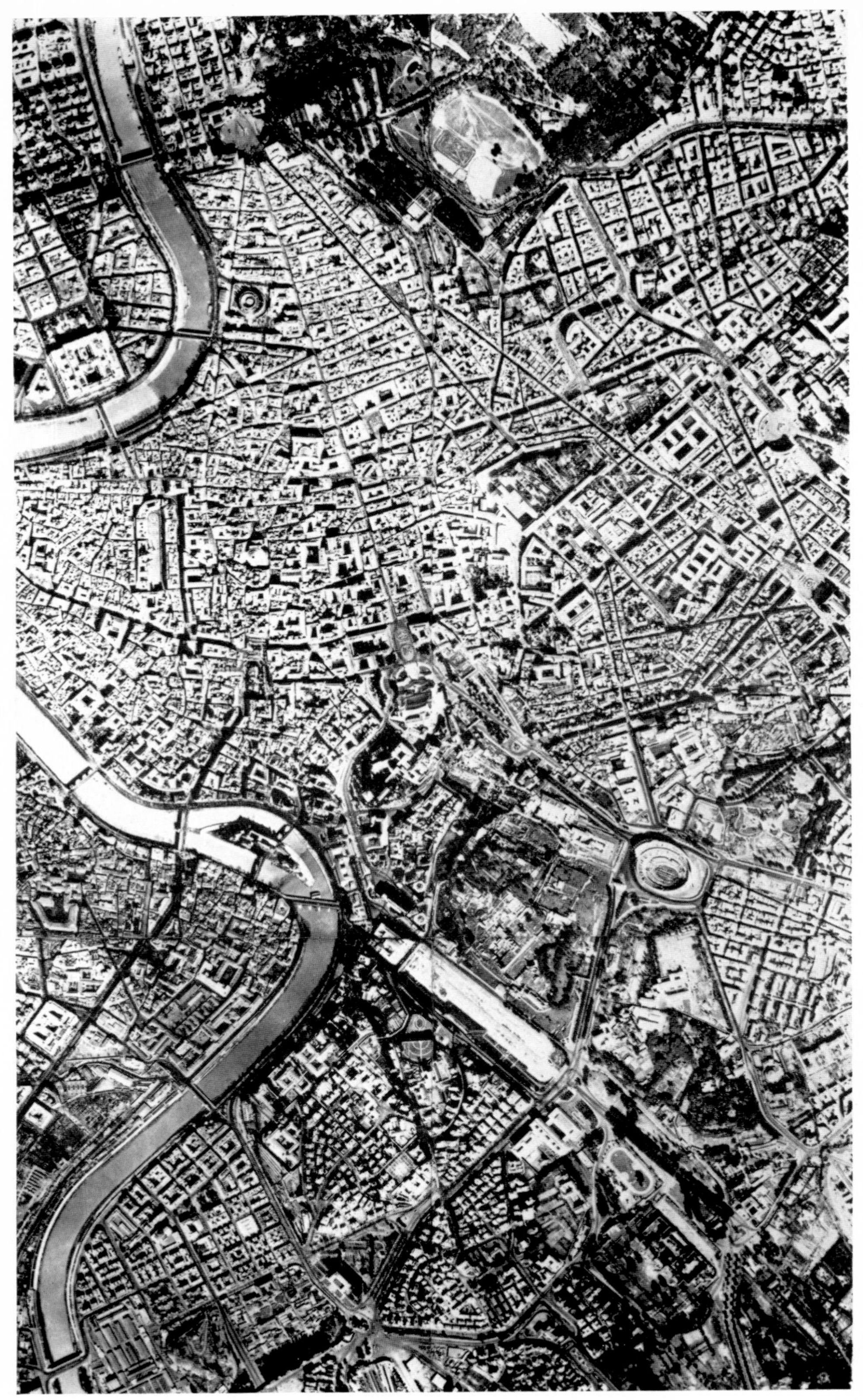

110. AIR PHOTOGRAPH OF MODERN ROME. See facing page.

INDEX OF ANCIENT AUTHORS
INDEX OF INSCRIPTIONS
INDEX OF NAMES
INDEX OF PRINCIPAL PLACES

---

110. AIR PHOTOGRAPH OF MODERN ROME. Much can be seen of ancient Rome in this high level air photograph of the heart of the modern city.

At the bottom left stands out clearly the artificial mound of the Monte Testaccio—the rubbish dump of pottery, etc., cast up from the ancient warehouses and ships. To its right a section of the Aurelian Walls leads to the Porta Ostiensis, with the pyramid of Gaius Cestius just discernible as a white triangle to its left. To the E. of this again the Thermae of Caracalla are seen as a dark rectangle, the long axis S.E.–N.W.: both *exedrae* are visible. North-west of this the Circus Maximus is the most conspicuous object in the whole city. North-east again, almost equally obvious, the Colosseum. Flanking the Circus Maximus on the N.E., the Palatine with the ruins of the Imperial Palaces. The 'Hippodrome' is clearly seen; opposite on the E., and across the road, the aqueduct of the Aquae Claudiae comes in at a right-angle. W.N.W. of the Colosseum, the Temple of Venus and Rome; at its top left hand corner, the Basilica of Constantine: below this, the Forum Romanum, leading to the Capitol. Detail eludes the naked eye: a glass will bring out the ground plan of Basilica Julia, the Arch of Septimius Severus, the Tabularium and the statue of Marcus Aurelius in Piazza del Campidoglio. The N.W. end of the Circus Maximus points to the Insula Tiberina, with the two ancient bridges of Pons Cestius and Pons Fabricius. The next bridge but one up-stream, the modern Ponte Sisto, corresponds to the Pons Aurelius. Immediately down-stream from the island, note the Ponte Palatino; the street running directly to it through the heart of Trastevere is on the line of the Via Aurelia. N.E. of the Tiber Island, the Theatre of Marcellus shows up as a D: N.E. again we reach the modern Victor Emmanuel Monument and Piazza Venezia. From here, N.N.W., the Via del Corso runs on the line of the ancient Via Lata and Via Flaminia to the Piazza del Popolo, the longest stretch in Rome where an ancient and a modern road coincide. The Obelisk of Augustus and its shadow show up clearly in Piazza del Popolo. Another ancient road shows S.S.W. from that piazza along the line of the modern Via Ripetta and Via della Scrofa: halfway along it, on the right, is the Mausoleum of Augustus. To the S.W. again, Piazza Navona preserves the outline of the Stadium of Domitian. A little to its right, the dome of the Pantheon, the *oculus* showing as a black pin-point. From the N. end of Piazza Navona, an ancient road goes due W. to the river along the line of Via delle Capelle and Via dei Coronari. Opposite Piazza Navona, but almost on the right-hand edge of the photograph, note the semi-circle of Piazza dell'Esedra, and the Thermae of Diocletian. North of this, Via Venti Settembre is clearly seen, running S.W.–N.E. along the line of Alta Semita. Finally, at the top of the picture, a long stretch of the Aurelian Wall runs from Porta del Popolo to the Porta Pinciana, and thence on the S. of the Corso d'Italia to the edge.

INDEX OF ANCIENT AUTHORS

INDEX OF INSCRIPTIONS

(IM refers to inscriptions illustrated in Atilius Degrassi *Imagines*, 1965)

OTHER SOURCES

INDEX OF NAMES

INDEX OF PRINCIPAL PLACES

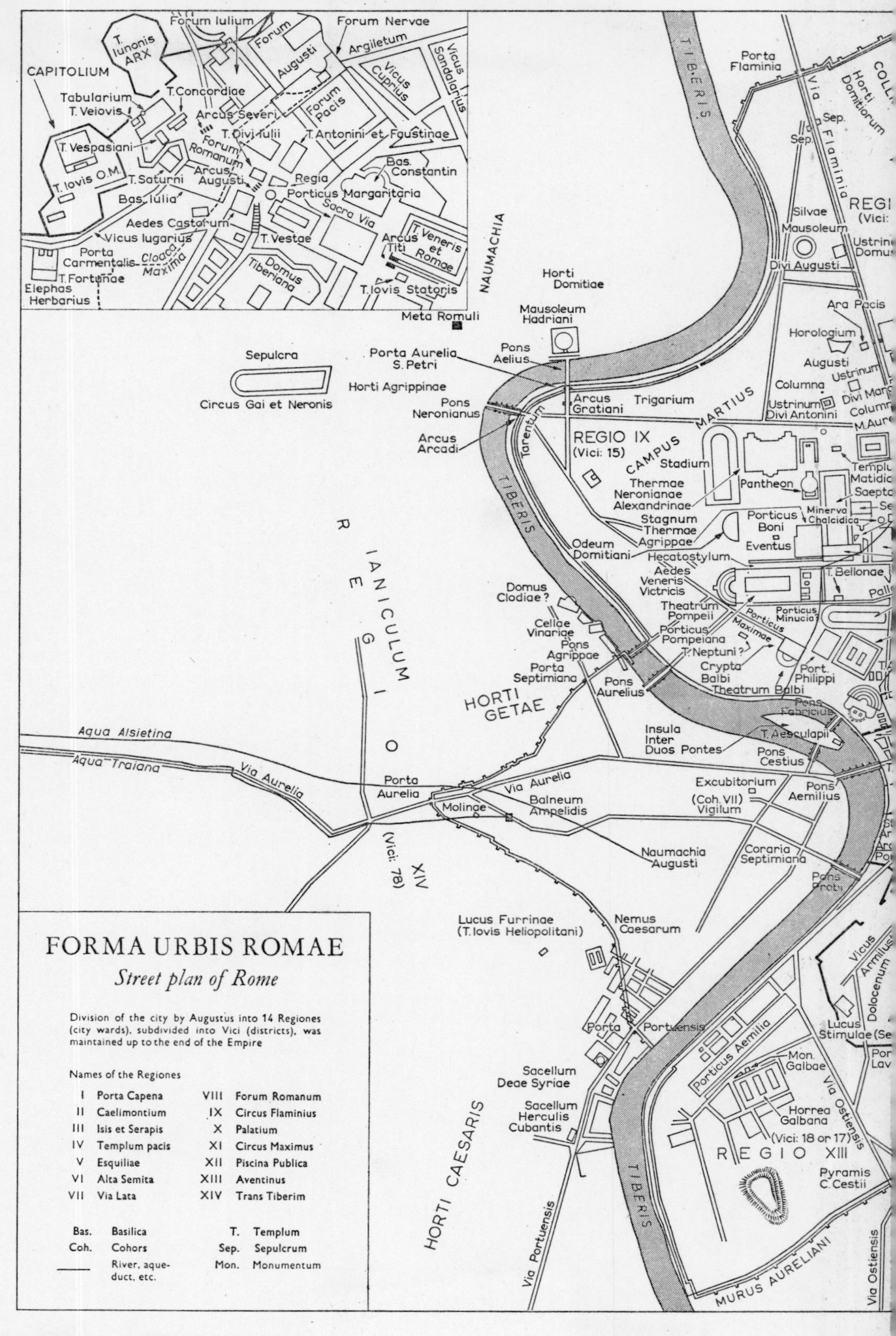

FORMA URBIS ROMAE
Street plan of Rome
Division of the city by Augustus into 14 Regiones (city wards), subdivided into Vici (districts), was maintained up to the end of the Empire
Names of the Regiones
I Porta Capena
II Caelimontium
III Isis et Serapis
IV Templum pacis
V Esquiliae
VI Alta Semita
VII Via Lata
VIII Forum Romanum
IX Circus Flaminius
X Palatium
XI Circus Maximus
XII Piscina Publica
XIII Aventinus
XIV Trans Tiberim
Bas. Basilica
Coh. Cohors
River, aqueduct, etc.
T. Templum
Sep. Sepulcrum
Mon. Monumentum
Forum Iulium
Forum Nervae
T. Iunonis ARX
CAPITOLIUM
Forum Augusti
Argiletum
Vicus Sandalarius
Vicus Cuprius
Tabularium
T. Veiovis
T. Concordiae
Arcus Severi
Forum Pacis
T. Vespasiani
T. Divi Iulii
T. Antonini et Faustinae
Forum Romanum
Bas. Constantin
T. Iovis O.M.
T. Saturni
Arcus Augusti
Regia
Porticus Margaritaria
Bas. Iulia
Sacra Via
Aedes Castorum
T. Veneris et Romae
Vicus Iugarius
T. Vestae
Arcus Titi
Porta Carmentalis
Cloaca Maxima
Domus Tiberiana
T. Fortunae
Elephas Herbarius
T. Iovis Statoris
NAUMACHIA
Meta Romuli
Horti Domitiae
Mausoleum Hadriani
Sepulcra
Porta Aurelia S. Petri
Pons Aelius
Circus Gai et Neronis
Horti Agrippinae
Pons Neronianus
Arcus Gratiani
Trigarium
Arcus Arcadi
Tarentum
REGIO IX
(Vici: 15)
CAMPUS MARTIUS
Stadium
Thermae Neronianae Alexandrinae
Pantheon
Stagnum
Thermae Agrippae
Porticus Boni Eventus
Minerva Chalcidica
Odeum Domitiani
Hecatostylum
Aedes Veneris Victricis
T. Bellonae
Domus Clodiae ?
Theatrum Pompeii
Porticus Minucia?
Porticus Maximae
Cellae Vinariae
Pons Agrippae
Porticus Pompeiana
T. Neptuni ?
Porta Septimiana
Crypta Balbi
Port. Philippi
Pons Aurelius
Theatrum Balbi
Pons Fabricius
HORTI GETAE
Insula Inter Duos Pontes
T. Aesculapii
Pons Cestius
IANICULUM
R E G I O
Aqua Alsietina
Aqua Traiana
Via Aurelia
Porta Aurelia
Molinae
Balneum Ampelidis
Excubitorium
(Coh. VII) Vigilum
Pons Aemilius
XIV
(Vici: 78)
Naumachia Augusti
Coraria Septimiana
Pons Probi
Lucus Furrinae
(T. Iovis Heliopolitani)
Nemus Caesarum
Porta Portuensis
Porticus Aemilia
Mon. Galbae
Sacellum Deae Syriae
Sacellum Herculis Cubantis
Horrea Galbana
(Vici: 18 or 17)
REGIO XIII
Via Ostiensis
HORTI CAESARIS
Pyramis C. Cestii
Via Portuensis
TIBERIS
MURUS AURELIANI
Porta Flaminia
Via Flaminia
Horti Domitiorum
Sep.
Silvae
Mausoleum Divi Augusti
Ustrina Domus
Ara Pacis
Horologium Augusti
Columna
Ustrinum Divi Antonini
Vicus Armilus
Dolocenum
Lucus Stimulae